LESSONS IN LEGITIMACY

LESSONS IN LEGITIMACY

COLONIALISM, CAPITALISM, AND THE RISE OF STATE SCHOOLING IN BRITISH COLUMBIA

Sean Carleton

UBCPress · Vancouver · Toronto

© UBC Press 2022

All rights reserved. No part of this publication may be reproduced, stored in a retrieval system, or transmitted, in any form or by any means, without prior written permission of the publisher, or, in Canada, in the case of photocopying or other reprographic copying, a licence from Access Copyright, www.accesscopyright.ca.

31 30 29 28 27 26 25 24 23 22   5 4 3 2 1

Printed in Canada on FSC-certified ancient-forest-free paper (100% post-consumer recycled) that is processed chlorine- and acid-free.

LIBRARY AND ARCHIVES CANADA CATALOGUING IN PUBLICATION

Title: Lessons in legitimacy : colonialism, capitalism, and the rise of state schooling in British Columbia / Sean Carleton.
Names: Carleton, Sean, author.
Description: Includes bibliographical references and index.
Identifiers: Canadiana (print) 20220280479 | Canadiana (ebook) 20220281262 | ISBN 9780774868075 (hardcover) | ISBN 9780774868082 (paperback) | ISBN 9780774868099 (PDF) | ISBN 9780774868105 (EPUB)
Subjects: LCSH: Education—British Columbia—History. | LCSH: Education and state—British Columbia—History. | LCSH: Education—Social aspects—British Columbia—History. | LCSH: Public schools—British Columbia—History. | LCSH: Church and education—British Columbia—History. | LCSH: Indigenous peoples—Education—British Columbia—History. | CSH: Indigenous peoples—British Columbia—Residential schools—History.
Classification: LCC LA418.B7 C37 2022 | DDC 370.9711—dc23

Canadä

UBC Press gratefully acknowledges the financial support for our publishing program of the Government of Canada (through the Canada Book Fund), the Canada Council for the Arts, and the British Columbia Arts Council.

This book has been published with the help of a grant from the Canadian Federation for the Humanities and Social Sciences, through the Awards to Scholarly Publications Program, using funds provided by the Social Sciences and Humanities Research Council of Canada.

Printed and bound in Canada by Friesens
Set in AkzidenzGrotesk and Fournier by Artegraphica Design Co.
Copy editor: Deborah Kerr
Proofreader: Carmen Tiampo
Indexer: Emily LeGrand
Cover Image: Image B-00342, South Fort George School, courtesy of the Royal BC Museum
Cover designer: Alexa Love

UBC Press
The University of British Columbia
2029 West Mall
Vancouver, BC V6T 1Z2
www.ubcpress.ca

Contents

List of Illustrations	vii
List of Abbreviations	ix
Preface	x
Acknowledgments	xiii
Maps	xvi
Introduction	3

Part 1: Colonial Origins, 1849–71

1	Creating Common Schools	21
2	Settler Anxiety and Missionary Schooling	48

Part 2: Ruling by Schooling, 1871–1900

3	Public Schools for the People	81
4	Inventing Indian Education	110

Part 3: Reform and Resistance, 1900–30

5	Reforming Public Schools	145
6	Revising and Resisting Indian Education	178
	Conclusion	207

Appendix 1: Growth of Public Schools 213

Appendix 2: Growth of Indian Education 214

Appendix 3: Indian Day Schools, 1930 215

Appendix 4: Indian Residential Schools, 1930 217

Notes 218

Bibliography 283

Index 308

Illustrations

Maps

0.1	Indigenous Peoples in British Columbia	xvi
0.2	Regions of British Columbia	xvii
0.3	Indian Day Schools and Indian Residential Schools in British Columbia	xviii

Figures

1.1	Fort Victoria, c. 1860	24
1.2	Colonial Administration Buildings, Victoria, c. 1860s	26
1.3	Craigflower School, c. 1850s	29
1.4	Reverend Edward Cridge, c. 1870s	31
2.1	A mission school in Quw'utsun territory, c. 1860s	50
2.2	Governor James Douglas, c. 1860s	54
2.3	Reverend J.B. Good and his school, c. 1860s	73
3.1	Superintendent John Jessop, c. 1870s	85
3.2	The Cache Creek Provincial Boarding School, c. 1870s	87
3.3	Hastings Sawmill School, c. 1886	96
3.4	Port Alberni School, c. 1887	96
3.5	Bamfield School, c. 1895	97
3.6	Hazelton School, c. 1899	97
3.7	Sooke schoolchildren, c. 1880s	98
3.8	Sooke schoolchildren and teacher, c. 1890s	99
3.9	Children going to school, c. 1890s	102
4.1	Metlakatla, c. 1880s	112

4.2	Port Essington Indian Day School, c. 1890	125
4.3	Alberni Indian Boarding School, c. 1896	126
4.4	St. Mary's Indian Boarding School, c. 1880s	132
4.5	Kuper Island Indian Industrial School band, c. 1900	135
4.6	Port Simpson students with Thomas Crosby, c. 1890s	139
5.1	Sidney schoolchildren, c. 1910s	150
5.2	Ella Gladstone, c. 1925	154
5.3	South Fort George School, c. 1911	155
5.4	Capilano School, c. 1920s	156
5.5	Capilano School, c. 1920s	156
5.6	Technical class, c. 1910s	160
5.7	Sewing class at King Edward High School, c. 1918	162
5.8	Victoria High School under construction, c. 1912	165
5.9	Cadets at Boys' Central School, c. 1918	171
5.10	Woodpecker School, c. 1925	174
6.1	Ucluelet Indian Day School, c. 1900s	185
6.2	Songhees Indian Day School, c. 1910s	186
6.3	Williams Lake Indian Residential School, c. 1920s	193
6.4	Kootenay Indian Residential School, c. 1920s	197
6.5	Alert Bay Indian Residential School, c. 1930	202
6.6	Sechelt Indian Residential School, c. 1920s	204

Abbreviations

ARSP	Annual Report of the Public Schools
BCA	British Columbia Archives
BCPP	British Columbia Provincial Police
BCTF	British Columbia Teachers' Federation
CMS	Church Missionary Society
CO	Colonial Office, United Kingdom
DIA	Department of Indian Affairs
HBC	Hudson's Bay Company
IDS	Indian Day School
IRS	Indian Residential School
LAC	Library and Archives Canada
MONOVA	Museum and Archives of North Vancouver
NA	National Archives, United Kingdom
NCTR	National Centre for Truth and Reconciliation
NWMP	North West Mounted Police
OMI	Missionary Oblates of Mary Immaculate
RCMP	Royal Canadian Mounted Police
SPG	Society for the Propagation of the Gospel
TRC	Truth and Reconciliation Commission of Canada

Preface

I have spent much of my life learning, and subsequently trying to unlearn, colonial legitimacy. As such, I would like to preface this study by positioning myself and acknowledging how this struggle with legitimacy has shaped my life and the making of this book.

I am a settler Canadian. My ancestors' roots are in Ireland and England, and my working-class family came to what is today known as Canada in the early 1900s, settling first on the Prairies and then moving to the west coast. I was born in Vancouver, British Columbia. I grew up in Lynn Valley, North Vancouver, on the ancestral and unceded territory of the Coast Salish, specifically the Sḵwx̱wú7mesh, səlílwətaɬ, and xʷməθkʷəy̓əm Nations. North Vancouver is a segregated urban environment. There are three Indian reserves on the North Shore, but I had few interactions with Indigenous Peoples growing up, aside from playing hockey with a Sḵwx̱wú7mesh teammate who sometimes talked about his life on the reserve and the racism he experienced at a local public school. But overall, I was ignorant about enduring Coast Salish culture and lifeways. I learned very little about Indigenous Peoples at the public schools I attended.

I knew nothing, for example, about the famous North Shore Indians lacrosse team or about the persistent activism of Coast Salish leaders fighting for land and rights, from Joe Capilano, Andrew Paull, and Simon Baker to Chief Dan George, Mazie Baker, and Ta'ah Amy George. My family lived near where the Squamish Indian Residential School operated between the 1890s and 1950s, and I passed by that site many times without knowing about the school's history and ongoing legacy. I understood nothing about how settler capitalism, more broadly, created my home very recently and provided me with a number of privileges that profoundly shaped my life.

I did not think critically about my experience growing up as a settler until I attended university, where I took courses on the history of Indigenous Peoples and British Columbia. These courses, and conversations with Indigenous students and professors, helped me realize how much of what I had learned, formally and informally, justified settler colonialism and normalized the creation and ongoing maintenance of British Columbia's capitalist society as commonsensical. As I began to question these lessons in legitimacy, I committed myself to a decolonizing practice/process of unlearning and relearning how to live in a better way.

As well, I learned about the history and ongoing legacy of Canada's Indian Residential School system from a new family member, Patrick, a Kwakwa̲ka'wakw Survivor of the St. Michael's Indian Residential School at Alert Bay, off the northeast coast of Vancouver Island. Through our conversations, I understood more about the nature of schooling in colonial settings such as British Columbia. I realized that it played a "destructive and creative" role, to borrow from anti-colonial theorist Albert Memmi, in our respective lives and prepared Patrick and I to take up very different positions in British Columbia's capitalist settler society.[1] As a result, I wanted to research the origins of state schooling for Indigenous and non-Indigenous people and its role in supporting settler capitalism and the making of British Columbia.

After many conversations, Patrick gifted me a sacred bundle with an eagle feather – a symbol of truth and leadership – and asked me to learn more about this history. The gift was also a responsibility. It came with the expectation of ongoing reciprocity. Patrick wanted me to share what I learned with others to help put truth before reconciliation and create pathways for healing and justice. I agreed. Yet, I took on the task with misgivings about my role in telling the story. I felt comfortable examining the origins of public schooling for settlers like me, but how could I write about colonial schooling for Indigenous Peoples?

In his book *A National Crime*, historian John S. Milloy explains that Indian Day Schools and Indian Residential Schools were "conceived, designed, and managed" by settlers. "The system is not someone else's story," Milloy writes, "it is *our* history."[2] I would slightly amend his words, with the work of Indigenous Studies scholar Aileen Moreton-Robinson in mind, to emphasize that it is *shared* history.[3] Nevertheless, Milloy insists that settlers need to take responsibility and learn more about their role in colonial schooling "as a site of self-knowledge from which we can understand not only who we have been as Canadians but who we must become if we are to deal justly" with Indigenous Peoples.[4] Moreover, he challenges non-Indigenous historians to continue asking critical questions about colonial schooling, such as how did it happen and why did it happen? This book addresses these questions and helps people understand the relationship between settler capitalism and the rise of state schooling for Indigenous and non-Indigenous people in British Columbia between 1849 and 1930.

Researching and writing this book taught me an important lesson: colonial legitimacy is neither natural nor inevitable. It is learned, and it can therefore be unsettled and unlearned to clear the path for decolonization and meaningful reconciliation. As Stó:lō writer Lee Maracle explains, "once we understand what kind of world [colonizers] have created, then we can figure out what kind of world we can re-create."[5] I hope this book can help support the work of creating a better world.

Acknowledgments

Books are collective accomplishments, and many people have helped me complete this project. I gratefully acknowledge the funding I received from the Social Sciences and Humanities Research Council of Canada (SSHRC). As well, I thank SSHRC for awarding me a Michael Smith Foreign Study Supplement, which supported my time as a visiting research scholar at the London School of Economics. Examining colonial papers at the National Archives in the United Kingdom shaped my understanding of the connections between empire, missionary imperialism, and education. I also appreciate the funding that I received from the Ontario Graduate Scholarship Program, Trent University, the Frost Centre for Canadian Studies and Indigenous Studies, the Symons Trust Fund for Canadian Studies, and the History Education Network at the University of British Columbia. Mount Royal University and the University of Manitoba contributed funds that helped me finish the book.

A number of scholars, colleagues, and friends enriched and pushed my thinking during the research and writing process. Thank you to the staff at Library and Archives Canada, the British Columbia Archives, the National Archives, the Museum and Archives of North Vancouver, and the National Centre for Truth and Reconciliation. Thank you to the Skwx̱wú7mesh Úxwumixw (Squamish Nation) and Yúusnewas project team members for inviting me to be the historical consultant on the work looking into the legacy of the Squamish Indian Residential School in North Vancouver. Yúusnewas means to take care of everyone and each other, and working with the Nation and the team has taught me much about how to do this important work in a good way that is focused on healing and creating a positive environment for future generations. I also thank colleagues at Trent University, including Kristi Allain, Dimitry Anastakis, Meaghan Beaton, Jeannine Crowe, Caroline Durand, Michael Eamon, Julia Harrison, Marg Hobbs, Janet Miron, Cathy Schoel, Jim Struthers, John Wadland, and Shirley Williams. John S. Milloy, Bryan D. Palmer, and Joan Sangster were exceptionally helpful. I am especially grateful for Bryan's mentorship and ongoing personal and professional support. This book is better because of his generous and constructive feedback.

Many colleagues offered guidance and encouragement. I thank Funké Aladejebi, Kristine Alexander, Sarah Carter, El Chenier, Penney Clark, Wallace Clement, Merissa Daborn, Mylène Gamache, Mona Gleason, Jane Griffith, Nancy Janovicek, Mary-Ellen Kelm, Madeline Knickerbocker, Peter Kulchyski, Emma LaRocque, Erica Violet Lee, Jessie Loyer, Roberta Lexier, Kristina Llewellyn, Michael Marker, Eryk Martin, Ted McCoy, Chris Minns, Ian Mosby, Sarah Nickel, Kirk Niergarth, Alison Norman, Thomas Peace, Roxanne Panchasi, Leo Panitch, Lisa Pasolli, Jennifer Pettit, Deanna Reder, Niigaan Sinclair, Hugh Shewell, Timothy Stanley, Waaseyaa'sin Christine Sy, Anne Toews, David Tough, Eliot Tretter, Renae Watchman, Andrew Woolford, and others. As well, I thank Jean Barman, Jarvis Brownlie, Jason Ellis, Crystal Gail Fraser, Laura Ishiguro, Mark Leier, David Parent, Adele Perry, Helen Raptis, and the anonymous reviewers for their helpful feedback on earlier drafts. UBC Press was wonderful to work with, and I am thankful for James MacNevin and Meagan Dyer's editorial guidance.

Love and support from my friends and family sustained me while I worked on this project. I thank all of them for their patience and constant support. I am especially grateful to my mom, Karon, my dad, Gordon, my sister, Kelly, and the extended Carleton and Smith families. This book would not be possible without my partner, Julia, who is a loving companion and comrade. Thank you.

Finally, I thank Patrick for sharing his story and asking me to learn more about the history of schooling and colonialism in British Columbia.

Sadly, Patrick passed away as this book went to press. In his honour, I have directed UBC Press to send royalties from the sale of the book to the Indian Residential School Survivors Society (www.irsss.ca) in North Vancouver.

Maps

FIGURE 0.1 Indigenous Peoples in British Columbia. | Cartography by Eric Leinberger

MAPS xvii

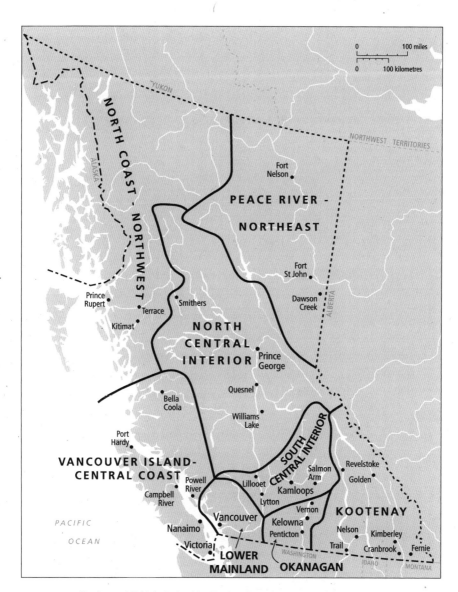

FIGURE 0.2 Regions of British Columbia. During the 1850s and 1860s, most common schools were situated in southern Vancouver Island and the Lower Mainland. By 1930, more than a thousand public schools were operating throughout the province. | Cartography by Eric Leinberger

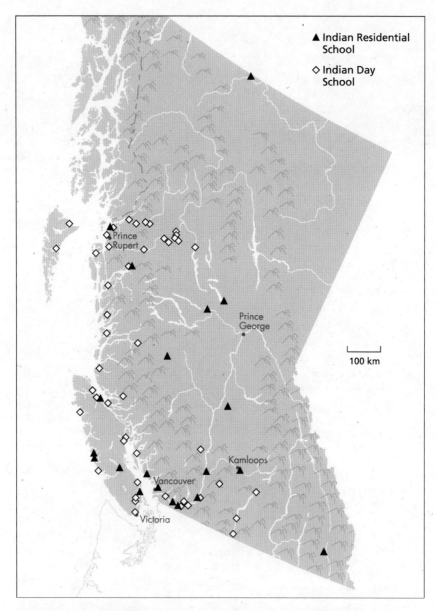

FIGURE 0.3 Indian Day Schools and Indian Residential Schools in British Columbia, c. 1930. By 1930, 3,291 Indigenous students were enrolled in 63 schools (46 day schools, 16 residential schools, and 1 combined school). | Cartography by Eric Leinberger

LESSONS IN LEGITIMACY

Introduction

In light of the Truth and Reconciliation Commission (TRC), many Canadians are coming to terms with Canada's history of schooling and colonialism.[1] After years of extensive research and consulting Survivors, the TRC released its final report in 2015 to raise public awareness about the history of the Indian Residential School (IRS) system. The report revealed that approximately 150,000 Indigenous children and youth attended more than 130 federally funded and church-run boarding schools across the country between the 1880s and 1990s. Separated from their families, thousands died, and many were mentally, physically, and sexually abused by staff in institutions that the Government of Canada, in its 2008 apology to Suvivors, acknowledged were designed to "kill the Indian in the child."[2] The TRC's conclusions shocked many settler Canadians but confirmed what generations of Indigenous Peoples experienced:

> For over a century, the central goals of Canada's Aboriginal policy were to eliminate Aboriginal governments; ignore Aboriginal rights; terminate the Treaties; and, through a process of assimilation, cause Aboriginal peoples to cease to exist as distinct legal, social, cultural, religious, and racial entities in Canada. The establishment and operation of residential schools were a central element of this policy, which can best be described as "cultural genocide."[3]

The TRC's findings challenged Canadians to grapple with the "complex truth" that their own government, in partnership with various churches, devised, deployed, and defended a genocidal school system for more than a century.[4]

The TRC's focus on "truth determination" and "truth-telling" was meant to correct Canada's long history of denying or downplaying the devastating effects of schooling and colonialism for Indigenous Peoples.[5] Its final report, complete with ninety-four Calls to Action, stressed that Canadians must confront their country's colonial history before reconciliation, or the process of "establishing and maintaining respectful relationships" with Indigenous Peoples, can begin.[6] Though many individuals and institutions are responding to the Calls to Action, the TRC chair, Murray Sinclair, voiced concerns that Canada is rushing reconciliation and leaving the truth behind. Some Canadians want to skip to redemption without acknowledging the root of the problem. According to Sinclair, refusing to recognize historical injustices is a recipe for disaster. "This history is not going to stay in the past," he remarked, "it is going to get critical."[7]

Sinclair's prediction became a grim reality in 2021, when the Tk'emlúps te Secwépemc Nation announced that it had located approximately 215 potential unmarked graves on the site of the Kamloops Indian Residential School in the interior of British Columbia. This revelation, and similar announcements by other Indigenous Nations, sparked an international outpouring of grief and outrage, as well as renewed calls for Canada to reckon with its colonial past and present.[8] Recent events thus confirm the TRC's conclusion that if settler Canadians are serious about repairing relations with Indigenous Peoples, the full extent of Canada's history of education and colonialism – including schooling for settlers – must first be understood and addressed.[9] There are no easy shortcuts. We need truth *before* reconciliation.

This book contributes to the important project of truth telling about Canada's history of schooling and colonialism. Specifically, it examines the role played by various kinds of schooling in helping to build British Columbia, first as a British colony and then as a Canadian province, between 1849 and 1930. Because of its large Indigenous population and rapid socioeconomic development, British Columbia offers a compelling microcosm of Canada's colonial project.[10] My central argument is that colonial and then provincial and federal governments gradually and strategically took on greater responsibility for educating Indigenous *and* non-Indigenous people. They administered various kinds of primary and secondary schooling – such as public schools, Indian Day Schools, and Indian Residential Schools – in ways that helped catalyze and legitimize the making of British Columbia as a capitalist settler society.[11] Indeed, as Helen Raptis and and members of the Ts'msyan Nation argue, residential schooling was just "one plank" of the larger colonial project, and a more comprehensive accounting of the history of schooling and the creation of British Columbia is sorely needed.[12] *Lessons in Legitimacy* addresses that need.

Building on the work of historians such as Adele Perry and Laura Ishiguro, I place the making of British Columbia in a transnational context, and I situate my study in relation to international literature that examines the history of education and imperialism in the British Empire.[13] Historians show how British colonies used schooling – "as and for legitimacy," in the words of M. Kazim Bacchus – to help build capitalist settler societies.[14] Anti-colonial theorist Albert Memmi contends that in colonial settings, it is impossible for colonizers "not to be aware of the constant illegitimacy" of their status. Memmi explains, "In order for the colonizer to be the complete master, it is not enough for him to be so in actual fact, but he must also believe in his legitimacy."[15] As a result, colonizers, particularly those who possess the most social, economic, and political power as Aileen Moreton-Robinson points out, developed various techniques of rule to legitimize colonial hegemony.[16] "Ruling by schooling," as sociologist Bruce Curtis calls it, was one such technique.[17] Schooling had a "hidden curriculum," or what I call lessons in legitimacy: the formal and informal teachings that justified the colonial project and normalized the unequal social relations of settler capitalism as commonsensical.[18] Schools, in short, served as important laboratories for learning colonial legitimacy throughout much of the British Empire in the late nineteenth and early twentieth centuries.

In many British colonies, education for Indigenous and non-Indigenous people developed in distinct yet overlapping ways.[19] Colonial governments supported schooling for Indigenous children and youth, often overseen by Christian missionaries, as a "civilizing" project aimed at disrupting and delegitimizing Indigenous lifeways and recalibrating pupils for subordinate roles in the new colonial society.[20] Historian Catherine Hall shows that Europeans who emigrated to British settler colonies also needed to be "civilized" and trained to be effective colonizers, and so colonial governments supported the creation of schools for their children.[21] Hall suggests that these schools were key sites of making colonial subjects and subjectivities that supported ongoing colonization.[22] Students got lessons in everything from history and civics to home economics and calisthenics in ways that built their character and prepared them for their future roles as loyal subjects and defenders of empire. Schooling not only preserved social order in the colonies, it actively helped produce and reproduce – and legitimate – that order. In this way, schooling for Indigenous and non-Indigenous people played different but complementary roles in expanding the British Empire and securing what Eve Tuck and K. Wayne Yang call "settler futurity."[23]

Shifting the focus to Canada, and to the vast and varied province of British Columbia, *Lessons in Legitimacy* examines the relationship between colonialism, capitalism, and the rise of state schooling in a different corner of the empire. This book unsettles the conventions of education history by bringing schooling for Indigenous and non-Indigenous people, often studied separately, into one analytical frame.[24] To do so, I draw on literature in the fields of education history and Indigenous history. Historians R.D. Gidney and W.P.J. Millar point out that though schooling shares national characteristics, education in Canada comes under provincial jurisdiction.[25] As a result, a rich body of literature looks at the history of schooling in British Columbia, which I engage directly.[26] Important new books by Timothy J. Stanley and Helen Raptis examine various aspects of education and colonialism in British Columbia, though they focus on the twentieth century and do not fully interrogate the nineteenth-century origins of schooling.[27] In fact, no book-length study has investigated the province's early schooling history since 1964, when F. Henry Johnson published his survey, *A History of Public Education in British Columbia*.[28] His book helpfully documents the development and expansion of state-run schooling, but it does so uncritically. It also advances an "onward and upward" Whiggish narrative, in which it wrongly assumes that "the more schools there are, the bigger they become and the greater the number of children attending them, the better everything was supposed to be getting."[29] In contrast, recent works by Paul Axelrod, Mona Gleason, Amy von Heyking, Bruce Curtis, Jason Ellis, and Funké Aladejebi understand schooling more as a project of rule, an important but contested process of socialization and subject formation.[30] However, no book-length study builds on the insights of this literature to critically re-examine the origins of schooling in British Columbia. *Lessons in Legitimacy* does this.

I also draw on works of Indigenous history that investigate the relationship between education and Indigenous Peoples.[31] Under the terms of the British North America Act and due to the quirks of Canadian federalism, schooling is a provincial jurisdiction, but what is known as "Indian education" was the official responsibility of the federal government. Important works by historians such as J.R. Miller and John S. Milloy carefully interrogate Canada's IRS system as a project of colonial rule, but significant gaps remain. First, as Gwichyà Gwich'in historian Crystal Gail Fraser points out, most studies tend to focus only on residential schools and do not give enough attention to the early mission schools that predated them or to the Indian Day Schools that operated concurrently and often accommodated as many or more students.[32] Second, most historians either trace the national contours of the IRS system or closely examine one school. As a result, the provincial perspective is largely neglected or presented in incomplete ways.[33] Third, the majority of scholarship disconnects the experiences of Indigenous and non-Indigenous students by treating their histories of schooling as separate subjects.[34] Though researchers unconsciously reproduce this approach as they follow scholarly convention and archival ordering, the result is that most strictly adhere to official policy lines that in practice were blurred, broken, and challenged in everyday life. British Columbia's public schools, for example, often accommodated both Indigenous and settler children. Public school classrooms are thus better understood as what Mary Louise Pratt calls "contact zones" or "social spaces where cultures meet, clash, and grapple with each other, often in contexts of highly asymmetrical relations of power, such as colonialism."[35] By examining the various kinds of schooling for Indigenous and non-Indigenous people and showing how they sometimes overlapped, this book, as a kind of "experiment in historiography" to borrow E.P. Thompson's phrase, offers a different way of understanding the history of education in Canada.[36]

It also builds on theoretical insights from Critical Indigenous Studies, historical materialism, and political economy to comprehend the braided histories of colonialism, capitalism, and state schooling in British Columbia. I draw on Critical Indigenous Studies literature to acknowledge the centrality of land and dispossession/white possession to examinations of colonialism, specifically what Cree scholars Gina Starblanket and Dallas Hunt call the "structures and operations" of settler colonialism.[37] Patrick Wolfe makes clear that the "elimination" and "erasure" of Indigenous Peoples from the land to gain "access to territory" is the "primary motive" of settler colonialism, and Sioux scholar Nick Estes argues that colonialism in the Americas has always been "about the land: who stole it, who owned it, and who claimed it."[38] The same holds true for British Columbia, where colonizers have "come to stay."[39] Indeed, Secwépemc leader Arthur Manuel stresses, "It began with our dispossession: our lands were stolen out from underneath us."[40]

Similar to the enclosures in eighteenth-century Britain, the "British Columbia Clearances" consisted of the mass expropriation of territory and resources that directly led to the creation of a new capitalist society.[41] Colonizers stole, surveyed, sold and resold, and (re)settled Indigenous lands, remaking them into what is now known as British Columbia. Scholars such as Dene political theorist Glen Sean Coulthard and Michi Saagiig Nishnaabeg writer Leanne Betasamosake Simpson argue that land is not simply a resource or a commodity for Indigenous Peoples. Instead, it is a reciprocal relationship that imparts crucial lessons to human and non-human beings about interconnection and interdependence.[42] Acknowledging the land as a lifeforce enables us to understand that the deliberate attempts of colonial dispossession to sever that relationship were – and still are – devastating for Indigenous Peoples. Indigeneity is enduring, and organized resistance to land theft is ongoing, as Kanaka Maoli scholar Kēhaulani Kauanui and Secwépemc historian Sarah Nickel emphasize, but Arthur Manuel and Grand Chief Ronald M. Derrickson put the consequences of dispossession/white possession in stark terms: "Indigenous lands today account for only 0.36 per cent of British Columbia territory. The settler share is the remaining 99.64 per cent."[43]

It is important to recognize, however, that settler colonialism is not only about colonizers showing up and stealing land. Colonial invasion, as Wolfe writes, is a "structure not an event." It "destroys to replace."[44] Ojibwe political scientist Heidi Kiiwetinepinesiik Stark states that it "is not just reductive, it is *productive*, actively producing both the settler state and its accompanying legitimizing narratives."[45] Colonizers reproduce and reaffirm, in the words of Moreton-Robinson, their "ownership, control, and domination" through "perpetual Indigenous dispossession."[46] Drawing on the insights of geographer Cole Harris, I thus argue that colonial dispossession in British Columbia serves a specific purpose: restricting Indigenous Peoples to small reserves and transforming their territories into private property to be possessed – sold and controlled – by government for the purposes of resettlement and capitalist accumulation.[47] Indeed, Coulthard clarifies that in Canada, "the ends [of colonial dispossession] have always remained the same: to shore up continued access to Indigenous Peoples' territories for the purposes of state formation, settlement, and capitalist development."[48] To better theorize settler capitalism and the making of British Columbia, then, I build on the recent engagement of Indigenous scholars with historical materialism to analyze the connections between dispossession – commonly referred to as "primary" or "primitive" accumulation – and the exploitative economic system that the newcomers developed.[49]

Drawing on historical materialism, I examine settler colonialism alongside other kinds of coercive dispossession to better understand the process of destruction and development that helped build British Columbia. Instead of disaggregating the "colonial-relation" and the "capital relation," as some scholars do, I employ a dialectical appreciation of how colonial dispossession fed capitalist accumulation and the creation of new markets in the mid- to late nineteenth century only to have new forms of capitalist expansion in the early twentieth century require renewed dispossession.[50] Land pre-emption policies and the creation of private property and Indian reserves went hand in hand with the processes of proletarianization and pauperization that divorced most working-class settlers and many Indigenous Peoples from the land, though in uneven ways as Coulthard emphasizes.[51] Separated from the land, the vast majority of settlers, and an increasing number of Indigenous Peoples, had little choice but to live by selling their labour power in exchange for wages to purchase goods and services from the emerging market economy.[52] But advancing capitalism in the late nineteenth and early twentieth centuries also required new waves of dispossession, including the "cutting off" and sale of Indian reserve lands, as well as the imposition of taxes and rents, the increased regulation of women and the poor, and the introduction of new methods of education to further disrupt Indigenous lifeways and compel the growing masses into wage labour.[53] To be clear, so-called primitive accumulation was neither a one-time invasion nor a simple handmaiden of capitalism; various kinds of coercive dispossession sustained accumulation and social formation over the *longue durée*. In the pages that follow, I build on David Harvey's concept of "accumulation by dispossession" and present it as a permanent and dialectial force. It is a simultaneously destructive and generative process facilitating the *ongoing* development of British Columbia as a capitalist settler society.[54]

To clarify the role of the state and schooling in this process, I turn to political economy as a "way of seeing" to determine who benefits the most from socioeconomic development in colonial settings.[55] Locating and defining "the state" in British Columbia, especially for the late nineteenth and early twentieth centuries, is a task that Perry describes as akin to catching a "slippery fish."[56] Admittedly, as the coming pages reveal, many overlapping jurisdictions and competing kinds of state power were at play – imperial/colonial, federal, provincial, and municipal – all in various stages of development.[57] Though some historians have recently downplayed the power of the state in Canada, political economists have demonstrated the instrumental, and distinctly interventionist, role that state actors, in an evolving network of institutions, including government, bureaucracy, judiciaries, and the police and military, play in continued accumulation by dispossession.[58]

Political economists have shown that the state is not a neutral arbiter between social groups. Instead, scholars such as Leo Panitch illustrate that differing levels of government and state agencies act on the behalf, but not at the behest, of dominant or ruling classes. A range of state actors carries out various duties, consciously or unconsciously, in ways that serve the dual roles of facilitating capitalist accumulation and ensuring the continued development and legitimation of society.[59] Moreover, institutions such as schools, as "agencies of legitimacy," are administered by state actors such as government officials, superintendents of education, inspectors, and trustees in overt and covert ways that help to secure hegemony.[60] Indeed, political theorist Antonio Gramsci argues that the state in capitalist socities can be understood "as an educator" and that "every relationship of 'hegemony' is necessarily an educational relationship."[61] Building on these insights, I deploy a dual view of the state and schooling as a kind of domination – a project of rule – as well as a site for struggle.[62] Schooling, as Terry Wotherspoon shows, can reinforce and reproduce oppressive social structures but can also be an arena for contestation and possible social transformation.[63] By employing a political economy approach, which takes both top-down and bottom-up perspectives into account, I emphasize agency and highlight instances of conflict, compromise, and resistance by various individuals, including politicians, reformers, school officials, Indian agents, teachers, parents, students, and community members. I present the rise of state schooling in British Columbia as a powerful but negotiated and contested historical phenomenon.

In terms of methodology, key tools of the historian – examining context, interpreting causality, and tracing the contours of change over time – are central to this book.[64] Equally important, however, is incorporating Indigenous methodologies that emphasize the role of relationships and respect in producing knowledge about the past in the present. As I explained in the Preface, I am a white settler scholar who is a "continuing beneficiary" of Canada's colonial project, and thus it is essential that I engage respectfully with Indigenous methodologies to guide my work as it relates to Indigenous history.[65] This is important because, as Métis political scientist Adam Gaudry argues, academic research on Indigenous Peoples is "often an extractive process" that can "reproduce tired colonial narratives that justify occupation and oppression."[66] This need not be the case. Mary-Ellen Kelm and Keith D. Smith stress that historical thinking and Indigenous methodologies can be seen as "nested practices" to produce "new and better ways to understand the past."[67] Similarily, Māori scholar Linda Tuhiwai Smith argues that *"coming to know the past has been part of the critical pedagogy of decolonization. To hold alternative histories is to hold alternative knowledges."*[68]

In *Decolonizing Methodologies,* Smith outlines a number of projects for researchers. I take up the project of "reading" to critically interrogate the archival records produced by governments, churches, and schools that I use as evidence in this book.[69] Writers such as Ann Laura Stoler suggest that scholars approach the archives as producers of colonial knowledge and power.[70] We must read along and against the archival grain, she suggests, to understand how the archive is coded in colonial common sense and how it makes available some knowledges while serving to bury others.[71] In the context of British Columbia, historians such as Perry, Nickel, and John Sutton Lutz show that the archival record largely privileges settler conceptualizations of history but can nevertheless offer an important window onto the past.[72] Building on the work of Kelm and Smith and Mary Jane Logan McCallum and Perry, I aim to consult and "converse" with archival sources in ways that challenge colonial common sense and the erasure of Indigenous Peoples and their perspectives on the past.[73] In this way, *Lessons in Legitimacy* draws on and reads a range of sources along and against the grain. I examine public school and Department of Indian Affairs (DIA) records, Colonial Office (CO) correspondence, church records and missionary accounts, newspapers, photographs, educational materials such as textbooks and curriculum documents, and newly digitized school files and church records related to the creation and administration of mission schools and Indian Day Schools and Indian Residential Schools. As well, I consult Indigenous autobiographies and published oral histories as a way of showcasing Indigenous Peoples challenging and talking back to the colonial archive.[74]

I also engage Smith's project of reframing to offer a different perspective on the educational past.[75] Instead of consulting colonial sources to document progress, I critically examine my sources to better understand the central tendencies, or what Gidney and Millar call the "structural functions and operating procedures," of schooling.[76] Unlike Gidney and Millar, though, I am interested not only in explaining "how schools worked" but also in examining why they operated as they did to determine who benefitted most from the rise of state schooling. In doing so, I ask: What factors influenced the shift from voluntary education around the middle of the nineteenth century to compulsory state schooling in the early twentieth century? Who paid for schooling and why? How did colonial officials, church agents, provincial administrators, DIA staff, reformers, school trustees, teachers, parents, community members, and students debate, shape, and influence the meaning and outcomes of schooling? Why were Indigenous and non-Indigenous children mostly schooled separately, and how did the different school systems develop? What accounts for examples where Indigenous and non-Indigenous children and youth attended the same schools? How were relationships between and hierarchies of colonial, patriarchal, and capitalist rule normalized and legitimized but also resisted and subverted between 1849 and 1930? The pages that follow address these questions.

Responding to Cree political scientist Kiera Ladner's call to re-story Indigenous-settler relations in ways that reject narratives of convergence/assimilation, I use a parallel structure to trace the distinct but overlapping histories of Indigenous and non-Indigenous schooling.[77] *Lessons in Legitimacy* is organized chronologically into three parts that correspond to phases of colonization and the building of British Columbia. Each part consists of two chapters: the first examines settler schooling and the second discusses Indian education, but they are intended to be read contrapuntally, as a totality.[78] I also draw attention to instances where colonial binaries and the official boundaries between the systems were challenged and traversed. Overall, I show how different schooling projects for Indigenous and non-Indigenous people played complementory roles in catalyzing and legitimizing the making of British Columbia's capitalist settler society.

Part 1 explores the emergence of schooling in the colonies of Vancouver Island and British Columbia between 1849 and 1871. Chapter 1 shows that it shifted from ad hoc education for the offspring of elite Hudson's Bay Company (HBC) officers to a government-supported system of common schooling that was open to all classes of mostly, though not exclusively, settler children. HBC and colonial officials reluctantly agreed to pay for schooling, in exchange for increased power over education. Chapter 2 reveals that officials invited missionaries to start schools for Indigenous Peoples in the context of settler anxiety about their resistance to colonization.[79] Their purpose was to convince Indigenous Nations to accept colonization and develop skills to contribute to the new economy.

Part 2 looks at the rise of state schooling between 1871 and 1900. Chapter 3 shows that the provincial government transformed common schooling into a centralized public system after British Columbia joined Canada in 1871. During the early 1870s, the government agreed to cover almost the entire cost of the new system in exchange for increased power over education. By the late 1880s, it still retained this authority but started to shift costs and some administrative responsibilities to local levels. In response, municipalities taxed the property of ratepayers to raise funds for schooling. Thus, accumulation by dispossession — taxing stolen and occupied Indigenous lands — underwrote the growing school system. Chapter 4 discusses the federal government's new system of Indian education — which consisted of day, boarding, and industrial schools — that took root in British Columbia by the late 1880s and early 1890s, as part of its strategy to expand Canada's capitalist confederation.

Part 3 shows that provincial and federal governments reformed schooling in the early 1900s to support the development of an industrial capitalist economy. As Chapter 5 outlines, the provincial government normalized mass public schools by making attendance mandatory and introducing new educational methods to better prepare students for their eventual roles as citizens and wage workers. Chapter 6 examines Ottawa's continued commitment to Indian Day Schools and Indian Residential Schools as a way of disrupting and delegitimizing Indigenous lifeways to support ongoing settler capitalism and Canadian nation building. This chapter looks at the federal government's insistence on making Indian education compulsory and the emphasis on industrial training, but it also highlights what Mohawk scholar Audra Simpson calls Indigenous "refusal" as well as resistance. Such episodes, Simpson argues, strike at the heart of colonial hegemony and call state authority and its legitimacy into question.[80] Taken together, Chapters 5 and 6 show that Indigenous and non-Indigenous schooling played an important, though still contested, role in the consolidation of British Columbia by 1930.

This study ends in 1930 for a number of reasons. Obviously, neither school reform nor the making of British Columbia halted at that point. However, by the late 1920s and early 1930s, British Columbia's transformation to successful province was largely complete. New phases of colonial dispossession, proletarianization, and capitalist accumulation continued, of course, and regional development proceeded in uneven ways, but by this time the foundations were firmly established. Moreover, mass schooling had become the norm by the late 1920s, and the onset of the Great Depression slowed school reform efforts, federally and provincially, with few major educational changes occurring in British Columbia schools until after the Second World War.[81]

For the Conclusion, I synthesize my major findings. Stepping back to evaluate the book as a totality, I highlight the lessons learned from presenting separate but similar — and sometimes overlapping — histories of Indigenous and non-Indigenous schooling in tandem. I also connect these lessons to the present and to the calls made by the TRC and by Indigenous leaders such as Arthur Manuel for Canadians to put truth before reconciliation.[82]

In 2015, as the TRC prepared to release its final report, Murray Sinclair pointed out that "education is what got us into this mess," but he added that new kinds of education, including learning how to reckon with and address the colonial past and its ongoing legacies, are "the key to reconciliation."[83] Building on the work of the TRC, and bringing the histories of schooling for Indigenous and non-Indigenous people into one analytical frame, this book contributes to the project of truth telling about Canada's history that is required to support decolonization and meaningful reconciliation.

PART ONE

COLONIAL ORIGINS, 1849–71

BY THE MID-NINETEENTH CENTURY, Britain had created a number of settler colonies in the South Pacific, such as New Zealand and New South Wales, but its territorial claims in the Pacific Northwest were more tenuous. Between the 1770s and 1820s, Spanish and British explorers had reconnoitred the region, and traders intermittently competed over furs and exchange with numerous Indigenous Nations, notably the Nuu-chah-nulth.[1] By the 1830s, the Hudson's Bay Company (HBC), a London-based fur-trade business, had established a network of forts along the Columbia River and in the northern mainland known as New Caledonia; however, its focus was on producing private profit rather than engaging in international diplomacy and extending British sovereignty. At the same time, the United States was rapidly colonizing new territory in North America, including in Oregon Country, as it aggressively pursued westward expansion.

To protect their trade interests, and without consulting the numerous Indigenous Nations in the region, Britain and the United States signed the Oregon Treaty in 1846, dividing the Pacific Northwest in half. At the stroke of a pen, Britain claimed the northern portion, which included Vancouver Island, Haida Gwaii, and the large mainland area between 49° and 54°40.' Nevertheless, some British officials worried that if it were not properly colonized, the United States would annex the entire region. These fears were exacerbated by a series of gold rushes and the sudden influx of miners and settlers to the west coast. As a stopgap, Britain created two colonies: the Colonial Office in London established Vancouver Island in 1849 and British Columbia in 1858. In 1866, they merged to create the single Colony of British Columbia as part of the growing British Empire.

Britain's colonization efforts were also part of a new phase of global imperialism spurred by socioeconomic changes in the metropole. In the aftermath of the Industrial Revolution (1820s–40s) and the 1848 revolutions that shook Britain and much of Western Europe, and in the midst of the Great Famine in Ireland (1845–49), British officials saw a renewed commitment to imperialism as sound policy. Colonization, they argued, could offer the growing numbers of dispossessed and discontented in Britain the opportunity to improve their lives and status abroad, thus relieving political pressure at home. As scholars such as Ellen Meiksins Wood reveal, mass emigration through colonization also stimulated capitalist development by expanding overseas markets for British goods and creating global trade linkages.[2]

Conditions in the remote British colonies on the west coast, however, were rough and characterized by the booms and busts of uneven development. At first, only a handful of settlers, mostly with ties to the HBC, clustered around Victoria, the capital of Vancouver Island. Their emerging political culture was dominated by a small elite group, and the nascent government was controlled by colonial officials and HBC men with means, to the frustration of new settlers.[3] These arrivals, most of whom were white men from Britain, the United States, and British North American colonies, initially amounted to only a few thousand. They were greatly outnumbered by a diverse Indigenous population of more than sixty thousand, who possessed their own economies, cultures, and lifeways developed on the land and waterways since time immemorial. The limited colonial economy was structured around mercantile capitalism and the export of staples, such as minerals, animal products, and lumber, which were sought-after items in the global market. Traders exchanged imported commodities from the metropole, such as guns, tools, and utensils, for Indigenous subsistence products such as fish and furs. These economic activities were augmented by independent commodity production, as well as modest forms of agriculture and wage labour in fledgling resource industries such as mining and logging.[4]

Some Indigenous Nations, such as the ləkʷəŋən near Victoria, welcomed trade with the newcomers, whereas others, such as the Nlaka'pamux on the mainland, resented colonization and experienced it as an invasion that upset their subsistence economy and brought mass death through the spread of infectious diseases.[5] One particularly deadly outbreak of smallpox in 1862–63 decimated Indigenous Peoples, killing upward of thirty thousand people or approximately 50 percent of the population, which contributed to distrustful relations with newcomers.[6] Many prospective colonists viewed Vancouver Island and British Columbia as unstable and undesirable, opting instead for other parts of the British Empire.

Hoping to attract more settlers, HBC and colonial officials established key infrastructure, or what Ned Blackhawk calls the "mechanics of colonial rule" – everything from roads, bridges, and telegraph cables to police forces, post offices, banks, and courthouses – and they also gradually supported the creation of common schools.[7] As Chapter 1 shows, education shifted from an ad hoc HBC initiative to an organized common school system by the late 1860s, which offered basic education and was designed for working-class settler children. Partially funded by the government, it played an important role in encouraging settlers of modest means to put down roots and raise their families in the colonies. In this way, common schooling helped to assert British sovereignty and to establish a non-Indigenous population that numbered more than ten thousand by 1871.

Chapter 2 examines how colonial officials entered into agreements with missionaries to support separate schooling initiatives targeting Indigenous Peoples. Indigenous people negotiated the coming of Christianity as active agents, but missionaries, with assistance from colonial officials, sought to gain spiritual influence in ways that undermined Indigenous sovereignty and aided colonization. As settler anxiety intensified regarding Indigenous resistance to colonization, authorities hoped that missionaries would cultivate cordial relations and help avoid conflicts and costly military campaigns, ultimately strengthening British control in the region. Like common schools, colonial officials supported mission schools as part of their strategy for safeguarding the colonial project. Together, Chapters 1 and 2 show how government-assisted schooling, designed for Indigenous and non-Indigenous people, often overlapped and supported the seizure and settling of what became known as British Columbia in the mid-nineteenth century.

CHAPTER | ONE

Creating Common Schools

In 1847, James Edward FitzGerald, a British Museum employee in London with political ambitions, wrote to Britain's Colonial Office to propose a plan for colonizing the Pacific Northwest. The area was only informally secured by the fur-trade operations of the HBC, and thus he stressed Britain's need for "possessing some strong dependency" to protect its interests against possible advances by Russians in Alaska and Americans in Oregon Country.[1] FitzGerald argued that Vancouver Island and specifically Victoria, because of its temperate climate and good harbour, could benefit the growing British Empire by becoming a hub for trade in the Pacific.[2] He was adamant, however, that colonists must not be sent "to a desolate territory – without means – without organization."[3] They required an organized society, a "structure" in the words of Patrick Wolfe, that could sustain them.[4] As a result, he called on the British government to assist in establishing the necessary institutions, specifically schools to help socialize settler children and teach them how to be colonists.[5] His only stipulation was that trained personnel, not HBC employees, should be put in charge of overseeing the project.[6]

The Colonial Office, comprised of some thirty people working under the secretary of state for the colonies in two houses on Downing Street in London, agreed with many of FitzGerald's proposals, including the need for schools. Nevertheless, it did not share his lack of confidence in the HBC. Thus, when Britain created the Colony of Vancouver Island in 1849, the company was granted a ten-year lease to the new territory. FitzGerald was furious. He spoke out publicly against the decision, and he even wrote a book on the subject insisting that the HBC could be trusted only to secure higher profits for its shareholders to the detriment of extending British sovereignty.[7] The Colonial Office saw things differently. Because the HBC was already in the area and had established trade relations with Indigenous Peoples, it was strategically positioned to oversee immediate colonization. Having just moved its operations north in 1843 from Fort Vancouver on the Columbia River to Fort Victoria at the southern tip of Vancouver Island, the HBC was in the right place at the right time. There was one important caveat to this arrangement, however: if the company did not promote colonization, its lease would be revoked. As part of its settlement plan, the HBC gradually supported the creation of schools and an organized educational system.

This chapter details the development of schooling and colonization on the "edge of empire," as Adele Perry calls it, between 1849 and 1871.[8] Drawing on political economist Terry Wotherspoon's dual view of schooling "as a story of domination and struggle," it challenges the consensus thesis advanced by historians who contend that a general public agreement was reached regarding the role of education in society.[9] Instead, it shows that the creation of the common school system in mid-nineteenth-century British Columbia is best understood as a product of negotiation, struggle, and compromise. On the one hand, many colonists wanted an organized, non-denominational school system paid for by the colonial government. On the other hand, the government was willing to concede on the religion issue – despite preferring Anglican schooling – and agreed to take on more financial responsibility. In exchange, the government assumed almost total power over public education. This compromise set the stage for the nascent state to use its authority over education to create and administer a centralized school system – as a tool of legitimation – to support colonization and shape British Columbia's social formation into the 1870s.

EARLY SCHOOLING ON VANCOUVER ISLAND

By the 1820s, the HBC had started to support schooling initiatives in North American colonies such as Red River. The company also provided education for its employees and their children – almost all of Indigenous ancestry (and specifically Métis) – in the Pacific Northwest.[10] Sporadic schooling began in 1832 at Fort Vancouver, and employees in the new fort at Victoria, named after the queen, desired similar facilities. In 1848, a year before the island became a colony, the HBC selected Anglican clergyman Robert John Staines to fill the dual office of company chaplain and schoolmaster at the salary of £200 and £340 per year, respectively.[11] Staines, who had taught in England and Ireland, sailed out from London with his wife, Emma, who was also a teacher. In the spring of 1849, they arrived in Victoria and quickly discovered the colony's rough conditions. In speaking of their arrival, HBC clerk Roderick Finlayson recalled,

> At this time there were no streets and the traffic cut up the thoroughfares so that everyone had to wear sea boots to wade through the mud and mire ... It was my duty to receive the clergyman, which I did, but felt ashamed to see the lady come ashore. We had to lay planks through the mud in order to get them safely to the fort. They looked wonderingly at the bare walls of the building, and expressed deep surprise, stating that the Company in England had told them this and that, and had promised them such and such.[12]

Victoria was not what the couple had expected.

Nonetheless, they took up their duties, teaching approximately twenty elite children, boys and girls, in the rooms of Fort Victoria, including the Mess Hall and the Bachelors' Hall. Emma, generally thought to be a better teacher than her husband, taught the girls and served as the matron to the children, who slept above the Bachelors' Hall.[13] The students sometimes poured water through cracks in the floor onto the heads of the bachelors below.[14] The school was envisioned as a kind of private boarding facility where the children of elite fur-trade officers would receive a proper education at the cost of £20 annually per child for room and board. The company wanted to use private education, increasingly popular in Britain after the Industrial Revolution, to reproduce the class hierarchy of the Old Country in the new colony.[15] Schooling also ordered rank and class according to gender and racialization. The colony was heterogeneous, and as Perry and Sarah Carter make clear, many HBC officers established intimate relationships with Indigenous

FIGURE 1.1 Fort Victoria, c. 1860. On the left are the residence of the chief factor and the Mess Hall. On the right are the Bachelors' Hall (below) and the school dorm (above). The fort, known briefly as Fort Albert, was established by the HBC in 1843. It was built byləkʷəŋən labourers. | Courtesy of the Royal BC Museum, Image A-04098, British Columbia Archives

women.[16] Nick Estes argues that fur traders sought out Indigenous women's bodies to increase their "access to new markets through their kin – and by extension, land, capital, and political and economic influence."[17] As a result of such unions, some of the early pupils in the private school were elite and Indigenous.

Staines faced many challenges in his new position. According to James Anderson, one of Staines's pupils, the teacher was a disciplinarian but had a difficult time controlling the class.[18] Though Staines attempted to impart an appreciation for the game of cricket, Anderson and his classmates preferred an assortment of rough activities including "rounders, horse racing, fighting Indian boys, worrying Indian dogs, some surreptitious shooting with our antiquated flint-lock musket, besides any occasional mischief such as boys alone are capable of conceiving."[19] Staines, in short, had his work cut out for him. In October 1850, Fort Victoria chief factor James Douglas wrote to A.C. Anderson, the chief trader at Fort Colville, Washington, whose children attended the private school. He reported, "The children have greatly improved in their personal appearance and one thing I particularly love in Staines is the attention he bestows on their religious training. Had I a selection to make he is not exactly the man I would choose; but it must be admitted we might find a man worse qualified for the charge of the school."[20]

As this mixed review intimated, Staines's stay on Vancouver Island was contentious. According to physician John Sebastian Helmcken, who married Douglas's daughter Cecilia in 1852 and later became a prominent British Columbia politician, a "fairly rigid class structure" emerged in the colony.[21] Reinforced by the private school, it became known as the "family-company-compact" because it privileged HBC officers and their children (such as the Douglasses, Works, Tolmies, Finlaysons, and Tods). Staines may have been good enough to teach children of the elite, but he was never accepted into the colony's inner circles of power. Thus, he sided with disgruntled colonists and former HBC employees who were frustrated with company rule. In particular, poor colonists objected to the high cost of land, arbitrarily set by the company at £1 per acre, with a minimum purchase of twenty acres, which had the effect of driving settlers into wage labour, just as popular colonization theorist Edward Gibbon Wakefield had recommended.[22] Staines also frequently wrote and signed petitions calling on the Colonial Office to revoke the HBC lease and to assert proper imperial authority on the island. Richard Blanshard, its first governor, who arrived after Staines, shared many of these frustrations and resigned from his post after less than two years. In 1851, Staines helped draft a petition to oppose Douglas's appointment as governor. His efforts were in vain. The Colonial Office opted for Douglas.

Bad blood soon developed between Staines and the elite. In the eyes of some parents, his political activity – especially in challenging the authority of the new governor – made him unfit to teach their children. In

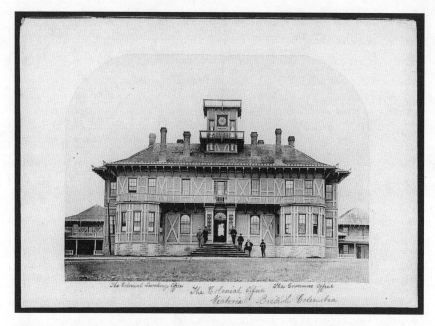

FIGURE 1.2 Colonial Administration Buildings, Victoria, c. 1860s. Architect H.O. Tiedemann designed a series of six government buildings in an ornate style that some observers thought resembled birdcages. The buildings, including the Colonial Office (pictured), were thus nicknamed "The Birdcages." The Colonial Secretary's Office is on the left. The Governor's Office is on the right. | Courtesy of the National Archives, Image 1069/271

1853, they criticized his conduct and petitioned Douglas to fire him. On February 1, 1854, Douglas and HBC chief factor James Work complied, dismissing Staines from his posts as schoolmaster and HBC chaplain.[23] Staines was outraged. A few days later, a delegation of discontented colonists selected him to carry petitions to London expressing their grievances with company rule. He soon boarded the *Duchess of San Lorenzo* at Sooke, bound for San Francisco en route to London, but the ship foundered and sank in the Salish Sea. All on board drowned. Given the hard feelings between her husband and the HBC elite, Emma Staines decided to return to London. So ended the first sustained schooling experiment in the colony, though it was soon resumed, and new private schools, such as the Collegiate School for Boys, Angela College, and St. Ann's Academy, were opened in Victoria for pupils "of the middle and upper sort."[24]

Common Schooling in the Colony of Vancouver Island

In the early 1850s, hoping to address the complaints of malcontented colonists, Governor Douglas turned his attention to the children of lower-class HBC employees. Most of these workers were craftsmen, interpreters, and labourers (many with Indigenous families), and according to Douglas, their children were "growing up in ignorance, and the utter neglect of all their duties to God and to society."[25] He envisioned a new system of common schooling, denominational in character, whereby the HBC would furnish "the sites and [provide] such pecuniary assistance as they may deem necessary."[26] Douglas explained that the new public or "common schools" were "intended for the children of the laboring and poorer classes," and that "children of promising talents, or whom their parents may wish to educate further, may pursue their studies and acquire the other branches of knowledge at the company's school."[27] As historical sociologists Philip Corrigan, Bruce Curtis, and Robert Lanning argue, such early schooling experiments were less about education per se and more about "making selves" – of informing, improving, and transforming people – through "subjectification and embodiment."[28] Education historian Charles E. Phillips also notes that religious schooling for the poor played the important role of justifying social and economic inequality "by attributing it to God."[29] On the island, Douglas envisioned a two-tiered, denominational educational system based on class distinction and predicated on payment by parents. The common schools would teach lower-class children and would be lightly subsidized by the colony. Private schools would service HBC officers, as well as labourers whose children showed "promising talent" and who could afford to pay the fee. Moreover, the colony would take a mostly hands-off approach to administering education. Douglas's hope was that the ad hoc common schooling system could mollify complaints about company rule while still reinforcing and legitimizing the colony's rigid class structure.

In 1852, Douglas opened the first common school. Situated in temporary quarters, its pupils were the male children of HBC servants in Fort Victoria. Charles Bailey, a company labourer, was appointed as schoolmaster. In a letter to HBC headquarters in London, Douglas explained,

> Mr. Charles Bailey the young man who acted as schoolmaster for the Emigrants during the outward voyage of the *Tory* having conducted himself with great propriety since his arrival here and not being particularly useful as a mere labourer I have opened a day school for boys, the children of the Company's labouring servants at this place, who are growing up in ignorance of their duties as men and Christians. It is now attended by 18 boys, who are making fair progress in learning.

Parents paid £1 annually per child, which went into a fund to support the teacher in purchasing supplies. In addition, Douglas clarified that the teacher received "his wages and provision from the Company, who are put to no other expense for the institution."[30] The next year, Robert Barr replaced Bailey at the school, which moved to the first purpose-built schoolhouse in the colony at Minie's Plain about a mile away from the fort. In October 1853, Douglas informed the colonial secretary that "Mr. Barr resides on the premises, and has thirty-three pupils, who are making satisfactory progress."[31]

Subsequent common schools were planned for nearby settlements at Esquimalt and Maple Point, but they were put on hold by Douglas, who felt that the coal-mining community of Nanaimo should be the next priority. Having learned about coal deposits from citizens of the Snuneymuxw Nation and recognizing the potential profit of resource development in the area, the HBC encouraged upward of eighty labourers and their families to emigrate from England to Nanaimo, on eastern Vancouver Island, to begin mining.[32] This industry would later become a key component of British Columbia's capitalist economy.[33] As FitzGerald had anticipated, the miners soon made demands for their children's education. Eager to retain them as colonists, Douglas opened the second common school, in Nanaimo in 1853. He transferred Bailey there to serve as schoolmaster. Historian John Douglas Belshaw notes that though many miners were initially enthusiastic about the school, "there are reasons to think that the miners and their families became increasingly alienated from the whole idea."[34] Belshaw argues that miners came to resent the erosion of parental authority over education and rejected

FIGURE 1.3 The Craigflower School's first class, with parents, c. 1850s. Craigflower Farm was established in 1853 by the Puget Sound Agricultural Company, a subsidiary of the HBC. The farm supplied fresh produce to nearby Fort Victoria. The Craigflower School opened in 1855 and was the colony's third common school. | Courtesy of the Royal BC Museum, Image D-03648, British Columbia Archives

the pay-for-service model by refusing to reimburse the HBC or the colony for the teacher's salary. In protest, some families even kept their children at home.[35] Nanaimo, then, is a good example of how common schooling was provided, initially at cost to company and colony, as a strategy to support colonization. It also reveals that schooling was a contested and negotiated process from the start.

The colony's third common school was the Craigflower School, near the Craigflower Farm, an agricultural settlement a few miles northwest of Fort Victoria. The Craigflower School officially opened its doors in 1855, with Charles Clarke from England as its first schoolmaster. The two-story building consisted of a single classroom on the ground floor and six additional rooms upstairs for the teacher, his family, and a few student boarders. Almost a half-century later, Thomas Russell, who taught at the school in the 1860s, reflected on the coming of the Clarkes and the opening of the school: "Shortly after their arrival the school was opened with due form and ceremony, the enrolment consisting of eight boys and six girls from our own little party. The school gradually grew in strength and continued to flourish under Mr. Clarke."[36] Thus, by the mid-1850s, the HBC had opened and partially funded three common schools, mostly for the labouring classes, on Vancouver Island, where pupils learned to read, write, and accept their lower standing in the colony's emerging social order. The early growth of common schooling was, as historian Thomas Fleming points out, greatly shaped by the HBC penchant for "paternalism and centralized authority."[37] In the earliest days, Governor Douglas even attended the annual examinations and awarded prizes to deserving students to encourage their continued enrolment.

Once Robert and Emma Staines were gone, the HBC hired another Anglican clergyman in the mid-1850s to teach at the Fort Victoria private school and to supervise the common school system. Reverend Edward Cridge accepted the terms and conditions of the position, including an annual salary of £300, with an additional £100 to act as HBC chaplain. He made the voyage out from England to Victoria with his wife, Mary. The Cridges arrived in 1855 during a time of transition in the colony. After six years of HBC rule, and a number of petitions sent to London by dissatisfied settlers, Britain granted the island a legislative assembly – the Council of Vancouver Island – the first elected assembly west of what is today known as Ontario. Its opening session was held in the Mess Hall at Fort Victoria, one of the buildings where Staines had taught. Such are the origins of British Columbia's rudimentary state structure. Most individuals who were eligible to vote for council members – men with property – were still inextricably linked to the HBC, but the balance of political power started to shift.[38] The council created new positions, whose holders were accountable to it. One of its first orders of business was to appoint Cridge as the superintendent of education, a position he held for nearly ten years.[39] Cridge took his responsibilities seriously, producing a series of detailed reports that catalogued the successes and failures of the common schools.[40]

Cridge's reports revealed that the common school system was plagued by problems of poor attendance, improper facilities, and inadequate

FIGURE 1.4 Reverend Edward Cridge, c. 1870s. In addition to his teaching and religious duties for the HBC, Cridge served as the colony's first superintendent of education between 1856 and 1865. | Courtesy of the Royal BC Museum, Image A-01202, British Columbia Archives

educational materials. A number of variables explained the low attendance. Weather was one. In his 1860 report, Cridge explained that twenty six students had left the Victoria school during the winter "on account of the state of the weather, intending as the teacher understood, to return in the spring." Tuition fees, ranging anywhere from five to twelve dollars per year, also posed a barrier for some poor families and contributed to irregular attendance. During the winter of 1857, the classroom at the Victoria school was unusable. Cridge recorded that "the scholars were at present taught in the Kitchen ... the Schoolroom being too cold for winter occupation." Teachers developed creative strategies to address such challenges, including sending some students out for recess while teaching the remainder in the school building.[41] Despite these rough conditions,

Cridge noted that the students who managed to attend received a satisfactory education in the basics of reading, writing, arithmetic, grammar, and geography, with some religious instruction as well.[42]

Cridge's reports also showed that the student body of some schools was more heterogeneous than has previously been thought. Reflecting on his experience at the Victoria school, Edgar Fawcett remembered, "our school might be aptly termed a mixed one ... There were white boys and black boys, Hebrews and Gentiles, rich and poor, and we all sat close together to economize room."[43] Cridge reported that twelve "colored" students attended in 1864–65, including "Peter Lester" and "Isabella Lester." The category of "colored" might have included Iroquois and Pacific Islanders, or Kanakas, who worked for the HBC, but the Lesters were probably the children of Peter Lester, a Black leader of the National Negro Convention Movement in California who fled north to Victoria.[44] Though "colored" is the only racialized designation to appear on the school lists, simply to assume that all the other children were "white" would be a mistake. Below the Lester children on the roll is listed "James Douglas Govrs Son." The Indigenous ancestry of Douglas's children, including his son James, was widely recognized in the colony. Perry notes that the Douglas children grew up enmeshed in "elite Creole-Metis life."[45] Douglas himself was likely born in Demerara, now Guyana, to a Scottish father and a Creole mother who was classified as a free woman of colour from Barbados. His wife, Amelia Connolly, was the Métis daughter of an influential fur trader with ties to the Red River settlement in what is now Manitoba.[46]

Similarly, other children listed in the 1860s attendance records cannot simply be assumed to be white.[47] In the words of critical theorist Homi K. Bhabha, they were "not quite/not white."[48] Indeed, Perry argues that "whiteness was far from given or salient" in mid-nineteenth-century British Columbia.[49] The attendance records list Isaac Tod as "HBC Farmers Son," and William Tod has only "HBC" scribbled beside his name. Isaac and William were the sons of HBC chief trader John Tod and his Indigenous wife, Sophia "Martha" Lolo. Student David Work was the son of John Work and his Indigenous wife, Josette Legace. Work moved his family from Fort Simpson on the Northwest Coast to Fort Victoria specifically so that his children could attend school.[50] In analyzing fur-trade societies, historian Sylvia Van Kirk argues that it is "important to differentiate racism along sex lines because prejudice affected males in different ways and usually earlier than it did their female counterparts."[51] Sons of fur-trade marriages, sometimes racialized as "half-breeds," were often denied access to elite society.[52] This can explain why Douglas's son attended a common school, whereas his daughters went to private schools. Douglas even enrolled his youngest daughter, Martha, in a prestigious private school in England and counselled her to keep her Indigeneity a secret.[53]

Cridge's reports also reveal that teaching in the colony was a prized but underpaid occupation. In 1862, he spoke very highly of W.H. Burr's teaching efforts at the Victoria Colonial School, though he admitted that Burr had difficulty supporting his family on a teacher's salary.[54] In 1863, Cornelius Bryant, the new teacher at the Nanaimo school, took matters into his own hands by demanding a pay raise. In a letter to Douglas, he reasoned, "Owing to the increasing importance and responsibilities of my duties as School Teacher at this place I am induced to humbly petition your Excellency to be pleased to grant me an increase in salary. ... As I understand the Teachers of the other Colonial Schools are receiving this year an advance on their former salaries of £50 per annum," he noted, "I hope that my humble request for a similar favour may meet with your Excellency's kind consideration."[55] As the school system grew, so too did teachers' expectations for greater remuneration.[56]

Despite its many challenges, Vancouver Island's common school system started to congeal in the 1860s. In 1866, roughly five hundred students were attending the Victoria, Nanaimo, and Craigflower schools, as well as newly established ones at Esquimalt, Cedar Hill, Lake District, South Saanich, and Cowichan. However, many children still went to private institutions. Some labouring parents, for religious reasons, pressed for strictly denominational education for their children, and elite parents preferred private schooling to pass on the privileges of rank and class to preserve the status quo.[57] Moreover, some children did not attend school at all. In 1864, a Victoria newspaper lamented that approximately fifty to a hundred children were still "running through the streets ... acquiring street education that will prepare many of them in after years for every description of crime and depravity."[58]

In 1864, Arthur Kennedy replaced Douglas as governor and raised concerns about the future of schooling on the island. If it were to be useful in furthering colonization, reform was needed. Many parents agreed. In March, a large public meeting was held in Victoria. Those in attendance, supported by outspoken teachers such as John Jessop and politicians such as Israel Wood Powell, demanded the establishment of tuition-free, non-denominational common schools. This public pressure pushed elected representatives to pass the Common Schools Act, 1865, which implemented a completely free system of common schooling paid for by the government in Victoria. In addition, it was to be based on non-sectarian principles.

After fifteen years of largely ad hoc, fee-based, and mostly denominational education, the school act established a free, non-denominational system. It also created a highly centralized administrative structure to run the system. The governor was still in charge, though he could now appoint nine board members to oversee all things educational. As before, he could also appoint teachers, but the board outlined their duties and had the authority to inspect schools. The governor also appointed a superintendent of education with an annual salary of $1,500. In 1865, Kennedy chose Alfred Waddington, a prominent politician and advocate of free education, to replace Cridge. Many people welcomed these changes, but there was by no means a consensus. Free schooling was a compromise as well as a strategy of rule on Vancouver Island. The government saw the new school act as a double-edged sword. On the one hand, free schools would encourage settlers to stay and support colonization. On the other hand, the colony was deeply in debt and the government promise to pay for schooling exacerbated financial problems during a time of economic depression in the mid-1860s. Indeed, Kennedy was alarmed at the growing expenditure for education, rising from about $5,000 in 1865 to almost $25,000 in 1866, and he noted that administering the system was "rapidly degenerating into a monster job."[59]

Common Schooling in the Colony of British Columbia

Schooling on the mainland developed differently and more slowly than on the island. In 1858, in the midst of a gold rush, British Columbia became an official Crown colony. In a brash move, and one of the largest land grabs in history, the British government ended the ten-year HBC lease early and asserted its sovereignty over the mainland without consulting Indigenous Nations.[60] Its power play was orchestrated by the colonial secretary in London, Sir Edward Bulwer-Lytton, to secure control of the resource-rich region. The new colony officially came into being on August 2, 1858, and the Colonial Office appointed Douglas as governor of both colonies on the condition that he resign from the HBC to avoid a conflict of interest. Douglas agreed. In claiming control over the mainland, Britain benefitted from the gold rush (from both the export of gold and the opening of new markets for its goods), but the Colonial Office made it clear that the new colony was to be financially self-sufficient. Thus, it took a hands-off approach to assisting social development. Once again, facilitating colonization was left to Douglas. Reflecting on the job at hand, he noted, "to create a great social organization, with all its civil, judicial, and military establishments, in a wilderness of forests and mountains, is a herculean task."[61] The mainland was not, however, an empty landscape, as Douglas and other colonial officials would soon realize. Many Indigenous Nations already lived there, having inhabited it for time out of mind.

As the gold rush intensified, and thousands of miners poured in, the need to assert authority became clear when the Fraser Canyon War broke out between invading miners and the Nlaka'pamux in the summer of 1858.[62] Historian Keith Thor Carlson writes that the "gold rush constitutes a particularly violent moment" in the history of British Columbia. "Given the speed of the event, the number of people involved, the size of the Indigenous population affected, and the extent to which the latter held firm concepts of property ownership," he explains, "violence was inevitable."[63] Indeed, Karl Marx noted that the "discovery of gold" and conflicts with Indigenous Peoples in the Americas were among the "chief moments" of so-called primitive accumulation and the birth of capitalism.[64] In the case of the Fraser Canyon War, Nlaka'pamux citizens complained that American and European miners from California and Oregon Country were impinging on their territories and taking gold, salmon, and other resources. They also harassed Nlaka'pamux women. Sicangu scholar Virginia Driving Hawk Sneve shows that white men's violence against Indigenous women is a defining feature of transient all-male communities, often referred to as "man camps," that are based on resource exploitation.[65] As a mining colony consisting mostly of men, British Columbia had the homosocial characteristics of a man camp and the Indigenous Nation perceived the link between settler violence against Nlaka'pamux women and violence against its lands.[66]

Tensions boiled over in August 1858 when a miner raped a Nlaka'pamux woman. In response, the community killed him and put his body into the Fraser River.[67] Miners organized volunteer militias to mount a show of force. Deadly conflict erupted. As the militias travelled up the canyon, they met the Nlaka'pamux in battle and burned a number of villages upon their return to Yale. Local Indigenous Nations gathered to determine their response. Meanwhile, the Pike Guards, a militia led by Captain H.M. Snyder, set out to enter into peace talks.[68] Snyder carried a white flag and brokered deals with various chiefs at Lytton, including Chief Emmitt Liquitem of the Stó:lō and Chief Cexpe'nthlEm (David Spintlum) of the Nlaka'pamux.[69] Stories passed down to Nlaka'pamux Elder Mary Williams give a different version: "They arrived with one of their headmen, and told the Lytton people to gather ... Every one of the White men had loaded rifles, ready to shoot the people ... The Whites said that all the old people were going to be killed off – only the young women were to be kept." According to Williams, Cexpe'nthlEm intervened, shouting, "Stop right there! End that talk right there! I am going to give you some land ... The white people agreed. They put down all their guns and shook hands with the Indian people and went back to where they came from, back to Yale."[70]

Alarmed by reports of conflict in the canyon, Douglas sent out a small force from Vancouver Island, the Columbia Detachment of the Royal Engineers, to keep the peace and lay the foundation for colonization on the mainland. The engineers and their families were stationed at

Sapperton, which lay on the slope above the Fraser River near a Qayqayt village. It was just east of what would become Queensborough, the colony's capital, later renamed New Westminster by Queen Victoria. The engineers, or "sappers," were tasked with keeping order, protecting settlers, and assisting with surveying land and constructing the roads and bridges that were essential to the new colony's development. Like the miners at Nanaimo, they soon asked the colony for financial support to educate their children. In examining the engineers and their families, Laura Ishiguro notes that "young people were central to, rather than distractions from, the settler colonial project."[71] In 1861, Colonel Richard Moody, head of the engineers and lieutenant governor of the mainland colony, asked for school aid. Douglas forwarded his request to the Colonial Office in London. Moody asked for the sum of £85 to cover the educational costs for thirty-one children.[72] An informal school had been in operation at Sapperton before 1861, probably as early as 1858 or 1859, mostly under the direction of Reverend John Sheepshanks, the acting chaplain for the sappers.[73] Emily Herring, stepdaughter of an engineer named Philip Crart, had been hired as its first official teacher but was dismissed in 1861, and the school was in jeopardy. Moody thus asked Britain's War Department to provide "aid towards the schooling of soldiers' children" in the "sum of thirty pounds per annum with free rations."[74] Moody's request was forwarded to the War Office for consideration and approved at the rate of £18 per year, confirming the linkages between war, money, and empire, as outlined by political economist David McNally.[75] The local colonial government also contributed a grant of £50. With these new funds, from metropole and colony, the school was reopened in 1863. Anne Moresby, a widow from Victoria, was hired as its teacher.

Later that same year, the detachment was disbanded on Douglas's orders, and the Sapperton school transitioned into a general common school. Moresby was kept on as teacher. In November 1864, Arthur Thomas Bushby, a public servant in the colony, wrote to the Colonial Office to explain that "a petition unanimously signed by the inhabitants of the camps" was presented regarding "the necessity for the continuance of the school and praying for pecuniary help to that purpose. The result was that Ms Moresby was re-appointed for twelve months at a salary of £72 per an. with allowance." In addition, Moresby could collect school fees to use as she saw fit. The status quo at the Sapperton school was mostly maintained. Bushby elaborated:

> The school for some time past has been attended by an average of twenty-five children (boys & girls) from the ages of four to ten. The school hours are from 9:30am to 12am and from 1 to 3pm with half holy day on Wednesday and Saturdays ... The course of instruction consists of reading, writing, spelling, history, grammar, geography, and arithmetic, in most of which branches I found the children very fairly proficient considering their ages and scanty appliances Ms Moresby has at her command for imparting such knowledge.[76]

Bushby confirmed that the local colonial government paid £72 for Moresby's salary and that she collected a $1 fee per student per month from parents. Partly due to the lack of white women and the demographic dominance of men, especially in the backwoods, an organized system of schooling did not develop as quickly on the mainland as it did on the island.[77] Nevertheless, by the mid-1860s both colonies possessed common schooling systems that were supported by government funds and fees paid by parents.

Around the time that the Sapperton school became a common school, a new school at New Westminster was opened in April of 1863, with James McIlveen as teacher. At the prodding of a petition signed by concerned parents, Governor Douglas provided funding in the form of £100 to help construct a suitable building. Soon the new venture had over twenty pupils, who were taught reading, writing, arithmetic, geography, grammar, and English history. It operated along non-sectarian lines. Though the colony provided a plot of free land for the school and an annual grant of £100 for upkeep and the teacher's salary, attendance was by no means free. As at Sapperton, parents were expected to pay for their children's education through fees. By 1865, the Sapperton and New Westminster schools were proving that a demand for education existed in the young colony, even if parents had to shoulder some of the costs.[78]

Little is known about the conditions of British Columbia's other early common schools, at locations such as Langley, Yale, and Douglas. However, some records do provide glimpses. In 1868, Bushby included a report from the Langley school in a letter to the Colonial Office in London. Its unnamed author, probably the teacher, stated that twenty-six children between the ages of seven and fifteen attended the school from April to December in 1867. The writer explained, "Except my own children, none could read. With the above exception none speaks anything but Chinook. Of those who have attended regularly, quite a number can read and spell tolerably, and a few can write fairly."[79] As John Sutton Lutz shows, Chinook Jargon, or chinuk wawa, was a prominent hybrid language that emerged in the Pacific Northwest for trade purposes and was based loosely on the language of the Chinook people.[80] And though language cannot be assumed to be a signifier of identity, given that Langley started as an HBC fort, many of the students were probably Indigenous.[81] Indeed, Barman explains that the fort was a representative mix of HBC employees, including Canadiens, Indigenous Hawaiians, and Iroquois who had travelled west to work in the fur trade.[82] The author of the report on the Langley school stated that it received $250 via a government grant and the rest of the $434 was paid by a local committee through parental subscriptions and monies raised by charging $1 per scholar per school term.[83]

What we know about the first teachers in British Columbia comes from their own sporadic reports, which often discussed teaching conditions and pay grievances, and even rarely commented on the racial composition of classes. Little is known about the school at Douglas, at the head of Harrison Lake on an early route to the Cariboo gold fields, but because of a grievance over wages, we have a record for its teacher, Mrs. Sarah Brown, and her class. By 1866, as the gold rush waned and a depression ensued, the population of Douglas had decreased. In May, Chief Inspector of Police Chartres Brew informed the local colonial secretary that its school had only five pupils. He argued that if the government were determined to close it down, Mrs. Brown should still receive her salary for work completed.[84] Soon afterward, Brown wrote to Brew: "I venture to address you upon the subject of my salary; as I have performed the duty of School Mistress for two months and a half I would certainly be glad to know what steps the Committee or the Government are going to take in the matter."[85] It was decided that Brown would continue as teacher at the rate of $25 per month, so long as the number of pupils was sufficient to justify payment. To prove that her school was meeting this requirement, Brown compiled a list of its eight students in July 1866, recording their names, area of residence, and racialization:

Joseph Smith – 29 Mile House – white
Josephine M. Donald – Douglas – white
Minnie Parker – Douglas – white
Kate Parker – Douglas – white
Alfred M. Donald – Douglas – white
Alfred Smith – Douglas – white
Frederick M. Donald – Douglas – an infant – white
Benjamin Franklin (half Jew, half Siwash) – Douglas.[86]

"Siwash," the Chinook word for "Indian," was sometimes used as a slur in the nineteenth century, and the Douglas Nation, or Xz'xtsa, is a subgroup of the St'át'imc. British Columbia's early common schools, then, like those on the island, are best understood as "contact zones" with a more heterogeneous student body than was previously believed, confirming Perry's observations about the colony as a whole.[87]

By the mid-1860s, only four common schools were officially in operation on the mainland: Sapperton, New Westminster, Yale, and Langley. The Sapperton school was taught by Moresby and was attended by twenty-five students, ten boys and fifteen girls. Run by H. Burr, New Westminster had sixty pupils, forty boys and twenty girls. At Yale, A. Burr taught twenty-six, twelve boys and fourteen girls, and at Langley, A. Kennedy taught thirty, fifteen boys and fifteen girls.[88] Though public demand for schooling was growing throughout the colony, an official explained in 1866 that "no general system of public education exists at present" and that the government was committed to avoiding Vancouver Island's costly "free" system of common schools.[89]

Two Visions, One System

In 1866, the two colonies merged to form the united Colony of British Columbia. It was a marriage of convenience.[90] In the wake of the gold rush, Vancouver Island was suffering the effects of a depression, and the resource-rich but deeply indebted colony needed more administrative support. The union, however, was a rocky one. Each colony had cultivated its own procedures, and they disagreed on the proper direction of policy. What to do about schooling was a particularly contentious question. Vancouver Island officials pointed to the mainland's scanty school system as ineffective for supporting colonization, whereas their mainland counterparts criticized the free education scheme as extravagant and advocated for fee-based schooling. Given the two conflicting visions, the need for a unified approach to school reform quickly became apparent. In the meantime, the status quo – of free schools on the island and for-pay schools on the mainland – continued.

In the mid- to late 1860s, a fight for school reform arose, most notably championed by the editors of the leading newspapers, the *British Colonist*'s Amor De Cosmos in Victoria and the *British Columbian*'s John Robson in New Westminster. Both men were political reformers, advocates for a single non-sectarian school system, and proponents of British Columbia's eventual confederation with Canada in 1871. They played influential roles as state-builders, later served as premiers of British Columbia, and are numbered among the founders of its public education system.[91] Though they disagreed on certain issues, including that of school fees, they sparked a popular debate about the future of schooling in the colony. Like many settlers who had travelled west from the Maritimes and Ontario, De Cosmos and Robson brought their education experiences and ideals with them, and they saw an organized school system as key for supporting colonization and British Columbia's continued social and economic development.

Born William Alexander Smith, Amor De Cosmos fancied himself a "lover of the universe." De Cosmos, whom Johnson calls the "most eccentric, colourful, and controversial figure" in the history of British Columbia, was born in Nova Scotia and reaped the benefits of an organized system of common schooling before attending Dalhousie University, where he was exposed to the ideas of political reformer Joseph Howe.[92] After a stint in the California gold fields, he came north to Victoria, where he founded the *British Colonist* to sound off on pressing issues. His weapon of choice was the sharply worded editorial.[93] His favourite targets were the HBC, the Church of England, and the power of the local elite. In only a few short years, De Cosmos became an important political reformer, and he routinely advocated for free, non-denominational schooling for all. One of his key ideas was that education should be paid for through the sale of public lands, which had been usurped from Indigenous Peoples through colonization. He lobbied for the government to set aside school land reserves in every township and suggested that proceeds from their rental or sale could be put into a common endowment to pay for education costs, to be supplemented with a tax as needed.

As a result of his work in the colony, De Cosmos was elected to the Vancouver Island legislature in 1863, and he continued to advocate for free schooling on the island. In an 1865 editorial, he stated his views on the importance of education for social development:

> For the first time since the colony of Vancouver Island came into existence the blessing of education has been presented to the poorest as well as to the richest child ... Poverty has at length ceased to be an excuse for idle and ignorant childhood ... In a young community like ours the education of youth is a subject of even more tender solicitude than it is in older countries. We are forming the minds of those who are not only to become responsible for the material progress of the country, but who are to build it up, if not indeed lay the foundation of the social as well as political fabric of British rule on this side of the continent. There is a power in the public system of education of creating a national sentiment and

inculcating an earnest patriotism almost unknown in the private schools of instruction.[94]

According to De Cosmos, schools were crucial tools not just of colonization and legitimation, but also of cultivating an interest in industry and social progress.

On the mainland, his educational equal was Robson, who was similarly attracted to the coast by the lure of the gold fields. When his luck ran out, Robson decided to settle in British Columbia, where he became an advocate for representative government. Growing up in Upper Canada, he was exposed to the ideas of reformers such as Egerton Ryerson, who played an instrumental role in implementing public schooling in Upper Canada and who also called for separate industrial schools for Indigenous children. In British Columbia, Robson became a newspaperman, the mayor of New Westminster, and an outspoken advocate for school reform. In the *British Columbian,* he argued that with increased immigration to the colony, schooling was necessary to harness the power of its population growth. Robson believed, much like FitzGerald twenty years earlier, that an organized school system was essential for recruiting and retaining desirable colonists. Though he favoured inclusive, non-denominational education and argued that the fees were "entirely too high for the working classes," he did not approve of free schooling.[95] He believed that to "throw free education open to everyone was a serious principle, it caused people to forget the advantages that were bestowed on them and rendered the parents careless as to the attendance of the children at school. There could be no doubt that making the parents pay one-half of the cost of educating their children was the true principle."[96] In his opinion, no one could complain about the use of public money for education if schools were non-denominational and open to all. Moreover, he agreed with De Cosmos on the appropriation of public lands – setting aside every fifth or tenth lot surveyed in a townsite for school purposes. The lots would be sold or rented to establish an endowment fund for education, which would be supplemented, as needed, with government grants and school fees.

De Cosmos and Robson's calls for reform garnered a lot of public support, especially from parents and guardians. But the British Columbia government mostly preferred the status quo.[97] Frederick Seymour, governor of the newly amalgamated colony, initially opposed school reform. In the first session of the legislature, he addressed the public's demands.[98] He protested, "the Colony is not yet old enough for any regular system of Education to be established." On the subject of free schools, he stated that

> any man who respects himself would not desire to have his children instructed without some pecuniary sacrifice on his own part. The State may aid the parent, but ought not to relieve him of his own natural responsibility else it may happen that the promising mechanic may be marred, and the country overburdened with half-educated professional politicians or needy hangers-on of the Government.[99]

Barman summarizes Seymour's logic succinctly: "Unnecessary education, likely if it be free, would only result in individuals unhappy with their destined place in the social order."[100] Seymour noted that the duty of government was only "to assist in giving to all elementary instruction, and then to offer inducements to those who are able to come to the front in the intellectual struggle with their fellow men."[101] Many elite parents who favoured class-based, denominational schooling shared his opinion. If education were free, they argued, the lower classes might forget their proper place in the social hierarchy. As a result, the government held firm that it should not bear the entire financial burden of an expanding school system.

By the late 1860s, however, a growing population and persistent demands by parents, guardians, and reformers such as De Cosmos and Robson pressured the government to reconsider. Now, it admitted that the time had come to "establish a uniform system of Public Education."[102] On February 24, 1869, the Legislative Council of British Columbia passed the Common School Ordinance, 1869. A stopgap measure, it acknowledged limited state responsibility to provide public education. The government also conceded on the issue of non-denominational schooling. In return, the new act gave it unprecedented power over the administration of public education. Drawing on examples from across the British Empire, it wanted a highly centralized management model.[103] A Governor-in-Council was appointed, who had the authority to create new schools, choose teachers, hear complaints, and ensure that proper textbooks were used, among other duties. The government also assigned certain responsibilities to local school boards, including calling public meetings, dealing with maintenance and repair issues, and, most importantly, deciding how to raise additional funds.

The school act stipulated that the government would provide $500 per year for each qualified common school throughout the colony. This funding, largely generated through selling Indigenous land, licencing, or by imposing taxes on exported resources and on all imported goods, would pay for things such as teacher salaries. Any remaining costs would still be borne by parents in a manner that local school boards could decide, usually through a fee (often a dollar per month), a poll tax (two dollars per year on all male residents over eighteen), or some combination of the two. In reality, enforcing compliance proved problematic for school boards, and many had a difficult time in collecting the necessary money. In 1870, the government amended the school act to concentrate educational power in the hands of an inspector-general of schools. If it were going to pay more for schooling, it wanted even more oversight. Edward Graham Alston, previously a member of the General Board of Education on Vancouver Island, was appointed to the position. Alston instituted new procedures for approving the qualifications of teachers and for ensuring that their classes were conducted in accordance with the "Rules and Regulations for the Management and Government of Common Schools," which listed authorized textbooks and set hours of instruction, vacation periods, and teaching duties. These policies established an organized system for monitoring and evaluating students and teachers in British Columbia's common schools.

Conclusion

Though the new school ordinances signalled a shift in policy, the government saw them only as makeshifts. As one official explained, "The

Common Schools Ordinance was a tentative measure ... It was roughly and hurriedly thrown together, but served its purpose by initiating the proposed system, and will, no doubt, be altered and amended as occasion demands."[104] In the spring of 1870, Anthony Musgrave, the former governor of Newfoundland who replaced Seymour as governor of British Columbia, wrote to the Colonial Office in London and described the colony as a "peculiar community" consisting of a few thousand people clustered in "small knots separated by great distances." He noted, "any educational measure can be in the existing circumstances of the colony only a very rudimentary character." Musgrave added, "there are no common schools in any District existing without the aid of the government," and he explained that the amended school act of 1870 was passed "not as a perfect measure, but as another step towards the establishment of a more satisfactory system."[105] In a report, Henry Pering Pellew Crease, the colony's attorney general, argued that "a more perfect system, the yearning of the settler after an education for his children, if possible superior to his own, [is needed for] a population to take root in the soil."[106] By the end of the colonial era, the government had assumed a more active role in supporting schooling to achieve this aim and promote settlement.

By the early 1870s, schooling had transitioned into an organized system of voluntary common schools supported financially by the government. In 1870, the colony possessed more than twenty schools accommodating 570 students. Common schools were established, or were in the process of being opened, on Saltspring Island, and there were ten more on Vancouver Island at Cedar Hill, Craigflower, Esquimalt, Lake, Saanich, Metchosin, Nanaimo, North Cowichan, South Cowichan, and Victoria. On the mainland, school was in session at Burrard Inlet, Cariboo, Chilliwack, Clinton, Hope, Langley, Lillooet, Lytton, New Westminster, Sumas, and Yale. Overall, funding this system cost the government an estimated $15,000 by 1871. All the schools received approximately $500 per year from Victoria and all took in extra fees, either in the form of voluntary subscriptions or a local tax – with many school promoters advocating for a property tax – to cover remaining costs.[107] The end result was a strategic compromise in which the government wielded greater power over public education – as a tool of legitimation – in return for providing partial financial support for non-denominational schools that were open to all. On the eve of Confederation, the foundation for a highly centralized public school system was laid. State schooling took root in the colonial era, but it did not flourish until later in the nineteenth century.

CHAPTER | TWO

Settler Anxiety and Missionary Schooling

On October 31, 1851, Governor James Douglas wrote to assure the Colonial Office in London that all was calm on Vancouver Island. Douglas, whom Cole Harris pronounces "a master of the colonial despatch," noted with pride that nothing had occurred to "disturb the tranquillity" of the far-flung colony since its founding in 1849.[1] This sanguine assessment, however, masked his growing concern about security, particularly his anxiety about the potentially disastrous consequences of conflict with Indigenous Peoples, which had almost broken out on two occasions.[2] Indeed, Douglas would later describe local Indigenous-settler relations as "a smouldering volcano, which at any moment may burst into fatal activity," and he admitted that "probably the worst calamity that can befall this colony in its infant state is the hostility of the Native Tribes."[3] Officials and colonists on this edge of empire were living on edge.

A garrison mentality had developed by the early 1850s.[4] At mid-century, more than thirty thousand Indigenous people surrounded just a handful of colonists, who numbered not more than a thousand.[5] Given this great imbalance and the fact that some Indigenous Nations had acquired firearms through trade, Douglas feared that further attempts to promote colonization could risk arousing Indigenous resistance that would jeopardize the colony's existence, as had occurred in other parts of the British Empire.[6] Though the Colonial Office sent gunboats to patrol the bays and inlets of the Northwest Coast (with some ships even shelling Indigenous communities to assert dominance), Britain was reluctant to dispatch soldiers to defend the colonial outpost.[7] Lacking the funds to support a military force, Douglas deemed it strategically necessary to "cultivate [the] good will" of Indigenous Peoples while the colony found its footing. Thus, he wrote to Earl Grey, the colonial secretary, to discuss how to contain and control the Indigenous population to avoid conflict and safeguard British sovereignty in the region.[8]

Schooling was one solution. In his letter to Grey, Douglas wrote, "I am led to regret that the Missionary Societies of Britain, who are sending teachers to so many other parts of the world have not yet turned their attention to the natives of Vancouver Island."[9] He suggested that if they could send out missionaries, "schools might be established for the moral training and instruction of the Aborigines, to the manifest advantage of the Colony."[10] Douglas hoped that missionaries would use schooling to win over Indigenous Peoples and, in the process, discourage their organized resistance to colonization. Indigenous Nations negotiated the arrival of Christianity as active agents, as historian Susan Neylan shows; however, missionaries played an important role in slowly shifting the balance of power.[11] Encouraged by the results of similar experiments in other British colonies, the Colonial Office saw promise in Douglas's proposal, so it approached missionary societies about sending agents to the region.

This chapter shows that colonial officials and missionaries entered into various arrangements to provide schooling for Indigenous Peoples between 1849 and 1871. As was the case for common schools, government assistance for mission schools ranged from grants of free land to direct financial aid. Historians have highlighted the connection between church, state, and colonization in Canada, though most scholars suggest that this partnership developed later in the nineteenth century on the west coast than elsewhere in Canada.[12] Scholars such as Robin Fisher argue that missionaries in British Columbia "worked within a framework of governmental coercion," but I show that, in part to assuage settler anxiety over Indigenous resistance, the government called upon and assisted missionaries to help establish that very framework or "structure."[13] Bolstering security, and not benevolence or a sense of religious devotion, was its primary objective in doing so.[14] As Dakota Sioux scholar Vine Deloria Jr. explains, it recruited missionaries, armed only with Bibles, to serve as the shock-troops for settler colonialism.[15] As was the case with common schools, it gradually took on an active role in supporting missionary schooling. Thus, common and mission schools need

FIGURE 2.1 A mission school in Quw'utsun territory on Vancouver Island, c. 1860s. Methodist, Catholic, and Anglican missionaries competed for converts in the colonies of Vancouver Island and British Columbia. Colonial officials gave free land grants and money as incentives to work in the area. Many missionaries used church buildings as schools. | Courtesy of the Royal BC Museum, Image F-08506, British Columbia Archives

to be understood as parallel projects, helping to build and legitimize colonial British Columbia.

First in the Field

The first missionaries travelled to the west coast in the 1820s and 1830s, with little government support. Here too, the Hudson's Bay Company (HBC) played a decisive role. One of the earliest missionaries was Reverend Herbert Beaver of the Church Missionary Society (CMS), who arrived in 1836 at Fort Vancouver on the Columbia River. The HBC sent Herbert, accompanied by his wife, Jane, to serve as the fort's chaplain and as a missionary to local Indigenous Peoples. The Beavers were unimpressed by their new surroundings. As Anglicans, they disapproved of the large number of Catholic employees at the fort, and they were outraged at the country marriages – unions between Indigenous women and non-Indigenous men – entered into by company officers such as John McLoughlin, Peter Skene Ogden, and James Douglas.[16] "Marriage," argues Adele Perry, "has always mattered to empire."[17] As strict zealots in a more flexible and forgiving environment, the couple did not fit into fur-trade culture. Herbert believed that "mixed-blood" wives of fur traders were purveyors of "vice and immorality," and Jane refused to associate with the Indigenous wives of traders.[18] Relations at the fort became irreparably damaged when Chief Factor McLoughlin attacked Herbert with a cane after he denigrated McLoughlin's wife in public. McLoughlin later apologized for the assault, but the Beavers had had enough. They left the area in 1838, having accomplished very little.[19]

1838 also marked the arrival of Catholic missionaries. The bishop of Quebec sent out Fathers Francis N. Blanchet and Modeste Demers to create a mission at Fort Vancouver. With the fort as a base, Demers travelled extensively throughout the region. In 1841, he journeyed north to Fort Langley, on the Fraser River, and in the following year, he accompanied a supply brigade to the hinterland posts of New Caledonia. Also in the 1840s, Father Pierre de Smet, a Jesuit priest, visited Indigenous Peoples in southeastern New Caledonia, and Father John Nobili worked in the north. As the HBC prepared to move its headquarters from Fort Vancouver to Fort Victoria, Father Jean-Baptiste Bolduc accompanied Douglas on a reconnaissance mission to Vancouver Island and worked among various Indigenous communities.

Though Reverend Robert John Staines had come to Vancouver Island in 1849, he did not actively preach to Indigenous people, except for the Indigenous children of HBC officers who attended the private school. That job was taken up by his Catholic counterpart, Father Honoré Timothy Lempfrit, who also arrived in 1849.[20] Lempfrit immediately started teaching HBC servants, the Indigenous wives of traders, and interested children from a nearby ləkʷəŋən settlement. The company initially furnished him with a makeshift building, but he later erected a small house in Victoria to use as a classroom and chapel, teaching upward of twenty-five pupils. The HBC provided moral support but no financial aid. Instead, he relied on donations from his parishioners. Lempfrit laboured in the colony for two years, and according to Royal

Navy officer Fairfax Moresby, he was a "very intelligent and earnest missionary" who was generally "on good terms with the community."[21]

But Lempfrit's relations with the ləkʷəŋən soon soured, which caused a great deal of consternation. In 1851, Moresby stated, "the good Padre [became] the cause of anxiety to the settlement, through a misunderstanding with the Indians, when the tribe assembled round the fort in a threatening manner."[22] Lempfrit's contact with the ləkʷəŋən was endangering security. In the wake of the incident, Douglas asked him to abandon his mission in Victoria. Complying with the request, Lempfrit travelled northwest to live among the Quw'utsun, who were rumoured among settlers to be warlike.[23] Douglas saw this as a tactical error. He explained to the colonial secretary that Lempfrit had set off without "a single white assistant, and without any pecuniary means to defray the expense of an establishment, as he trusted entirely to his Indian converts for support; a plan that could hardly be expected to succeed."[24] Unsurprisingly, Lempfrit's mission did not last long. In 1852, Douglas informed the secretary that "we were ... lately alarmed by a reported outrage committed by a party of Cowegins" on Lempfrit. According to Quw'utsun leadership, Lempfrit fathered a child with a local woman against the wishes of the community.[25] Douglas "immediately dispatched an officer and a small force, with orders to bring Mr. Lempfrit" back to Victoria.[26] Upon his return, Lempfrit decided to leave the colony altogether, and he was eventually expelled from the Oblates for "scandalous conduct" in the Diocese of Vancouver Island.[27]

In light of this debacle, Douglas questioned the wisdom of allowing missionaries to work among Indigenous Peoples in the young colony.[28] Given the small size of the settler population and the limited resources, he thought that sending missionaries to other parts of the island without any formal support "would be a mere waste of energy."[29] Officially, the colony did not aid religious bodies so as to avoid the denominational disputes and allegations of sectarian favouritism that plagued the British North American colonies. Douglas also believed that encouraging missionaries to work among remote Indigenous Nations would merely expose them to danger, potentially sparking "Indian difficulties" and drawing the colony "into the contest."[30] In stopping missionaries from overreaching, he was following "the only safe course, by taking every possible precaution, to prevent the occurrence of difficulties."[31] Douglas was no humanitarian, as some scholars still insist; he pursued colonial statecraft strategically.[32] Nevertheless, many colonists resented his conciliatory approach to Indigenous-settler relations, which some disparagingly termed a "squawtocracy."[33]

WAR AND PEACE AND PRIMITIVE ACCUMULATION

Douglas's approach, and the prospects for missionary work, shifted in the fall of 1855, when news reached Victoria of the outbreak of the Puget Sound War. This armed conflict was a struggle over land rights between Indigenous Nations (Nisqually, Muckleshoot, Puyallup, and Klickitat) and colonizers in Washington Territory, just across the Salish Sea. "Indian difficulties" had become a reality. In a letter to Douglas, James Tilton, the acting governor of Washington Territory, explained that the clash was a "determined combination among the various Tribes to make war upon us."[34] He asked for help, and Douglas answered the call: "I most cordially acknowledge the moral obligation which binds Christian and Civilized nations to exert their utmost power and influence in checking the inroads of the merciless savage."[35] Though lacking in supplies, he purchased fifty rifles and secured ten barrels of gunpowder and a supply of ball that he immediately sent on the *Traveller*. Extra ammunition was delivered later on the *Beaver*, which happened to employ a number of Indigenous labourers as woodcutters and stokers. The ship stayed on to patrol Puget Sound. Douglas hoped that the "moral effect" of its visit "will be powerfully felt by the Native Indian Tribes, and may contribute in some measure to confirm their wavering allegiance and to detach them from the general Indian confederacy."[36] His response to the Puget Sound War was in keeping with his early "Indian policy," which historian Barry Gough contends was "essentially crisis management."[37]

Douglas monitored the war closely. In a letter to the Colonial Office, he expressed hope that Indigenous Peoples in Washington Territory would "receive a timely check, or the evil spirit may spread among the aboriginal population of the British Territory."[38] If the spirit of insurrection

FIGURE 2.2 Governor James Douglas, c. 1860s. Believed to have been born in Demerara, now Guyana, in 1803, Douglas became an influential fur trader and colonial official. He served as Governor of the Colony of Vancouver Island between 1851 and 1864 and as Governor of the Colony of British Columbia between 1858 and 1864. |
Courtesy of the Royal BC Museum, Image A-01227, British Columbia Archives

spread, the island "would have to bear the brunt of an Indian war, which I trust a kind Providence may avert."[39] The Indigenous residents on the island remained "quiet and friendly," but they were nevertheless "powerfully moved in favour of their race, a feeling which may exercise a mischievous influence on their excitable minds." Douglas was anxious. He lamented that the colony could not afford to play a more active role in the war but hoped that Indigenous Peoples would nevertheless "soon be made to yield to the palm of victory."[40] By year's end, it appeared that hostilities would not spread to the island.

A few months later, however, Isaac Stevens, the governor of Washington Territory, wrote to Douglas with concerning news – "Northern Indians" were planning to attack various southern settlements.[41] Alarming rumours of such attacks soon spread throughout the colony.[42] Douglas even received a petition by a "deputation of the most respectable inhabitants of the Colony," probably written by Edward Cridge, asking that a warship be sent to Victoria for protection.[43] The petition read,

> May it please your Excellency we the undersigned inhabitants of Vancouver Island beg most respectfully to call your most gracious attention to the Indian war that is now raging on the American shores within a few miles of our own homes. From the most recent accounts the attacks of the Indians have been most frightful and daring atrocities have been committed on the persons of women and children. We are aware that a large number of Indians are on their passage here from the north and it is impossible for any person to calculate to what extent they may be influenced by the accounts. They must undoubtedly hear from the neighbouring Indians. Under these circumstances and from a knowledge that we have no efficient force on the Island and cannot possibly organize such a force for some considerable time if at all, we deem it an imperative duty ... [to ask] that one of Her Majesty's ships should be sent here for our protection.[44]

At the request of the Colonial Office, the Admiralty sent a frigate, the *President*, to Vancouver Island as a precaution. Douglas, too, shared the fear that northern Indigenous Nations might join the fray: "[Recent] events prove how formidable an enemy the Indian may become and react powerfully on the minds of the natives within the British Territory who naturally feel elated at the courage and success of the colored races."[45] In the end, the attacks failed to materialize, but the Puget Sound War proved a powerful catalyst for change in the colony, as did the fear that northern Nations, especially the Haida, might attack scattered

European settlements. This confirms Western Shoshone historian Ned Blackhawk's observation about the American West that fears of violence and colonial social formation often progressed hand in hand. He explains, "Violence enabled the rapid accumulation of new resources, territories, and subject peoples. It legitimated the power of migrants, structured new social and racial orders, and provided the preconditions for political formation."[46]

International pressure played a role as well. As news of the Puget Sound War, and the Fraser Canyon War discussed in Chapter 1, made its way back to the metropole, the Aborigines' Protection Society, a so-called humanitarian organization in Britain, wrote to the Colonial Office in 1858 "invoking the protection of Her Majesty's Government" over the Indigenous inhabitants of the Pacific Northwest.[47] Although London approved of Douglas's actions during the Puget Sound and Fraser Canyon Wars, he himself believed that more needed to be done to cultivate the goodwill of Indigenous Peoples and shore up security. Upon learning that the Colonial Office had approached the Society for the Propagation of the Gospel (SPG) about sending out missionaries to British Columbia, as he had earlier requested, Douglas responded, "I am glad to learn such is the intention of this society." He added, "I shall be most happy to render every assistance in my power to the clergymen when they arrive." During the early 1850s, Douglas had taken a cautious approach to bringing in evangelists, but now he proclaimed that they would find "an extensive field open to missionary enterprise, as vast among the white population as amongst the native Indian tribes."[48]

Nonetheless, both Vancouver Island and the new mainland colony were severely cash-strapped. The solution to this problem lay in land. Perry notes that "land lay at the heart" of the colonial project in British Columbia; it was the "medium through which colonial society aimed to reconstitute itself."[49] Indeed, David McNally and Glen Sean Coulthard stress that land is "foundational" to settler capitalism because so-called primitive accumulation "pivots on the theft, enclosure, and parcelization of the earth."[50] Accordingly, some colonial officials justified usurping Indigenous lands by invoking the doctrine of discovery and viewing the region as *terra nullius* – empty and free for the taking.[51] The local government was already taxing certain exports (such as gold and coal) and imposing tariffs on all imported goods to generate revenue for public spending, but now the Colonial Office encouraged it to steal and sell off Indigenous lands, at a high price, to raise additional funds to support various initiatives, including schools.[52] This is how, as Aileen Moreton-Robinson points out, the "possessive logics of patriarchal white sovereignty" were "operationalized, deployed, and affirmed" in the British Empire.[53] Herman Merivale, permanent under-secretary for the Colonial Office, explained the scheme:

> Might it not be desirable to suggest to the Governor that in any funds acquired from the Sale of Indian Reserves – which it might be intended to appropriate in the service of the Indians – a good portion should be set aside for the purpose of a school for the education of the children ... As V. Couver's Isld and B. Columbia advance in prosperity they should not overlook the civilization & interests of the Indian, which so far as I can see can be best promoted by the establishment of industrial & educational Schools for the younger members of that race.[54]

As in other settler colonies throughout the British Empire, Merivale's proposition became policy: portions of reserved and stolen lands were sold, and part of the proceeds went to the creation and funding of schools that could teach new generations of Indigenous people to accept colonial authority and to contribute to the emerging capitalist economy.[55] Colonial Secretary Lord Carnarvon confirmed as much in an 1859 letter to Douglas:

> In the case of the Indians of Vancouver Island and British Columbia ... I would enjoin upon you, and all in authority in both Colonies, the importance of establishing Schools of an industrial as well as an educational character for the Indians, whereby they may acquire the arts of civilized life which will enable them to support themselves, and not degenerate into the mere recipients of eleemosynary relief.[56]

Douglas agreed.

The first laboratory for the new policy was Victoria, where two recently arrived Anglican clergymen, Reverend Alexander Charles Garrett of the SPG and William Duncan of the CMS, worked among the ləkʷəŋən, as Lempfrit had almost a decade earlier. Garrett came to Victoria in 1859 and quickly rose to prominence. An ordained priest, he was elected principal of the newly created Indian Improvement Committee, and Duncan, a lay cleric, became its secretary. In 1860, Garrett wrote on behalf of the committee to request that Douglas "be good enough to grant a site on the Indian reserve for a school house and master's residence, for the benefit of the Indians" near Victoria.[57] Given that the project needed "some substantial and reliable source from which to draw the necessary funds," he suggested that

> a grant of money at least equal to the amount that the Committee may be able to raise, would be required to meet the expenses of erecting the necessary buildings and also that one half the amount of expenditure for the maintenance of the Institution, should be secured by the Government from some source local or otherwise, the Committee to raise the other half.[58]

In essence, Garrett proposed a cost-sharing agreement between missionaries and the government, a model that became standard for Indian education in Canada by the 1880s. He assured Douglas that in supporting the initiative, he could help Victoria become "the seat of a flourishing and efficient establishment for Missionary and Industrial enterprise."[59]

It is unclear where exactly Douglas expected the money to come from. Journalist Alexander Begg claimed that £100 was collected at a public meeting to be used to create a schoolhouse for ləkʷəŋən children and that Douglas personally contributed a significant portion of it.[60] In addition, a government grant was probably given to the Church of England to work on the reserve, which was part of an ad hoc system of Indian reserves being created.[61] Regardless, Garrett received the necessary financial assistance to open a school for ləkʷəŋən children in 1860. In 1861, he explained the resulting situation:

> The Songhees Indians have now for a long period been watching with a jealous eye the occupation of their reserve by the whites. They have consented to this occupation because they have been repeatedly informed by authority, that the funds would be obtained to be devoted to their own benefit, and especially to the education of their children and the care of the sick and aged.

Garrett proposed that the funds be used in the following ways:

> 1. All children of the Songhees tribe attending school shall have two suits of clothes a year.
> 2. A lavatory to be attached to the school where they shall be required to wash daily and attend to the general cleanliness of their persons before entering the school.
> 3. If any be very irregular in attendance, or refuse to comply with the regulations of the lavatory, they shall be excluded from any benefit.

He also suggested that the funds would pay for industrial training:

> An industrial training school to be established as soon as possible, in which the young and rising generation of Indians shall be taught those various useful arts which shall make them independent of savage needs of life.
> This institution to be conducted as follows:
> 1. One or more tradesmen to be engaged, either for the whole or part of the time, according as the funds will allow. The first should be a tailor, the second a shoemaker, the third a carpenter.
> 2. Materials to be supplied.
> 3. The Indians to receive a small remuneration according to the merit of their work.
> 4. The articles made to be sold, and the proceeds returned to the general fund.[62]

Garrett's proposal made clear that schooling was intended as a civilizing project and that industrial training, in particular, was a good investment.

Few records survive for the Victoria mission school, but in 1862 Garrett wrote that of the $256.50 appropriated from the fund by the commissioners of the Victoria Indian reserve, $98 went to clothes for fourteen pupils, seven boys and seven girls. Boys received a "red jacket, dark trousers and one pair of shoes each," and girls got a "dark dress, red petticoat and one pair of shoes." These clothes were distributed to the "seven boys and seven girls who have been in regular attendance at school." Apparently, the government approved of this use of the fund, and Garrett informed the local colonial secretary that "the feeling in the tribe in consequence of this action of the Government is on the whole very good."[63]

EXPANDING THE FIELD

By the late 1850s and early 1860s, government-supported missionary work had taken root in Vancouver Island and British Columbia. The three most active denominations – Methodist, Catholic, and Anglican – carved out separate spheres of spiritual influence, or what Lynn A. Blake calls "denominational geographies."[64] Methodists, the smallest in number, concentrated on the lower Fraser Valley, Vancouver Island, the Northwest Coast, and Haida Gwaii. Lay Catholics were active on the island, and the Oblates of Mary Immaculate dominated the mainland, especially the interior and the lower Fraser Valley. Anglicans divided into two major groups – those sent by the High Church-oriented SPG and those by the evangelical, Low Church CMS – and took over the Northwest Coast and the Fraser Canyon. These denominational delineations were, of course, fiercely disputed, a fact that significantly shaped missionary schooling in the colonial period and beyond.[65] Nevertheless, these missionaries – all directly assisted, in differing ways, by the government until the late 1860s – collectively started an assault on Indigenous Peoples and their lifeways that resulted in a gradual shift in the balance of power in favour of colonial society. Missionary schooling helped form what Frantz Fanon labels the "tightly knit web of colonialism" and Andrew Woolford calls the "settler colonial mesh" that "operates to entrap Indigenous Peoples within the settler colonial assimilative project."[66] Missionary activity, then, can be understood as part of what

Coulthard terms "Canada's repeated attempts to overtly uproot and destroy the vitality and autonomy of Indigenous modes of life" through institutions such as schools.[67]

Methodist Missionaries

In 1858, after the Puget Sound War and in the midst of the gold rush, the Methodist Church sent its first agents, Reverends Ephraim Evans, Edward White, Arthur Browning, and Ebenezer Robson (brother of John Robson), to the west coast. They established themselves at Victoria and Nanaimo, as well as at Hope, New Westminster, and Chilliwack.[68] Though originally focused on the white population around Victoria, they became increasingly concerned about the state of Indigenous Peoples. As historian Kenton Storey notes, some island colonists, steeped in racism, worried that poor conditions were breeding grounds for degradation and disease that could prompt Indigenous Peoples to exact revenge through violent attacks.[69] In 1861, Thomas Crosby answered a call in a Methodist newspaper for missionaries to travel to the region. He came to Victoria in April 1863.[70] Like his colleagues, Crosby was concerned about the state of Indigenous Peoples in and around Victoria. Reverend Garrett, however, was already at work with the ləkʷəŋən, so the Methodists looked elsewhere.

Encouraged by the success of Garrett's work in Victoria, the government sanctioned other missionary activity, including that of the Methodists. In 1860, Douglas told the colonial secretary in London that he was doing everything in his power "to promote the good cause, by encouraging the residence of an ordained and educated Clergy in British Columbia ... Having no authority to apply any part of the Public revenue to the aid and support of Churches," Douglas clarified, "there was little in my power to bestow, beyond the sincerest sympathy and advice, in aid of the zealous Clergy of the Church of England and the Methodist Episcopal Church, who first entered the field of missionary labour in British Columbia." Moral support was the primary means of early government assistance. But Douglas also provided, on application, a free acre to local representatives of "the Church of England, and of the

Methodist Episcopal Church, respectively, in the Towns of Yale, Hope, Derby, Douglas, and New Westminster." He argued, "A grant of land to that extent would not be burdensome to the colony, and would nevertheless form an attractive inducement for Christian churches to devote their attention to the country, until population increases, and other provision is made for the maintenance of a Christian clergy, and the erection of places of Christian worship."[71] Douglas offered free grants of stolen Indigenous land to religious societies that were willing to send missionaries to work in the region.

One of the first enclaves that Methodist missionaries carved out was Nanaimo, Snuneymuxw territory. After a brief stint in Hope, on the south bank of the Fraser River, Reverend Ebenezer Robson moved to Nanaimo in the early 1860s, where he built a school for Indigenous children. In 1863, Crosby was sent there to teach. At first, his inability to speak the local language was a barrier:

> One of the first difficulties was my ignorance of their language. Hence I had to use the language of signs. Beckoning and pointing to the school-house, I sought to persuade them to come into school. They would look at me, laugh at my efforts, and make a bolt for the bushes nearby. Sometimes I made an attempt to capture them, but they would run like wild hares, and I could not get near them. I had always a love for children, and prided myself on my ability to win them; but these, I was afraid, were going to outdo me.

To coax children into his school, Crosby resorted to bribery. Foraging in the forest for material, he built a swing. "Then I started again with my sign language," he said, "and at last succeeded in getting one of them into the swing." He continued,

> As I swing the little fellow to and fro I noticed the others peeping out curiously from among the bushes. Pointing to the swing and then to the school-house, I beckoned to them, as much as to say, "If you come here and have a swing you will have to go to school." By this means I got acquainted with them and won their confidence.

As Crosby learned the language, his classroom attendance grew. The first sentence he mastered was "All children come to school."[72] Armed with this basic phrase, he walked through the village, shouting it and encouraging children to follow him to school.

Most Snuneymuxw parents, however, were indifferent to his efforts. They "showed little appreciation" for his work and frequently took their children away on hunting and fishing trips, interrupting lessons. Whereas colonists often lobbied the government to take their children's education more seriously, many Indigenous parents adopted a different approach. After Crosby had been in Nanaimo for some time, they lobbied *him* about the matter of pay, asking how long their children must attend his classes before he provided compensation. Crosby was confused. He responded, "Oh, I couldn't pay you. In our country the people pay the teacher." But this was not his country. Unimpressed, the parents answered, "we cannot let them go much longer unless you pay us." These kinds of complaints continued into the 1870s and 1880s.

Snuneymuxw children also resisted the school. Crosby's swing, signs, and singing did attract some, but many more stayed away, especially in the summer. Crosby reasoned,

> What boy or girl likes to attend school on a hot day? When I started to round them up they made for the beach, and when I drew near they would slip off their blanket or simple dress and make a bolt for the salt water. In they would go, the tide being up, diving and swimming away out of reach of everybody. For a little you would lose sight of them, then away in the distance you would see two or three little fellows pop up, shake their heads, rub their hands over their faces, and cry out, Ha! Ha! Ha![73]

In 1866, Crosby left Nanaimo to become a travelling preacher on the mainland and was subsequently assigned a permanent post at Chilliwack in 1869.[74] In the early 1860s, Reverends Robson and White had visited the Stó:lō at Chilliwack and had promised to send a missionary. Writing many years later about his missionary experiences, Crosby explained that other Indigenous communities on the Fraser River had also asked for schooling. Nonetheless, he noted that because the Stó:lō were "scattered at such distances, and so few children in any one place, the only real teaching we could do was when we got them all together in a big rough house, put up for that purpose, near Atchelitz church not far from Chilliwack, and here we gave them instructions every Sabbath." For Crosby, this was merely the first step, and as he noted, "it became evident to all concerned that we must have an industrial or boarding school."[75] The foundation was laid for a boarding school, and the Coqualeetza Industrial Institute was opened in the 1880s. After almost ten years, with assistance from the colonial government in the form of free land grants, Methodist missionaries had established a presence at Victoria, Nanaimo, New Westminster, Hope, and Chilliwack.

Catholic Missionaries

The Methodists were a marginal force compared to Catholic missionaries, who dominated the field in the 1850s and 1860s. After the mostly unsuccessful work undertaken by Lempfrit, Bishop Modeste Demers invited the Sisters of St. Ann to establish a private school in Victoria in 1858 for Indigenous and non-Indigenous children. Two of Douglas's daughters were briefly enrolled, and the nuns continued to manage the school throughout the colonial period.[76] Demers also invited the Oblates of Mary Immaculate. Under the direction of Oblate Superior Louis-Joseph d'Herbomez, they established a station at Esquimalt, an agricultural settlement and naval base, and started to visit other Indigenous communities on the island. As Dakelh historian Allan Downey outlines, the Oblates instituted the "Durieu system," named after Bishop Pierre-Paul Durieu, that sought total control over their missions to eradicate unchristian behaviour.[77] A split soon developed between Demers and d'Herbomez, prompting the Oblates to relocate to the mainland. Overall, Catholics made the most advances in missionary schooling, and they received substantial encouragement as well as financial support from the government to carry on their work.

Oblate missionaries gradually shifted their activities to the Colony of British Columbia. Following some delay in the selection of a location,

Fathers Charles Pandosy and Pierre Richard opened a mission in 1859 near Kelowna in Syilx territory. Another Oblate establishment was created in 1860 at New Westminster, where two chapels were built, one for whites and one for Indigenous people. In 1861, Father Leon Fouquet founded the St. Mary's mission exclusively for Indigenous Peoples and selected a site near the mouth of the Harrison River, now known as Mission City, that was halfway between New Westminster and Hope. This spot, on the north bank of the Fraser, was chosen because it allowed a variety of Coast and Interior Salish people to travel to the mission by canoe. In 1862, Brothers Janin and Félix Guillet built a residence for the first priest, Father Florimond Gendre. A boarding school for Indigenous boys was started in 1863. St. Mary's would go on to become the longest-serving Oblate mission school in British Columbia.[78]

Initially, the government displayed little interest in St. Mary's. Father Fouquet wrote to Douglas on April 11, 1864, informing him of his efforts and requesting aid:

> The mission of St. Mary's, to which your memorialist belongs has already an educational and industrial school at the Lower Fraser, where there are at present forty-two boys of the aboriginal tribes, supported and provided for by the Mission, and taught the usual branches of common education, viz. Reading, writing, arithmetic ... Arrangements have been made for establishing a school for girls ...
>
> For consideration of the foregoing mentioned exertions for the amelioration and improvement of the aborigines, your memorialist respectfully requests that some portion of the money appropriated by the Legislature for educational purposes, may be granted to St. Mary's Mission.[79]

Fouquet laid out his case, but with the school already operating at capacity, the cash-poor colony had little incentive to offer aid. Douglas was in the process of retiring as governor, and he appears not to have responded to Fouquet. As with the Puget Sound War, however, Indigenous resistance to colonization proved an impetus for political change that would shape the future of both St. Mary's and missionary schooling in British Columbia.

When Frederick Seymour, former governor of British Honduras, took over from Douglas in the spring of 1864, many Indigenous leaders were worried. As outlined in Chapter 1, Seymour tended not to favour government support for schooling, but he was eager to fill his predecessor's shoes and to court the goodwill of Indigenous Peoples. His commitment to diplomacy was quickly tested. In late April, just weeks after Fouquet asked for government funding, Tsilhqot'in citizens waged war on settlers at Bute Inlet, killing nineteen men. A wagon road was being built through their territory, without their consent, to connect with the Cariboo Road on the way to Barkerville and the gold fields in the interior. As road construction continued on to Bute Inlet, a group of Tsilhqot'in attacked the crew and then moved farther north, killing foreman William Brewster and three others, as well as William Manning, a settler at Puntzi Lake. As John Sutton Lutz shows, the Tsilhqot'in resented the intrusion of whites into their territory and some sought to exact revenge for certain hardships, including the recent spread of a deadly smallpox outbreak.[80]

When news of the resistance reached Seymour, he took immediate action. Under a false amnesty, eight Tsilhqot'in were arrested, five of whom – Klatsassin, Piell, Tellot, Tahpit, and Chessus – were charged with murder.[81] Klatsassin protested that the killings were acts of war, not murder, a kind of "redirection" of violence back against colonizers invading Tsilqot'in homelands.[82] Supreme Court Judge Matthew Baillie Begbie, later nicknamed the "Hanging Judge," interpreted the events differently and sentenced all five to death by hanging in what is today known as Quesnel.[83] The Tsilhqot'in declaration of sovereignty was ignored, and the executions were used as public spectacles to solidify colonial rule. Afraid that Indigenous Nations might unite in a mass uprising, the government wanted to send a message that violence against colonists would not be tolerated. However, this approach was not without cost. The proceedings drained upward of approximately $80,000 from the already depleted colonial coffers.

Despite Seymour's swift action, rumours of an imminent "general insurrection" of Indigenous Peoples continued to circulate.[84] In an attempt to establish friendly relations and avoid further costly conflicts, Seymour organized the first of many gatherings of Indigenous people at New Westminster to mark Queen Victoria's birthday in May 1864. As Keith Thor Carlson notes, Seymour hoped that such a summit, dressed up as a birthday celebration for the queen and rife with imperial pageantry, could strengthen relations with Indigenous Nations and ease tensions.[85] The governor invited approximately six thousand Indigenous people to attend the first summit to prove that he had "succeeded to all the power of my predecessor [Douglas] and to his solicitude for their welfare."[86] At the gathering, he announced,

> I am glad to see you and to find that so many have come down to show their loyalty to our Queen. You are right. The Queen has a good heart for the good Indians. I shall be good to them but harsh and severe to the bad ones. I will punish them as they deserve ...
>
> I am glad that you wish to be civilized and raised to an equality with the white man. Cultivate your lands, send your children to school, listen to what the clergymen tell you and believe in it.[87]

Seymour, in short, saw sagacity in Douglas's strategy of trying to contain Indigenous Peoples by cultivating their goodwill, and he identified missionary schooling as an important tool of legitimation.

In the aftermath of the Tsilhqot'in War, Seymour took greater interest in missionary work, especially the nearby St. Mary's school. In the spring of 1865, he travelled up the Fraser River to investigate it. Upon his return to New Westminster, he reported to the colonial secretary, offering a rare look at one of the first Indian industrial schools in western Canada. He commented on the forty-eight pupils in attendance:

> Their ages ranged from eight to fourteen years. Their fine healthy appearance and good clothing at once satisfied me, that in this institution at least the native race was not weakening and dwindling by contact with Europeans. Indeed the pupils appeared more robust and active than the boys of their age whom I had seen in the forests and their cheerful faces presented an agreeable contrast to the worn

and anxious countenances of the seniors who came to be present at the inspection.[88]

Furthermore, "The school room was large, clean and well ventilated. It had been decorated with flags, boughs, and ribbons by the boys."[89] Concerning pedagogy, Seymour observed, "I found them on examination to have made very considerable progress in arithmetic, geography, and spelling. Some of the handwriting was extremely good. The priests have almost entirely thrown aside the inconvenient Chinook medium and teach the boys in English. Even better than the writing was the singing."[90] In fact, the pupils at St. Mary's developed a reputation as excellent musicians. Seymour remarked, "I have not heard in any school with which I have officially come into contact, here or elsewhere, any piece of music so well delivered as was one Catholic hymn by these Indian boys."[91] Overall, Seymour's visit convinced him that "the native race can thrive and improve under civilised habits. Mind and body seemed to have expanded together, and the cultivation of the brain, if one could judge by the demeanour of the students towards their preceptors, to have improved the impulses of the heart."[92]

He was so impressed with the boys at St. Mary's that he invited them to attend the second summit of Indigenous Nations in 1865.[93] In his view, they were a symbol of success. For the benefit of the colonial secretary, he described the 1865 celebrations. Unfortunately, "it rained heavily on the morning of the 24th of May," he explained, "but a procession was formed of nearly one thousand canoes, extending from one bank of the Fraser to the other. Each boat had its flag and the more civilised of the natives sang a Catholic hymn, which had a very fine effect proceeding from thousands of voices upon the water."[94] As part of the spectacle, "God Save the Queen was sung by the Indian boys of St. Mary's Mission, and the Indians generally cheered vociferously."[95] The festivities went well. Seymour concluded, "I allow myself to hope that the native conflicts will soon cease throughout the wide extent of the colony, and the white man will be able to travel anywhere without molestation."[96] Like Douglas, Seymour understood that "civilizing" efforts such as missionary schooling played an important role in strengthening colonial security.

Against this backdrop, Fouquet renewed his request for financial support for St. Mary's. That summer, he asked Seymour for funds to "be granted for the benefit of the children."[97] The governor, who was simultaneously resisting paying more for common schooling in the colony, authorized a grant of £50 and then a subsequent grant of £250 for St. Mary's.[98] Fouquet's report for 1865–66 confirmed, "The grant we have received from the Government in August 1865 has enabled us to admit ten additional boys from amongst the numerous applicants who were most anxious to become partakers of a good education and thus we increased our number to an average of sixty boarders."[99] Fouquet's report includes a rare example of a student voice in the form of an address made to a government official. It was probably prepared, or at least approved, by a church authority, but it remains an example of students acknowledging the government funds received by the school: "We are most happy of having another opportunity of thanking you as the representative of Her Majesty as well for your kind visits and for the pecuniary assistance which we have already received and which shall always be remembered by us with feelings of the most sincere gratitude."[100] By the mid-1860s, the government viewed Catholic schools such as St. Mary's as providing an invaluable service that warranted financial support.

Anglican Missionaries

Anglican missionaries, specifically those from the SPG and the CMS, also received government aid. Garrett of the SPG continued to labour among the lək̓ʷəŋən in Victoria, but he was soon eclipsed by William Duncan, who founded a mission at Fort Simpson on the Northwest Coast. In 1856, as the Puget Sound War wound down, the CMS sent Duncan to Victoria as its first agent. He was later joined by Reverend Lewin S. Tugwell, also of the CMS, and his wife.[101] After working briefly in Victoria, Duncan and the Tugwells set sail for Fort Simpson to work among the Ts'msyan, arriving in October 1857. Duncan had hoped to return to Victoria after getting Tugwell acclimatized, but Garrett soon sent word that he was not needed in the capital. Moreover, Tugwell's poor health soon necessitated his return to Victoria, so Duncan was left to labour on his own. Accepting his situation, he learned to speak Sm'algyax from hereditary chief and HBC employee Arthur Wellington Clah, and his mastery of the language supported his efforts.[102]

To spread his influence, Duncan established a school at Fort Simpson, probably the first on the mainland, predating the Sapperton school discussed in Chapter 1 by at least a year. In the summer of 1858, the school was built outside the fort walls and Duncan began teaching there the next year. The students, upward of 140 children and adults, were taught a variety of subjects, including reading, writing, and singing, in addition to religious teachings. Schools such as Duncan's were important institutions of acculturation that gave missionaries daily access to Indigenous Peoples in their efforts to transform their lifeways. Yet, as Susan Neylan demonstrates, it is important to see missions – and their schools – as "sites of hegemonic struggles," where Christianity was contested and negotiated by Northwest Coast peoples. Neylan concludes that "the Christian mission was intrusive, coercive, and destructive, but it never achieved absolute control nor completely realized its aims amidst competing Native agendas concerning Christianity."[103]

Duncan's early success was not restricted to Fort Simpson. Many of his students travelled to Victoria for trade purposes, where they, with their good behaviour, caught the attention of Douglas. In early 1860, Douglas recruited Edward Cridge, his trusted advisor, to learn more about Duncan's school. As Cridge wrote to Duncan, the governor wished to "express to you the great gratification he has received from conversing with several of the Indians who have been under your instruction at Fort Simpson, and who are now at Victoria, and his pleasure at witnessing the great improvement of manners, learning and religion, which you have succeeded in effecting in their condition."[104] Having been taught a sharp lesson by the Puget Sound War, Douglas was interested in learning more about how Duncan's "civilizing" methods could be replicated by other missionaries to prevent future hostilities. In the spring, he even invited Duncan to Victoria to consult on what might be done to ease settler anxiety and ameliorate the conditions of Indigenous Peoples in the area. Duncan's labours were starting to pay off.

He seized the opportunity to travel to Victoria for a tête-à-tête with the governor to emphasize the benefits of his missionary work. Though he spoke enthusiastically of the Fort Simpson school, he desperately desired an independent settlement far away from the distractions of fort life and its poor hygienic conditions, which were thought to contribute to the spread of devastating diseases such as smallpox. He wrote to Cridge, as an intermediary, to ask Douglas for support to establish a separate community. Duncan believed strongly that promising converts, especially the "rising generation," must be "removed from the evil influence" of the fort. He felt a "growing anxiety for a safe retreat."[105] This "anxiety" also likely stemmed from an incident where an armed Ts'mysan leader, supported by various community members, "burst into the schoolroom at Fort Simpson" and threatened to kill Duncan unless he closed the school during an important ceremony.[106] Douglas, though, thought highly enough of Duncan to forward the idea to the Colonial Office in London. He asked for imperial sanction to "reserve several hundred acres" to "enable Mr. Duncan to carry this useful and benevolent plan" into effect.[107] The Colonial Office approved:

> It would be a bright future in British Colonization; and an example to the United States if we can succeed in converting to Christianity and introducing to civilization the native inhabitants, or any portion of them, of British Columbia. To grant a reserve of land as a missionary settlement for converts seems to me a very proper and justifiable proceeding.[108]

"Missionary work and land acquisition," Deloria contends, "always went hand in hand" in North America.[109] It is important to note that this land theft led to bitter relations with some Ts'msyan and would later play a role in Duncan's undoing, as Chapter 4 discusses.[110] For now, he had secured a free grant of land for his purposes, but two years would elapse before he attempted the move from Fort Simpson.

To relocate his followers, Duncan required some additional funding, and once again, he turned to Cridge to broach the subject to Douglas. Separation from the poor influence of the fort was key:

> I can then take a child or two from each of the surrounding tribes under my care and I have a hope of sending them back to teach in their own people; but this I cannot do at Fort Simpson. Parents have frequently told me that they feel afraid to have their children in this heathen camp, but will have no fear of their being with me under this new arrangement.

Like the Oblates, Duncan desired total control over his converts. On the subject of funding, he wrote,

> When I was last in Victoria I had a long conversation with his Excellency the Governor which turned principally on this subject viz. promoting industry among the Indians at their own homes. He assured me that the government would render what assistance they could to promote so considerable [sic] work. Hence I thought of writing to him and begging some government aid ... Will you kindly take the favourable opportunity of mentioning the matter to him?[111]

In the context of growing settler anxiety about possible conflict with Indigenous Peoples, aiding missionary education seemed a reasonable course of action to the governor. He was in favour of missionaries creating English-style villages to convert Indigenous people to Christianity and to introduce them to British culture.[112] On June 21, 1862, Cridge informed Duncan that he was to receive a grant of £50 to aid the founding of his settlement, in addition to the free land reserve offered earlier. Duncan and his followers then moved to his chosen site of Metlakatla on the Northwest Coast, which means "saltwater pass" in Sm'algyax. "We have succeeded," he wrote to Douglas, "in erecting a strong and useful building capable of containing at least 600 souls which we use as Church and School."[113] He explained further: "I have about 100 children who attend morning and afternoon and about 100 adults (often more) in the evening. I occupy the principal part of the time with the latter in giving them lectures on the following subjects – Geography, astronomy, natural history, or morals – these lectures they seem greatly to prize."[114] In 1868,

FIGURE 2.3 Reverend J.B. Good and his mission school in Nlaka'pamux territory, c. 1860s. Good was an SPG missionary who worked in Nanaimo, Yale, and Lytton. He continued his missionary work until his death in 1916. | Courtesy of the Royal BC Museum, Image D-03971, British Columbia Archives

Cridge travelled from Victoria to Metlakatla to inspect Duncan's work and, despite rumours of the missionary's intimate relations with female Ts'msyan students, spoke favourably of the school.[115] Metlakatla soon had a population of a thousand.

Although Duncan was the most celebrated Anglican missionary in the region, he was not alone. From the early to mid-1860s, new SPG agents became active at Victoria, Cowichan, Saanich, Nanaimo, Comox, Alberni, New Westminster, Yale, and Hope. The most successful was Reverend J.B. Good, who was based mostly in the Fraser Canyon area, specifically at Lytton, where the Fraser and Thompson Rivers converge. His mission at Lytton was considered to be second only to Metlakatla. Yet, Good soon discovered that government support came with strings attached. The onset of an economic depression after the gold rush changed the government's willingness to pay for missionary activity.

Good came to Victoria in 1861 and then started a mission at Nanaimo to compete with the Methodists who were already there. After five years, Anglican bishop George Hills posted him to Yale at the foot of the Fraser Canyon. Upon his arrival, Good wrote to Chief Commissioner of Land

and Works Joseph Trutch to apply for a grant of land near the Indian reserve at Yale "for the purposes of erecting thereon a building to be used as a school for the instruction of Indians and as the residence of the teachers." Although the response has not survived, Trutch, whom Fisher calls the "archetypal colonist," summarized his thoughts in a letter to the colonial secretary:

> I have the honor to state that I am of the opinion that it is not advisable to make further free grants of Public Land in the colony to religious bodies for any purposes whatever. There can be no doubt that good results might be anticipated from the establishment of the school proposed by Mr. Good, but I do not estimate these prospective advantages highly enough to warrant a free grant being made to the Church of the site for such a school house. Which would as it appears to me establish a precedent for many future applications of similar character and lead to much embarrassment. I want to further recommend that instead of a free grant a lease be granted of a lot of land for a term of seven years conditional on the erection thereon of a schoolhouse.[116]

Not only did this shift policy away from granting free land to missionaries, but it discouraged Good from continuing his work at Yale. Instead, at the invitation of three Nlaka'pamux communities, he moved north to Lytton. During the first months, he started a school for boys to instil "habits of instant obedience."[117] By the late 1860s, SPG missionaries such as Good had established a presence in the lower mainland to compete with the Catholic missionaries.

The greatest missionary success for Anglicans, however, continued to be that of the CMS on the Northwest Coast. In 1864, the society sent out Robert Doolan, a deacon, to establish a mission among the Nisga'a, which would be modelled on Metlakatla. Using Metlakatla as his base, Doolan travelled up the Nass River and founded his settlement at Quinwoch, one of five major Nisga'a villages. As at Metlakatla, schooling played a prominent role. Historian E. Palmer Paterson II claims that at Quinwoch a "day school was conducted with children and adults present, the latter coming out of curiosity. The formal atmosphere of the schoolroom was very difficult to establish and maintain. There was much coming and going and moving about, and there was the problem of keeping the building comfortably heated."[118] According to Doolan's journal, his average daily attendance was thirty-five students.[119]

The CMS also dispatched missionary Robert Tomlinson, who arrived at Metlakatla in May 1867. In June, he, Doolan, and Cowcaelth – a Nisga'a citizen who was baptised and renamed Philip Latimer – travelled approximately twenty-five kilometres from Quinwoch, where they picked a site for a new settlement called Kincolith. Under Tomlinson's tutelage, Kincolith became known as the "eldest daughter" of Metlakatla. He and a core of Nisga'a supporters built a church, school, and residences for the missionaries. In total, nine houses were constructed for the first Nisga'a living in the new settlement. The school trained young Indigenous men to evangelize nearby communities.

While Kincolith was being established, Tomlinson asked the government for financial assistance, as other missionaries had done throughout the 1860s. In particular, he wrote to Trutch to apply for a site for the mission buildings and a reserve similar to what Duncan had received. He asked for a free land grant to be held in trust by the government for the CMS.[120] Trutch informed Tomlinson that the governor was pleased to authorize his request. Given the government's previous support for missionary activity, this was not surprising. Yet, the practice had come under attack in the mid-1860s by critics such as Amor De Cosmos and John Robson, who argued that state funds would be better spent on other things, including the common school system.[121] Trutch thus informed Tomlinson, as he had told Good earlier, that the land was not to be given for free: it would be leased to him for a seven-year period at the rate of ten dollars per year.[122] This was the interwoven nature of accumulation by dispossession in late 1860s British Columbia: the government leased stolen Indigenous land to churches and used the funds to help pay for colonization, including common schooling for settler children. Early officials had recruited missionaries to help cultivate friendly relations with Indigenous Peoples, but by the late 1860s the colony was no longer willing to give missionaries handouts. The churches were effectively cut off. Tomlinson, like his Methodist, Catholic, and Anglican counterparts, managed to adapt and navigate the changing situation to continue missionary work into the 1870s, but without direct financial assistance from government.

Conclusion

By the late 1860s, it was evident that the colonial government no longer wanted to fund missionary schooling. Trutch made this clear in an 1870 letter to William Green of the Aborigines' Protection Society: "the government although giving cordially to these missions every countenance and moral support in its power has found it impractical to grant them any pecuniary aid."[123] As it agreed to assume more control over common schooling for settler children, it shifted financial responsibility for missionary schooling for Indigenous Peoples back to religious bodies. In the 1870s, this lack of funding opened a window for the dominion government to intervene and take on more responsibility for Indian education, which profoundly altered the missionary landscape and resulted in devastating effects for many Indigenous Peoples, as examined in Chapter 4. Indeed, as Part 2 of this book reveals, British Columbia's addition to the Dominion of Canada in 1871 significantly shaped its schooling projects.

PART TWO

RULING BY SCHOOLING, 1871–1900

IN JULY 1871, BRITISH COLUMBIA became the sixth province to join Confederation. The decision was contentious, but the government in Victoria saw it largely as a matter of convenience. The remote and beleaguered colony was broke. By the early 1870s, its economy was severely depressed after the gold rush boom, and its debt skyrocketed as the government struggled to support a sparse and scattered settler population. The Colonial Office in London wanted to maintain a strategic presence, but it was largely indifferent to the financial woes of the small and distant colony. Britain was far more focused on expanding its imperial influence and creating new markets in China, India, and Southern Africa.[1]

At the same time, the Dominion of Canada made it clear that western expansion was one of its primary objectives: it acquired Rupert's Land in 1869 and organized against the Métis Nation's Red River Resistance in 1869-70. Its expansionary ambitions were threatened by the 1867 American purchase of Alaska, which bordered on British Columbia, a fact that spurred negotiations to bring the colony into Confederation. In joining Canada, British Columbia became a self-governing province, and Ottawa wiped out its debts. In return, the dominion secured access to the Pacific Ocean, and the federal government promised to build a transcontinental railway to link the province to the rest of Canada and connect east-west trade to international shipping and trade routes throughout the British Empire.[2]

With its debts settled, the new provincial government set its sights on schemes to spur socioeconomic development. It imposed a legal framework over the province, including creating a series of small Indian reserves. Restricting the land base of Indigenous Peoples was intended to drive them into wage labour and would open up their territories, whose sale would generate revenue and accommodate the expected spike of immigrants after the completion of the Canadian Pacific Railway in 1886.[3] On the eve of Confederation, British Columbia's non-Indigenous population was approximately 10,000. By 1900, it jumped to almost 150,000, with the majority – from Britain, the United States, and Canada, as well as some from China and Japan – being from poor and working-class backgrounds. The intent of most, to secure employment and raise enough money to buy property, helped transform the emerging economy.

Previously, it had been connected to the fur trade and mercantilism, but now it started to transition into an industrial capitalist economy, linked to wage labour and rooted in resource extraction and export to global markets.[4] Moreover, white supremacy and racist politics – seeking to marginalize Indigenous and Chinese people in particular – played a role in creating a consciousness of British Columbia as a "white man's province."[5]

To support the transformation from struggling colony to thriving capitalist settler society, the provincial government invested in a range of infrastructure projects, from new roads and communication technology to a centralized system of public schools. As historian Paul Axelrod explains about mid-nineteenth-century education, "economic progress required civil order, and schools had a key role to play in ensuring political stability in a period of profound social change." Schools – as tools of socialization and legitimation – could "cultivate the students' sense of citizenship, loyalty, respect for property, and deference to authority."[6] Chapter 3 looks at how the provincial government, at great expense during a time of global recession (1870s–90s), created a system of free public schools as part of its strategy to build British Columbia. Schools would help to attract settlers and encourage them to stay. They would also produce loyal subjects and effective citizens, who would contribute to the province's development. Public schooling was an important part of the emerging structure of settler capitalism.

Indigenous Peoples responded to British Columbia's socioeconomic development in various ways. Sḵwx̱wú7mesh living around Burrard Inlet augmented their subsistence practices with seasonal wage labour, whereas other Nations such as the Tsilhqot'in in the interior initially refused to participate in the new economy, mostly preferring isolation and independence.[7] The Indigenous population hovered at around twenty-five thousand, but it decreased from 70 percent of the total population in 1871 to just 16 percent by 1900, as a result of mass settler immigration. Although the newcomers now greatly outnumbered the original inhabitants, settler anxiety over potential conflict with Indigenous Peoples did not diminish. These fears were exacerbated by Indigenous grievances about stolen land and problems with the newly created reserve system, and the government tried to contain Indigenous resistance to safeguard continued colonization. Here the federal government played an interventionist role. As per the terms of Confederation, it assumed responsibility for Indigenous Peoples and sought to assert its authority over the numerous and diverse Nations west of the Rocky Mountains. Chapter 4 shows how Ottawa worked with missionaries, cut off from funding by the colonial government during the late 1860s, to support and expand their experiments in schooling. In the early 1880s, it also formally partnered with churches to open new day, boarding, and industrial schools for Indigenous students as part of its attempt to disrupt Indigenous lifeways and recalibrate Indigenous Peoples to contribute to capitalist development and Canadian nation building. Chapters 3 and 4 trace the rise of state schooling in British Columbia and show that government-supported public schools and day, boarding, and industrial schools developed as distinct but overlapping projects of ruling by schooling.

CHAPTER | THREE

Public Schools for the People

British Columbia entered Confederation, according to historian F. Henry Johnson, "with the most centralized school system on record."[1] In the early 1870s, the ad hoc system of fee-based common schooling was transformed into a province-wide system of free public education that was paid for and administered by the government. Moreover, British Columbia was the first province in the dominion to establish a strictly non-sectarian system. In the eyes of some officials – including noted school promoter and Victoria MLA Amor De Cosmos – this was a key component of continued colonization and province/nation building. They hoped that free schooling, open to all without prejudice, would aid in attracting new settlers, a process that would help expand and legitimize provincial control over the vast and varied territory.

The legislature passed An Act Respecting Public Schools (The Public School Act, 1872) on April 11, 1872.[2] The *Daily British Colonist* applauded the measure:

> The deplorable condition of the public schools – perhaps it would be more correct to say the absence of them – long constituted one of British Columbia's chief grievances, and no measure was more distinctly or more unanimously demanded than a system of free non-sectarian education. Listening to the unequivocal voice of the people, it was one of the earliest acts of the new government to introduce a bill for the purpose of supplying this great public want ... The new School Bill, although making no pretentions to perfection, was admitted on all hands to present a fair basis to work upon; and the country rejoiced at the near prospect of having a free education placed within the reach of every child.[3]

Many parents put great faith in public schooling as an instrument of social mobility for their children. As a result, some people praised the legislation for creating "schools of the people."[4] In 1872, Victoria began to assemble what it called the "educational machinery" – an apparatus of administrators, inspectors, teachers, curriculum, and, of course, new schools – to establish schooling throughout the province.[5] Between 1872 and 1900, it gradually put this machinery in motion, resulting in an overall increase in classroom attendance. There was a boosterish quality to British Columbia during the period, a spirit that was captured in an 1887 newspaper editorial: "We cannot afford to stand still, progress is our watchword, if we desire others to make their homes with us, we must give them streets and sidewalks, water and light, sewage and protection from fire, schools and hospitals."[6] Schooling played an important part in this endeavour.

Historians like Johnson, suggest that Victoria simply listened to the "unequivocal voice of the people" and offered to pay for and provide schooling as a progressive public good.[7] This chapter, however, argues that the new system was not "of the people." Instead, it was a project of rule that was designed *for* the people. The government assumed full financial responsibility for public schooling in exchange for increased power over education as a tool of legitimation. Although some parents were entitled to vote for school board trustees, the state gradually assumed greater authority. Once the apparatus was in place, the system was reformed to aid the continued development of British Columbia's capitalist settler society. Indeed, Leo Panitch points out that ruling classes in places such as British Columbia, where class factions had difficulty finding unity in political parties or economic coalitions, "used the provincial state to express their interests."[8] In the struggle over who controlled education, the government won the day, selling what Bruce Curtis calls "ruling by schooling" to British Columbians as being in the best interests of the people.[9]

A NEW ACT TO FOLLOW

Despite the changes in the late colonial period, British Columbia's common school system was in a shambles by 1870. Some teachers were not even being paid. The system's failings were particularly pronounced in Victoria, where two teachers – one of them noted school promoter John Jessop – announced they were withdrawing their services to protest non-payment.[10] The colony was insolvent. By 1872, with its debts paid by Ottawa, the new government in Victoria could no longer claim financial ruin as a reason to download school costs onto parents and guardians. As a result, it passed the Public School Act, 1872, and assembled a plan to provide free public education to all children and youth between the ages of five and sixteen, based loosely on models elsewhere in Canada (specifically Ontario), the United States, and Europe.

The school act provided the foundation for a highly centralized system and for the establishment, maintenance, and management of non-denominational public schools throughout British Columbia, to be paid for by the government.[11] Local officials, though, were not powerless. Ratepayers in each school district could elect three trustees to their school board as stewards. Trustees were responsible for calling meetings, maintaining premises, and collecting taxes for educational purposes. Eventually, they were empowered to hire and fire teachers and to determine their salaries. Interestingly, the act said nothing about denominational private schools, which remained "unassisted and unregulated" by the provincial government until the mid-twentieth century.[12] A new private school for boys, Lorne College, opened in New Westminster in 1883, but it closed in 1887 due to lack of support in the face of a burgeoning public school system. Though some parents preferred private education, private schools accommodated not more than 3 percent of school-age British Columbians during the late nineteenth and early twentieth centuries.[13] The school act thus ensured that government-controlled, non-denominational public schooling would become the dominant mode in the new province.

In 1872, Victoria approved a budget of $40,000 to cover the costs of schooling and spent just over $10,000 on education in the first year. By 1900, it was spending more than $300,000 annually.[14] As was the case for other provincial expenditures, the necessary funds were raised, in part, through an evolving system of land sales, taxation, and pre-emption predicated on the logics of white possession and the processes of accumulation by dispossession, which geographer Cole Harris points out was at the heart of British Columbia's settler capitalist project.[15] Selling and licensing stolen Indigenous land to settlers and companies, the government developed forms of taxation to generate additional revenue that would pay for public services, including schooling.[16] In addition to applying basic operating grants to local schools, it awarded communities free or cheap plots of land as an incentive to establish schools, just as colonial governments did for missionaries in the 1850s and early 1860s. Moreover, toward the end of the century municipalities worked with local school trustees to raise supplemental funds – to pay for everything from teacher salaries and educational materials to constructing buildings – by taxing ratepayers' property in school districts.[17] Public schooling was thus paid for through funds accumulated and generated by settler capitalism, as David McNally notes.[18]

The new school system was placed under the jurisdiction of the Lieutenant-Governor-in-Council, the representative of the British Crown. The first person to occupy the position was Joseph Trutch, who also played a key role in creating provincial Indian reserves. Among other duties, Trutch appointed "six fit and proper persons" to staff a central Board of Education that would serve under him and administer the system.[19] Its wide-ranging responsibilities included everything from appointing and examining teachers to selecting learning materials such as textbooks. Trutch's most important duty, though, was to appoint a superintendent of education to chair the board and to promote and oversee the development of the school system. The superintendent reported to the provincial secretary until 1891, when it became customary to have a minister of education.[20]

The job of superintendent was entrusted to outspoken teacher John Jessop. Born in Norwich, England, he grew up in Canada West (Ontario), where he became acquainted with its system of state-supported common schooling and the ideas of school promoter Egerton Ryerson.[21] In 1859, after receiving his teaching certificate from the Toronto Normal School, Jessop put his pedagogical career on hold to travel to the Cariboo gold fields. Failing to strike it rich, he stayed on in Victoria and soon turned his attention back to education. In 1861, unable to secure a teaching post

FIGURE 3.1 John Jessop, British Columbia's first superintendent of education, c. 1870s. Jessop ran a successful private school in Victoria before becoming superintendent. | Courtesy of the Royal BC Museum, Image G-00297, British Columbia Archives

at a common school, he opened a successful non-sectarian private school in Victoria. Given his experience, the government appointed him as principal of the Victoria common school in the mid-1860s. As an established expert, Jessop was consulted on drafts of the Public School Act, 1872, by the provincial government, and he emerged as a natural candidate for the position of superintendent. Like Ryerson, Jessop was given the opportunity to create a system of free public schools.[22]

Jessop held the post of superintendent from 1872 to 1878. It came with an annual salary of $2,000, but it was not a symbolic position. It entailed gruelling toil, travel, and, as Jessop would unhappily discover, paper pushing. He started his work energetically in the spring and summer of 1872. He paid off the outstanding salaries of teachers, reopened schools in Victoria, and embarked on his first tour of duty to inspect and survey existing schools. Logging hundreds of kilometres on foot, on horseback, and by canoe, he examined schools as far north as Barkerville and as far east as the Okanagan Valley.[23] In an effort to simplify administration, he collected information on each one, a task that made the school-aged population "legible," in the words of political scientist James C. Scott, and thus controllable and manageable.[24]

Jessop's initial observations of the schools painted a bleak picture. As of July 31, 1872, only fourteen public schools were in operation, a drop from the twenty-one common schools counted the previous year. The number of students on the rolls was just 286, with an aggregate attendance of 201 (117 boys, 84 girls), though Jessop suggested that the total population for the year, counting children between the ages of five and sixteen, was 534. By his best estimate, there were approximately 1,768 school-aged children in the province and that "there are, therefore, fully 900 children not attending any school; more than 200 are in the Upper Country, where, at present, there are no schools within their reach."[25]

Common schools in established areas such as Victoria and New Westminster successfully transitioned into public schools, but the true test was expanding to all parts of the province. Jessop and the Board of Education tried to increase attendance by passing new legislation. In 1873, an amendment to the school act allowed trustees to create by-laws compelling parents and guardians to send their children to school.[26] In 1874, the government passed a new set of rules and regulations that attempted to tie teachers' salaries to attendance records, in hopes that teachers would pressure parents to send their children to school regularly. In 1876, it amended the school act again to give the existing measures more teeth by empowering trustees to lodge formal complaints with a magistrate against any parents or guardians who regularly kept their children at home. If found guilty, they could be fined upward of ten dollars. These efforts, including early attempts to introduce local taxes for schooling, were mostly unsuccessful, as trustees, teachers, and parents could either ignore or creatively subvert such punitive measures if they wished. In the 1870s, provincial state power was very "weak," as historian E.A. Heaman observes.[27]

The problem of poor attendance was worst in rural areas.[28] Putting a school in every hamlet was considered impractical, given the small and scattered settler population, so the government decided to create a boarding school at Cache Creek in the interior that would take in rural British Columbians. On the surface, the idea was about extending education to the far corners of the province. Yet, the underlying ambition, as Jessop explained, was actually to put the government "in a position to insert a COMPULSORY CLAUSE in the School Act; which certainly will become a *necessity* as soon as the means of education can be placed within the reach of every family."[29] Jessop's efforts to increase rural attendance must be understood as part of the state strategy to use schooling as a tool of legitimation and a project of rule.

In June 1874, the government opened the Cache Creek boarding school. Its initial enrolment was eighteen pupils, a mix of boys and girls, many of whom were Indigenous.[30] Their number soon expanded to

FIGURE 3.2 The Cache Creek Provincial Boarding School, c. 1870s. The Cache Creek school was a boarding school run by the provincial government. The government hoped that a boarding facility would entice parents in remote areas to send their children to school. The Cache Creek school opened in 1874 and closed in 1890. | Courtesy of the Royal BC Museum, Image A-03501, British Columbia Archives

thirty-six, each student paying eight dollars per month for room and board. Jessop reported that most were starting "at the very bottom of the ladder of learning."[31] Nevertheless, he recognized the institution's early advances: "The school has been going on for some days previously, while arrangements were being made for the opening; eighteen pupils, of both sexes, were then enrolled. The number has since increased to thirty-six, about as many as the building can accommodate. The success of the Boarding School experiment is now placed beyond a doubt."[32]

However, the school was soon mired in controversy. After only two years, Jessop fired the schoolmaster, T.T. Jones, who was discovered to have neglected his teaching duties, using the school as a hostelry on the Cariboo Road. He also occasionally worked as a teamster instead of delivering his lessons. Jessop hired new staff, and everything appeared to be going smoothly until the spring of 1877. At that time, the new principal revealed that a number of the Indigenous students had been impregnated by male pupils.[33] The fact that students were having sex at a school shocked many British Columbians, and the local trustees promptly fired the staff for dereliction of duty. Jessop supported the firings and managed to save the reputation of the school, which allowed the experiment to continue until a decline in enrolment forced it to close in 1890.[34]

Jessop, who was not infallible, become a lightning rod for criticism near the end of his tenure as superintendent. In 1876, the leader of the Opposition, George Anthony Walkem, targeted him for having an unnecessarily extravagant salary.[35] Jessop managed to survive the crisis and he hung on for two more years, but when Walkem was elected premier in June 1878, his days were numbered.[36] In August, a resolution was placed before the legislature to reduce Jessop's salary by more than half, from $2,000 to $750. As justification, Walkem suggested that Jessop was "unfit in point of education for the position." His proof? Jessop's annual school report for 1876 apparently contained more than three hundred grammatical "blunders."[37] Instead of accepting the pay cut, Jessop resigned.

On balance, his stint as superintendent was successful. The number of school districts almost doubled from twenty-five in 1872–73 to forty-five in 1877–78. Student enrolment had expanded as well, from 1,028 to 2,198. The average daily attendance had risen from 55.93 percent to

63.59 percent by 1877–78 (see Appendix 1). This growth is partly explained by modest population gains and by the fact that education was becoming more accessible and standardized, thanks especially to Jessop's attention to rural schooling. The government also maintained its commitment to pay for the system, with the total expenditure rising to $43,334.01 by 1878.[38] Though most people felt that the new schools were better than the chaotic common schools of the past, improvement was still needed to justify additional government spending and to broaden the state's educational reach throughout the province.

Expanding Education

From the late 1870s to 1900, the work continued apace. As the educational system widened its influence, the state tightened its grip on administration. In the lead-up to Jessop's resignation, the Board of Education resigned to protest Walkem's bullying behaviour. Waiting until Jessop was out of the picture, the Walkem administration responded by passing the Public Schools Act, 1879, in which it abolished the board and effectively transferred its duties to the superintendent. Now paid a much-reduced salary, the superintendent would be assisted only by two civil servants to help with the examination and certification of teachers. Such changes made the school system even more centralized and firmly concentrated power in the hands of the superintendent.

Colin Campbell McKenzie and Stephen D. Pope succeeded Jessop as the next two superintendents, and they mostly shared his vision for expanding public schooling.[39] Born in 1836 at Fort Vancouver, Oregon Country, to Métis fur-trading parents, McKenzie was educated at St. Peter's College in Cambridge.[40] He was the principal of the Victoria Boys' Public School from 1872 until being appointed superintendent in September 1878. Pope was born in the United States, but he attended Queen's University in Kingston, Ontario. After graduation, he travelled to British Columbia to become a teacher. In 1884, he replaced McKenzie as superintendent and remained in the position until 1899. Administering and extending the school system was left largely in the hands of these two men, though a Council of Public Instruction was created in 1891 to set the curriculum, authorize textbooks, create school districts and define boundaries, and lay out the general rules and regulations for schools and teachers.[41]

Additional administrative positions were also created in the 1880s and 1890s, and new forms of reporting were established. As part of the 1879 shake-up by Walkem, and to lighten the duties of the superintendent to justify the reduction in salary, the government appointed a school inspector. He took over the superintendent's travel schedule and reported on "the progress and average attendance of the pupils, the discipline and management of the school, the system of education pursued, the mode of keeping the school registers, the condition of the buildings and premises and such other matters as he may deem advisable in furtherance of the interests of the School."[42] As Bruce Curtis and Thomas Fleming demonstrate, inspectors played an important role as the eyes and ears – and the most visible symbols – of the educational state, performing the necessary surveillance to ensure that things ran smoothly.[43] David Wilson, previously employed as the principal of the boys' school in New Westminster, was hired in 1887 as the first inspector. By the late 1890s, he was joined by other inspectors, who helped oversee schools to ensure compliance.

By the 1899–1900 school year, there were four inspectors on staff: Wilson, S.B. Netherby, F.M. Cowperthwaite, and William Brown. During their visits to all parts of the province, they collected valuable information and statistics on school matters. They often arrived unannounced, much to the surprise of teachers, even though informal networks tried to warn them. Journalist Jan Gould recounted one such experience:

> At Spences Bridge in the 1890s, young teacher Miss Hopkins ran over to her neighbour, Jessie Ann Smith, complaining that a strange man appeared to be following her everywhere. What should she do? Mrs. Smith advised her to open the school as usual and promised to send her husband to the school to keep an eye on everything. No sooner had Miss Hopkins started the day's work than she glanced out of the window and saw the stranger marching up the school path. With the help of the larger children in the class, she pushed hard against the door. The stranger pushed from the other

side. Harder and harder she and the children pushed until finally they gave up and stepped back. The stranger staggered into the room and fell to the floor: "I am Mr. Cowperthwaite," he said slowly as he picked himself up. "The school inspector."[44]

Teachers like Hopkins had little job security and could not afford to be ill prepared or behind in their lessons. The fear of surprise reviews pressured them always to be prepared and to exercise diligence in teaching the authorized materials. By the late 1880s, they were required to keep detailed records and to complete monthly reports on their school's progress. Such reporting provided the government with useful information for planning the future and, as Scott suggests, for devising strategies of "simplification" to monitor and manage the population.[45]

By 1900, British Columbia's school machinery was firmly in place. An expanded system helped it accommodate a spike in population leading up to, and especially following, the completion of the Canadian Pacific Railway in 1886. In 1882, four years before the railway reached the coast, there were 48 school districts, with a total enrolment of 2,571. Not ten years later, by 1891, there were 141 districts, with an enrolment of 9,260 and an average daily attendance of 5,134. By the 1899–1900 school year, 231 districts had a total enrolment of 21,531 (see Appendix 1).[46] As the settler population increased, classrooms swelled with new students.

Contact Zone Classrooms

The schoolroom was an important laboratory of socialization that sorted children, both formally and informally, according to class, gender, and racialization. It helped to fix their places in the emerging capitalist and heteropatriarchal society of the province. Officially, public schools were open to all, but the vast majority of students came from the working class. The children of the affluent mostly continued to attend private schools, which, as Jean Barman and John Porter note, reproduce the ranks of the elite and entrench class privilege and social exclusivity.[47]

For everyone else, public schools were the best option. Historian Alison Prentice explains that nineteenth-century education was "at once the best means to rise [one's social position] and the only real insurance against social and economic decline."[48] Rather than abolishing class inequality, public schools normalized the unequal relations of capitalism, presenting them as the natural outcome of a fair and open competition. Many working-class parents wanted their children to be educated, but some viewed public schooling with suspicion, seeing it as a way of undercutting the family economy and breaking up the informal transmission of teachings and training directly from themselves to their children.[49] In other words, they felt that children's labour at home was more beneficial than regular attendance at school. By the 1890s, however, this resistance had started to decrease as, in the midst of a global depression, the threat of financial penalty for truancy forced many parents to comply and send their children to school. Within a generation, many had embraced both public schooling and the government's power over education as essential for promoting social mobility. This consent, as Jessop explained in the 1870s, was the necessary precondition for Victoria's eventual implementation of a clause to compel attendance.

British Columbia's classrooms were also profoundly gendered spaces. In the 1870s, the government still felt public pressure to keep boys and girls in separate classrooms, ideally in different schools altogether. Under the Public School Act, 1872, the Board of Education had the power to "establish a separate School for females in any District where they may deem it expedient to do so."[50] Though some education officials preferred to separate boys and girls, this made little sense in the sparsely populated province, where many schools initially struggled to attract enough children to stay open. Gender segregation also had its fierce opponents. In 1877, a letter to the editor of a Victoria newspaper, probably written by teacher and suffragist Agnes Deans Cameron, outlined the issue: "If we are to march forward and break down the senseless division walls that exist between male and female in the formation of society, then the system of teaching boys and girls in the same classes is more calculated to accomplish the object than anything I know."[51] Public pressure dovetailed with economic necessity to establish combined classrooms as the norm by the 1880s and 1890s. In 1899–1900, the reported school population was 21,531 (11,076 boys and 10,455 girls).[52] It must be noted, however, that schooling remained profoundly gendered, and boys enjoyed special access to higher education as a gateway to sought-after professions and upward mobility.

Public schools were also open to children of all backgrounds.[53] Scattered attempts to establish segregated schools based on racialization failed, and Black, Kanakas, and Chinese children attended late-nineteenth-century public schools in places such as Saltspring Island, Vancouver, Victoria, and Barkerville. Indigenous children also found their way into the schools. Indeed, as sociologist Renisa Mawani writes, this kind of heterogeneity "in and of itself was generative of new racial orders."[54] According to the terms of British Columbia's union with Canada, Indigenous Peoples fell under the jurisdiction of the federal government, and the province was not supposed to provide for their education. Yet, in the 1870s and 1880s Ottawa lacked the power, influence, and staff to adequately take control of Indian affairs in the Pacific Province, as Chapter 4 explores more thoroughly. Moreover, Constance Backhouse, Mary Jane Logan McCallum, and Adele Perry all note that who was considered to be an "Indian" by the state is not always easy to comprehend.[55] As Mawani points out, Ottawa's legal definition excluded both the non-status Indians who did not live on reserves and those disparagingly racialized as "half-breeds," or people of Indigenous and European decent.[56] Both were often treated as if they were Indians, but they did not fall within the government's legal category. As a result, they paid taxes and could – and did – send their children to public schools. All of these jurisdictional and juridical complexities challenged what Anne McClintock terms "sanctioned binaries" of "colonizer-colonized, self-other, dominance-resistance" in the province.[57]

Though Ottawa established a separate school system for Indigenous children in the 1870s – which is the subject of Chapter 4 – many Indigenous students continued to attend public schools in British Columbia.[58] Jessop's records from his school tours are filled with references to Indigenous students. In 1874, he visited Breyegers Bay School, finding only six pupils in attendance. In taking stock of the local school-aged children, though, he counted twenty-three, "3 whites" and "20 half-breeds." His reports from other schools, mostly on Vancouver Island and the Gulf Islands, offered comparable findings. Griffith settlement had eight children, all of whom were "halfbreeds"; Maple Bay had "7 whites, 4 halfbreeds"; Cowichan Flat had "3 whites, 8 halfbreeds"; Saltspring Island had a number of "half breed" and "coloured" children; and on Gabriola Island, he "found 16 children in attendance. All halfbreeds but well-behaved."[59]

On the mainland, the situation was similar. The teacher at Moodyville on the north shore of Burrard Inlet noted that at least half of her students were "half breeds."[60] In May 1876, Thomas S. of Lillooet wrote to Jessop, explaining, "The majority of the scholars is half-breed children ... All the half-breed children of school age that I know anything about with but one exception have attended the school."[61] A month later, Alex Deans wrote to Jessop to clarify that "there are 6 or 8 Indian children of school age in the immediate vicinity [of Lillooet] whose parents express a willingness" to send them to school.[62] Similarly, in October Jane Trenaman, the teacher at Hope, wrote to Jessop about her Indigenous students, asking whether she should have permitted the children to attend:

> Once again I have to trouble you as I am so inexperienced in school matters I do not know what I ought to do in the case. It is this: a week ago an Indian boy sent another boy to me to get a book as he wanted to learn to read. I sold him the book and his cousin (a half-breed coming to school) told me he wanted to go to the mission but his father would not allow it. So I told her if he ... [wants] to learn he could come to school as long as he behaved properly. He has come ever since and is acquainting himself creditably ...
>
> Since then another Indian boy has come to me wanting to come. I permitted him to do so with the same conditions.[63]

Jessop's diary and correspondence confirm that Indigenous students also attended public schools in Vancouver, the Fraser Valley, the Cariboo, and the Okanagan. Moreover, Jean Barman shows that men with Indigenous wives and children of school age served as school trustees in North Saanich, North Cowichan, and South Cowichan on Vancouver Island;

on Saltspring Island; and at Maple Ridge, Cache Creek, Nicola Valley, and Moodyville on the mainland.[64] In the late nineteenth century, British Columbia's public schools accommodated, in varying and uneven ways, Indigenous and non-Indigenous pupils.

Underutilized sources such as school photographs can shed new light on this subject, offering a unique view of early contact zone classrooms. Cameras, of course, are not objective instruments, and photographs can simultaneously depict and distort reality. Scholars such as Sherry Farrell Racette, Carol Williams, Paige Raibmon, and Kristine Alexander stress that photographs in colonial settings often reproduce and reinforce a colonial gaze that relegates Indigenous Peoples to the margins.[65] Yet, they can also reveal what was obscured or not otherwise documented, as recent studies show.[66] Indeed, Dakota Sioux scholar Philip Deloria argues that they can capture "Indians" in "unexpected places" and push back against erasure and prove their presence in the historical record in ways that subvert expectations and unsettle colonial ways of thinking.[67] In British Columbia, class pictures were part of the state's attempts to document growing school attendance to justify its increased educational expenditure. Nevertheless, those images also "unexpectedly" document the Indigenous students who attended public schools even though they were expected to enrol in federal institutions such as day, boarding, and industrial schools.

The textual evidence for Indigenous students attending public schools in British Columbia is supported by numerous school photographs. An 1886 class picture identifies "whites and Indians" at the Hastings Sawmill School in Vancouver, which is not surprising as the nearby mill employed a number of Indigenous men as labourers (Figure 3.3).[68]

Similarly, Figures 3.4 and 3.5 are class photos taken at public schools near Indigenous communities on western Vancouver Island during the late 1880s and early 1890s – before federal Indian schools were established in the area. They too show Indigenous students in attendance.

Figure 3.6 is an 1899 class picture from the school in Hazelton, in northwestern British Columbia. It shows students who appear to be Indigenous. These sources are, of course, imperfect and partial reflections of Indigeneity, but considered in context and alongside textual

FIGURE 3.3 Indigenous and settler students outside of the Hastings Sawmill School in Vancouver, c. 1886. Many Indigenous Peoples worked at lumber mills and on the docks around Burrard Inlet and some sent their children to local public schools. | Courtesy of the Royal BC Museum, Image D-05546, British Columbia Archives.

FIGURE 3.4 Port Alberni School in Hupacasath and Tseshaht territory, c. 1887. | Courtesy of the Royal BC Museum, Image D-04590, British Columbia Archives

FIGURE 3.5 Bamfield School in Huu-ay-aht territory, c. 1895. | Courtesy of the Royal BC Museum, Image C-03733, British Columbia Archives

FIGURE 3.6 Hazelton School in Gitxsan territory, c. 1899. | Courtesy of the Royal BC Museum, Image B-01336, British Columbia Archives

evidence they further suggest that British Columbia's public schools were not homogeneous spaces reserved only for white settler children.

Victoria's stance on whether Indigenous children should attend public schools was also inconsistent. As historian Timothy J. Stanley notes, "Racisms do not have fixed essences, but change with time and place."[69] On August 11, 1884, Superintendent Pope clarified to John Robson, now provincial premier, that the public schools were "free to all without distinction of race or creed."[70] A few years later, in response to a query raised by Thomas Holchey of the Merns public schools, Pope wrote, "As to admission of Indian children, allow me to state that they may be admitted as pupils."[71] Thus, it appears that Indigenous students were sometimes allowed to attend classes to boost numbers and keep schools open, especially in rural areas. In the late 1880s, however, a noticeable shift occurred. Because Indian education was a federal responsibility, provincial authorities preferred local school boards to comply with this

FIGURE 3.7 Sooke schoolchildren, c. 1880s. | Courtesy of the Royal BC Museum, Image A-09148, British Columbia Archives

arrangement as a convenient cost-cutting measure. "Indian children are wards of the Dominion Government," Pope wrote in an 1889 letter, "and are not presumed to be entitled to attend the Public Schools of the Province."[72] By the 1890s, as an economic depression set in, Pope's position hardened. In 1892, a settler parent in Sooke, identified only as "Mr. White," complained that Indigenous children were attending the local school (they were probably the offspring of Iroquois fur-traders who had settled in Sooke and married into the T'Sou-ke Nation).[73] In response, Pope instructed trustees that they could now bar Indigenous pupils from attending a public school if a single parent in the district objected to their presence.[74] Nevertheless, Indigenous children continued to find their way into public schools well into the twentieth century, though they – like other classmates of colour – still experienced racism and informal segregation, such as being seated together in separate parts of the room or let out of school before their white classmates.[75]

FIGURE 3.8 Sooke schoolchildren and their teacher, c. 1890s. | Courtesy of the Royal BC Museum, Image A-09151, British Columbia Archives

Tightening Control

Though increasing numbers of children from all backgrounds were going to school by the 1880s, the average attendance rose by just 12 percent between 1881 and 1900, from 51.21 to 63.5 percent.[76] In his 1890–91 school report, Pope lamented, "The percentage of average attendance was 55.45. This is a very credible showing; however, when we take into consideration that fifty-five per cent of regular attendance means forty-five per cent of irregular attendance, it is to be hoped that improvement in this respect will be made."[77] Irregular attendance threatened to blunt the effectiveness of ruling by schooling. For his part, Pope started to crack down on non-compliant school districts. "As the average daily attendance of your school for the past month has fallen below the requirement of Statute," he informed a Nanaimo school official,

> it is my duty to close the same forthwith. I regret the loss to the children of school facilities and trust that the Trustees will at an early day, be in a position to make application for the re-opening of the school, which they can do when they feel assured that the average daily attendance required by the school act (10) will be maintained.[78]

Somewhat counterintuitively, Pope was willing to close schools in order to induce higher attendance numbers.

Inconsistent attendance was a persistent problem throughout the period. "Irregularity of attendance, although decreasing year by year, still continues to be a hindrance to progress in many of our rural schools," wrote Inspector William Burns in 1895. He continued,

> this is no doubt frequently unavoidable at certain seasons of the year. By it, not only are those who have been absent unable to keep up with the classwork, but those who have been present are compelled to go over work already known, for the benefit of those absentees, or the teacher is obliged to devote additional care and attention to them by individual teaching.[79]

Waging war on tardiness and truancy demanded creative tactics, and officials tried various methods of recruiting parents and teachers to the cause.

In the 1870s, Jessop argued that success in schooling was dependent on more than government action from above: the cooperation of parents and guardians on the ground was also essential. Consent, rather than coercion, was most effective. As he wrote, "A little judicious pressure brought to bear upon negligent parents in our school districts, by Trustees, will soon make chronic non-attendance almost a thing of the past." He suggested that "public schools are entirely a new feature; and parents themselves, in some instances, require to be *educated*, in order properly to realize the fact that instruction is requisite of their offspring."[80] Jessop explained that

> in my visiting and lecturing tour this autumn, I shall endeavour to awaken a more lively interest in the education of the young; to show parents and guardians that everything possible is being done for them, and that it is their bounden duty to avail themselves of the very great educational privileges already provided for the benefit and advancement of those committed to their charge.[81]

This is consistent with Antonio Gramsci's idea of the state "as an educator" and confirms Philip Corrigan, Bruce Curtis, and Robert Lanning's argument that nineteenth-century schooling was focused on "making selves" in ways that normalized social rules and legitimated state power.[82]

However, the resistance of parents and guardians to mass compulsory schooling did not always arise from simple ignorance regarding "educational privileges." Indeed, opposition existed throughout the province and was at least partly responsible for sporadic attendance. In his 1874 school report, Jessop cited one example from North Saanich on Vancouver Island, where a school was closed due to the "persistent refusal of two heads of families, representing at least seven children of school age, neither of whom are more than two and a half miles from the school house, to send their children to the school."[83] Poor weather, the

FIGURE 3.9 Children going to school on horseback, c. 1890s. Many students, especially in rural areas, lived far from their schools. Before the adoption of school buses made getting to school easier, factors such as geography and weather greatly influenced attendance in many parts of the province. | Courtesy of the Royal BC Museum, Image B-07190, British Columbia Archives

need for family labour, and long distances to schools all contributed, in varying measures, to some parents' refusal to send their children to school regularly. Strained parent-teacher relations also led to truancy. In 1894, Pope wrote to Miss M.R. Smith, a teacher, about recent difficulties at her school: "I regret that your relations with some of the parents of the district are not as pleasant as you would wish them to be. It is well for the teacher not to be too sensitive and to be willing to throw the mantle of charity over remarks made that are annoying or even offensive."[84]

Because parents played such an important role in their children's lives, officials tried to make them feel responsible for the success of schooling. Women, and mothers in particular, were targeted in the attempt to break down resistance. In the 1880s, Victoria amended the school act so that "the wife of every voter" could now cast her municipal ballot for school trustee. According to Pope, this move "contributed to the awakening of no little enthusiasm in both civic and rural districts."[85] Legislation was also passed so that women could serve on school boards and as trustees, at first only in city districts, though historian Lara Campbell notes that successive provincial governments "expanded and contracted" the right to vote and the ability to stand for election.[86] Joan Sangster also argues that some women, including suffragist Maria Grant, who successfully ran for the Victoria Board of Education in 1889, justified their activism in maternal terms as taking care of their families and looking out for the best interests of society.[87] In his 1890–91 report, Superintendent Pope suggested that the progress of pupils owed a great deal to the attitude of their parents: "Every parent is, or should be, solicitous for the progress of his children at school. The success of the child does not alone depend on the ability and energy of the teacher; the parent is a very important factor in the matter."[88]

Parents and guardians had significant responsibilities, but recruiting and training suitable teachers was also essential. The 1872–73 school report gave a detailed list of their duties: teaching all the required branches of knowledge; keeping a daily, weekly, and monthly register; maintaining "proper order and discipline"; and classifying students according to their abilities. Teachers were also expected to promote "CLEANLINESS, NEATNESS, and DECENCY. To personally inspect the children every morning, to see that they have their hands and faces washed, their hair combed, and clothes clean." Developing children of good character was important, but so too was instilling a respect for authority. Teachers were "to pay the strictest attention to the morals and general conduct of the pupils; to omit no opportunity of inculcating the principles of TRUTH and HONESTY; the duties of respect to superiors, and obedience to all persons placed in authority over them."[89] They were to enforce a regular schedule. From April to September, school was to run from 9:00 a.m. to noon and from 1 p.m. to 3:30 p.m. From October to March, it ran from 9:30 a.m. to noon and 1:00 p.m. to 3:00 p.m. Every morning, students had a fifteen-minute recess.

Teachers were vitally important, but they were not treated equally.[90] Their profession was hierarchical and highly stratified by rank, status, and gender. Rank was based on a rigorous government certification process whose purpose was to control and standardize their work. To acquire a certificate, potential candidates had to arrange an examination to be overseen by the superintendent and one member of the Board of Education, and later a Board of Examiners, that tested them on various branches of knowledge. There were six levels of certification correlating to the percentage of correct answers: "First Class (A), 80 per cent.; First Class (B), 70 per cent.; Second Class (A), 60 per cent.; Second Class (B), 50 per cent.; Third Class (A), 40 per cent.; Third Class (B), 30 per cent."[91] By the 1899–1900 school year, 218 certificates had been issued in British Columbia.[92]

Certificates also dictated salary scales, with first-class teachers receiving the highest pay. The 1872 school report listed twenty-nine teachers who were employed in public schools. The best-paid was McKenzie, the future superintendent, who held a certificate from the Board of Education and received $100 per month. The lowest monthly salary, of $40, went to seven teachers, most of whom held third-class certificates. Room and board cost between about $16 and $25 a month. In 1876, teachers made an average annual salary of $644.41, which, though comparable with that of their Ontario counterparts, was still less than for other professions in British Columbia.[93] According to the 1899–1900 school report, 494 teachers were paid a total of $196,077, for an average salary of approximately $396, or just $30 per month. Some were listed as earning this amount, but most made between $40 and $60 a month. A few, who worked in Victoria and New Westminster, earned up to $125.[94] The profession was also ordered by gender. Women, many of them just out of school themselves, taught in lower divisions and were paid a fraction of what male teachers took home.[95] Some, such as Clara Smith Starrett, worked at remote rural locations before chasing other job opportunities, including at a boarding school for Indigenous children at Metlakatla.[96] Overall, teachers were expected to be role models, helping their students to develop a good character.

Though examples of outright student resistance to schooling are rare, there are glimpses of non-compliance in the archive. Children at the Granville school in the 1870s and 1880s were said to be "unruly." Conditions worsened to the point where they are reported to have "hog-tied one teacher and then thrown him into the bush."[97] Other incidences of opposition, including sexual misconduct, appear in records regarding corporal punishment. Barman documents a number of cases where boys whom teachers disciplined for using bad language subsequently lashed out, including harassing and even sexually abusing female classmates.[98] For students who did not conform to discipline, repression was often the result.

Punishments varied in form and frequency, and by school and teacher, but it seems likely that some form of physical punishment – be it the strap or a spanking – was used to police students in this period. In his 1894–95 report, Pope provided a few statistics:

> The number of cases of corporal punishment reported for the past school-year does not show any perceptible decrease. The number of cases reported for all the schools was 2,446. These figures do not speak well for the teachers of those schools in which the rod would appear to be the chief means employed to obtain necessary discipline. It is very proper to state, however, that more than half of the cases of corporal punishment reported are credited to less than twenty schools; one Graded Rural School reporting 108 cases.

In 1899, the principal of Victoria High School was fired for punishing a student too severely. Harsh chastisement, then, was doled out unequally, with some unlucky students disproportionately paying the price. Pope remarked,

> It is to be feared that the use of the power of moral suasion in obtaining good government in the schools is neglected, in great part, by a few of our teachers. Physical force is certainly not the only nor the best means at the command of the teacher for securing good discipline. The teacher who uses moral suasion effectively in the government of his school will accomplish the *best* results, not only in the moral training of the pupils but in their intellectual advancement.[99]

Although the state preferred moral instruction as the chief method of discipline, children who created cultures and practices of resistance were not spared the rod.

Learning Legitimacy

School officials also authorized new educational materials to teach students about colonial legitimacy and prepare them for citizenship. Initially, the curriculum – outlined in an official programme of studies – was quite rudimentary, and lessons were based on textbooks and exercises in writing and recitation. In the mostly one-room schools, students were categorized according to their reading level. In 1872, Jessop authorized the textbooks that were approved by the Board of Education. By 1874, he reported that all teachers were using them. Students purchased them from the school. These volumes, particularly the Canadian Series of School Books popularly known as the Red Series, reflected the religious, moral, political, economic, social, and cultural ideas of nineteenth-century settler society.[100] Harro Van Brummelen argues that most of them stressed the dignity of labour, the importance of religious devotion, and the virtue of overcoming hardships through sheer determination. They encouraged children to "construct an ideal world for themselves. As long as they worked hard, obeyed the moral law, contributed to family life, were diligent in their studies and shunned the evils of alcohol and tobacco their lives were to be happy even if they were not wealthy."[101] Soon, however, it became obvious that a basic elementary education would not sufficiently train children to take up their roles in an increasingly industrialized society.

To meet this need, the government created high schools and expanded the curriculum in the late 1870s and early 1880s. Some schools had experimented with higher levels of education in subjects such as bookkeeping, algebra, and philosophy, but not until 1874 did Jessop recommend that two high schools be established, one in Victoria and one in New Westminster. They offered advanced education at a cost to promising pupils, and they also served as "Training Institutes" for teachers, increasingly female students, in the absence of a provincial normal school, or teachers' college.[102] Victoria High School opened its doors in August 1876 and the New Westminster High School welcomed its first cohort in 1884. As both the population and demands for more schools increased, high schools were founded in Nanaimo in 1886 and Vancouver in 1890.

New courses were also created. Canadian history was introduced to shape an emerging national identity by rationalizing colonization and the development of Canada as a natural and inevitable process linked to building the British Empire. Given that Canada and its provinces were relatively new entities, history courses tended to focus on English history. Consequently, textbooks such as William Francis Collier's *History of the British Empire* had little to say about Canada, save for brief mentions of of the dominion's membership in the British Empire.[103] By the late 1880s, however, interest in Canadian history was growing, so it was added to the prescribed course list in 1887, specifically for high schools.

History education was envisioned as a tool of colonial subject formation. In his 1894–95 report, Pope explained that

> the immediate object of the study, so far as the school is concerned, is to give the pupil some acquaintance with the history of his own country; so that he may sympathize with its traditions and its fame, appreciate its laws and institutions, and love its soil and inhabitants. According to this view, history, particularly that of one's own country, furnishes the best training in patriotism.[104]

Despite the subject's perceived usefulness, no textbook on Canadian history was deemed suitable for schools until W.H.P. Clement published *The History of the Dominion of Canada* in 1897.[105] Like school history lessons generally, it offered a whitewashed account of the past that demonized and dehumanized Indigenous Peoples as bloodthirsty savages to present colonization and Christian nation building as a peaceful process that students should contribute to for the good of society. Indeed, history textbooks, as a powerful form of what Gina Starblanket and Dallas Hunt call "storying," helped to legitimize colonization and instructed students to take up their roles as subjects and defenders of empire, an emphasis that increased after the Boer War (1899–1902) and during the First World War.[106]

In the early 1890s, a growing number of social reformers and some parents called for manual training in schools (broadly understood as consisting of hand work, hand-and-eye training, constructive work, and industrial education).[107] During the late 1880s and the 1890s, students were expected to leave school in their teens, after which they would work for wages in the emerging resource extraction and manufacturing sectors. Given this, some officials felt that basic academic education should be supplemented with more specific manual training. Book learning needed to be augmented with physical training. To orient students, mostly boys, for the demands of an industrializing society, more modern methods were required. A major influence in this regard was the Macdonald-Robertson Movement. James Wilson Robertson worked his way up in the federal civil service as an agricultural expert in the Department of Agriculture, and he lobbied the Ontario government to implement a more practical education. In 1897, he met William Christopher Macdonald, a Montreal tobacco tycoon who also favoured educational change. The two men shared a common interest in school reform as a method for promoting greater socioeconomic development. In particular, they believed that manual training in Canadian schools could spur and sustain nation building and capitalist development. Macdonald's wealth supported Robertson's vision, and together their efforts started a national movement for practical training in schools.[108] The basic plan was to purchase industrial machinery for schools and provide the requisite salaries for professionals to teach the skills, mostly in wood- and metalwork, that children could use as workers once they graduated. Overall, the intent of the Macdonald-Robertson Movement was to prove to provincial governments that supporting practical training in schools had distinct benefits. This somewhat blurs Leo Panitch's distinction, in which the state works on behalf of capitalists and the elite, not at their behest.[109]

By the 1890s, the ideas of Robertson and Macdonald had reached British Columbia. In an industrializing society, some school officials thought that manual training could support the transition from farming or independent commodity production to wage labour in shops, factories, or the resource sector. In November 1900, Robertson visited the province to make the necessary arrangements with the Education Department to introduce manual training in Vancouver and Victoria for a trial period of three years. The aim was to illustrate the usefulness of such training in orienting children to the demands of physical labour at an early age. If they were to contribute to the economy as adults, schools needed to prepare them for this role.[110] By 1900, the government had agreed to include manual and industrial training in the curriculum, which would be greatly expanded in the early twentieth century.

Conclusion

By 1900, many British Columbians had accepted the new public school system as essential to socioeconomic development. In only thirty years, the sporadic system of fee-based common schools, with just over five hundred students and a few schools and teachers, had been replaced by a rapidly expanding system of hundreds of government-controlled schools that accommodated over twenty thousand students from a variety of backgrounds. This process, which supported the seizing of the area by settlers, was tightly controlled by a highly centralized educational bureaucracy, aided, to varying degrees, by teachers and parents. In the face of some resistance, the state successfully combatted truancy and increased student attendance, while implementing new learning materials that helped prepare students for wage labour. By the beginning of the twentieth century, the state had created schools for the people and was in a position to consolidate its power over public education – as a tool of socialization and legitimation – to further the development of British Columbia's capitalist settler society.

CHAPTER | FOUR

Inventing Indian Education

In November 1882, "riotous proceedings" broke out at the Metlakatla mission on the Northwest Coast, provoked by a dispute over its school for Ts'msyan children.[1] The conflict revolved around questions of money and autonomy. For twenty years, William Duncan, as one of the most respected CMS agents in the field, relied on government support to build and run his remote mission settlement. By 1870, however, the British Columbia government was no longer funding missionaries. When the colony joined Canada in 1871, Ottawa saw its chance to assert greater influence over Indian education by subsidizing the work of missionaries such as Duncan. As a result of securing new funding from the dominion, Metlakatla – particularly its school – flourished and was held up as a model throughout much of the British Empire. Duncan even became a trusted advisor to the federal government on Indigenous issues related to land and education.[2]

By the early 1880s, however, Duncan had fallen out of favour with Ottawa. Duncan, it was believed, fathered a child with a young Ts'msyan woman whom he forced to live in his mission house at Metlakatla.[3] The government also came to distrust him due to his unwillingness to follow its new policies.[4] His funding came with strings attached. Resenting the increased oversight, Duncan refused to send reports to the Department of Indian Affairs, which were required if his school were to qualify for annual funding. Ottawa subsequently branded him a renegade. To make matters worse, when the Diocese of British Columbia was split into three in 1879, William Ridley, the newly appointed bishop of Caledonia, chose Metlakatla as his base. He wanted to displace Duncan as its spiritual leader, and control over the school became a focal point in a power struggle between bishop, missionary, and community members. Ridley declared that Duncan's refusal to follow government policy, while still accepting federal money, meant that he no longer possessed authority over the building. He was an illegitimate leader. On these grounds, Ridley asserted control over the school as a way of separating Duncan from his followers. And it worked. Two Ts'msyan teachers quit and sided with Ridley, forcing Duncan to abandon the school. In response, he and some loyal Ts'msyan supporters posted a public notice threatening the bishop. "Unless you promise at once to remove your school house," they warned, "we shall ... take it down."[5]

When Ridley ignored this threat, Duncan and his followers started dismantling buildings. Ridley read the riot act, but to no avail. In an effort to save the schoolhouse, he armed himself with a rifle and occupied the building along with CMS missionary William Collison, who later became an Indian agent. Duncan interpreted this as a trick to scare him and his followers, perhaps even a plot to kill them. He and a group of Ts'msyan confronted Ridley and Collison on the school grounds, where tempers flared and threats of violence – including murder – were exchanged. In the end, cooler heads prevailed and the building was spared, but the mission was now firmly under Ridley's authority. The school became a symbol for local autonomy, and Duncan's loss of control signalled the start of a new era of increased outside interference. Many Ts'msyan were frusterated by the fiasco, and Duncan fled north with some of his followers to start a rival Metlakatla in Alaska. Meanwhile, Ridley continued the settlement, with increased financial support from the Canadian government. In the late 1880s, the school building was retrofitted to become British Columbia's first federally funded and church-run Indian industrial school.[6]

The events at Metlakatla were symptomatic of Indigenous-settler relations in Canada during the final three decades of the nineteenth century, as Ottawa asserted its authority over Indigenous Nations.[7] During this period, it forged stronger relations with churches to invent new schemes of Indian education as a technique of colonial rule. As settler anxiety about Indigenous resistance increased in the 1870s and 1880s, especially in the North-West Territories and British Columbia, Ottawa used schooling to undermine Indigenous lifeways and facilitate settler

FIGURE 4.1 Metlakatla, c. 1880s. William Duncan, a lay CMS missionary, started the Metlakatla settlement in the 1860s. Buildings included a town hall, a trade hall (large building on the far left), a school house, St. Paul's Church (centre), a court house, and a jail. | Courtesy of the Royal BC Museum, Image B-03571, British Columbia Archives

capitalism and nation building. At first, it concentrated on supporting existing mission day schools, but in 1883 it also created a new system of federally funded and church-run boarding and industrial schools on the Prairies. New day schools were also opened. Despite early warning signs about poor conditions, death and disease, and outright resistance by Indigenous parents and students, the system was expanded to British Columbia in the late 1880s, starting with Metlakatla. By 1900, the Pacific Province had the most industrial schools in Canada.[8]

INDIAN AFFAIRS AND MISSION SCHOOLING

British Columbia's amalgamation with the Dominion of Canada in 1871 initially made little difference to the federal government's management of Indian affairs. According to the terms of union, specifically article 13, the trusteeship and management of Indigenous Peoples shifted, in principle, from the Colonial Office in London to the Department of the Interior in Ottawa. Indigenous Peoples now lived within provincial borders but fell under federal jurisdiction. In the early 1870s, however, the federal government possessed neither the power nor the staff to assert its authority in British Columbia. As historian W. Kaye Lamb notes, the province was in Canada but not yet of it.[9] As a result, the status quo from the late colonial period endured for practical reasons. At the time, the Indigenous population of British Columbia numbered approximately thirty thousand, more than double that of any other province. As well, over four thousand kilometres separated Ottawa from Victoria. British Columbia was "physically and psychologically" distant from the "centres of imperial and dominion power," to use historian Laura Ishiguro's phrasing.[10] Moreover, clear lines of transportation and communication between the two capitals were not immediately established and remained slow even after the completion of the Canadian Pacific Railway in 1886. As Jean Barman puts it, British Columbia was truly the west *beyond* the west.[11] The federal government therefore devised an ad hoc solution: simply extend existing Indian policy, as it was applied to Ontario and Quebec, to newly acquired territories, including British Columbia.[12]

The government quickly realized that this simplistic solution was inadequate. Like its provincial counterpart, which developed an "educational machinery" to manage public schools in the 1870s and 1880s, it needed its own administrative apparatus – new policies, procedures, and staff. Colonialism, as Marx notes, requires both "brute force" and an organized bureaucracy to harness the power of the state to support ongoing accumulation by dispossession.[13] Thus, Ottawa established the Indian Branch in 1873, under the authority of the minister of the interior. Its main task was to oversee the implementation of the new Indian policies, which eventually included the 1876 Indian Act.[14] The act was amended in 1880, upgrading the branch to the Department of Indian Affairs (DIA). The title of "superintendent general of Indian Affairs" was given to the minister of the interior, a position Prime Minister Sir John A. Macdonald chose to hold from 1878 to 1887 and again briefly in 1888. In practice, though, Macdonald did not run the DIA. Day-to-day decision-making responsibilities fell to Lawrence Vankoughnet, who served as deputy superintendent general between 1874 and 1893. Vankoughnet was replaced by soldier-turned-politician Hayter Reed, who stayed in the position until James A. Smart took over in 1897. DIA expenditure, always a matter of partisan debate, was paid for through a mixture of grants acquired via taxation and from an Indian Trust Fund set up by the government and generated by the sale of Indigenous lands surrendered in the treaty-making process.[15] Once again, accumulation by dispossession helped pay the bills, as Brian Gettler and David McNally demonstrate was the case in Canada and other colonial settings.[16]

To grow the department, new "inside" civil servant positions were created at the DIA headquarters in Ottawa, including that of chief clerk, an accountant, and various other clerical posts. The government also established a contingent of "outside" employees across the country, most notably Indian agents who, along with other duties, supported the rise of Indian education by acting as intermediaries between the government, schools, and Indigenous Peoples.[17] By 1900, the DIA employed almost five hundred people. Regional Indian Affairs boards were established in Winnipeg and Victoria. Under the purview of lieutenant governors, they consisted of a few paid staff and were led by a local superintendent. These men were the primary contacts on Indigenous matters in their jurisdictions, and they liaised with Indian agents and forwarded quarterly reports to the DIA.[18] Like the school inspectors examined in Chapter 3, they helped the state to "see" and "simplify" Indigenous Peoples for the purposes of management.[19] Yet, as historian Daniel Rück argues, it is important to stress that Canada's DIA was not always a smooth and efficient bureaucracy; it was defined by "effective inefficiency." Rück explains that Indian policy in Canada "has sometimes been effective and brutal" in accomplishing its goals of undermining Indigenous sovereignties, but it has also been marked by "absurdity" and "inconsistency, confusion, inefficiency, and contradiction."[20]

In British Columbia, the new DIA machinery arose slowly and haphazardly. In 1872, the federal government appointed physician and politician Israel Wood Powell, who had been a school promoter on Vancouver Island during the 1860s, to the position of DIA superintendent for British

Columbia. A year later, a Board of Indian Commissioners was established under Powell's direction at Victoria. A personal friend of Macdonald, Powell was also appointed lieutenant-colonel of the militia because the federal government believed that an air of colonial authority would help him in his dealings with Indigenous Peoples. Powell took his duties seriously, often wearing his military uniform to the office. He pushed paper with pomp and panache.[21] A key part of his job was dividing the province into a number of Indian agencies and appointing agents to staff them. Due to British Columbia's vast size and its large Indigenous population, Powell was overwhelmed by the work. As a result, a secondary superintendency was created in 1874 and awarded to James Lenihan, who worked in the interior until his position was cut in 1880. In 1889, after seventeen years of service, Powell was replaced by A.W. Vowell as the sole superintendent. He held the position until 1910, when it was eliminated.

The federal government maintained that the key to managing Indian affairs in British Columbia was to "begin right."[22] The terms of Confederation stipulated that it would apply an Indian policy "as liberal as that hitherto pursued by the British Columbia government."[23] Ottawa wanted to pacify Indigenous Peoples with promises of protection, as it was trying to do on the Prairies, in its attempts to end the so-called Indian problem. In settler colonial contexts such as Canada, Audra Simpson notes, "the desire for land produces 'the problem' of the Indigenous life that is already living on the land."[24]

In British Columbia, much had been made of James Douglas's earlier attempts to establish cordial relations with Indigenous Peoples, and Powell wanted to use similar tactics. Victoria, however, favoured a more belligerent approach to colonization. Powell butted heads with provincial officials, most notably Lieutenant Governor Joseph Trutch, who had abandoned Douglas's tact and was pursuing more aggressive manoeuvres, including unilaterally adjusting or "cutting off" and reducing the size of Indian reserves to open them up to Euro-Canadian settlement.[25] Ottawa cautioned against such measures and urged the Province to cultivate consent rather than use coercion and possibly provoke conflict with Indigenous Nations. However, as Leo Panitch points out, provincial jurisdiction in Canada's federalist system is strong, and thus Ottawa could only try to work through Powell to pressure Victoria to take a judicious approach.[26] Indian education would play a key role, and Powell advocated for its strategic use.

For help with Indian education, the federal government turned to missionaries. As was the case for public schooling, the prospects for missionary schooling in British Columbia did not look promising in the 1870s. In 1874, at least eight mission schools were in operation at Comox, Cowichan, Nanaimo, Victoria, Fort Simpson, Lytton, Metlakatla, and Mission.[27] Ten teachers were recorded, seven men and three women. They had a total of 472 pupils, roughly the same number as British Columbia's public schools at the time. Most mission schools had ongoing problems with irregular attendance. Nevertheless, DIA officials such as William Spragge remained optimistic, arguing that missionaries of the "leading religious denominations" – Methodist, Catholic, and Anglican – were providing "praiseworthy and successful efforts" that would be "for the lasting good of the Indians of British Columbia."[28]

As discussed in Chapter 2, Victoria had stopped funding missionaries in the late 1860s, and thus Ottawa saw an opportunity: in exchange for more authority over Indian education, it would work with religious agents to expand and improve missionary schooling. As Powell explained, "the various Mission Societies already established in the Province will take measures to increase the number of schools, and take advantage of the material assistance afforded by the Government in granting a sum of money to every school which can show a certain average attendance of Indian pupils."[29] Though some schools continued to be funded by missionary societies, most began to accept a $300 federal grant in the early to mid-1870s.[30] To qualify for the grant, a school needed to demonstrate a daily attendance of thirty pupils. For comparison, the provincial government required its schools to have between ten and fifteen students to receive funding. The DIA's higher attendance threshold meant that many early schools struggled to obtain the necessary funding, which negatively affected learning and living conditions for students.

Irregular attendance thwarted most teachers' attempts to attain the required number of Indigenous pupils. In brainstorming how to grow the school system, Powell suggested that if the attendance requirement were dropped from thirty to fifteen, "a greater number of schools would soon be commenced, and of course much larger benefits secured in promoting education among the natives."[31] However, the Indian Branch did not immediately alter the funding formula, and many mission schools closed as a result. By 1877, the total number of Indigenous children attending mission schools had actually dropped from 472 to 402. Eventually seeing the error of its ways, the branch created a new policy and changed the funding arrangement to a simple per-capita grant.[32] Under this arrangement, Ottawa agreed to pay $12 per annum per Indigenous pupil in daily attendance up to a total of not more than $300 per school. This new money incentivized missionary outreach during the late 1870s, as churches now saw the opportunity to further profit from expanding their preaching and teaching work.

Inventing Indian Education

By the late 1870s and early 1880s, Ottawa had concluded that missionary day schools, albeit adequate stopgaps, did not equip Indigenous children for work in the emerging capitalist economy. A different scheme was needed. Thus, schools would be used, not just for religious instruction and primary education, but also for industrial training. Though calls to develop such a program increased during the late 1870s and early 1880s, they were not new. In fact, schools with an industrial focus, such as Duncan's school at Metlakatla and the Mount Elgin, Mohawk Institute, Shingwauk, and Wikwemikong industrial schools in Ontario, were already in existence across the dominion.[33] They were models for what was possible in a school system that combined basic instruction with boarding facilities to incarcerate and re-educate Indigenous children and youth.

Ottawa also looked abroad for examples. In 1878, Deputy Minister of the Interior J.S. Denis submitted a memorandum to Prime Minister

Macdonald, suggesting that Canada should consider adopting American-style manual labour boarding schools for Indigenous Peoples. In response, Macdonald awarded his friend and fellow Conservative Party member Nicholas Flood Davin with a one-person commission to travel to Washington to learn more about the schools.[34] Davin also visited a boarding school for Indigenous children in Minnesota and consulted with a number of church officials in Winnipeg. On March 14, 1879, he released his findings as the "Report on Industrial Schools for Indians and Half-Breeds," often referred to as the Davin Report.[35] Most of it summarized what Ottawa already knew, but it served as the catalyst for Macdonald and his government to implement what is now known as the Indian Residential School (IRS) system. The release of the report corresponded with Macdonald's plan to "settle the west" as part of his National Policy platform.[36] During the 1870s, because the federal government had promised to provide schooling for Indigenous Nations on the Prairies as stipulated by the Numbered Treaties, some missionary associations, such as the CMS, began to focus their efforts on other parts of the world. Missionary societies hoped to spend their money elsewhere. In this situation, Davin felt that Ottawa had a moral responsibility to pick up the slack. Moreover, by the late 1870s, some of the Indigenous leaders who had negotiated the treaties began demanding that the government fulfill its schooling promises. According to the Davin Report, it had a "sacred duty" to invent and implement a new system of Indian education.[37]

The system should be based on the industrial schools of the United States.[38] As the report explained, in America, "the industrial school is the principal feature of the policy known as that of 'aggressive civilization.'" Canada should create similar institutions, which could incarcerate Indigenous children and re-educate them for their future work as labourers and producers.[39] Davin stated, "At the industrial school, in addition to the elements of an English education the boys are instructed in cattle-raising and agriculture; the girls in sewing; breadmaking, and other employments suitable for a farmer's wife."[40] Quoting an American official, he noted that what "the Indian needs most is to be taught to work."[41] Unlike most mission day schools, where children went home after class, boarding and industrial schools separated them from their communities and instructed them "in industry and the arts of civilization."[42] They would be disconnected from the land and divorced from their lifeways and economic practices rooted in what Glen Sean Coulthard calls "grounded normativity."[43] Mary Jane Logan McCallum argues that this kind of education must be understood as "violence enacted by the state" on Indigenous children.[44]

Davin sketched two ways of running the proposed school system. In the first, Ottawa would take control of the schools and would administer them through the Indian Branch, as was done in the United States. This, however, would greatly strain the burgeoning Indian Branch bureaucracy and would exponentially increase government spending. In the second method, the government would partner with missionaries, who would continue running existing schools and would create new ones. With direction and financial assistance from Ottawa, missionaries would administer schooling at the local level. Davin conceded that the American commissioner of Indian Affairs was not in favour of this option, because "the children at schools under contract do not, as a rule, get sufficient quantity of food." That caveat should have been a red flag. Nevertheless, Davin proposed that Canada follow the state-church model to offer schooling "of the cheapest kind."[45] Day schools would continue to operate, but new boarding and industrial schools would be established and run by churches on the cheap, as an effective means of schooling Indigenous children and youth. The churches supported this arrangement because it gave them a more secure financial footing to expand their work.

After federal officials negotiated contracts with church officials, Macdonald prompted parliament to budget $44,000 to set up new industrial schools.[46] In 1883, three government-funded trial schools were opened in the North-West Territories at Qu'Appelle, Battleford, and High River.[47] Speaking as prime minister and DIA superintendent general, Macdonald defended the new system in the House of Commons:

> When the school is on the reserve the child lives with its parents, who are savages; he is surrounded by savages, and though he may

learn to read and write his habits, and training and mode of thought are Indian. He is simply a savage who can read and write. It has been strongly pressed on myself, as the head of the Department, that the Indian children should be withdrawn as much as possible from the parental influence, and the only way to do that would be to put them in central training industrial schools where they will acquire the habits and modes of thought of white men.[48]

Macdonald was not alone in this thinking. He was supported by a wide network, including various church officials, DIA bureaucrats such as Vankoughnet, and other politicians, including Minister of Public Affairs Hector-Lewis Langevin, who made a similar speech in the House praising the system and Macdonald's position.[49]

The early results of the three schools were mixed. At Battleford, there was considerable opposition: Indigenous parents were unhappy at being separated from their children, and some pupils disobeyed orders and ran away. But the DIA was undeterred. Its 1883 annual report noted,

The Indians show a reluctance to have their children separated from them, but doubtless, time will overcome this obstacle, and by commencing with orphans and children who have no natural protectors, a beginning can be made, and we must count upon the judicious treatment of these children by the principals and teachers of the institutions eventually to do away with the objections of the Indian parents to their children being placed under their charge.[50]

Historian James Redford confirms that many of the first residential schools, including those in British Columbia, had a high number of orphans, or children with at least one deceased parent.[51] In late-nineteenth-century Britain, it was common practice to prey on vulnerable children and incarcerate orphans or send them, as "home children," to various parts of the British Empire to help rural families and assist with colonization schemes.[52] Overall, politicians and church leaders in Canada suggested that success in Indian education would take time and that the best results would be obtained only if the system were expanded throughout the dominion. The prime minister agreed. Between 1878 and 1882, he was also the MP for Victoria, having been parachuted into the riding for the 1878 general election. Given this, he had good reason to heed Powell's pleas for new boarding and industrial schools in British Columbia.

Expanding Indian Education

Thus, in 1884, the DIA announced that it would be opening new boarding and industrial schools in British Columbia. In the early 1880s, only seven federally funded mission schools were operating in the province, including boarding schools at Metlakatla, Port Simpson, Yale, Chilliwack, and Mission, with a total enrolment of 544 students, 322 boys and 222 girls.[53] In the opinion of local DIA officials, Metlakatla was the most desirable spot for an industrial school because it already had the necessary infrastructure. It was also the epicentre of growing Indigenous resistance on the Northwest Coast.

Though the conflict at Metlakatla that opened this chapter ended in 1882, tensions persisted in the community and surrounding area. Indigenous Peoples were frustrated at the failure of government to prevent further settler encroachment on their lands. In response, Ts'msyan and Nisga'a citizens created new political organizations to fight back and assert their sovereignty.[54] In fact, DIA officials who wanted to open new schools on the Northwest Coast often heard complaints from parents, including, "what we want from the Government is our land, and not schools."[55] Moreover, news of the 1885 war between Canada and the Métis and allied Cree, Assiniboine, and Saulteaux communities made its way over the Rocky Mountains. W.H. Lomas, the Cowichan Indian agent, confirmed the growing danger: "Rumours of the Metlakatla land troubles and of the North-West rebellion have been talked over at all their little feasts, and not often with credit to the white man."[56] Lomas warned that the provincial government's disregard for Indigenous Peoples was tantamount to playing with fire and that action should be taken immediately to dissuade further dissent and prevent a general uprising. The "smouldering volcano" of Indigenous-settler relations once again threatened to erupt. Settler fears about Indigenous resistance, as

Ned Blackhawk argues, directly inform colonial policy.[57] In this context, and with Duncan out of the picture and Bishop Ridley in charge, the Metlakatla school was retrofitted to become the province's first official industrial school.

John R. Scott, who had taught in Australian schools for Indigenous children, was chosen as its first principal. When he reported for duty in 1888, he found its condition unsatisfactory. There was no furniture to accommodate the pupils. After securing proper lodgings, Scott toured neighbouring communities to convince Indigenous parents to send their children to the school. He travelled to Fort Simpson and Kincolith and also visited a number of fishing camps along the Nass River. Of his journey, he wrote, "At these places I called at nearly all the huts and houses, and wherever I saw any children I explained to their parents the objects of the school and the provision made by the Government for educating Indian boys." Some parents were interested, but Scott's efforts were mostly met with indifference. Unfazed, he took in four boys, and two more pupils followed shortly thereafter. On May 13, 1889, he officially opened the Metlakatla school with just six students. By the end of the year, fifteen boys, four Nisga'a, eight Ts'msyan, and three Haida, were attending.[58]

Ottawa soon deemed the Metlakatla experiment a success and began preparations for new schools in the province. As in the colonial period, Anglican, Methodist, Presbyterian, and Catholic missionaries competed over newly available federal funds.[59] Given the widely known difficulties with mission day schools, Powell proposed that boarding and industrial schools be established in strategic locations throughout the province as "the more desirable and advantageous course."[60] Considerable debate ensued among the churches and the DIA about the number and most suitable locations for such schools, with Powell and Indian agents relentlessly lobbying the DIA. In the end, three schools were established in 1890: Kamloops in the interior, Kuper Island, off the east coast of Vancouver Island, and Cranbrook in the southeastern mainland. Allocated per-capita grants of $130 per annum per pupil based on annual attendance, all three were run by Catholic missionaries and staffed by the

Oblates of Mary Immaculate. All three were also situated in areas with significant Indigenous opposition to colonization.

In the late 1870s, Kamloops was identified as a hotbed of discontent over the provincial government's land policy. In the summer of 1877, when two reserve commissioners arrived to investigate Secwépemc complaints, they quickly fired off an alarmed telegram to the Indian Branch in Ottawa: "Indian situation very grave from Kamloops to American border – general dissatisfaction – outbreak possible."[61] Kuper Island and the parts of Vancouver Island that were located in the Cowichan Indian Agency also had a reputation for resistance. Most notably, Indigenous Nations were angry over the state's attack on the potlatch, a ceremony and important economic gathering that Ottawa outlawed via an 1884 amendment to the Indian Act. In the late 1880s, the Kootenay region was also seen as troublesome. In 1887, provincial reserve commissioner Peter O'Reilly, Trutch's brother-in-law, laid out reserves in the Cranbrook area in an unsatisfactory way, and Ktunaxa citizens, particularly Chief Isadore, were dissatisfied.[62] A detachment of the newly formed North-West Mounted Police (NWMP) under the command of Sam Steele was sent out from nearby Lethbridge, Alberta, as a show of force to deter further conflict. As tensions eased and the police were redeployed, the barracks that had been built for them were updated "for industrial school purposes in the interests of the Indian children."[63] The fact that Indigenous children were to be institutionalized in an old NWMP barracks established to check the power of their parents confirms that the structures of settler colonialism in British Columbia developed in the shadow of colonial conflict over the land, as Blackhawk shows was the case in the American West.[64] Indeed, the principal of the Kootenay Indian Industrial School, Nicolas Coccola, acknowledged that when the school opened in 1890, the Ktunaxa were "on the eve of breaking out into war with the whites."[65] State schooling thus emerged in what Blackhawk calls the "maelstrom of colonialism."[66]

The new school system was tiered, and the funding available to schools depended on their rank and utility to the DIA. At the bottom of the hierarchy were the Indian Day Schools. Given their high rates of irregular attendance and inability to separate children from their parents and communities, they were seen as inefficient but still necessary stopgaps. Thus, most day schools received only a few hundred dollars of federal funding, barely enough to cover a teacher's annual salary. Paying the remaining costs was left to the churches. Nevertheless, by 1890, ten were in operation, mostly on the coast, at Alert Bay, Bella Bella, Clayoquot, Cowichan, Hazelton, Kincolith, Lakalsap, Masset, Nanaimo, and Port Essington. By 1900, their number had jumped to twenty-eight in all parts of the province (see Appendix 2). Securing regular attendance remained an issue, however. In 1884, Harry Guillod, the Indian agent for the West Coast Agency, informed the DIA of a disturbing incident:

> Rev. Father Nicolaye has had trouble with the Indians. He, as a punishment, shut up two pupils for non-attendance at school, and some sixty of the tribe made forcible entry into his house, and three of them held him while others released the boys ... It is very uphill work trying to get the children to attend school, as the parents are indifferent, and are away with them at other stations for months during the year.[67]

Far from being agnostic about schooling, Indigenous parents organized against the teacher and advocated for education on their terms. Gwichyà Gwich'in historian Crystal Gail Fraser notes that Indigenous parents often "understood the implications" of Indian education "while demonstrating their awareness that their complicity within the system did not equate to unqualified approval." Parents and guardians actively negotiated their circumstances and "proved remarkably successful in their capacity to transform, to greater and lesser degrees, emerging state structures and policies around schooling."[68] Still, such activity convinced the DIA that boarding and industrial schools were necessary to separate children from their parents and communities to facilitate re-education and assimilation.

Indian Boarding Schools, originally designed for younger children and located on or near Indian reserves, were a step above day schools in the DIA ranking. According to state officials, they had the advantage of being able to house children and establish some distance from parents for

INVENTING INDIAN EDUCATION 125

FIGURE 4.2 Port Essington Indian Day School, c. 1890. The school was opened by the Methodist Church on the Skeena Reserve in Port Essington in 1885. It closed in 1947. | Courtesy of the Royal BC Museum, Image B-05843, British Columbia Archives.

much of the year to disrupt Indigenous lifeways. Indeed, Métis historian Allyson D. Stevenson argues that "disruption and dispossession figure prominently in the colonization of Indigenous kinship."[69] Their per-capita grant was usually in the range of sixty to eighty dollars, and some also received free or cheap land grants to open new facilities. In 1890, boarding schools were operating at Coqualeetza, Port Simpson, Mission, and Yale. The All Hallows Boarding School at Yale originally accepted Indigenous and white pupils, the latter mostly the daughters of Anglican families in the Diocese of New Westminster who were unhappy with the non-denominational public school system being implemented across the province. As Jean Barman writes, All Hallows was unique in that it was both a boarding school for Indigenous girls, complete with DIA funding, and a private Anglican school for white pupils who paid fees.[70] By 1900, there were seven boarding schools, with new institutions being

FIGURE 4.3 Alberni Indian Boarding School, c. 1896. The school was opened by the Presbyterian Church in 1893 a few kilometers outside Port Alberni. It was taken over by the United Church in the 1920s. It closed in 1973. | Courtesy of the Royal BC Museum, Image I-31563, British Columbia Archives

established or recognized by the DIA at Alberni, Alert Bay, and North Vancouver (see Appendix 2). Most incarcerated Indigenous children from many different Nations from across the province.

The highest rank in the new system was reserved for the Indian Industrial Schools. The first schools were mostly paid for by the federal government, but an Order-in-Council of 1892 shifted substantial costs back to the churches. Missionaries were now expected to operate the institutions on per-capita grants that were below the then-current level of expenditure, usually $130. The government assumed that teaching would be done on a volunteer basis or would be covered by churches. The inadequate funding simply exacerbated existing problems. Nevertheless, by 1900 new industrial schools at Alert Bay, Coqualeetza (which was upgraded to an industrial school), and Williams Lake joined Metlakatla, Kuper Island, Kamloops, and Kootenay.[71] Within twenty years, the number of Indigenous children attending federally funded schools of all kinds — day, boarding, and industrial — had doubled, reaching a total of 1,568 by 1900 (see Appendix 2).[72]

Learning to Labour

As the federal government extended its reach, it increasingly emphasized industrial training for Indigenous Peoples.[73] This kind of training was introduced in Indian education much earlier than in British Columbia's public school system. DIA official Edgar Dewdney explained the rationale:

> It would be highly desirable, if it were practical, to obtain entire possession of all Indian children after they attain the age of seven or eight years, and keep them at schools of the industrial type until they have had a thorough course of instruction, not only in the ordinary subjects taught at public schools, but in some useful and profitable trade.

"Were such a course adopted," he predicted, "the solution of that problem, designated 'the Indian question' would probably be effected sooner."[74]

Generally, boarding and industrial schools used a half-day system whereby mornings were devoted to religious and elementary instruction and afternoons to learning a trade or performing manual labour related to the school's operation. The lessons were in English, French, or Latin, and students were mostly forbidden to speak their own language, so many were forced to live in the school and learn and study in a second language. Curriculum and teaching in the early schools varied widely. In an effort to standardize instruction, the DIA issued an official "Programme of Studies for Indian Schools" in 1896. Students were now to be taught a range of subjects and at varying levels, or "standards," from 1 to 6 that roughly corresponded to the authorized lessons for public schools. Teachers, often with little formal training, tutored students in the basics of writing, reading, and arithmetic, as well as introductory history lessons and subjects such as ethics.[75] At the first level for ethics, students learned about "the practice of cleanliness, obedience, respect, order, neatness." The intermediate levels dealt with the importance of "Industry" and "Thrift," as well as the evils of "Pauperism." And the most advanced level covered "Patriotism," "Enfranchisement," and "Labour" as the "law of life," as well as the "relations of the sexes as to labour."[76]

Most of these lessons assumed that Indigenous Peoples were racially inferior and that they had no choice but to accept their lower status in society. Barman argues that the new curriculum might have improved education "had not children been expected to get through it in less time each day than was allowed their counterparts in provincial schools."[77] Indeed, because half of the school day was devoted to manual labour or learning a trade, students typically spent only two or four hours on the curriculum, instead of the five or more that were the norm in public schools. By the 1920s, the vast majority of Indigenous children never advanced higher than Grade 1 or 2. This is why Barman states that full assimilation into mainstream settler society was never the goal of policy makers. Instead, Indigenous students in British Columbia, as elsewhere, were "schooled for inequality."[78]

Indian education was also profoundly gendered. Leanne Betasamosake Simpson argues that in colonial schools the "gender binary is introduced," Indigenous girls "are domesticated into the role of Victorian housewives," and boys are "domesticated into the wage economy and taught their only power is to ally with whitemen in the oppression of Indigenous women through church, school, law, and policy."[79] Initially, industrial schools were intended only for boys, with an emphasis on agricultural and manual training. At Metlakatla, Principal Scott claimed that "thirteen boys received some instruction in carpentry – the trade likely to be of the greatest service to them on leaving – and the most of these exhibit an aptitude for the work."[80] At the Kootenay Indian Industrial School, Principal Coccola noted that the "boys have been taught sawing and splitting firewood, clearing land, gardening, and housework in their own apartments."[81] At the Kuper Island Indian Industrial School, Principal George Donckele stated, "Five boys take lessons in shoemaking, and Mr. Renax, their instructor, is well pleased with the aptitude of his apprentices; two of his pupils are now able to turn out a new shoe, all but the cutting of the leather."[82] Because industrial equipment was expensive, training remained rather rudimentary, and boys were mostly accustomed to the discipline and drudgery of manual labour that directly benefitted the school.

Training was gradually extended to girls, as they were admitted to the schools in the late nineteenth century. Preparation work for them, centred mostly on domestic labour, similarly blurred the lines between training and chores. As McCallum notes, the DIA boarding and industrial schools were "training grounds for domestics."[83] Like the boys, girls were groomed to perform the unpaid labour necessary to keep their schools running. At the Kootenay school, Coccola reported that the fifteen female students

> have been taught housework, cooking, baking, washing, ironing, sewing, mending clothes, dairy work and gardening. Five of the largest girls have become able to bake good bread, also to cook ordinary victuals. Their progress in sewing is no less worthy of mention. Three of them, apart from the cutting out, can make their clothes well, whilst the others are trying to improve in that branch of education.[84]

Making clothes was a particular focus of schools that incarcerated girls. At Kuper Island, Donckele produced an extensive list of sewing projects:

> During the course of the last year the following articles were made at the institution, exclusive of mending the children's clothes: Fifty jumpers, three suits, forty-eight sheets, thirty-one pillow cases, fifty-one aprons, forty-seven dresses, twenty-four chemises, twelve collars, one pair trousers, thirteen skirts, ten napkins, twenty-four night dresses, twelve rollers, six dish towels, twenty-five night shirts and nine pairs stockings. The making of these articles is estimated at one hundred and fifty dollars.[85]

In short, Indigenous children and youth were trained to take up gender roles that would aid the school's basic operation as well as support the rise of a heteropatriarchal capitalist settler society.

By the mid-1890s, many church and state officials concluded that Indian education was achieving its objective. The St. Joseph's Indian Industrial School in Williams Lake was so successful that it began selling student-made items, such as saddles, a practice that raised the ire of local business owners. In 1893, Principal A.M. Carion at Kamloops explained, "The greatest difficulty we experience with the pupils is to overcome their natural repugnance to work of any kind; but I have no doubt that they will gradually be made to look upon work as a necessary and healthy occupation."[86] At Kootenay, which took in children from southeastern British Columbia as well as southern Alberta, Coccola noted that "although brought up with their people in idleness and in perfect ignorance of all sorts of work, the active life of this industrial school is soon cheerfully embraced by the new comers." He added, "They show a real desire to become qualified for some trade or employment, as they commence to understand that the roaming habits of their people will have soon to be done away with on account of the game becoming more and more scarce."[87] Indeed, DIA deputy superintendent general Hayter Reed argued,

> It has justly been said by one greatly interested in Indian industrial training that no system of Indian training is right that does not endeavour to develop all the abilities, remove prejudice against labour, and give courage to compete with the rest of the world. The Indian problem exists owing to the fact that the Indian is untrained to take his place in the world. Once you teach him to do this, the solution is had.[88]

In 1897, Coccola stated that his school's efforts to "instil into the children a love of labour" had "been crowned with success."[89] The next step was obvious, as Reed pointed out: "If the schools be regarded as the chief factors of the great transformation that is being wrought, it would seem a natural and logical sequence to establish as many as the country's finances will admit."[90]

Disease, Death, and Everyday Acts of Resistance

Some students did have positive individual experiences with Indian education. For example, Cornelius Kelleher, who attended St. Mary's Indian Boarding School in the 1880s, had fond memories of Easter Passion plays, brass band competitions, sports day gatherings, and even skipping class to ride the first CPR locomotive to pass by the school.[91] Genocide scholar Andrew Woolford notes that it is "not contradictory that former students remember these moments, when desires for connection, entertainment, excitement, and the like were fulfilled, as good times at the school."[92] Overall, however, the archival record clearly reveals that the system was deeply flawed from the start. As Woolford explains, that some Indigenous Peoples have positive recollections does not take away from the fact that Indian education was a "manifestation of a collective settler attempt to address the Indian Problem through the elimination of Indigenous groups [... and schools] were part of an infrastructure, a settler colonial mesh."[93]

Instead of producing strong and healthy students, as historian Mary-Ellen Kelm explains, schools "tended to endanger them through exposure to disease, overwork, underfeeding, and various forms of abuse."[94] Most of these indicators were simply ignored or overlooked by church and state officials, who continued to see the schools through a humanitarian lens. Constant remarks about high rates of disease, death, and acts of resistance – by parents and students – appear in the DIA reports from the 1890s. In reading these sources along and against the grain, as Ann Laura Stoler recommends, we can comprehend the problematic origins of Indian education, specifically boarding and industrial schooling, in British Columbia.[95] Attempts to disconnect Indigenous children from their families and communities and delegitimize their grounded normativity disrupted group life and had genocidal consequences for Indigenous Peoples. The schools themselves were also often intimidating and disorienting spaces for Indigenous students, as Woolford and Geoffery Paul Carr argue, because the buildings were large and imposing and were "meant to impart the superiority of European culture in both their grandness and style."[96]

FIGURE 4.4 St. Mary's Indian Boarding School, c. 1880s. OMI missionary Leon Fouquet founded St. Mary's Mission in 1861 on the north bank of the Fraser River. A boarding school for boys was established in 1863. New school buildings were constructed in 1882 (pictured) and 1933. St. Mary's closed in 1984. | Courtesy of the Royal BC Museum, Image D-08840, British Columbia Archives

Sickness plagued both the schools and the bodies of children from the beginning. Waves of disease and death had always accompanied European colonizers, and boarding and industrial schools were beset by episodes of devastating illness.[97] Poor conditions on many reserves, manufactured by major land losses as a result of the reserve system, catalyzed many illnesses that students took with them to school. As well, the poor conditions of many schools, including overcrowding and poor ventilation and sanitation, created by a lack of funding and careless management by church officials, proved breeding grounds for new diseases that students took back to their communities during holidays. In 1891, Scott reported that at Metlakatla, "the epidemic influenza known as 'la grippe' visited the Indian village here, and shortly afterwards extended to this institution."[98] Similarly, "la grippe," influenza, affected thirteen children at the Kuper Island school in the same year. The disease ravaged the Kootenay school the next year, which dismissed many children and allowed them to return home. Given that schools took in children from a variety of communities, sending them home when they were sick spread diseases throughout the Indigenous Nations. Influenza was not the only illness to break out at the schools. Students also suffered from tuberculosis, measles, whooping cough, chicken pox, and diptheria. Woolford notes that the widespread presence of disease likely confirmed the opinion of officials that Indigenous Peoples were genetically inferior and more prone to getting sick. In this way, he argues, "disease was also complicit in the racist degradation of Indigenous peoples and served as a further rationalization of and legitimation for policies of assimilation and aggressive civilization."[99]

Whereas many DIA reports talked proudly of rehabilitating sickly pupils, others reluctantly logged student deaths. Some children died at school, and their deaths were recorded by the staff. Other deaths went unmentioned, especially as schools were still trying to convince communities that the boarding and industrial institutions were safe.[100] Some sick students were sent home to be treated, as Bev Sellars confirms in her memoir, and some died there or during transit.[101] Some of these deaths went unrecorded. Nevertheless, the records paint a deeply troubling portrait. In 1891, Coccola claimed, "The 'grippe' has severely affected several pupils, although the best care has been taken by the Sisters to avoid all fatal results; still one boy became a victim of it."[102] At the Methodist Port Simpson Girls' Home in 1899, six of the forty pupils died – 12 percent of the student body – "three from tubercular meningitis, and three from pulmonary tuberculosis."[103] The next year, three more died, "one of consumption, one of tubercular meningitis, and one of kidney disease."[104] Overall, between 1890 and 1900, boarding and industrial schools officially reported sixty deaths among the students. Many more probably went unrecorded, and because the cost of transporting their bodies across the province was high, some children were likely buried near the schools rather than being sent home. Historian John Douglas Belshaw points out that morbidity and mortality rates in general were high during this period, particularly among the Indigenous population, but the death rates at the schools were especially alarming.[105] Thus, the DIA hired Dr. Peter Henderson Bryce in the early 1900s to investigate conditions at the schools. A few years later, Bryce reported that 34 percent of pupils admitted between 1892 and 1909 were dead.[106] Responding to his report, one official decried the "scandalous procession of Indian children to school and on to the cemetery."[107]

Indigenous parents and students resisted in various ways. Just a few months after the Kamloops Indian Industrial School opened, its first principal, Michel Hagan, wrote that "the natural affection of Indian parents for their children leads such of them as have children at the school to make frequent visits to it, and their camping nearby has caused a restless feeling among the children in attendance."[108] Anti-colonial writer Albert Memmi, who attended a boarding school in a different colonial context, described his crushing feeling of loneliness and lack of affection: "Deprived of the protection of my parents and of their physical presence, I found myself, for the first time, cast alone on the world."[109] Sellars, who attended the school in Williams Lake, confirms that she and other students felt similar feelings of isolation and loneliness.[110] In an effort to protect their children, some Indigenous parents refused to send them back to school after designated holidays – if holidays were permitted – or organized to withdraw them at other times of the year. Principal Scott of the Metlakatla Indian Industrial School explained in 1892 that some children "were withdrawn because they were needed at home, others through anxiety on the part of parents. That anxiety arose from their sons being far away from home during the prevalence here, about a year ago, of the influenza epidemic."[111] Scott also reported that some parents told him bluntly, "we have come to an agreement among ourselves not to send any of our children to the school." When he pressed for their reason, they replied, "We mean to keep our children at home if the government will not give us back our country, of which we have been despoiled by whites."[112] These examples show how Indigenous parents and community members tried to negotiate the terms of school attendance as active and involved agents.

Students, too, found ways to resist. As Woolford stresses, Indigenous students "did not passively submit to the settler colonial mesh. They sought to tear open this mesh to create gaps in which they could assert and perform their identities."[113] They developed cultures of everyday resistance, or what Anishinaabe scholar Gerald Vizenor calls

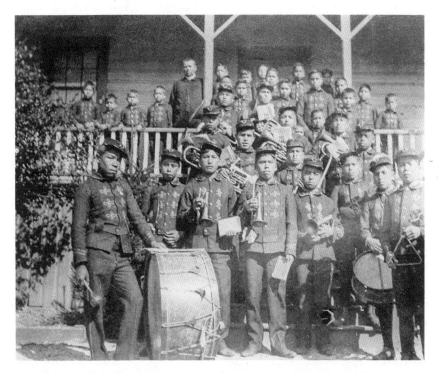

FIGURE 4.5 Kuper Island Indian Industrial School band, c. 1900. The Catholic Church opened the Kuper Island school in 1889 on Kuper Island (now Penelakut Island), near Chemainus. The school was well known for its band (pictured) but also for its strict environment. Some Survivors called the school "Canada's Alcatraz." It closed in 1975. | Courtesy of the Royal BC Museum, Image D-05991, British Columbia Archives

"survivance," a mixture of survival and resistance that ranged from speaking their own language and refusing poor food to shirking chores and even setting fire to the building.[114] Shortly after the Kuper Island school opened, Donckele wrote,

> Considerable dissatisfaction concerning the school seemed to exist amongst the pupils as well as amongst the Indians in general. It is difficult to say whether their uneasiness was grounded on any real cause, but due allowance must, of course, be made for the many difficulties incidental to the organization of an institution of this kind amongst the various tribes of Indians unaccustomed to school life and discipline.[115]

Although Donckele's official reports painted a rosy picture, documentary evidence tells a different story. A "Conduct Book" from the early years of the school shows that many students lived in a culture of fear. They were punished for "talking Indian," "disobedience," "coming late," "fighting," and "wrestling." The various penalties for such transgressions included confinement and "work at recess." Manual labour was both preferred pedagogy and punishment. In 1892 alone, Harry, "Inmate No. 5," was disciplined twenty-eight times for "misdemeanour," "laziness," "playing forbidden games," "talking in bed," "breaking bounds," and "fighting," always with "work at noon." Other punishments included "kneeling down at recess" and "bread and water for super." Of course, incidents of misbehaviour may just have been part of daily life at the school. But they could also be understood as what James C. Scott calls a "hidden transcript," in which oppressed people subtly critique their oppressors.[116] Probably they were a combination of both.[117] Indeed, Scott lists an arsenal of techniques used by relatively powerless groups to express resistance, including "foot dragging, dissimulation, desertion, false compliance, pilfering, feigned ignorance, slander, arson, sabotage, and so on."[118] Student resistance, whether conscious or unconscious, was documented by church and state officials simply as bad behaviour that could sometimes lead to a student's expulsion.

Students could also run away, a solution that was particularly rampant at the Kamloops school. As Mvskoke/Creek historian K. Tsianina Lomawaima points out, Indigenous children and youth consistently "marshaled personal and shared skills and resources to create a world" within the confines of boarding schools, and "they occasionally stretched and penetrated school boundaries."[119] In 1891, Principal Hagan noted the first incident: "Two of the Shuswap boys, Martial and Daniel, brothers, ran away and after a time were brought back by parents; same boys left again and no effort was made to have them return."[120] The next year, Hagan reported that a female student who had escaped during the winter had frostbitten feet as a result.[121] In explaining why children fled from the Williams Lake school, Principal J.M.J. Lejacq cited their "ill-feeling towards manual labour." Boys were required to receive outdoor instruction in labour, which some saw as "disagreeable." It "created a kind of uneasiness" at the school. Lejacq confessed that its beginning was "a little stormy." Because "the children used to run where they liked, and do what they pleased," they "found it hard at first to be corralled in by the routine of the house."[122] The Indian agent for the Cowichan agency similarly remarked at the opening of the Kuper Island school that "at first, as before reported the boys could not stand confinement and several ran away."[123]

Other students turned to arson, which occurred on multiple occasions. In late 1895, Donckele reported that a number of boys tried to burn down the Kuper Island school. Its daily journal entry for November 15, 1895, stated, "fire is discovered in the boys' building and successfully extinguished in half an hour. Cause unknown. The damage is light."[124] The next day, another fire was discovered, this time in the basement of the boys' building. Who detected it and who was held responsible are unclear. Shortly afterward, however, school staff reported, "The conduct of some of the boys was reprehensible, 3 of them attempted to set fire to the boys building."[125] On order of the superintendent, the three boys were expelled. In 1899, Scott noted that a firebug had hit Metlakatla, too, though he stated that the fire was due to "the carelessness of one of the boys."[126]

The archival record from this period rarely provides glimpses of violence, mistreatment, and student resistance. One source, however, departs from this pattern, a detailed and damning letter written by Elizabeth Shaw, a missionary who worked at the Port Simpson school. It had been founded by Thomas Crosby, a Methodist missionary who, as mentioned in Chapter 2, taught in Nanaimo and Chilliwack before establishing boarding facilities for Indigenous Peoples at Port Simpson.[127] A home for girls was created in 1879, and one for boys was opened in 1890. Shaw spent five weeks as a matron at the homes in the late 1890s, and her letter, written to a church official, chronicles the culture of abuse, violence, and repression she observed there.[128] Shaw wrote that the children were deliberately kept in "a culture of fear," which she blasted as "wrong and unnatural." She confessed,

> I can truthfully say that I never was in any place where I saw so little manifestation of love and sympathy as in that Mission Home at Port Simpson. "Never trust an Indian" was a quotation I heard very frequently and truly it seemed the rule in that Institution. None of the boys were treated and right well they knew this lack of faith in them. One of the big boys put the matter in a nut shell when he said "We never receive anything here but a threat or a command."

Shaw also remarked on the poor health and sanitation of the school, noting prevalent cases of skin disease and an "insufficient diet." She wrote,

> I was compelled to set meat before the boys that my brothers would not set before their dogs ... It was nearly rotten that the smell of it when cooking was so bad that I really could not stay in the kitchen, and the boys, hungry as I am sure they were, said that they could not eat it, this, when there was abundance of good wholesome food in the house, seemed to me inexcusable.[129]

Shaw did not restrict her condemnation to the boys' school. The girls' school, "conducted on pretty much the same principles," fared little better in her assessment. She felt compelled to describe one particularly disturbing incident. It involved a young Indigenous woman named Nellie, a resident in the girls' home who "caused a great deal of trouble. It happened that her father wished to take her away from the Home before she had stayed the requisite length of time." Nellie was returned to the Port Simpson home but shortly thereafter snuck out to a nearby village without permission to spend the night with a girlfriend. School staff went to collect her, and shortly after midnight Shaw was awakened by "awful screams from downstairs." She recalled,

> As soon as I had recovered from my fright I awoke to the fact that Nellie, a full grown young woman, engaged to be married, was receiving a severe thrashing at the hands of the man who was the spiritual and temporal over-sight of the Boys' Home ... My blood

FIGURE 4.6 Port Simpson, c. 1890s. Thomas Crosby stands on the top step (left) with students. He is accompanied by Henry Tate (far left), interpreter and assistant teacher, and Miss Hargrave (far right), teacher. Crosby started the school in the 1870s, as part of his Methodist missionary work on the Northwest Coast. The school started receiving government funding in 1893. It closed in 1948. | Courtesy of the Royal BC Museum, Image A-04182, British Columbia Archives

nearly froze in my veins as the shrieks of the unfortunate woman rang through the house, and to my dying day I shall never forget the agony in her voice as she pleaded, "O Mr. Richards, pray for me."

Nor would Shaw forget Mr. Richards's response: "Pray for you? I am tired [of] praying for you." When Richards was finished with his beating, he threw Nellie into a "little stuffy pantry off the kitchen without air or light." According to the matron, she was kept there for days, with nothing but an old mat and a blanket, which was particularly egregious because she "was suffering from a large running sore on one of her hips." The horrors that Shaw encountered at Port Simpson, which "upset" all her "preconceived ideas of Missionary work," were "burned" into her heart.[130] She was a canary in the coalmine. Shaw tried to blow the whistle on the Port Simpson school, but her letter – and its early warning – was ignored by church and state officials, as were the persisting complaints of Indigenous parents and students.

Conclusion

Despite mounting evidence of poor conditions in many of the new schools, as well as growing resistance by Indigenous parents and students, Ottawa continued to expand its scheme for Indian education. By 1900, 297 schools were in operation throughout the country, with an enrolment of almost 10,000 students. In British Columbia, the growth was especially significant. During the early 1870s, roughly 400 pupils attended fewer than 20 schools in the province. By 1900, that number had trebled to a total of 1,568 children, 840 boys and 728 girls, at 42 schools: 28 day schools, 7 boarding schools, and 7 industrial schools (see Appendix 2).[131] Vowell, the DIA provincial superintendent, claimed that Indian education was creating "the most favourable results" in the Pacific Province. He stated, "the feeling of uncertainty on the part of the parents and guardians of the pupils as to the benefits likely to accrue to their offspring or wards from such a course of training has almost entirely disappeared." Vowell even suggested that in some retail outlets, "I have seen Indian boys who have been educated at the industrial schools, acting as clerks and book-keepers most successfully."[132] In the view of many officials, the project of transforming Indigenous Peoples into useful subjects was succeeding, and the schools, especially the boarding and industrial schools, were playing their necessary part in building the Canadian nation. As DIA deputy superintendent general Reed put it, because "the permanent elevation of the race depends upon the education of the young, the cost [of these schools] may be regarded as not only inevitable but, when viewed with relation to the future interests of the country, as an excellent investment."[133]

PART 3

REFORM AND RESISTANCE, 1900-30

By the turn of the twentieth century, British Columbia's transformation from underdeveloped colony to prosperous province was rapidly accelerating. Population growth played a pivotal role. In the early 1880s, the non-Indigenous population – mostly of British, Canadian, American, Chinese, and Japanese origin – numbered only 20,000, but by 1930, it had grown to more than 600,000. Meanwhile, the Indigenous population remained relatively stable at around 25,000, though Indigenous Peoples comprised just 3.5 percent of the population by 1930, down from 70.8 percent in 1871. John Douglas Belshaw refers to the birth of British Columbia as a process of "depopulation and repopulation."[1] Cole Harris summarizes the effects of the cataclysmic changes: "immigrants and capital had abruptly de-territorialized the prior [Indigenous] inhabitants of British Columbia and had re-territorialized themselves."[2] Many Indigenous Peoples continued to resist the ongoing colonization of their homelands, as historians Paul Tennant and Sarah Nickel emphasize.[3] However, by the early 1900s British Columbia was firmly established as a capitalist settler society connected to the Dominion of Canada and enmeshed in the wider web of the British Empire.

British Columbia was an industrializing but still unevenly developed province, with an economy defined by dependence on extractive industries, particularly forestry, fishing, and mining. However, employment was growing in transportation, manufacturing, professional and white-collar work, and public services. New railways were built, with government support, to connect salmon canneries on the Northwest Coast, silver mines in the Kootenays, cattle ranches in the Cariboo-Chilcotin, and fruit orchards in the Okanagan to the Lower Mainland, with its emerging home markets and growing urban population (comprising over 50 percent of British Columbians by 1930).[4] Aided by the opening of the Panama Canal in 1914, which connected the Atlantic and Pacific Oceans and opened new trading routes, Vancouver became a world-class port. This allowed powerful companies such as R. Dunsmuir and Sons, H.R. MacMillan Export, and Rogers Sugar to more easily ship coal, timber, and sugar to export markets by sea. Even Vancouver's changing soundscape signalled industrialization: sawmills buzzed, trains whistled, trollies clanged, and ships whooshed and tooted in the busy harbour. Every evening, the Nine O'clock Gun – a twelve-pound British muzzle-loader installed at the entrance to Stanley Park during the 1890s – boomed, as a signifier of capitalist time/work discipline, so that Vancouverites could set their clocks and arrive at work on time the next day.[5] The nightly blast also served as a sonic reminder of colonial rule to nearby xʷməθkʷəy̓əm, S̱ḵwx̱wú7mesh, and səl̓ílwətaɬ communities.

Though some white women had gained limited forms of the franchise by the early 1900s, white, property-owning men, mostly from British or Canadian backgrounds (but with a growing number born in British Columbia), still controlled the province's political system. As historian Robert A.J. McDonald outlines, politicians showed an increased willingness to use state authority to impose social, cultural, and economic structures that normalized patriarchal power and white supremacy while marginalizing Indigenous Peoples and immigrants of colour.[6] As the settler population grew, it was increasingly stratified by gender and racialization but also by class into a majority of landless labourers and a small group of capitalists, who rapidly accumulated property and private wealth.[7] Capitalists, many of them taking turns in provincial politics, used government subsidies and cheap land – stolen from Indigenous Peoples – as well as an abundant labour supply to establish new enterprises to extract and export the rich staple resources. In 1860, the gross value of minerals produced in British Columbia was just $2.4 million. In 1900, that number rose to $16.4 million, and it jumped to $61.5 million by 1925.[8] With the exception of a slowdown in the 1910s, the economy was thriving at the start of the new century.

In this context, many British Columbians viewed improved education as key to continued socioeconomic growth. In the early 1900s, the government revised schooling to train an expanding workforce and to assist with the development of Canada. In Victoria, as Chapter 5 outlines, the provincial government made a number of changes to public schooling, including introducing modern educational methods designed to keep students in class longer and to transform them into productive workers and socially efficient citizens. By the 1920s, in the aftermath of the First

World War, many British Columbians had started to accept improved but compulsory and government-controlled education as a normal and necessary part of life.

Although some Indigenous children continued to attend public schools in the early 1900s, Chapter 6 shows that the federal government, amidst growing resistance by Indigenous parents and students, expanded Indian education. It hoped that a stronger emphasis on industrial training in Indian Day Schools and Indian Residential Schools could transition Indigenous Peoples from wards of the state into productive wage workers. Chapter 6 also highlights that some Indigenous parents and students continued to challenge federal schooling schemes, with varying levels of success. Overall, Chapters 5 and 6 reveal how provincial and federal efforts to assert greater authority over schooling for Indigenous and non-Indigenous students overlapped and played essential roles in helping to legitimize and consolidate British Columbia's capitalist settler society by 1930.

CHAPTER | FIVE

Reforming Public Schools

In 1905, the federal government selected New Westminster to host the Dominion Exhibition, a national fair that was held annually in Canadian cities between 1879 and 1913. Like the Great International Exhibitions (London in 1851, Paris in 1867, Chicago in 1893), it showcased local industry and agriculture and functioned as a kind of provincial and national advertising.[1] In Ottawa's eyes, British Columbia's rapid socio-economic development since the late 1880s made it a deserving choice to host the exhibition. No longer an isolated and underdeveloped colonial outpost on the edge of empire, the Pacific province was ready to be thrust into the spotlight. Between September 27 and October 7, thousands of people from across Canada and around the world visited the fair, enjoying everything from industrial displays and agricultural demonstrations to musical contests and special sporting events. Except for a few bouts of rain, entirely fitting for coastal British Columbia, the ten-day spectacle was a celebrated success.[2]

Of its many highlights, an exhibit on public education stood out as "one of the most attractive features" to David Wilson, who was hired in 1887 as the province's first school inspector.[3] The exhibition's organizing committee called on the Education Department to solicit schoolwork from teachers, parents, and students to be displayed. Thousands of samples – from art and essays to agricultural products and manufactured goods – were assembled on the top floor of the Industrial Building. The display itself covered more than eight thousand square feet.[4] In his 1905–06 report, Wilson expressed pride in the final product. "It was something that the public should have had satisfactory proof that the schools of the Province are giving a just return for the large amounts of money annually spent on their maintenance," he wrote, "and it meant a great deal that the visitors from abroad should be favourably impressed with the educational facilities which this Province affords."[5] For Wilson, the exhibit reinforced the belief that social progress in British Columbia was tied to schooling and vice versa.

This chapter examines how the provincial government reformed public schooling in the early 1900s in ways that continued to legitimize and support British Columbia's socioeconomic development. At the turn of the century, education experts argued that industrialization necessitated a new kind of education, and they called for reforms to modernize the system.[6] Accordingly, Victoria passed legislation making school attendance mandatory, and schools introduced new methods and courses designed to train children and youth for socially efficient citizenship. The outbreak of the First World War in 1914 galvanized this change, with reformers and parents pressing the government to make schooling more practical to prepare children – as future citizens and subjects of the British Empire – to contribute to society and to defend it if necessary. By 1930, as historians R.D. Gidney and W.P.J. Millar explain, getting a good public education was normalized as a necessity for social advancement.[7] With the fees for private schools proving too expensive for many of British Columbia's mostly working-class families, there were few alternatives to public schooling.[8] Revising and reforming the system ultimately helped the provincial government consolidate its power over education, as a tool of socialization and legitimation.

A System under Strain

By 1900, the school machinery that dated from the 1870s was starting to show signs of strain. In that year, British Columbia had a few hundred schools, with 20,000 students – now placed in graded divisions (1–12) with corresponding curriculums, exams, and authorized textbooks – and approximately 600 teachers. By 1930, there were more than 1,000 schools, with over 100,000 students being taught by 4,000 teachers.[9] To help manage the rapidly expanding system, the supervisory structure also ballooned to include almost forty administration positions.[10] In 1920, Victoria created the Department of Education, which was overseen by its own minister, to handle all things educational. The public school system, however, was still largely controlled by one person: the superintendent of education. Alexander Robinson held the post between 1899 and 1919, and Samuel J. Willis took over from him and served in the position until 1945.[11]

Like previous superintendents, Robinson and Willis anchored the education department and sought to identify and eliminate barriers to a fully functional, compulsory system of mass public schooling in the province. In particular, school officials targeted irregular attendance or absenteeism. As the settler population spiked, so too did the number of students attending school. Yet, average daily attendance grew only modestly. The total enrolment for the 1890–91 school year was 9,260, but the average daily attendance was just 55.45 percent.[12] By 1900, enrolment had more than doubled, jumping to 23,615, but attendance was still only 63.93 percent.[13] By the beginning of the twentieth century, the average for irregular daily attendance hovered around 40 percent and had increased by just 10 percent despite large-scale population growth. This was hardly a sign of success. Inspector S.B. Netherby agreed. "The people, to get the full benefits of the instruction given to them," he stated, "must send their children regularly and punctually."[14]

Aside from student illness, resistance from parents and guardians remained a major cause of absenteeism. Some objected to poor teachers and the use of corporal punishment, whereas others complained about the long distances and inadequate roads between their homes and the school.[15] Some kept their children at home, or sent them intermittently, because they objected to paying additional fees or could not afford to provide their children with shoes, winter coats, and other necessary supplies. Others, many of whom did not oppose schooling, simply counted on their children's labour to contribute to the family economy, especially in rural areas.[16] Indeed, as an urban-rural divide widened in British Columbia, public schooling could seem more useful to urban parents than to those in the countryside. Rural and assisted schools (often one-room schoolhouses with educational costs paid for entirely by the provincial government) generally had the highest truancy rates.[17] "The parents are oftentimes responsible," explained Inspector A.C. Stewart, adding,

> It is frequently found that parents keep their children at home on the faintest pretext of work to be done on the farm, and at the same time expect them to make the same rate of progress as pupils who attend regularly, and find fault with the teachers when their children fail to make the advance and progress which they unreasonably expect.[18]

Like their counterparts in the 1880s and 1890s, school officials in the early 1900s stressed the need to convince parents about the benefits of schooling. Some even resorted to public shaming to get results. The principal at Kaslo, in the Kootenay region, insisted that his teachers rank their students in order of merit and published the results in the local newspaper. Superintendent Robinson appreciated his initiative but demanded that the practice be discontinued.[19]

A more effective method of improving attendance was by introducing legislation to make it mandatory. Educational officials had already tried to compel attendance but lacked proper enforcement mechanisms, and the state had opted for the careful cultivation of public consent instead. However, this started to change by the 1890s and early 1900s, as the population increased and some parents, especially in cities, saw education as necessary for their children's upward mobility. Coercive measures, within reason, could now be introduced and enforced without inciting a popular revolt. This confirms Paul Axelrod's observation that in English Canada, "Compulsory-school legislation ... tended to follow, not precede, large-scale participation in public schooling."[20] In 1901, Victoria amended the school act to require children between the ages of seven and twelve in city districts to attend class.[21] In 1912, it increased the age to fourteen.[22] In 1920, it made attendance mandatory throughout the province, including in rural districts (which accommodated 20 percent of pupils). The compulsory age was raised to fifteen the next year.[23] In urban centres such as Vancouver, trustees authorized truant officers to prosecute the parents of absentee children. As well, as historian Diane L. Matters notes, Victoria created provincial industrial schools for boys and girls to combat a perceived crisis in youth delinquency.[24] Partly due to increased immigration and partly because the growing cohort of inspectors, trustees, and truant officers enforced the relevant legislation, attendance rose dramatically during the first three decades of the twentieth century.[25] Enrolment almost quintupled, from 23,615 (12,069 boys and 11,546 girls) in 1900–01 to 111,017 (56,125 boys and 54,892 girls) in 1929–30. The average daily attendance jumped from 63.93 to 86.65 percent over the same period (see Appendix 1).[26]

Classroom Composition

Increased attendance created new problems and put more strain on the growing school system. In 1902, Principal J.C. Shaw explained that "another natural consequence of the growth" in enrolment was "the over-crowding of our present quarters."[27] In 1900–01, classes across the province averaged 57.0 students per teacher; classes in Nanaimo averaged 76.5 pupils per teacher.[28] Inspector H.H. MacKenzie offered his own assessment of the "dark and disturbing" trend of overcrowding.[29] "To argue that under existing conditions the intellectual progress of the pupils is not being retarded is to give vent to mere sophistry," he wrote, "and to state that the health and physical well-being of these children are not being impaired is to ignore the inexorable laws of a universe whose maker and builder is God."[30] To hammer home his point, MacKenzie repurposed a well-known nursery rhyme: "The old woman who lived with her numerous progeny in a shoe had large, spacious, and luxurious quarters compared to those in which thousands of benighted children spend their hours of school."[31]

Overcrowding was partly a product of the government funding structure. Prior to 1906, government aid to schools was based on average daily attendance, much like the DIA funding to day and boarding schools during the same period. Designed to bolster attendance, this scheme encouraged local districts to place large numbers of pupils under each teacher to cut costs and have teacher salaries completely covered by the government grant. Taking this approach meant that property taxes would not need to be increased. After receiving numerous complaints from parents and school officials, the government shifted funding from a simple grant per pupil to a grant per teacher. As a result, school boards had less incentive to pack classrooms full of students, but overcrowding remained a significant issue in many locations during the early 1900s.

Though all school-aged children were encouraged to attend class, arguments about overcrowding often dovetailed with racist attempts by school boards and white parents to bar students of colour. The provincial government wanted to avoid the political tensions associated with segregated and sectarian schools elsewhere in Canada, and most state officials insisted on equal access to education, at least in theory, to promote the assimilation of new immigrants.[32] Yet, as historians Patricia Roy and Timothy J. Stanley show, school boards in Victoria and Vancouver nonetheless tried to limit access for children from Asian backgrounds because of fears that schooling would allow them to unfairly compete with white settlers in the labour market.[33] In Vancouver, parents of Japanese ancestry still pushed to have their children attend public schools, but they also sent them to the Nippon Kokumin Gakko (Japanese National School) for additional lessons between 1906 and 1922. In 1909, after

FIGURE 5.1 Sidney schoolchildren, c. 1910s. Many of British Columbia's public schools can be understood as contact zones, or social spaces where students from various backgrounds navigated and negotiated everyday life. | Courtesy of the Royal BC Museum, Image G-06020, British Columbia Archives

repeated attempts to stop Chinese students from attending a Victoria school, the Chinese Consolidated Benevolent Association opened the Chinese Imperial School to take in children who wanted a more supportive environment.[34] In 1922, the Victoria School District attempted to establish separate schools for Chinese students, but Chinese parents and students staged a strike for the entire school year to challenge racism and school segregation.[35] Racism affected school attendance in different ways at different locations, but many children from a variety of backgrounds – Japanese, Chinese, Black, Kanakas, South Asian, Eastern European, and more – went to school alongside their classmates from British, Canadian, and American backgrounds throughout the early twentieth century.

It is often assumed that all Indigenous children were simply channelled into day and boarding schools by the early 1900s. Not so in British Columbia. Although the provincial government stressed that Ottawa was responsible for providing – and paying for – Indian education, some Indigenous students still found their way into the public system.[36] Correspondence between British Columbia's Education Department and a colonial official in South Africa offers insight into the provincial government's view at the turn of the century. In 1904, the superintendent, now Alexander Robinson, received an inquiry concerning the "Education of the native races" from A.D. Dunbar, the Private Secretary for the Education Advisor's Office in Johannesburg, Transvaal, South Africa. The Transvaal government was looking to former British colonies for policy recommendations in its efforts to establish an apparatus of institutionalised racist segregation and discrimination that would become known as apartheid. In response to the letter, the superintendent tried to explain Canada's jurisdictional nuances as they related to Indigenous Peoples and education: "The full blooded Indian children of British Columbia are wards of the Dominion Government and not of the Provincial Government ... The Provincial Government makes no provision whatever for their education." He continued, separate "schools are erected in various points of the Province and into these [day and boarding] schools the Indian children are gathered for purposes of instruction, but I am not in a position to give you full particulars regarding this instruction for the reason that our inspectors do not visit these schools." The superintendent clarified, though, that "half breeds (that is children of white fathers and Indian mothers) are wards of this Government and as such are educated in public schools exactly in the same way as are the white children." He concluded, "throughout the whole Province the half breed children as well as the children of the Chinese and Japanese are treated in our schools exactly the same as are the children of the whites. We find this plan acts wonderfully well."[37]

Just because provincial officials in the early 1900s were beginning to emphasise the federal government's jurisdiction over Indian education does not mean that Indigenous children stopped attending public schools. There were a number of pathways for Indigenous children to attend public schools in British Columbia. One way, alluded to in the superintendent's response to the South African official, hinged on the legal definition of a status "Indian" as a full-blooded Indigenous person who lived on a government-sanctioned reserve. Children racialized as "half-breeds" as well as those categorized as non-status Indians living off the reserve were still Indigenous but were not legally considered "Indians" according to the federal government's Indian Act and could thus attend public schools. As explained in Chapter 3, many non-status Indian parents and guardians demanded access to public schools precisely because they lived off-reserve, paid property taxes, and wanted their children to benefit from the institutions that their taxes supported. School officials, especially in rural areas, also often ignored the rules and admitted Indigenous students to boost their enrolment figures and secure provincial government funding to keep schools open.

Still other school boards petitioned Ottawa directly to pay for Indigenous children to attend public schools in the province. Eve Chapple and Helen Raptis show that at Telegraph Creek in the northwest, the provincial and federal governments collaborated to have Indigenous and settler children attend the local school together – known as a "combined school" – in the early 1900s.[38]

The public schools in the Okanagan are another case in point. Though some Syilx children went to the Kamloops and Kootenay boarding schools, in the 1910s, a number of Syilx children also attended public schools with settler children at Armstrong, Hedley, Larkin, Osoyoos, Penticton, Similkameen, West Bank, and Woods Lake. In 1913, Indian Agent Robert Brown explained, "Owing to the fact that there are no Indian schools in my agency, Indian children have to depend almost entirely on the public schools, and I am pleased to be able to report that a few of the more progressive Indians take advantage of the privilege."[39] This confirms Woolford's idea that space/territory can aid resistance, namely that the remoteness of the Okanagan from main hubs of settler power afforded Syilx communities the ability to force gaps in the settler colonial mesh and assert more control over education.[40] In fact, Indigenous communities in the area refused to allow day schools to open on reserves until the 1910s and 1920s. As a result, the DIA agreed to pay an annual tuition grant of twelve dollars per student, conditional upon regular attendance.[41] In 1915, Brown confirmed that at Woods Lake "there are five Indian children attending this school and the teacher reports that they are making good progress. ... At the Similkameen public school," he added, "there are eight Indian children in attendance." Eight Indigenous children also went to the school in Hedley, and two were enrolled at the Larkin school.[42] In addition, the high school in Armstrong admitted Henry Harris, a local Syilx teenager. The DIA made it clear, though, that it was unwilling to "assume the cost of higher education of Indians."[43]

But Harris was not the only Indigenous student to attend high school. In 1915, R.H. Cairns, the DIA inspector of schools, noted that another student, an unidentified girl, "passed the McGill matriculation, ranking seventy-sixth in a group of five hundred who were successful in the western provinces."[44] In 1923–24, Edgar Green and Elinor (Ella) Gladstone, two children who boarded at the Methodist Coqualeetza Indian Residential School, attended the nearby Chilliwack High School. Six Indigenous students had applied for admission, but the Chilliwack principal claimed to have "desks for two" only.[45] The DIA agreed to provide fifty dollars each for Edgar and Ella. Ella, a member of the Haida Nation from Skidegate who also sat on the first student council at Coqualeetza, was profiled in the boarding school's *Commencement Exercises* pamphlet in June 1925. She was chosen as class valedictorian. Her picture (Figure 5.2) was accompanied with the following caption: "We are pleased to show you our

Miss Elinor May Gladstone

We are pleased to show you our most advanced pupil, who is completing her second year at Chilliwack High School. Her standing is with honours. She hopes to matriculate, as did her sister, Sophia (now Mrs. Read of Victoria). Elinor is proficient in bookkeeping and is a fair typist; she also is a good pianist.

FIGURE 5.2   Ella Gladstone, c. 1925. After leaving school, Ella moved to Vancouver and became Secretary-Treasurer of the Coqualeetza Fellowship, a group of Coqualeetza alumni that supported Indigenous Peoples living in the city. She was also the aunt of Haida carver Bill Reid. | *Coqualeetza Residential School: Commencement Exercises, June 1925,* 10. Courtesy of Library and Archives Canada, RG 10, School Files, volume 6422, file 869-1, part 2, Library and Archives Canada

most advanced pupil, who is completing her second year at Chilliwack High School. Her standing is with honours. She hopes to matriculate, as did her sister, Sophia (now Mrs. Read of Victoria). Elinor is proficient in bookkeeping and is a fair typist; she is also a good pianist."[46]

Photographs, like that of Gladstone, provide further evidence of what Philip Deloria calls "Indians in unexpected places," showing that some Indigenous children attended British Columbia public schools well into the twentieth century.[47] A class photograph shows a number of Indigenous students outside the South Fort George School, a public school near Prince George (Figure 5.3).

FIGURE 5.3 South Fort George School in Lheidli T'enneh territory, c. 1911. | Courtesy of the Royal BC Museum, Image B-00342, British Columbia Archives

In North Vancouver, class photos show that Indigenous students attended public schools in Skwxwú7mesh, səlílwətaɫ, and xʷməθkʷəy̓əm territory near the community of X̱wemelch'stn, which is today known as Capilano Indian Reserve No. 5. Figure 5.4 shows a number of Indigenous students, as well as those of Kanakas and Asian ancestry. Figure 5.5 shows a young girl identified as "Nora Newman" (Newman is a common Skwxwú7mesh surname). As Carol Williams cautions, however, we must be careful with interpretations of pictures in colonial contexts.[48] Photographs cannot definitively prove Indigeneity. Yet, attendance records from the nearby Moodyville school, also in North Vancouver, confirm that many Indigenous children went to local public schools in this period. In 1909, a number of Skwxwú7mesh boys went to the school. Among them was Edward Nahanee, who became a noted longshoreman and an activist involved with the Native Brotherhood of British Columbia.[49] When presented in context and alongside textual evidence, photographs can unsettle expectations, as Deloria suggests. Functioning as "windows of opportunity," they reveal the complex reality that British Columbia's

FIGURE 5.4 Capilano School, c. 1920s. | Courtesy of Archives of North Vancouver, Image 6490, MONOVA.

FIGURE 5.5 Capilano School, c. 1920s. Nora Newman is in the bottom row, second from the right. | Courtesy of Archives of North Vancouver, Image 6496, MONOVA.

early public schools, as "contact zones," were more heterogeneous than previously thought.[50]

At times, the superintendent of education even approved of Indigenous attendance at public schools. In 1919, Robinson informed the secretary of the Mayne Island School Board that "Indian children living on Reserves are wards of the Dominion Government." Nevertheless, he added, "I may say, however, that this Department will offer no objections whatever to your Board admitting these children to your school. If your Board decides to admit the children of any family they should, I think be ready to admit others that might seek admission later."[51] Indigenous children and youth, then, like thousands of their peers across British Columbia, continued to attend public schools in the early twentieth century, which only added more students to an already strained system.

Modern Methods

In the early 1900s, some reformers and parents started to pressure or, to use the words of historian Neil Sutherland, prod, push, and cajole the government to improve schooling.[52] The public system, they argued, was out of touch with the demands of an increasingly urban and industrializing society. If students were to succeed in a fast-changing world, they needed more than a basic education. Simply put: more was required than books, facts, and memorization with occasional religious instruction.[53] The rise of industrial capitalism in the late nineteenth and early twentieth centuries generated a number of social problems related to urbanization and class polarization. Reformers – both inside and outside the school system – stressed that improved public education was the solution.[54] Politicians, businessmen, teachers, school administrators, and community members with a reformist agenda called on Victoria to update educational methods to make schooling more practical and relevant.[55] However, as Axelrod notes, "the changes introduced were not always consistent with the visions that inspired them."[56] Indeed, political economist Stephen Schecter points out that "school reform, then as now, had less to do with providing avenues of upward mobility and more to do with legitimizing a changing class structure."[57]

Efforts to reform and modernize public schooling in British Columbia coalesced around progressivism, also known as the "new education" movement, which emerged in the late 1880s and the 1890s.[58] Its core message was that if students were to become good citizens, schooling needed to be child-centred and should include practical instruction in manual and industrial work.[59] Sutherland contends that a "loose confederation of peoples, interests, and organizations gradually forged their ideas into a new public consensus" on what education should look like.[60] Yet, drawing on the work of political economists, we must ask: Who benefitted the most from progressivism?[61] In British Columbia, as elsewhere in Canada, education officials selectively adopted aspects of the movement to enhance schooling's power as a tool of legitimation.[62] It was controversial, but most proponents highlighted its potential to produce "useful" citizens who would propel socioeconomic development. In particular, as historian Timothy Dunn shows, some reformers argued that the introduction of manual and industrial training "could stem sources of conflict plaguing society by providing students with industrial work habits and matching youth to suitable jobs."[63] Though this form of education typically took a back seat to the academic curriculum, students were increasingly exposed to practical instruction that sought to prepare them for life and work in an industrializing world.

Reformers asserted that the need for such training was countrywide.[64] In 1910, William Lyon Mackenzie King, federal minister of labour and future prime minister, established the Royal Commission on Industrial Training and Technical Education, whose mandate was to make recommendations on how Canadian schooling could promote "industrial efficiency" to aid national prosperity.[65] The commission was headed by none other than James Wilson Robertson of the Macdonald-Robertson Movement, a campaign that emphasized manual training in Canadian schools. Unsurprisingly, its 1913 report urged the government to increase its support for industrial education.[66] It recommended that all children should receive practical training and that "the experiences of the school should tend more directly towards the inculcation and conservation of a love of productive, constructive and conserving labour."[67]

Though the report presented this step as being in the best interest of pupils, its ultimate aims were clear:

> The interest of the State, as such, is that the individuals who compose it should be healthy, intelligent, capable, animated by goodwill towards their fellows and that they should be able and willing to fill their places in the community, as citizens discharging their duties and preserving their rights, as individuals in the economy of life, and as earners contributing to the material prosperity of the State.[68]

The federal government, in short, had a duty to support practical training in schools as a way of preparing children, as individuals, for employment. "The demand is everywhere insistent," the report warned, "that the schools shall meet the larger duties which are now thrown upon them by the changed social and industrial conditions."[69] The commissioners noted that advanced countries such as England, the United States, and Germany were already using schooling to support industrialization. Canada needed to catch up.

Although the commissioners recommended that Ottawa should provide the financial support, they clarified that supplying the training itself must remain a provincial responsibility. Again, the idiosyncrasies of Canadian federalism meant that introducing manual training would ultimately be the prerogative of provincial governments. During the 1890s, Macdonald and Robertson had purchased industrial equipment for British Columbia schools, so the province was already ahead of the curve. In the early 1900s, Harry Dunnel, whom Macdonald brought out from England, was designated the inspector of manual training for British Columbia, and education officials authorized new courses in manual and vocational training as well as domestic science – later called home economics – as part of an expanded curriculum.[70] Dunn states that the intent was to promote individualism, idealize physical labour as honourable and noble, and train working-class students to see themselves as workers.[71] Indeed, as Karl Marx noted, "the positing of the individual as a *worker*, in this nakedness, is itself a product of *history*."[72] Initial

FIGURE 5.6 Technical class, c. 1910s. By the early 1900s, many public schools provided students with industrial training to prepare them to join the province's workforce. | Courtesy of the Royal BC Museum, Image B-03439, British Columbia Archives

experiments in Vancouver and Victoria proved successful, and smaller towns such as Nelson, Revelstoke, Kamloops, and Prince Rupert soon instituted similar training. By the 1910s, British Columbia's Education Department had decided to continue industrial training in public schools and agreed to pay the salaries of instructors.

Even if some reformers and officials refused to draw a straight line between the classroom and the shop floor, the new emphasis on practicality became inextricably linked to the employability of students.[73] Inspector Netherby wrote, "Education, to be of any service, must be something incorporated with the thoughts and habits of the scholar, not something to be performed like gymnastic exercises which are of little benefit in the ordinary pursuits of life."[74] "Keeping this view of education before the pupils," he explained, "I hope to find, as time progresses, a corresponding degree of efficient practical training, a training which will turn out matter of fact, practical men and women prepared to grapple with such difficulties as they may encounter in life, and to make themselves useful to society and their country."[75] Increasingly, practicality meant employability. According to Netherby, "the education that makes men and women great is that which enables them to rise to a higher place, whilst still content with a day's wage and perhaps a humble life. Much has been said about the ideas of education, but the true philosophy of life is to idealise everything with which we have to do."[76] In his opinion, practical public schooling would not only legitimize but also idealize everyday life in a capitalist settler society.

Some reformers insisted that insufficient education hindered pupils' prospects in the modern workforce and put society, and the economy in particular, at a disadvantage. Reformed schooling, oriented to changing market forces, was therefore necessary. In 1900–01, Inspector Wilson noted,

> The business man expects the boy from the Graded or High School to write the bold, rapid, character-displaying hand of the bookkeeper many years behind the desk. If the boy does not or cannot, writing in the schools is condemned. I feel justified in saying that never before has so much been expected of children in their school work as now, and, all things considered, well do they stand the test.[77]

By the 1890s, some schools had offered courses in bookkeeping and typing, but now reformers called for the implementation of more rigorous industrial training. Some government officials went so far as to claim that students, particularly boys, were being channelled into white-collar office jobs, instead of being trained to join the ranks of industrial workers in the growing resource sector, a fact that could only hinder economic development.[78] This confirms Schecter's point that the history of schooling can "be seen as an ongoing dialectic between educational reform and the transformation of capitalism."[79]

Practical training sought to habituate students to shop conditions and instill in them the value of hard work, discipline, and obedience to authority, but it was also markedly gendered. Courses in wood- and metalwork were typically restricted to boys, whereas girls were prepared for entry-level white-collar work, such as bookkeeping and stenography, and for their predetermined roles as mothers and homemakers in line

FIGURE 5.7 Sewing class at King Edward High School, c. 1918. Practical training enforced gender binaries. Boys took wood- and metalwork classes. Girls learned how to cook and sew in home economics courses. | Courtesy of the Royal BC Museum, Image C-07582, British Columbia Archives

with prevailing notions of the "cult of domesticity" and the assumed requirements of social reproduction in a patriarchal society.[80] *The Canadian Girl at Work,* a 1920 textbook, explained that their training was intended "to bring about in the life of a girl a satisfactory connection between paid employment and home-making, and to show home employments in their rightful place as occupations of the first importance."[81] To that effect, early domestic science courses were established in Victoria in 1903 and then in New Westminster in 1905. By 1925, John Kyle, the organizer for technical education, observed, "The work of home economics as a whole is well established in the Province ... Lessons on food, food values, and preparation of foods are for the most part grounded around the laws of health. Sewing and dressmaking are linked with a study of clothing and with a knowledge of materials."[82] Home economics was not straightforwardly about teaching girls to be servants. Instead, it asked them to internalize an idealized version of the domestic work that was required to raise the next generation and to reproduce society's labour power.[83]

Practical training prepared girls and boys for their unequal roles in a capitalist – and heteropatriarchal – settler society.

Hands-on training was essential, reformers argued, but so too was ideological instruction. As Terry Wotherspoon notes, "Schooling is ideological. It offers legitimacy ... to authority, domination and competition. Alternative visions, and challenges to the status quo, are discouraged and dismissed as irrelevant."[84] By the 1910s, civics courses were offered for the first time in public schools. The study of society, or "social studies," was to play an important role in supporting continued social formation and promoting class harmony, especially as the First World War and the 1917 Russian Revolution ignited popular demands for participatory democracy around the world.[85] Newly authorized textbooks such as R.S. Jenkins's *Canadian Civics (British Columbia Edition)* and James McCaig's *Studies in Citizenship* discussed the value of liberal democracy, but they also stressed the importance of work to modern society. In a chapter titled "Manufacturing" McCaig explained that "the great work of producing things to satisfy our needs is called *the production of wealth*."[86] His description was devoid of politics, side-stepping questions about the fair distribution of that wealth. Instead, he briefly touched on the processes of proletarianization and class polarization. A chapter titled "Capital and Labor" said that society "may be divided into two classes, those who employ and those who are employed, or, as we say, *employers* and *workers*."[87] *Studies in Citizenship* did not ask students to question the capitalist system; it merely aimed to orient them to it. This kind of education can be understood as what philosopher Ivan Illich calls the "New Alienation," whereby schooling "makes alienation preparatory to life."[88] Marx also explained that schooling aided the development of a working class by normalizing capitalism's coercive social relations as "self-evident laws."[89] In this way, civics courses helped acclimatize young children to work and taught them to accept, and even idealize, the exploitative relationship between workers and employers, thus equipping them to contribute to national prosperity and social harmony.

Teachers, as workers themselves, were tasked with delivering the authorized curriculum, including its lessons about work and society. To improve the educational system, the government established a provincial normal school to train teachers and introduce them to modern methods.[90] Before 1900, they were mostly untrained and, as Jean Barman argues, not necessarily committed to the profession.[91] Increasing state authority over their certification was an important aspect of reform. The first normal school opened in Vancouver in 1901, followed in 1915 by one in Victoria.[92] Though many teachers welcomed additional training, they were less pleased by their poor pay. In their opinion, modern teachers employing modern methods deserved more than modest wages. During the early 1900s, salary increases – often determined by local school trustees – did not keep pace with the rising cost of living, especially in urban centres but also in some rural districts. Complaints over low pay motivated many teachers to join the British Columbia Teachers' Federation (BCTF) after its formation in 1917.[93]

Teachers argued that their increased remuneration would greatly improve the quality and success of schooling throughout the province. In 1900–01, teachers in rural schools made an average annual salary of $631.92, whereas those in the city received $711.12.[94] By 1929–30, elementary school teachers earned an average salary of $1,393, which was not bad, given that the average annual salary for men in the province was roughly $1,200 and approximately $650 for women.[95] High school teachers took home considerably more, making on average $2,328. The calculation of "average" salaries, however, hides the real disparities of region and gender. High school teachers in cities were paid as much as $4,180 annually, whereas elementary teachers in rural districts received as little as $800.[96] Moreover, women, comprising the vast majority of the teaching force by the early 1900s, were paid substantially less than similarly qualified men for the same work.[97] As Axelrod notes, "The 'feminization' of teaching, then, owed a great deal to the employment of thousands of women at relatively low wages."[98] As in the nineteenth century, men monopolized twenty of the twenty-three better paying high school teaching positions in 1929–30, and all nineteen high school principals were men.[99] Embracing modernity did not mean jettisoning old-fashioned patriarchy. Indeed, many male school officials saw enforcing a gendered division of labour as an efficient way of paying for an expanding school system.[100]

More advanced secondary schooling was also proposed by reformers as being necessary to prepare students for the demands of the modern world. Basic elementary education was no longer sufficient. As early as 1903–04, Superintendent Robinson stated that the importance of high schools could "scarcely be overestimated."[101] In 1900–01, there were just five high schools, mostly in major cities, with a total of 584 enrolled students. By 1929–30, there were eighty-two, with 20,509 pupils.[102] Whereas boys consistently outnumbered girls at elementary schools, the opposite was true at high schools. "The great preponderance of girls," the 1903–04 school report explained, "is accounted for by the fact that these schools are largely preparatory schools for teachers, and the percentage of women engaged in our public schools is increasing every year."[103] For girls, a high school education was becoming an essential key to social mobility.

FIGURE 5.8 Victoria High School under construction, c. 1912. As the demand for secondary schooling increased in the 1900s, especially in urban locations, new schools were built throughout the province. Reform efforts influenced school architecture. Modern designs maximized efficiency but also prioritized students' health and hygiene, paying particular attention to proper lighting, ventilation, and fire safety. Schools also became prominent landmarks and symbols of pride for many communities and architects sought to convey their civic importance through new designs. | Courtesy of the Royal BC Museum, Image B-03433, British Columbia Archives

The demand for secondary education grew substantially during the 1910s, and new schools were established in Chilliwack, Cumberland, Kamloops, Kaslo, Nelson, Rossland, and Vernon.[104] In the early 1920s, the province introduced a specific programme of studies for junior high schools, and by 1929–30 secondary students could choose from a number of streams, depending on their plans for the future: matriculation (for university-bound graduates), normal school entrance (for prospective teachers), general (for the undecided), and commercial and technical (for those purposing professional or trades careers).[105] All streams shared core compulsory courses such as English, social studies, health, and physical education, and allowed students to choose an additional one or two courses from a list of electives that included agriculture, home economics, and industrial arts. Still, by the end of the 1920s, secondary school enrolment accounted for not more than 20 percent of the province's school population and was mostly, though not exclusively, an urban phenomenon.[106]

As British Columbians embraced modern methods and demanded better and higher levels of public schooling, the government saw an opportunity to download its costs. In response to rising expenditures – schooling was often the largest part of the provincial budget – it steadily reduced its share of funding from practically 100 percent in the early 1870s to 38 percent by 1924.[107] The process of offloading the bills, specifically in cities, started during the late nineteenth century. In 1888, Nanaimo, New Westminster, Vancouver, and Victoria were required to refund the provincial treasury for one-third of their teachers' salaries, which they achieved via a municipal property tax.[108] The school act was also amended to allow for the levying of tuition fees at local discretion, and soon urban school boards were required to reimburse the treasury for one-half of teacher salaries and to bear the full cost of expenditures on property, buildings, and other things. For a time, Victoria continued to pay all the costs in rural districts, but by the 1920s the superintendent was informing those areas that they needed to take on more responsibility and contribute financially through local assessment.[109]

In 1900, Victoria paid $307,479.00 and school districts, mostly cities, paid $81,888.39. By 1930, the government paid $3,765,920.69 and the districts paid $7,384,075.58.[110] The compromise brokered during the early 1870s — that the government would cover all costs in exchange for greater power over education — was breaking down. More correctly, Victoria was gradually and unobtrusively altering its terms. Most parents and guardians were primarily focused on securing the best education for their children, and so did not challenge or even recognize the subtle changes. The result was not a great "public consensus," as Sutherland and other scholars suggest, but rather the normalization of acceptance and accomodation. Hegemony was secured through a general acquiescence to struggle, and increasing public demands for practical education gave the government further licence to implement its vision for school reform.

In exchange for improved schooling, parents agreed to pay more for it through taxation, and school boards accepted increased control over the management of local schools. In the process, however, the public also ceded power over the direction and content of education to the government. Having consolidated its authority, Victoria introduced school reforms that did not democratize society or radically increase social mobility, in the ways that some parents had hoped. Instead, the reforms narrowed the aims of schooling — as a tool of socialization and legitimization — to more effectively reproduce the social relations necessary for socioeconomic development.[111] They strengthened the state's ability to rule through schooling.

THE SERVICE OF EDUCATION

The outbreak of the First World War in 1914 acted as a catalyst for school reform, sparking greater interest in public education across Canada.[112] Officials frequently talked about the "service of education" and believed that practical schooling should play a more prominent role in preparing children for war.[113] In his report for 1913–14, Inspector Arthur Anstey wrote,

> it may be said that the outlook is encouraging; people are taking greater interest in the work of the schools, and in their own responsibilities as regards the administration and financing of them ... And

> in spite of the depressing though temporary war conditions, there are indications that educational efficiency is coming to be regarded, more than ever before, as a prime factor in our struggle for national existence and supremacy.[114]

Moreover, Inspector John Martin explained,

> Since the beginning of the school-year our Empire has become involved in a great European war. Many of our male teachers, in company with patriots from every walk of life, have left their positions and home to do their part to uphold the cause of right and the honour of our beloved Mother-country. More will go if necessary to maintain the struggle, knowing that they are fighting on the side of justice in a more righteous way.
>
> We, as teachers, should as a lesson from the causes of the present war, endeavour to make the *spirit* of the school the first concern in its social and moral life. While teaching the truest patriotism and love of flag, we must instill in the minds of the children that to treat others with courtesy, forbearance, and justice; to sympathize with the weak and pity the unfortunate; to be honourable and truthful from principle – those transcend all other aims in the school, and pupils impressed with such ideals will grow up true citizens as well as efficient workers.[115]

For some, like Martin, the war was an opportunity to stress the necessity of training students to become better workers, loyal citizens, and dutiful subjects of empire.

Teachers were essential in making the war understandable to students. "The little pitchers with big ears have been taking in a good deal of war-talk," Inspector Wilson wrote in his 1914–15 report, "and public school teachers have naturally found a fresh interest in giving intelligent direction to these new ideas."[116] To guide their discussions, the Education Department purchased a number of pamphlets to stock in school libraries. It also ordered copies of a 1915 book for young readers, *The Children's Story of the War*, by Sir Edward Parrott. Like other propaganda, it downplayed the imperialist origins of the war, emphasizing the heroics of soldiers and their loyalty to king and country.[117] After 1914, new civics and Canadian history textbooks – now more readily available to students thanks to the creation of the Free Textbook Branch in 1908 – stressed the justness of the war as a valiant defence of the British Empire and included pictures of dramatic battle scenes to inspire respect for the soldiers overseas.[118] I. Gammell's *History of Canada* opened with a reproduction of Edgar Bundy's painting *The Landing of the First Canadian Division at St. Nazaire, 1915*, which depicts a group of jovial bagpipe-playing Canadian soldiers in full Highland regalia being welcomed by French officers and civilians. The image invokes the grandeur of war and none of its brutality. The book also informed students that the war had unified the subjects of the British Empire, including Canadians, "in spirit and in loyalty to the common Crown," and stressed that everyone had a duty to safeguard Canada and defend the empire.[119]

A corollary of boosting British imperialism was an increased emphasis on teaching students a romanticized history of colonization. School materials had always boasted about the British Empire. Many schools celebrated Empire Day (observed on the school day preceding the May 24 holiday for Queen Victoria's birthday), proudly flew the Union Jack, frequently sang "God Save the Queen/King," and displayed portraits of reigning monarchs and Mercator maps (with the British Empire shown in red) on the walls of classrooms. After the Boer War (1899–1902), however, a new series of Canadian textbooks more explicitly linked British imperialism and Canadian nation building.[120] Timothy Stanley shows that textbooks "were particularly important in transmitting a nexus of ideas about patriotism, citizenship, and 'character' which made [white] supremacist notions virtually impossible to challenge."[121] In British Columbia, Stanley contends that "above all textbooks fostered 'an ideology of difference' which legitimated the White occupation of the province as both natural and morally necessary, at the same time that it rendered First Nations people and Asians as 'Others' ... as morally depraved and illegitimate in their presence."[122] Textbooks, then, were a key site in which the destructive and creative aspects of colonialism played out in ways that helped students learn about its legitimacy.[123]

Textbooks typically praised European explorers for discovering and claiming Canada, and many included derogatory depictions of Indigenous Peoples, often in the initial pages, as a way of justifying colonization and Christian nation building. Gammell's *Elementary History of Canada* stated, "The story of Canada covers a period of four centuries. Its beginnings takes us back to a time when *our* country was a forest wilderness inhabited by a few wandering tribes of red men, when our forefathers lived in Europe and knew nothing of a continent beyond the Western Ocean."[124] Like other textbook authors, Gammell painted all Indigenous Peoples with the same racist brush as "cruel and revengeful" and described them as "skilled in woodcraft, warlike; cruel and revengeful; lazy and improvident; superstitious."[125] Students, including the Indigenous students who attended public schools at this time, were presented with an account of colonization as an epic tale in which settlers overcame a savage Indigenous population to create a new civilized society as part of the beneficent British Empire. This falsification of history became a significant part of promoting British imperialism and thus legitimizing Canadian and British Columbian society as worthy of defence.

Physical education and military training were also introduced in schools. It was not enough to cultivate loyal hearts and minds; strong hands to wield the weapons of war were also needed. A privately endowed agency known as the Strathcona Trust began to provide the necessary funds in 1910. The trust had been set up in 1909 with a $500,000 endowment by Lord Strathcona, Canada's high commissioner to Great Britain, at the insistence of Frederick William Borden, the minister of militia and defence.[126] In particular, it encouraged military drill – training in marching and the use of weapons – mostly for boys in public schools across the country. Borden wanted them to acquire "an elementary knowledge of military drill and rifle practice" should they ever need to "take part in the defense of their homes and country."[127] Drill, and the creation of cadet corps in schools, was thought to build up manliness while ensuring obedience, loyalty, and military preparedness. The Strathcona Trust also supported physical education for girls, though they were not permitted to become cadets.[128] Historian Mark Moss notes that "interest in both the drill and physical education reflected

REFORMING PUBLIC SCHOOLS   171

FIGURE 5.9 Cadets at Boys' Central School, Victoria, c. 1918. British Columbia had the second-highest number of school cadet corps in Canada. | Courtesy of the Royal BC Museum, Image B-03424, British Columbia Archives

the chauvinistic belief in Anglo-Saxon superiority, as well as the related ideals of nationalism, patriotism, character-building, and respect for authority."[129]

Not all British Columbians approved of this use of schooling, with parts of the labour movement and many pacifist Doukhobors voicing opposition.[130] Nevertheless, when war broke out in 1914, physical and military training was greatly expanded. By the end of the war, British Columbia had thirty-nine school cadet corps and 3,855 active cadets, the second-highest number in Canada.[131] Upon leaving school, some young men saw active duty during the war, including George Newman, a Skwxwú7mesh citizen who attended the Moodyville public school in the early 1900s and became a machine gunner.[132]

The service of education also took other forms. As historian Nancy Sheehan observes, education officials, teachers, and even students were asked to make a number of personal sacrifices to aid the war effort.[133] Many male teachers enlisted.[134] On the home front, teachers and educational officials were encouraged to make their own contributions by donating part of their salaries to the cause. The war also justified the further expansion of manual and industrial training. Commenting on the spread of vocational instruction in 1916–17, Inspector Anstey noted an "unmistakable tendency toward the establishment of a closer connection between school-work and the activities of the outside world."[135] Superintendent Robinson wrote to many schools, soliciting the help of teachers and female students in domestic science classes: "May I suggest that the girls of our schools who are now taking lessons in Domestic Science be required for a portion of each week to knit articles of use for our troops in England. By useful articles I mean of course such articles as socks, mitts, wristlets and stomach-bands."[136] Students also contributed produce grown in school gardens, which Macdonald and Robertson had earlier called on rural schools to create, as well as items made in school shops and kitchens. This tangible productivity demonstrated to the public the practical benefits of the new education that was being implemented in many schools.[137] After the war, in 1919, manual and industrial training received an additional boost when Ottawa passed the Technical Education Act, establishing a grant of $10 million to assist provinces in expanding practical training in schools to assist with the recovery.[138] Overall, the war, though horrific, helped convince the public of the pressing need for practical schooling that could better teach students – as future workers, citizens, and subjects of empire – how to contribute to and defend society.

Surveying the System

Although the war spurred educational reform and solidified the need for more practical education, many people still felt that the schools were out of touch with modern needs. Barman and Sutherland note that many British Columbians who hoped to rebuild and democratize society in the aftermath of war called for improved schooling.[139] In the early 1920s, the Union of British Columbia Municipalities and the BCTF advocated for an in-depth government survey of the school system to identify areas for improvement.[140] Both groups, for different reasons, asked for an independent review by experts. At first, the Department of Education was not prepared to marshal the necessary resources. However, partly in response to the end of the postwar depression and partly because of the BCTF's continued prodding, the government, led by Liberal premier John Oliver, authorized the survey. On July 5, 1924, it appointed two commissioners with significant educational experience to head the survey, Dr. J.H. Putman, a senior school official in Ontario, and G.M. Weir, the head of the Department of Education at the University of British Columbia, who would go on to become an influential education minister in the province.[141] Barman and Sutherland suggest that their findings were largely predetermined because both men were "already publicly acknowledged to be in the reform camp."[142]

Nevertheless, Putman and Weir travelled throughout British Columbia to hear from parents, teachers, and community members in urban and rural districts and to gather information about the "diversity of educational problems" in the province.[143] They logged over sixteen thousand kilometres, held 215 conferences, and inspected 160 public schools and 2 normal schools.[144] On May 30, 1925, they released their findings as the *Survey of the School System*, which historian Charles E. Phillips calls "the most thorough examination of any school system in Canada" at that time.[145] Their report offered an interesting and comprehensive snapshot of public schooling:

> The 86,000 elementary school pupils are housed and taught in buildings and environment of great variety and marked contrast. Some are in modern city buildings as complete as are to be found on the American continent. Others are modest but comfortable frame buildings in small towns or amid ideal rural surroundings. Many are in remote and lonely places beside a lake, under a towering mountain capped with snow, or on an arid plateau where all vegetation is brown and dusty. Some are on beautiful but lonely islands in the Pacific, where the settler is part farmer, part fisherman, and part lumberman. Some are on steep mountain sides in "Company Towns," where tall chimneys of pulp-mill or smelter form the centre of a busy industrial life. Some are close to the water on an arm of a canning-factory, and some stand on ground over coal-mines. Some have ideal surroundings, but the school buildings

themselves are primitive and very small. Many are built of logs. Some are not larger than 15 by 18 feet with a ceiling just above your head. Some have attractive grounds, some have bare and unattractive yards, and some are built on rocks. *In a number of them the children show unmistakeable signs of Indian blood.*[146]

That Putman and Weir noted how many schools were clustered around industrial activity and attended by children with obvious signs of "Indian blood" is worth underlining in light of the preceding pages.

In their report, Putman and Weir tried to make sense of the "bewildering maze" of British Columbia's educational issues and included a series of recommendations. *Survey of the School System* is best understood as the culmination of calls for educational change in the early twentieth century. Education historian R.S. Patterson argues that it "was another

FIGURE 5.10 A teacher and her class at the Woodpecker School in Dakelh territory, south of Prince George, c. 1925. | Courtesy of the Royal BC Museum, Image I-60775, British Columbia Archives

voice for change. It gave visibility and credence to many of the ideas which were gaining attention, not only in Canada, but throughout the western world."[147] Indeed, the Putman-Weir Report embraced elements of the new education and recommended reforms that would make schooling more practical and efficient.[148] It suggested changes to the normal schools and teacher training, and it also called for curriculum diversity in primary and secondary schooling that emphasized practical education. It insisted that IQ testing be used in schools and that manual and industrial training and home economics should become mandatory.[149]

Putman and Weir proposed that scattered rural schools should be amalgamated to better educate children in remote areas, and they stressed that students should attend school for an additional year.[150] The creation of middle schools, or junior high schools, would achieve this goal. Previously, grades were organized on an 8-3 system (eight grades in elementary and three in high school). Now, the system would be 6-3-3: pupils would attend elementary school for six years (Grades 1 to 6), middle school for three (Grades 7 to 9), and then high school for three more years (Grades 10 to 12), with the opportunity to continue to the post-secondary level, if desired.[151] In defending this scheme, the Putman-Weir Report argued that "in the increasing complexities of our modern society and industrial organization," secondary education, especially Grades 7, 8, and 9, "now represents the irreducible minimum of training necessary ... to the attainment of marked success in industry, commerce, or the art of home-making."[152] It also emphasized that compulsory secondary schooling could recalibrate students to the world of work and motivate them to contribute to society. This would be the "best insurance against anarchy and bolshevism" because it could best teach students lessons in loyalty and legitimacy that would be necessary for the "self preservation" of state and society.[153] Lastly, to the relief of the government, the report suggested that school boards should take on greater administrative responsibility and that the public should pay for education through a universal income tax.[154]

Though Putman and Weir described their recommendations as "radical," they were moderate in nature.[155] Rather than radically altering the province's educational structure, *Survey of the School System* mostly reinforced it and advanced reforms that were already being implemented.[156] As a result, historian Jean Mann labels it an essentially "conservative document."[157] Putman and Weir interpreted the new education rather narrowly. Although they mentioned John Dewey, one of progressivism's most notable figures, they never actually cited his work and did not embrace his more democratic philosophy.[158] Instead, they relied on lesser-known American thinkers who were noted for "the development and promotion of scientific efficiency, practicality and vocationalism, and testing and measurement in education," rather than any commitment to social transformation, justice, or democracy.[159]

Thus, *Survey of the School System* was critical of the means of public schooling in British Columbia but not of its ends. It did not question the suitability of state-controlled, compulsory mass education, seeking only to normalize and improve it. Putman and Weir praised officials for putting British Columbia's school machinery in place, and their 556-page report suggested that it merely needed a tune-up. Minor tweaks would ensure its sustainability in supporting ongoing growth and development. In the coming decades, various aspects of the system would be revised according to Putman and Weir's recommendations, but the basic schooling structure, established in the 1870s and consolidated by the mid- to late 1920s, remained largely unchanged until the 1970s.[160]

Conclusion

By 1930, British Columbia's public school system had grown dramatically. In 1872, as it transitioned from for-pay common schools to free public schools, there were only 500 students and a few teachers in schools scattered throughout the province. By the turn of the century, it was normalized as an essential institution, closely associated with social and economic progress, with over 100,000 children attending every day (see Appendix 1). Its growing success, as the 1905 Dominion Exhibition displayed, was a sign of rapid socioeconomic transformation. In the first three decades of the twentieth century, leading up to the Great Depression, which significantly slowed reform efforts, the provincial government managed to consolidate power over education with increased public support, all the while lessening its administrative burden and offloading costs.[161] By 1930, compulsory, mass public schooling was the norm, and it remained an effective tool of socialization and legitimization throughout the decades that followed.

CHAPTER | SIX

Revising and Resisting Indian Education

On February 10, 1902, Johnny Sticks, a Secwépemc man from Alkali Lake, made a gruesome discovery. He found the dead body of his eight-year-old son, Duncan, in a ditch at the side of a road. The snow around the boy's body was stained red with blood. Sticks was devastated. But he was also outraged. He had not been notified when, days earlier, Duncan and eight of his classmates ran away from St. Joseph's, the Catholic industrial school in nearby Williams Lake. Sticks was not surprised to learn that his son had run away. A year earlier, Duncan and two other classmates had fled the school. Sticks recalled that when his son made it home, he complained that "he did not get sufficient food – and that they whipped him too much."[1] Wanting Duncan to receive an education, Sticks reluctantly returned him to St. Joseph's but decided not to mention the boy's grievances, fearing reprisal. He checked in at the school during the summer and noted with relief that Duncan "seemed well and happy."[2] The next time Sticks saw him, however, was when he discovered his body.

With support from other Indigenous parents and community members, as well as a former teacher from the school, Sticks immediately called for a full investigation into the conditions at St. Joseph's.[3] A DIA-sanctioned inquiry was held a few weeks later. Two hearings took place, one at Alkali Lake and another at 150 Mile House. At the Alkali Lake hearing on February 28, Sticks reiterated his son's complaints about the abuse and poor conditions at St. Joseph's: "He was beaten with a [horse whip] – he said the food was bad and he could not eat it, and he was allowed no other food until he had eaten it."[4] These complaints were corroborated by other witnesses. Charlie Johnson said that his son ran away many times because "he was badly fed and beaten."[5] Christine Haines, a former student, ran away twice because she was fed rotten food. She said that she was sometimes stripped naked and beaten by the Oblate sisters, and she also complained about being hit in the face with a strap.[6] Other students, including Duncan's older sister, Mary, confirmed the abusive environment. "The sisters scolded me all the time – they gave me bad food – the beef was rotten," she explained, "I couldn't eat it – they kept it over and gave it to me next meal – they tied my hands and blindfolded me and gave me nothing to eat for a day." The nuns also hit her in the face with the strap for "not doing some needle-work."[7]

When the school was given the chance to address the charges, it downplayed or disputed the testimonies. The Oblates stated that great progress was being made at St. Joseph's and insisted that their work, at Williams Lake and other schools across the province, should be allowed to continue. Henry Boening, the principal, agreed. His annual report remarked glowingly that "too much praise cannot be given to the employees of the school, especially the kind Sisters, for the painstaking zeal with which they have worked."[8] After the inquiry, A.W. Vowell, DIA superintendent for British Columbia, promised to monitor the school closely, but no large-scale changes were implemented as a result of Duncan's death. A subsequent investigation headed by Vowell concluded that, in fact, the students were to blame for the problems.[9] The status quo at the school was maintained. This is an example of the DIA's preferred approach to problem-solving, which Daniel Rück calls "strategic indifference."[10] St. Joseph's remained in operation until 1981. A number of employees were eventually charged with various crimes, including more than twenty counts of sexual abuse.[11]

Despite early warning signs, such as Duncan's death and the letter written by missionary Elizabeth Shaw about the "culture of fear" at the Port Simpson school discussed in Chapter 4, the DIA chose to "expand and consolidate" its authority over Indian education in the early 1900s.[12] This chapter shows that it gradually introduced reforms, including increased vocational training, to grow and increase the efficacy of the system as a pillar of its Indian policy. The reforms did little to address the core problems, however. Settler colonialism's "structures of indifference," in the words of Mary Jane McCallum and Adele Perry, remained intact, and Indigenous Peoples continued to suffer the consequences.[13]

As a result, Indian Day Schools and Indian Residential Schools (as boarding and industrial schools became known by the 1920s) were resisted by various actors, who pushed back against what Audra Simpson calls the "stress and structure" of colonialism.[14] Settler civil servants called attention to underfunding and poor conditions in schools, Indigenous parents such as Johnny Sticks protested abuses, and students frequently ran away. In some cases, parents organized boycotts and kept their children at home, and students burned their schools to the ground. As one shíshálh student bluntly stated at a DIA inquest into abuses at the Sechelt Indian Residential School in the 1920s, "there should be a different system."[15]

Episodes of Indigenous resilience, refusal, and resistance, however, strengthened the resolve of church and DIA officials to revise Indian education and use it more effectively as a project of rule, as a way of trying to transform Indigenous Peoples from wards to workers. This was the dialectic of conflict and change, of resistance and reform. Even as it became apparent that the assimilation project was failing, the DIA and its agents continued to support Indian education. As Glen Sean Coulthard points out, Canada doubled down during this period on its "repeated attempts to overtly uproot and destroy the vitality and autonomy of Indigenous modes of life" through coercive institutions such as schools.[16] Rather than abandon a flawed and harmful system, church and state defended it precisely because they believed that it was achieving its most important objective: disrupting and delegitimizing Indigenous lifeways to support the ongoing development of Canada's capitalist settler society.

A Narrow Vision

By 1900, the DIA was undergoing significant restructuring. In the 1880s and 1890s, critics attacked John A. Macdonald's Conservative government for spending too much money on the department. Paying for boarding and industrial schools, in particular, was expensive. When the Liberals won the 1896 election, they "applied drastic surgery to Indian Affairs, reducing staff and budgets and reorganizing its structure."[17] Restraint became the watchword of subsequent regimes. Consequently, many civil servants were dismissed, and power was concentrated in Ottawa at the top of the DIA bureaucracy. Firing staff resulted in modest savings, but it also elevated select personnel to upper-level positions, most notably a "staunch British imperialist" named Duncan Campbell Scott, the DIA accountant.[18] A bookkeeper-turned-policy-wonk whose missionary father was a close friend of John A. Macdonald, Scott worked his way up the ranks to establish himself as "the principal architect of [Canada's] Indian policy" in the early twentieth century.[19] After a stint as DIA superintendent of education between 1909 and 1913, he served as deputy superintendent general of Indian Affairs between 1913 and 1932. Andrew Woolford emphasizes that "multiple actors" shaped DIA policy during this period.[20] He cautions against seeing Scott as a lone wolf. Nevertheless, Scott had a lot of power to bring about his narrow vision for managing Indian affairs: to get rid of the so-called Indian problem. As he explained to a parliamentary committee in 1920, the goal was "to continue until there is not a single Indian in Canada that has not been absorbed into the body politic, and there is no Indian question, and no Indian department."[21] This was the core of Canada's genocidal logic of elimination and white possession.[22]

Asserting greater authority over Indigenous Peoples in British Columbia was one of Scott's top priorities, as the province was still a smouldering volcano in terms of Indigenous-settler relations. The federal and provincial governments continued to quarrel over who controlled Indigenous lands. Many Indigenous Nations — notably the Nisga'a and Sḵwx̱wú7mesh — grew angry at the arrogance and inaction of state officials at all levels, and some leaders established new political organizations to press their demands.[23] As historian Keith Thor Carlson shows, some even travelled to London in 1906 to meet with Edward VII at Buckingham Palace. They "drew attention to the injustice of Canadian Indian policy in British Columbia as whole," but the king mostly ignored their demands.[24] Back in Canada, in 1910, chiefs representing the Secwépemc, Syilx, and Nlaka'pamux Nations met with Prime Minister Wilfrid Laurier at Kamloops to push for treaties and compensation for land theft.[25] Though no formal action was taken, the federal government renewed its calls for Victoria to transfer Indigenous lands to itself to administer, as had been done in other provinces. As mentioned earlier, provincial governments in Canada possess a great deal of jurisdictional authority, including over land management, and Victoria simply refused to comply with Ottawa's commands.[26] Instead, it continued to sell, lease, and tax stolen Indigenous land, using the revenue to pay for things such as roads and public schools to promote further settlement and socioeconomic development.[27]

In 1913, frustrated by the impasse, Ottawa and Victoria launched the Royal Commission on Indian Affairs for the Province of British Columbia, also known as the McKenna-McBride Commission. Its purpose was to investigate the land question and propose a solution. As Cole Harris explains, the hope was that engaging in discussions with Indigenous Peoples to alter and adjust their reserves would end their dissatisfaction.[28] This expectation was doomed to be disappointed. As they had since the time of James Douglas, Indigenous representatives pushed for the recognition of their land and title rights, something the commissioners were reluctant to entertain.[29] In the end, the 1916 McKenna-McBride Report recommended that the province relinquish control over Indigenous lands to the federal government, which it did, though not for another twenty-two years.[30] Victoria's intransigence persisted in the period immediately following the commission's report. For its part, Ottawa amended the Indian Act to undermine the potlatch and curb the savvy political organizing of Indigenous leaders such as Peter Kelly and Andrew Paull and by groups such as the Nisga'a Land Committee and the Allied Tribes of British Columbia.[31] In short, the colonial status quo mostly prevailed in British Columbia during the early 1900s. Although the McKenna-McBride Commission focused on the land question, many Indigenous representatives took advantage of the hearings to raise additional grievances, including the desire for school reform.[32] Capitalizing on their requests, some church and state officials concentrated on improved schooling, hoping that it would pacify Indigenous Peoples and entice them to accept DIA authority and control of Indian education.[33]

Education remained the cornerstone of Canada's Indian policy in the early twentieth century, and the DIA introduced a series of reforms to make it more efficient.[34] But again, drawing on political economy, we must ask: Who benefitted most from these reforms? Influenced by the growing discussion of the "new education" movement, as outlined in Chapter 5, DIA education superintendent Scott wanted more practical kinds of training in Indian Day Schools and Indian Residential Schools. Such changes could help the Indigenous student take up future roles as "a producer and as an industrial worker side by side with his white neighbour."[35] In British Columbia, there were signs that increasing numbers of Indigenous Peoples were embracing wage work. Department reports spoke proudly, and paternalistically, of Indigenous men who "live and work like white men" in occupations such as logging, canning, longshoring, mining, and construction.[36] Indigenous women, too, were employed in canneries and as domestics, nurse maids, and general servants, where they gave "great satisfaction to their employers."[37] To better facilitate the desired transformation from ward to worker, then, church and state increasingly emphasized vocational instruction in the belief that the "absorption" of Indigenous Peoples into the "industrial life of the country will tend more to the solution of the Indian problem than any other cause."[38] Like many public school officials at the time, Scott viewed school reform as an opportunity to revise Indian education to better support Canada's continued socioeconomic development.

As part of its reform efforts, the DIA revisited the idea of compulsory schooling. Since the 1890s, church and state officials had tried to make attendance mandatory for Indigenous children but had approached the matter cautiously. This was a smart strategy.[39] The DIA knew how to play the long game. After the First World War, it felt that it had consolidated its power over Indigenous Peoples to the point where it could remove children from their communities, with force if necessary, and not risk widespread resistance. In 1920, Ottawa amended the Indian Act to compel Indigenous parents by law to send children between the ages of seven and fifteen (and in some cases up to eighteen) to state-supported and church-run schools across the country.[40] Like the legislation that made attendance compulsory in public schools, this amendment to the Indian Act – often enforced by police acting as truant officers – boosted attendance, but it also greatly worsened the harm done to Indigenous communities. In 1920, the enrolment in thirty-nine British Columbia

Indian schools was 2,312, with an average attendance of 62.98 percent.[41] By 1930, 3,291 students were enrolled in sixty-three schools (see Appendices 3 and 4), with an average attendance of 71.31 (see Appendix 2).[42] The average attendance in Indian Residential Schools – where most students lived for much of the year – was significantly higher, depending on the school and year, as historian James Redford outlines.[43] In 1930, the federal government spent $532,578.97 on Indian education in British Columbia, the most for any province or territory.[44] Though the DIA continued to be characterised by what Rück calls "effective inefficiency," the department assumed even more authority over Indian education during the early twentieth century, narrowing its focus to concentrate on reforming day and residential schools.[45]

Indian Day Schools

Reforming Indian Day Schools was no easy task, however. DIA officials argued that day schools, usually located on or near Indian reserves, were deficient but still significant institutions. Cheaper than boarding and industrial schools, they were seen as important stopgaps, capable of reaching many Indigenous communities across the province. Moreover, some Indigenous parents preferred them over boarding schools because their children could live at home. In 1900–01, there were twenty-eight day schools, with a total of 815 students (456 boys, 359 girls). The average daily attendance was just 50 percent, the lowest for any kind of state-supported schooling in British Columbia.[46] DIA school inspector R.H. Cairns often instructed Indian agents to use a police constable "to put on pressure" to induce parents to regularly send their children to the schools.[47] After thirty years of operation, the system showed moderate growth, though there was very little improvement in the statistical returns the DIA used to justify expenditure. In 1930, forty-six day schools had a total of 1,437 students (693 boys, 744 girls) (see Appendix 3). More children were attending, but the average daily turnout was only 47.6 percent, a slight decline from the previous year (see Appendix 2).[48] The schools may have been increasing in number, but they were not necessarily improving, a disconcerting thought for the DIA.[49]

Moreover, the problems often associated with boarding and industrial schools – issues of disease and death – also plagued day schools, with children getting sick while attending class. Two students of the Tsartlip Indian Day School died of tuberculosis in 1915, and two died from the same disease at the Kincolith Indian Day School in 1920.[50] In 1921, at the Bella Bella Indian Day School, two boys died of tuberculosis, and two others were reported to have contracted it.[51] Even though children did not live at the day schools, the DIA identified them as breeding grounds for illness. As a result, some parents and guardians refused to send their children regularly.

Unqualified teachers were also seen by the DIA as barriers to the system's success. Indian agents and church officials tried to attract capable teachers, paid for by the DIA, but this proved challenging given the low salaries and remoteness of many schools from settler hubs. Moreover, as the provincial government started requiring public school teachers to obtain formal training, those who lacked such credentials sometimes

FIGURE 6.1 Ucluelet Indian Day School, c. 1900s. The Presbyterian Church opened the school in the 1890s on the Ittatso Reserve 1 on the west side of Vancouver Island. The United Church took over in the 1920s. It closed in 1966. | Courtesy of the Royal BC Museum, Image B-04662, British Columbia Archives

FIGURE 6.2 Songhees Indian Day School, c. 1910s. In 1911, the ləkʷəŋən (also known today as the Esquimalt and Songhees Nation) were pressured by municipal, provincial, and federal governments to relocate from a reserve in Victoria to a new reserve near Esquimalt. In 1913, the Catholic Church opened an Indian Day School on the reserve. The school closed in 1965. | Courtesy of the Royal BC Museum, Image A-07690, British Columbia Archives

looked to Indian Day Schools for employment. Officially, the provincial and federal school systems continued to operate separately, with the exceptions noted in Chapters 3 and 5, but teachers often applied for employment in both. Nonetheless, they saw work in a day school as the less desirable option or perhaps a temporary assignment and stepping-stone to the public school system.[52] In addition, the DIA was unhappy that many day schools were staffed by Indigenous teachers, some of whom were graduates of Indian Residential Schools in the province.

In 1907, the department identified Indigenous teachers or teaching assistants working in almost 20 percent of the Indian Day Schools in British Columbia. As historian Funké Aladejebi similarly argues about Black women teachers in Ontario, this reality can complicate the mainstream view of teachers in Canada as "primarily 'white' and middle class."[53] Some church and state officials used racism to pass judgment on the practice of hiring Indigenous teachers and urged the appointment of "more qualified" instructors. For the Aiyansh Day School near Terrace, the school inspector for British Columbia, A.E. Green, reported, "Charles Morvin, an intelligent native, is the teacher. He is doing his best, but is not qualified to teach. A white teacher should improve this school."[54] We must ask, improve the school for whom? Surely, some students appreciated a teacher from the community who understood the unique pressures they faced, as Aladejebi demonstrates was the case in other contexts.[55] Moreover, as Chapter 5 noted, many white teachers were badly underqualified and not committed to the profession.

Nevertheless, in an effort to address the perceived inadequacies of the day schools, the DIA introduced a number of reforms in the 1910s. Some church and state officials saw boarding and industrial schools as overly expensive and suggested, as did many Indigenous parents, that local day schools be improved and expanded as the primary means of Indian education.[56] They would not become the DIA's preferred educational method until after the Second World War, but during the 1910s the department began to increase teacher salaries in hopes of attracting more qualified individuals.[57] In 1911, annual salaries for teaching at a day school ranged anywhere from $100 to as high as $600, with the average being about $300.[58] By 1930, wages had increased to between $750 and $1,150, with the average being $850.[59] For comparison, elementary teachers in British Columbia's most remote rural public schools made an average of $1,227 at the time. In other words, the highest-paid teachers at day schools made substantially less than those who held the least desirable positions in the public system.

The DIA also began providing lunch for children in some day schools as an incentive for parents to send them regularly.[60] As well, it started to offer shoes and weather-appropriate clothing so that children could attend in greater comfort. Where the distance to school was a significant barrier to regular attendance, the department procured rudimentary transportation services.[61] These reforms, in addition to the Indian Act compulsory clause in 1920, increased average daily attendance to almost 2,500 by 1930 (see Appendix 2).[62] In that same year, the federal government paid $60,509.33 to support Indian Day Schools in British Columbia.[63]

Additionally, the DIA recommended that the schools follow the public school curriculum, using the same modern methods and materials. In reality, however, day school pupils continued to receive a rudimentary education. In 1930, more than half were in "Standard I," the lowest level of instruction offered. Very few were afforded the opportunity to attain higher levels of education, especially in schools where attendance remained sporadic and teachers soon moved on. Moreover, it is unlikely that the many day schools, already struggling to attract qualified teachers, could actually afford the new textbooks and updated educational materials. The two kinds of schooling – federal Indian education and provincial public schooling – were thus equal in theory but profoundly unequal in practice.

Though lacking in modern supplies, many day schools nonetheless introduced manual and industrial training. In 1911, Scott noted that a few teachers were providing "instruction in plain sewing, knitting and mending with a practical beneficial result."[64] Domestic science, for boys and girls, was integrated into lessons in an attempt to improve the character of the children, but especially to prepare girls for possible careers as servants. In the Hazelton Day School, run by the Church of England, the girls were regularly "taught sewing, knitting and other domestic accomplishments."[65] In addition, many schools planted gardens, and children learned basic agricultural skills that could serve them well at home or, for boys, as farmhands. In 1924, the DIA recorded that day school teachers were making a "special effort" to offer "classroom exercises with vocational training."[66] The DIA annual report for 1930 spoke favourably of the "rapid development of technical education in British Columbia," thanks to a special grant of $8,617.82 made available for the endeavour.[67] The department continued to see day schools as deficient, but it gradually implemented reforms as part of its strategy to use schooling to prepare children for participation in the capitalist economy.

Indian Residential Schools

Attendance at Indian Day Schools greatly outstripped that at other educational institutions for Indigenous Peoples across Canada, but in British Columbia Indian Residential Schools were the dominant form of state-supported education for Indigenous students (boarding and industrial schools were collapsed into one boarding, or "residential," category in 1923).[68] However, the day and residential school systems were still connected, as some children started at day schools and then moved on to a residential school for more advanced training. The DIA annual report for 1907 stated that "the main advantage of boarding as compared with day schools ... is the avoidance of the retarding and retrogressive influences of the home upon the pupils. ... Moreover," the report clarified, "with regard to outlying districts, the boarding school system overcomes the otherwise insuperable difficulty of securing any regular attendance of children among tribes of roving habits."[69] In 1915, R.H. Cairns, DIA inspector of schools for British Columbia, similarly used racist rhetoric to defend the residential schools:

> The Indian people are distinctively nomadic in their habits. Because of this trait of character, boarding schools are a necessity. If the child is to get an education, in many cases the only way to accomplish it is to remove him from his parents and place him in a boarding school, where he will be in constant attendance. Here he receives training and care at the hands of those who have become experts in this work. Wonderful transformations take place in the appearance of these children in a short time.[70]

Because residential schools overturned what Glen Sean Coulthard calls Indigenous Peoples' grounded normativity, they were seen as particularly effective tools in fashioning Indigenous pupils into useful workers.[71]

Funding the expanding fleet of residential schools, however, was a matter of considerable debate. Even as early as the 1870s, before the federal Indian Residential School system was created, mission schools complained that they did not receive enough funding from Ottawa. Their protests intensified when some mission schools were converted into official boarding and industrial institutions during the 1880s and 1890s, many of them provided with per capita grants of $75 and capped at a total amount, sometimes as low as $300. By comparison, a modest private boarding school in British Columbia charged parents approximately $160 per year per student. An elite private school for white boys charged

$470 for boarders, $150 for day pupils.[72] DIA funding thus proved insufficient to cover the full costs of teacher salaries, food and clothing for staff and students, and services such as heat and proper sanitation. Budgetary shortfalls were to be corrected by private donations where possible, and this created a situation, as historian J.R. Miller explains, where many schools suffered financially and denominations battled each other for enrolment.[73] In the case of the All Hallows Boarding School at Yale – which operated simultaneously as a boarding school for Indigenous girls *and* an Anglican private school for white girls – the fees paid by the latter subsidized the operation. When the numbers of private pupils declined in the 1910s, the school's finances and future became uncertain.[74] All Hallows eventually closed and the Indigenous pupils were transferred up the Fraser Canyon to the St. George's Indian Residential School at Lytton.

Ultimately, Indigenous students bore the brunt of federal underfunding. To cut costs, school staff frequently denied them suitable food, proper clothing, and necessary educational materials, just as Nicholas Flood Davin had predicted if the federal government were to contract the schools out to churches.[75] By the early 1900s, many church officials felt that the Indian Residential School system would simply cease to function without a revised funding agreement. Even Duncan Campbell Scott, always the penny-pincher, felt that chronic underfunding had created a situation whereby the debt load of many churches significantly hampered the effectiveness of the schools and impeded DIA policy objectives. To be clear, he was not concerned about the children's well-being; underfunding undermined the state's investment in Indian education as a tool of legitimation and nation building.

In 1910, the DIA organized a conference in Ottawa to determine how the situation could be fixed. It was attended by DIA bureaucrats and representatives of the Anglican, Methodist, Presbyterian, and Catholic Churches.[76] More government funding was the answer. If the Indian Residential School system was key to Indian policy, it should be funded accordingly. In 1911, the department announced a "new financial arrangement" in hopes that "greater efficiency" could be achieved. Scott detailed the rationale: "The representatives of the churches accepted suggestions made by the government which were to result in more efficient management of the boarding schools and the payment of an increased per capita grant. It was provided that a contract should be entered into between the management of each school and the government with reference to the conduct of the school."[77] In essence, the DIA further consolidated its hold over Indian education by offering more money in exchange for increased authority and oversight, including a greater supervisory role for Indian agents and inspectors. The churches accepted these terms.

In the 1910s, the DIA introduced a new classification system for funding: residential schools that were designated as Class A would receive $125 per student, Class B $100, and Class C $80. To qualify as Class A, a school must be made of quality material, have a proper water supply, sewage disposal system, an area for the treatment of sick children, modern ventilation and heating systems, and land for farms and gardens. To acquire a Class B designation, a school must have proper ventilation for dormitories, medical equipment to care for sick children, and an area for agricultural and industrial training. Most British Columbia schools were Class A or B, and thus they received per capita grants of $125 or $100. In theory, this system increased the DIA regulatory power and forced the churches to improve and maintain schools in hopes of securing more funding.

In 1900, the DIA spent approximately $13,800 on per capita grants for seven schools in British Columbia. Most received funds at a rate of $60 per capita.[78] By 1930, the DIA was spending $214,830.01 on revised per capita grants of between $160 and $180 for sixteen schools (see Appendix 4). These grants ranged from $3,057.24 at Port Simpson to $35,904.84 at Kamloops. The total cost for British Columbia residential schools, covered by a parliamentary grant, was $462,517.45.[79] Nevertheless, as historian John S. Milloy notes, even these enlarged grants barely kept pace with inflation and proved entirely insufficient.[80] According to Miller, this arrangement, which was retained until the 1950s, put "an already inadequate system under severe financial pressure," which led to "a descending spiral of problems" related to underfunding, including overcrowding and a reliance on student labour in many schools.[81]

The DIA also attempted to reform residential schools by providing new funds for "vocational and recreational equipment" in "an effort to make the instruction more attractive." The equipment could also make the schools self-sufficient. In 1925, Scott wrote that "the Department of Indian Affairs and the churches interested have made special efforts during the year to give better vocational training to pupils at Indian residential schools. ... It is the aim," he added, "to make graduates of these institutions self-supporting members of their respective communities."[82] In truth, many boarding and industrial schools had already been providing various forms of industrial training since their establishment in the 1890s, with students spending at least half the school day performing manual labour. Nevertheless, an increased emphasis was placed on practical training, as well as promoting student participation in sports, the cadets, and organizations such as the Boy Scouts and Girl Guides, in the years after the First World War.[83] Unpaid student labour ensured the proper function of the schools, and their work – making clothing, produce, and preserves – could be sold for profit.[84] In 1923, a fifteen-year-old boy, Clayton Mack, was brought to the St. Michael's Indian Residential School in Alert Bay to work as a labourer. He recounted his daily routine:

> I feed the horses, clean the barn, feed the cows and later even milk the cows. I get up at four o'clock in the morning sometimes and go look for them cows. I had ten cows. I'd get up, round them up, put them in the barn, feed them bran and then milk them ... In the summer it was really hard work. When the school closed in the summer they gave me the girls' cows too! The girls had about eight milk cows. So I did, looked after the whole works for two years. I tried to go to school but there was not enough time. I worked most of the time. I went to Alert Bay for school and instead they put me in a job.[85]

Schools justified student labour as practical training that would prepare Indigenous Peoples for the demands of the job market, but it was also a convenient cost-cutting measure.[86]

As in provincial public schools, vocational training in residential schools was gendered.[87] Leanne Betasamosake Simpson shows that

REVISING AND RESISTING INDIAN EDUCATION   193

FIGURE 6.3 Williams Lake Indian Residential School, c. 1920s. Catholic missionaries opened the school, also known as St. Joseph's, in 1891. It closed in 1981. Duncan Sticks and his siblings attended the school in the early 1900s. | Courtesy of the Royal BC Museum, Image E-09990, British Columbia Archives

Indian boarding schools were primary sites of learning heteropatriarchy and the gendered division of labour in capitalist societies.[88] Barman writes that the nuns at All Hallows prepared their Indigenous female students to "go out into the world" and become "a very useful, permanent element of the working community of the Province," especially as servants.[89] In a 1903 report, Principal Joseph Hall of the Methodist Coqualeetza Industrial Institute wrote that whereas the boys were often employed in manual labour or learning carpentry or shoemaking, "the girls are trained in all the departments of good housekeeping."[90] At the Presbyterian Clayoquot Boarding School, Principal P. Maurus noted, "Three boys are learning the carpenter's trade." The girls, on the other hand, "attend to the general housework and take their turns in assisting the cook. Some of the girls are fully competent now to prepare the meals for the children, without the assistance from the cook proper." Moreover, "in the sewing department the girls receive regular instruction in hand and machine sewing, in cutting and finishing dresses, in knitting, darning, and mending."[91] In residential schools, students were trained in a variety of occupations, including farming, gardening, carpentry, shoemaking, stock raising, dressmaking, cooking, baking, and general housekeeping. Just as in the public school system, then, the ultimate goal of a modern education with an "essentially vocational foundation" was to encourage students to secure employment in one of the province's developing industries after leaving school.[92] Although Indian Residential Schools were quite costly, the DIA continued to point to their successes in this venture. Moreover, the department often gave special grants to support industrial training in British Columbia schools.[93]

Resistance

Some Indigenous Peoples supported Indian education, but others continued to resist and challenge it. This fits with Anishinaabe historian Brittany Luby's explanation of the range of Indigenous responses to settler capitalism in Canada, including adaptation, cooperation, and resistance.[94] Parents and students, and even some non-Indigenous civil servants, tried to stop what Lee Maracle calls the "accumulation of hurt" occurring in many schools.[95] In the process, Indigenous students and parents created their own cultures and everyday acts of resistance. They deployed a series of what James C. Scott describes as "low-profile techniques" to challenge the school's authority.[96] In the pages that follow, episodes of resistance are documented against the backdrop of tightening DIA control over Indian education. "Enmeshed within the painful fabric of global colonialism," as Ned Blackhawk points out, Indigenous Peoples "shaped the world around them, doing so under conditions not of their choosing."[97] Instead of highlighting Indigenous agency to offer a "colonialist alibi" that downplays the severity of residential schooling, these accounts, as Crystal Gail Fraser emphasizes, show that parents and students recognized the injustice of the system and tried to change it, with varying degrees of success.[98] Although church and state officials were always quick to point to the newest statistics about increasing attendance or to mention the productivity of ex-pupils, by the early twentieth century it was clear that much was wrong with Canada's system of Indian education.

Abuses in residential schools ranged from overcrowded quarters and substandard food to beatings or whippings by staff for a range of infractions, including stealing food, speaking an Indigenous language, and generally refusing to obey the draconian rules.[99] Although not all schools employed corporal punishment in the same ways, punishment permeated the system. Celia Haig-Brown's interviews with former students at the Kamloops Indian Residential School make this evident. One student, incarcerated at the school in 1907–08, recalled, "Some people got punished; they got to lay down on the floor. Just pure bread and water to eat, laying on the floor ... oh, I don't know how many days." Another student, who attended between 1927 and 1930, remembered, "I was punished quite a bit because I spoke my language ... I was put in a corner and punished and sometimes, I was just given bread and water ... Or they'd try to embarrass us and they'd put us in front of the whole class." Still another who attended during the 1920s recalled being given the strap publicly: "If we got caught, we really got punished and if that didn't work, we got sent to the principal's office. And that was lashes we got there, in front of the whole school: real humiliation."[100] School violence was used to discipline children and force their obedience.

Debilitating accidents, diseases, and death also pervaded residential schools in British Columbia, as elsewhere.[101] In terms of accidents, the Kuper Island Indian Residential School is a case in point. In 1904, a female student "ignited her clothes and got terribly scorched" while attending to the fire in the kitchen.[102] In 1911, a girl broke her ankle because she stepped into a hole in the floor, caused by a broken floorboard that had not been fixed.[103] The next year, a boy cut off two fingers with a saw during his industrial training.[104] Not only were students often overworked, but the tasks they had to perform were not always safe. Such incidents challenge us to see the schools as manual labour institutions, as Alexandra Giancarlo demonstrates.[105] They also connect to the growing literature on the "multiplicity of [workplace] violences" that Jeremy Milloy argues is an important new direction in histories of work and labour under capitalism.[106] Many of the accidents at residential schools were workplace injuries.

Students also contracted a variety of illnesses at school, from whooping cough and diphtheria to pneumonia, tuberculosis, and smallpox. Between 1896 and 1904, as many as twenty-five of an average of fifty-eight pupils at the Kuper Island school were on "sick leave" every year. In 1927, the St. George's Indian Residential School in Lytton saw 95 percent of students affected by influenza and the mumps, thirteen of whom eventually died.[107] In 1919, a serious occurrence of smallpox at St. Mary's Indian Residential School in Mission was exacerbated when twelve children, who had not been vaccinated according to DIA policy, were sent to their home reserves after showing symptoms. Furious at the resulting smallpox outbreak in St'át'imc and Stó:lō territories, the Indian agent wrote to his superior in Ottawa to inform him of the disastrous situation:

> I questioned the children and found that there had been some sickness in the school, and some of these now suffering had been sick for a few days in the school, so they were all sent off home. One child was taken off the train with the rash out on her and she stated the school authorities had not any doctor to attend her.[108]

The principal at St. Mary's denied any wrongdoing and claimed that his medical officer had followed proper procedure to avoid the spread of the disease. Satisfied, the DIA decided not to pursue the issue. The medical officer later admitted, however, that some children may have been sent home prematurely.

Although many students recovered from their illnesses, many others did not. Deaths were recorded each year and published in the DIA reports. In 1906 alone, nine of seventeen schools recorded student deaths, a total of sixteen. Between 1908 and 1922, forty-nine children died at the Elizabeth Long Memorial Home at Kitamaat in Haisla territory, and only fifty survived.[109] Overall, the total death toll is unknown, but it was probably much higher than school records indicate because many officials did not count sick students who were sent home once ill, as was likely the

FIGURE 6.4 Kootenay Indian Residential School, c. 1920s. The Catholic Church opened the school, also known as St. Eugene's, in 1890 near Cranbrook. A new school was built in the 1910s (pictured). It closed in 1970. | Courtesy of the Royal BC Museum, Image I-30599, British Columbia Archives

case at St. Mary's in 1919. In her account of Margaret Butcher, a Methodist missionary at the Kitamaat school, Mary-Ellen Kelm remarks that many "school staff refused to see the connections between school conditions, disease, and death. For officials it was not the material circumstances of schools that caused disease and death but the [savage] nature of the students and their parents."[110] McCallum and Perry similarly note that this "unwillingness of institutions to hold anything or anyone accountable (other than the deceased)" for the death of Indigenous Peoples is a defining feature of settler colonialism's devastating "structures of indifference."[111]

By the early 1900s, it was obvious that the system was in crisis. Indigenous parents had objected to the harm being done to their children from the start, but now even white officials were taking notice. This included Dr. Peter Henderson Bryce, who carried out a DIA-sanctioned investigation into the conditions of boarding and industrial schools in the Prairie provinces and published a damning report in 1907. In 1909, he expanded his investigation and included the Kootenay Indian Industrial

School in Cranbrook, where he found that 34 percent of the pupils admitted between 1892 and 1909 had died.[112] Although Bryce was later appointed the DIA chief medical officer, the department and the churches mostly disregarded his reports.[113] In 1921, he was forced to retire from the civil service. Angry at Scott and DIA attempts to silence his critique of the residential school system, Bryce published his findings in 1922 as *The Story of a National Crime: An Appeal for Justice to the Indians of Canada*.[114] Still, his objections were largely ignored.[115]

Although some of the DIA reforms – including increased funding and efforts to attract more qualified teachers – did diminish opposition to a certain extent, Indigenous parents and guardians continued to show great dissatisfaction with Indian education. In 1900, a Stó:lō couple were jailed for keeping their daughter home from the Coqualeetza Industrial Institute after she had been whipped.[116] At Sechelt, shíshálh parents who had initially fought to create its residential school complained that their children were ill with various diseases, fed inadequate food, and physically assaulted. When one parent went to the school to remove her child, she got into a war of words with the mother superior over the treatment of the students.[117] A number of Kwakwa̱ka̱'wakw parents complained that the Alert Bay Girls' Home had allowed their children to return home on holidays "with their heads in an unclear condition." When Inspector W.E. Ditchburn investigated the matter, he concluded that the complaints were "well founded," confirming that many children had lice.[118] In 1924, Dakelh parents demanded a police inquiry after Melanie Quaw died as a result of a beating she received at the Lejac Indian Residential School, south of Fort St. James.[119] Some Sḵwx̱wú7mesh families, as Elder Mazie Baker notes, even temporarily relocated to Washington State to work in hop fields and avoid sending their children to the Squamish Indian Residential School in North Vancouver.[120] This kind of border crossing was common for many Coast Salish peoples, as Paige Raibmon and Lummi education scholar Michael Marker show.[121]

When the DIA and the churches ignored, trivialized, or failed to adequately address the grievances of parents and guardians, students often took matters into their own hands. Some stole food or spoke their own language while doing chores, and some ran away.[122] Nick Estes explains that truancy can be understood not merely as fighting *against* settler colonialism but as struggling *for* Indigenous life and connection to land and human and non-human relations.[123] Characterized by what Unangax̂ scholar Eve Tuck calls "desire," students often ran *away* from their schools as much as they ran *toward* their communities.[124] Indeed, Simpson argues that Indigenous refusal and resistance can be reclassified as episodes of return, restoration, and reclamation of Indigeneity in the face of settler colonial oppression.[125] State and church officials saw things differently. In 1900, the principal of the Coqualeetza Industrial Institute responded to complaints by parents that their children ran away because they were being abused and "used like dogs." Like most settler officials, he disputed such claims. He defended the treatment of children at his school: "I deny most emphatically and unequivocally that the children of our Institute are abused by their teachers ... Corporal punishment is occasionally resorted to, but always with reluctance ... But in no instance has any child received treatment which could be properly called abuse. No bruises are inflicted." He further rationalized the school's conduct:

> The restraints of discipline in study and work in many instances they may not like; to roam about in idleness, riding about on horseback at their pleasure, galloping about from place to place and occupying themselves in unprofitable amusements they may prefer; but that any pupil ever had a reason for running away in his having received abuse or wrong treatment in the Home I must most emphatically deny.[126]

Via training and discipline, the taste for "unprofitable amusements" was to be replaced with a desire to contribute to capitalist settler society.

Schools often worked closely with local Indian agents and police to apprehend fugitive students. The role of police as truant officers across Canada requires more research; however, in British Columbia there are examples where police, as what Black scholar Robyn Maynard calls agents of state violence, worked with schools to capture runaways.[127] For instance, in 1906, the Victoria *Daily Colonist* printed a story about a female student who had run away from the Kuper Island school and returned to her family home near Ladysmith, about fifteen kilometres away. Working through the local Indian agent and the school, the DIA instructed Constable Cassidy of the British Columbia Provincial Police (BCPP) to apprehend her and return her to Kuper Island. He soon located her, but she "refused to return under any circumstances." In addition, she "was backed up in her refusal by both her mother and father." In response, Cassidy "obtained assistance" to "drag" her back to the school.[128] Nevertheless, like most British Columbia residential schools, Kuper Island continued to report runaways and regularly worked with Indian agents and police (both the BCPP and NWMP/RCMP) to return them.

Running away was not the only method of resistance. Student agency, of course, was circumscribed, but some pupils found other creative ways to refuse and resist. Secwépmec leader George Manuel, who served as chief of the National Indian Brotherhood, recalls a community member berating a teacher "for overworking the boys" at the Kamloops Indian Residential School, an action that inspired the boys to fight back: "A teacher would raise his yardstick to strike a student. The student would grab the stick from the teacher's hand and the rest of the class was instantly on top of the man. It was a crude and juvenile way of returning the violence to its source."[129] Such instances of male students physically challenging school staff are examples of how gendered teachings about masculinity could be redeployed as "acts of strenuous resistance."[130] Simon Baker (Khot-La-Cha), a noted Skwx̱wú7mesh leader and union activist, wrote about his frustration at being overworked and underfed at St. George's Indian Residential School during the 1920s. He and his classmates chose to strike in protest:

> The older boys were expected to do heavy work, and we did not feel like we were getting enough to eat so we could do these jobs. In other words, we were hungry! We wondered what we could do about this. There didn't seem to be any rights for the students. We certainly had no part in any decision-making. We were just told what to do all the time ... I knew something about strikes and I told

the boys that we'd go on strike. We were a bit afraid to take a chance ... I told the boys, "The only way it will work is if we are sure to stick together, all of us, with no one backing down." They wouldn't expel all of us.[131]

Baker and his classmates stopped work one morning and marched to the principal's office to make their demand. They reasoned, "we work like men so we should eat like men, so you better give us more food on our table." The principal caved. In this instance, direct action proved effective, but Baker always felt that the school officials "had it against me for promoting the idea of a strike."[132] Students such as Manuel, Baker, and Andrew Paull also mentioned that the practice at some schools of incarcerating students from various Indigenous Nations helped form networks that spurred pan-Indian political organizing afterward, something akin to what Simpson calls "Indigenous internationalism."[133]

Some students turned to more incendiary methods of resistance. If they could not escape or strike for better conditions, they could free themselves by burning their schools to the ground. Between 1900 and 1930, approximately twelve fires were reported to have destroyed or damaged school property in British Columbia.[134] Not all were confirmed as arson, but many occurred in institutions with noted abuses. In 1901, a fire at the Metlakatla Indian Residential School, known for its extensive vocational training program for girls, destroyed a number of outbuildings, including the girls' dormitory, the laundry, and the workshops. In 1916, parents accused the Alert Bay Girls' Home of overworking their children and treating them poorly. Inspector Ditchburn was instructed to look into the matter and speak with staff, but little was done to address the parents' concerns. Two years later, in 1918, a fire broke out at the school and two female students admitted under threat of legal charges and imprisonment to setting it. When pressed for a reason, they said "that if the home was burned they would have a good holiday before a new one could be built." After the principal used a cane to give them a "thrashing," they were further interrogated before staff and students in an effort to "impress upon them the seriousness of the misdemeanour, and inform them

FIGURE 6.5 Alert Bay Indian Residential School, c. 1930. The Anglican Church ran this school, also known as St. Michael's, for almost one hundred years. It started as a small boarding school in the 1880s. In 1894, it became an industrial school and received DIA funding. A new school was built in 1929 (pictured, centre). The Girls' Home is visible on the left. The school farm is on the right. The school closed in 1974. | Courtesy of the Royal BC Museum, Image H-02890, British Columbia Archives

if any such attempt is again made the Department will not shield them but that they will be criminally punished."[135] According to Ditchburn, the treatment was too lenient.

The Alert Bay fire was not an anomaly. In fact, there was a growing pattern of fires at residential schools in British Columbia. In 1916–17, five were torched on Vancouver Island alone, with confirmed arsons at Alert Bay, Ahousaht, and Clayoquot.[136] In 1921, the Crosby Home for Girls at Port Simpson, noted for its poor treatment of pupils as discussed in Chapter 4, was also destroyed by fire. In 1925, the Kamloops school, known for its high rates of runaways, was destroyed by fire. In 1924, the Alert Bay school witnessed two further arson attempts. During the first, on September 7, the fire was quickly discovered and put out. A week later, another was found and this time three girls were identified as the culprits. Officials determined that both fires were of "incendiary origin."[137] After interrogation, the girls admitted guilt and were publicly whipped before staff and students. In September 1928, two girls ran away from St. Mary's Indian Residential School but were captured and returned against their will. In response, they set St. Mary's on fire, "with the idea of being released from the school." But instead of sending them home, the principal flogged them and instructed the RCMP to arrest them and ship them off to the Provincial Industrial School for Girls in Vancouver. They were then transferred to the Kamloops Indian Residential School.[138]

Another form of resistance, and one most feared by officials, was a boycott in which parents collectively kept their children at home. By the 1920s, when it was obvious that the systemic problems in Indian education would not be addressed, many Indigenous parents risked jail time or fines by organizing boycotts to demand improvement. In 1922, several Haisla parents refused to send their children to the Elizabeth Long Memorial Home after another young girl died there. They met with the Indian agent and a local RCMP constable to pressure the school to improve conditions.[139] The next year, conditions at the Sechelt Indian Residential School had deteriorated to the point where parents felt that a boycott was the best way to resolve their grievances. Shíshálh leaders sent a petition to the Indian agent, explaining, "We are not satisfied with the education given in this school and want to change the principal and the teachers immediately. If this matter is not settled we are not taking our children to school till it is settled."[140] This kind of political organizing, which fits with what Simpson calls "refusal," made church and state officials anxious.[141] If it caught on widely, it could potentially jeopardize the entire settler colonial project.

In an effort to regain control of the situation, Inspector Cairns launched an official investigation and held a meeting in Sechelt at which the shíshálh could voice their concerns. Parents and students raised numerous grievances about abuse, neglect, and being overworked at the school. Tom Julian, a former student who was acting as an interpreter, also spoke: "I put nine years in this school and know how on some occasions the food was poor and couldn't be eaten. I have seen kids go out after meals and throw up their food to prevent being sick." He disputed

FIGURE 6.6 Sechelt Indian Residential School, c. 1920s. The school, also known as St. Augustine's, was originally built in 1903 by members of the shíshálh Nation. The OMI took over operation of the school the following year and it was funded by the federal government from 1905 onwards. Community members, however, were deeply dissatisfied with the results of the school. It closed in 1975. | Courtesy of the Royal BC Museum, Image B-00445, British Columbia Archives

staff assurances that the discipline administered was lenient, noting "in some cases the treatment goes too far. ... There should be a different system," he concluded.[142] According to the transcript of the meeting, which was composed by the Indian agent, the conditions at the school were obviously troubling.

Yet Cairns, a former principal of the Coqualeetza Indian Residential School at Chilliwack, ultimately chose to side with the staff in his official report and colluded with them to keep the school open. It was too important to shut down. He wrote, "We are convinced that the Indians of Sechelt were not justified in taking action as a Band, to force the recognition of their grievances which might easily have been remedied had the aggrieved parents presented them to the Principal." He admitted that the evidence from the hearing led "us to the belief that friction exists," but he concluded that a few reforms, including providing better food and increased funding, would "remedy in the main any grievances the Indians may have against the conduct of the institution."[143] In this way, episodes of resistance, especially direct actions such as boycotts that challenged the system's legitimacy, could pressure officials to make some key improvements. Such tactics, though, could also tighten the "web of colonialism" or the "settler colonial mesh" by strengthening the resolve of the churches and the DIA to consolidate their power over Indian education.[144] To be clear, this is not to suggest that Indigenous Peoples are somehow responsible for the genocidal schooling imposed on them during the decades that followed. Rather, it highlights the conundrum that many Indigenous Peoples faced – the "Catch-22 of colonialism" – in which their strategic engagement with colonial structures often "further entrenched colonial hegemony."[145] Still, as Frantz Fanon points out, intensifying colonial repression only fuels renewed resistance.[146] Indeed, incidents of truancy at the Sechelt Indian Residential School remained high into the 1940s, and parents regularly kept their children at home, citing rampant abuse and poor conditions until the school was finally shuttered in 1975.

Conclusion

More than twenty years after the inquiry into the death of Duncan Sticks, the hearing at Sechelt yielded similarly unsatisfactory results for shíshálh parents and children. Demands for a better system, articulated in myriad ways by a range of Indigenous and non-Indigenous people throughout the early 1900s, were routinely downplayed or ignored by the DIA and the churches. The department had no intention of abandoning day or residential schools or of radically altering its system of Indian education, even in the face of the many obvious problems. Why? As this chapter shows, church and state officials continued to believe that the system was helping to solve the so-called Indian problem by, if not achieving full assimilation, at least disconnecting Indigenous Peoples from the land and training them to join the workforce. Disrupting Indigenous lifeways through schooling ultimately helped legitimate and perpetuate settler capitalism and Canadian nation building.

In British Columbia, Indian Residential Schools continued to run until 1984, when St. Mary's, one of the first schools to open in the early

1860s, finally closed its doors. Indian Day Schools operated in many parts of the province for another ten years, with the final schools, at Fort Ware, Halfway River, Prophet River, and Takla Lake, closing in 1994. And the ongoing legacies of assimilative education and Indian policy, as Woolford and Stevenson stress, continue to negatively shape the lived experiences of many Indigenous Peoples today.[147]

Conclusion

Between 1849 and 1930, various levels of government oversaw colonization, aided capitalist development, and ultimately helped guide British Columbia's transformation from an underdeveloped British colony into a wealthy province in the Dominion of Canada. Born in 1887, Skwx̱wú7mesh leader and longshore worker Mathias Joseph witnessed the uneven effects of this process for Indigenous Peoples firsthand. In 1913, he commented, "A long time ago, the Indians depended on hunting and fishing as their only means of living. Now things have changed."[1]

The preceding chapters have shown how different kinds of state schooling supported this change by teaching Indigenous and non-Indigenous students, in overt and covert ways, to accept and adapt to British Columbia's emerging capitalist settler society. *Lessons in Legitimacy* has presented the histories of Indigenous and non-Indigenous education together to demonstrate that schooling — as a tool of socialization and legitimation — was essential in helping to build the province. The final product is a narrative of truth telling about schooling and settler capitalism in Canada.

In terms of the book's main lessons, the first is the importance of connecting this history to wider transnational accounts of education and empire. British Columbia may be a province, but its history is not provincial. Government officials drew on examples in Britain and its global empire to devise, deploy, and defend various kinds of schooling, for Indigenous and non-Indigenous people, as a technique of colonial rule.[2] Gunboats, militias, police, and land surveyors played important roles in colonization, but so too did schools as laboratories for learning legitimacy. Colonial officials, missionaries, and teachers travelled out from Britain and its colonies, bringing their ideas and experiences with them, as they sought to shape education in British Columbia. Indian boarding schools were patterned after American manual labour schools for Indigenous Peoples, and government officials drew on ideas from a transimperial network to implement school reforms during the early 1900s. Building on recent scholarly work by Adele Perry, Kristine Alexander, Laura Ishiguro, Erin Millions, and Funké Aladejebi, continuing to situate histories of schooling and settler capitalism in a transnational context will create new paths for comparative research that can grapple with the global connections between education and empire making.[3]

Another key lesson of this book is that colonization is not a one-time invasion, and that stealing, selling, and (re)settling Indigenous territories was not simply a transitional stage in the development of a capitalist economy.[4] Instead, force and fraud need to be understood as permanent features of settler capitalism. Colonial dispossession and capitalist development are dialectically intertwined, deeply enmeshed, and *ongoing* processes that require constant state legitimation through the invention and administration of various structures and techniques of rule, including education.[5] In short, schooling helped to catalyze and legitimize the making of British Columbia. In service of this goal, colonial officials supported education during the 1850s and 1860s, though somewhat reluctantly, in hopes of attracting settlers and safeguarding the colonial project by pacifying Indigenous Peoples with promises of schools. In the 1870s, governments gradually accepted more responsibility for education, as part of their ongoing efforts to fashion workers and socially efficient citizens, whether Indigenous or non-Indigenous. Moreover, settler colonialism helped to pay the bills: the imposition of property taxes on stolen Indigenous land bankrolled the provincial public education system. Similarly, treaty making, the introduction of new taxes and tariffs, and continual land theft by the federal government generated the funds to pay for Indian education. Still, more work is needed to examine the connections between money, taxation, and settler capitalism, following the lead of historians E.A. Heaman, David Tough, Shirley Tillotson, and Brian Gettler, as well as political economists David McNally and Utsa Patnaik and Prabhat Patnaik.[6]

Lessons in Legitimacy makes clear, however, that government control over schooling was neither predetermined nor straightforwardly imposed. Drawing from political economy and building on the work of R.D. Gidney and W.P.J. Millar, it offers a "long view" of the development of state-supported schooling as a struggle and negotiated compromise, not a consensus.[7] Colonial officials promoted colonization by building roads and bridges and establishing police forces and courthouses, but they also grudgingly agreed to assist schooling efforts in limited ways, especially for the labouring classes to appease disgruntled settlers. As more working-class families moved to British Columbia, many parents lobbied the government to fund non-denominational schooling. Unable to afford private schools, they eventually ceded authority over education to the provincial government. At the same time, the federal government, now responsible for Indian education, supported the expansion of missionary schooling for Indigenous Peoples and collaborated with churches to create a genocidal school system. Its goal was to eliminate the so-called Indian problem by delegitimizing Indigenous lifeways and preparing children to join the workforce. Finally, to justify their increased expenditure, both provincial and federal governments assumed even more authority over education while reforming mass, mandatory schooling. In less than a century, schooling in British Columbia shifted from mostly ad hoc and voluntary operations to compulsory state-controlled institutions designed to educate thousands of children, Indigenous and non-Indigenous, in ways that supported ongoing settler capitalism and Canadian nation building. Building on the work of Mary Jane McCallum, Crystal Gail Fraser, and Allyson Stevenson, more work is still needed that connects other kinds of state institutions and assimilative policies – such as tuberculosis hospitals, the child welfare system, and reform schools – to the development and ongoing maintenance of settler capitalism in Canada.[8]

Although the state had effectively taken control of education by the mid-1920s, it is important to emphasize that resistance was ever-present, even if it did not always bring about meaningful change. State power, like colonial hegemony, was totalizing but never totally complete, and ruling by schooling must be seen as a contested phenomenon. In British Columbia, some parents and guardians kept their children at home for various reasons: the school was too far away; they disliked certain teachers; or they needed the children's labour. Once in class, students often chafed against the authoritarianism that teachers were hired to impose. In most cases, the archive subtly records student resistance as "bad behaviour," and in many mission, day, and residential schools for Indigenous children, it can be detected by paying close attention to such behaviour. This could include arriving late, speaking an Indigenous language, running away, and even setting schools ablaze to protest poor conditions and a range of abuses. The stories of resistance presented in this book are reminders that schooling is continually contested and negotiated, even though the terms of engagement are deeply unequal, which was especially the case for Indigenous parents and children. Building on the work of Audra Simpson, I suggest that future researchers might read episodes of resistance as proof that colonial hegemony and legitimacy can simultaneously be learned and challenged in the classroom.[9]

Lessons in Legitimacy also demonstrates the value of unsettling the conventional approach of writing histories of Indigenous and non-Indigenous education independently, as entirely separate fields of study. Although this approach can be useful, it can miss much about the story of schooling and settler capitalism in Canada and contribute to Indigenous erasure. Taking its cue from important work by Jean Barman, Helen Raptis, and Philip Deloria, this book challenges that erasure by showing that the boundaries between Indigenous and non-Indigenous schooling were often broken or blurred in everyday life.[10] Indigenous students consistently attended common and public schools in greater numbers than previously thought, and some settler parents and government officials, provincially and federally, approved and at times even defended this practice. Individuals also frequently moved between differing educational spheres: residential school principals sat on public school boards; their students became teachers in day and residential schools; and public school graduates also taught in day and residential schools. As a case in point, during his career, R.H. Cairns served as a public school teacher, principal of the Coqualeetza Indian Residential School, and then as the DIA's school inspector for British Columbia. Thus, the complexities of colonial education can be brought into sharper focus when the two streams of schooling, for Indigenous and non-Indigenous people, are considered together. As Crystal Gail Fraser and Helen Raptis and members of the Ts'msyan Nation urge, Canadians need to grapple with a more comprehensive history of education to implicate many kinds of schooling, not just residential schooling, in the colonial project.[11]

Finally, though this book focuses on the past, its main findings are relevant to the present. In its final report, the Truth and Reconciliation Commission notes that "history plays an important role in reconciliation; to build for the future, Canadians must look to, and learn from, the past."[12] It adds that "reconciliation is not about 'closing a sad chapter of Canada's past,' but about opening new healing pathways of reconciliation that are forged in truth and justice ... Without truth, justice is not served, healing cannot happen, and there can be no genuine reconciliation."[13] In the same vein, Arthur Manuel, noted Secwepémc leader and residential school Survivor, suggests that if Canadians really want reconciliation they must first prioritize truth telling about the past. He explains, "reconciliation has to pass through truth. And we still have not had enough of that" from Canada as a whole.[14] In short, we must have truth before reconciliation. This book contributes to the process of acknowledging the "complex truth" about schooling and settler capitalism that is the necessary precondition for decolonization and meaningful reconciliation.[15]

Acknowledging the wrongs of the past and working to unsettle Canada and decolonize and dismantle its colonial structures is not an easy task, but there is hope for change. Writing shortly before his death in 2017, Manuel invited all Canadians to join in the work of transforming society: "I think you will find the route is not complicated and the only guide you will need is a sense of justice and decency ... I promise you again that this does not need to be a painful process. It can be a liberation for you as well as for us."[16] British Columbians, and all Canadians, must be courageous enough to unsettle and unlearn their own lessons in legitimacy and commit to what Lee Maracle calls "continued growth and transformation" if they are serious about developing respectful and reciprocal relations with Indigenous Peoples.[17] In heeding the calls of the TRC and Indigenous writers such as Manuel and Maracle, I believe that we all have much to gain from continuing to put truth before reconciliation and learning to work toward justice, decolonization, and our future liberation.

APPENDIX | ONE

Growth of Public Schools

Year	Number of school districts	Aggregate enrolment	Average daily attendance	Percentage of attendance
1877–78	45	2,198	1,395.50	63.49
1882–83	59	2,693	1,383.00	51.36
1887–88	104	6,372	3,093.46	48.54
1892–93	169	11,496	7,111.40	61.85
1897–98	213	17,648	11,055.65	62.64
1902–03	268	24,499	16,357.43	66.76
1907–08	189	33,314	23,195.27	69.62
1912–13	359	57,608	43,274.12	75.12
1917–18	575	67,516	54,746.76	81.09
1922–23	744	94,888	77,752.98	81.94
1927–28	788	108,179	91,760.56	84.82
1928–29	792	109,588	94,410.00	86.17
1929–30	803	111,017	96,196.00	86.65

Source: British Columbia, *Annual Report of the Public Schools*, 1929–30.

APPENDIX | TWO

Growth of Indian Education

Year	Aggregate enrolment	Average daily attendance	Number of day schools	Number of boarding/industrial/ residential schools
1878	648	397	4	4
1883	672	342	10	3
1888	512	259	12	2
1893	786	471	17	9
1898	1,550	954	27	11
1903	1,632	1,097	29	16
1908	2,036	1,261	40	17
1913	2,005	1,265	42	18
1918	2,320	1,463	48	17
1923	2,630	1,760	43 + 1 combined school	16
1928	2,857	1,984	42 + 2 combined schools	16
1929	3,144	2,213	45 + 1 combined school	16
1930	3,291	2,347	46 + 1 combined school	16

Source: DIA Annual Reports, 1878–1930.

APPENDIX | THREE

Indian Day Schools, 1930

School	Agency	Denomination	Aggregate enrolment	Average daily attendance
Fort Babine	Babine	Roman Catholic	35	15
Glen Vowell	Babine	Salvation Army	15	7
Hazelton	Babine	Church of England	39	18
Kispiox	Babine	United Church	33	16
Kitsegukla	Babine	United Church	32	13
Kitwanga	Babine	Church of England	33	9
Robert Déboulé	Babine	Roman Catholic	22	6
Bella Bella	Bella Coola	United Church	42	15
Bella Coola	Bella Coola	United Church	27	14
Kitamaat	Bella Coola	United Church	48	22
Klemtu	Bella Coola	United Church	20	9
Cowichan	Cowichan	Roman Catholic	27	8
Koksilah	Cowichan	United Church	17	8
Nanaimo	Cowichan	United Church	38	17
Songhees	Cowichan	Roman Catholic	13	7
Shulus	Kamloops	Church of England	18	11
Alert Bay	Kwawkewlth	Church of England	27	18
Kingcome Inlet	Kwawkewlth	Church of England	47	16
Fort Rupert	Kwawkewlth	Church of England	16	7
Mamalillikulla	Kwawkewlth	Church of England	23	8
Smith's Inlet	Kwawkewlth	United Church	10	6
Cape Mudge	Kwawkewlth	United Church	27	16
Boothroyd	Lytton	Church of England	17	13
Seabird	Lytton	Roman Catholic	20	15
Seton Lake	Lytton	Roman Catholic	15	8

School	Agency	Denomination	Aggregate enrolment	Average daily attendance
Chehalis	New Westminster	Roman Catholic	14	7
Katzie	New Westminster	Roman Catholic	15	8
Skwah	New Westminster	Roman Catholic	27	22
Okanagan	Okanagan	Roman Catholic	16	10
Osoyoos	Okanagan	Roman Catholic	13	8
Penticton	Okanagan	Roman Catholic	14	7
Masset	Queen Charlotte	Church of England	119	41
Skidegate	Queen Charlotte	United Church	48	29
Gitladamicks	Skeena	Church of England	44	21
Hartley Bay	Skeena	United Church	21	12
Kincolith	Skeena	Church of England	50	21
Kitkatla	Skeena	Church of England	52	26
Kitselas	Skeena	United Church	27	10
Lakalsap	Skeena	Church of England	49	27
Metlakatla	Skeena	Church of England	37	18
Port Essington	Skeena	United Church	27	14
Port Simpson	Skeena	United Church	101	50
Homalco	Vancouver	Roman Catholic	27	10
Sliammon	Vancouver	Roman Catholic	15	8
Squamish	Vancouver	Roman Catholic	34	24
Ucluelet	West Coast	Presbyterian	26	10
Total schools: 46	Total agencies: Babine: 7; Bella Coola: 4; Cowichan: 4; Kamloops: 1; Kwawkewlth: 6; Lytton: 3; New Westminster: 3; Okanagan: 3; Queen Charlotte: 2; Skeena: 9; Vancouver: 3; West Coast: 1	Total churches: Church of England: 14; Roman Catholic: 15; United Church: 15; Presbyterian: 1; Salvation Army: 1	Total enrolment: 1,437 (693 boys, 744 girls)	Total daily attendance: 685 (% of attendance: 47.66)

Source: *DIA Annual Report*, 1930.

APPENDIX | FOUR

Indian Residential Schools, 1930

School	Agency	Denomination	Aggregate enrolment	Average daily attendance
Kitamaat	Bella Coola	United Church	32	23
Kuper Island	Cowichan	Roman Catholic	101	93
Kamloops	Kamloops	Roman Catholic	254	225
Kootenay	Kootenay	Roman Catholic	86	71
Alert Bay	Kwawkewlth	Church of England	145	122
St. George's	Lytton	Church of England	174	154
Coqualeetza	New Westminster	United Church	237	207
St. Mary's Mission	New Westminster	Roman Catholic	133	115
Port Simpson	Skeena	United Church	18	18
Fraser Lake	Stuart Lake	Roman Catholic	170	165
Sechelt	Vancouver	Roman Catholic	86	80
Squamish	Vancouver	Roman Catholic	52	52
Ahousaht	West Coast	United Church	43	42
Alberni	West Coast	United Church	115	104
Christie	West Coast	Roman Catholic	101	95
Cariboo	Williams Lake	Roman Catholic	99	91

Total schools: 16	*Total agencies:* Bella Coola: 1; Cowichan: 1; Kamloops: 1; Kootenay: 1; Kwawkewlth: 1; Lytton: 1; New Westminster: 2; Skeena: 1; Stuart Lake: 1; Vancouver: 2; West Coast: 3; Williams Lake: 1	*Total churches:* Church of England: 2; Roman Catholic: 9; United Church: 5	*Total enrolment:* 1,846 (911 boys; 935 girls)	*Total daily attendance:* 1,657 (% of attendance: 89.76)

Source: DIA Annual Report, 1930.

Notes

PREFACE

1 Albert Memmi, *The Colonizer and the Colonized* (Boston: Beacon, 1965), 89.
2 John S. Milloy, *A National Crime: The Canadian Government and the Residential School System, 1879 to 1986* (Winnipeg: University of Manitoba Press, 1999), xviii (emphasis in original).
3 Aileen Moreton-Robinson, *The White Possessive: Property, Power, and Indigenous Sovereignty* (Minneapolis: University of Minnesota Press, 2015).
4 Milloy, *A National Crime*, xviii.
5 Lee Maracle, *I Am Woman: A Native Perspective on Sociology and Feminism* (Vancouver: Press Gang, 1996), 90.

INTRODUCTION

1 Truth and Reconciliation Commission of Canada, *Honouring the Truth, Reconciling for the Future: Summary of the Final Report of the Truth and Reconciliation Commission of Canada* (Toronto: James Lorimer, 2015), 23.
2 Government of Canada, "House of Commons Debates, 39th Parliament, 2nd Session," *Edited Hansard* 142, 110, June 11, 2008. For more on the Canadian government's 2008 residential school apology, see Audra Simpson, "Whither Settler Colonialism?" *Settler Colonial Studies* 6, 4 (2016): 438–44; and Eva Mackey, "The Apologizer's Apology," in *Reconciling Canada: Critical Perspectives on the Culture of Redress*, ed. Jennifer Henderson and Pauline Wakeham (Toronto: University of Toronto Press, 2013), 47–62.
3 Truth and Reconciliation Commission, *Honouring the Truth*, v. For more on the term "settler," see Emma Battell Lowman and Adam J. Barker, *Settler: Identity and Colonialism in Twenty-First Century Canada* (Winnipeg: Fernwood, 2015), 1–23.
4 Truth and Reconciliation Commission, *Honouring the Truth*, 23. On the IRS system and genocide, see David B. MacDonald, *The Sleeping Giant Awakens: Genocide, Indian Residential Schools, and the Challenge of Conciliation* (Toronto: University of Toronto Press, 2019). For a comparison between the Canadian and American use

of the boarding school as an instrument of genocide, see Andrew Woolford, *This Benevolent Experiment: Indigenous Boarding Schools, Genocide, and Redress in Canada and the United States* (Winnipeg: University of Manitoba Press, 2015). I agree with Woolford that using the term *genocide* in the Canadian context is not "intended to mire us in the past. Nor is it a term intended to lock Indigenous peoples into the role of victims. It is a term, rather, that asks us to think deeply about destructive relations (and not just symbolic relations, but material relations as well) between groups." Woolford, *This Benevolent Experiment*, 298.

5 For more on this subject, see MacDonald, *The Sleeping Giant*, 151–52; and Sean Carleton, "'I Don't Need Any More Education': Senator Lynn Beyak, Residential School Denialism, and Attacks on Truth and Reconciliation in Canada," *Settler Colonial Studies* (June 6, 2021), https://www.tandfonline.com/doi/full/10.1080/2201473X.2021.1935574.

6 Truth and Reconciliation Commission, *Honouring the Truth*, vi. "Reconciliation" is a contested concept. See, for example, Michael Asch, John Borrows, and James Tully, ed., *Resurgence and Reconciliation: Indigenous-Settler Relations and Earth Teachings* (Toronto: University of Toronto Press, 2018). On the importance of "truth telling" in the era of so-called reconciliation, see Paulette Regan, *Unsettling the Settler Within: Indian Residential Schools, Truth Telling, and Reconciliation in Canada* (Vancouver: UBC Press, 2010); and Eva Mackey, *Unsettled Expectations: Uncertainty, Land and Settler Decolonization* (Halifax: Fernwood, 2016). I use "Indigenous Peoples" expansively to refer to people identified as "Indians," "Native peoples," "First Peoples," "Aboriginals," "First Nations," "Inuit," and "Métis" in the historical record. I also use endonyms, the specific names Indigenous Peoples use to refer to themselves (e.g. Secwépemc), instead of anglicized exonyms used by newcomers (e.g. Shuswap) as part of a decolonizing practice. For more on respectful and empowering terminology, see Gregory Younging, *Elements of Indigenous Style: A Guide for Writing by and about Indigenous Peoples* (Edmonton: Brush Education, 2018), 50–73.

7 Murray Sinclair, quoted in Michael Swan, "Reconciliation Barely Getting Started, Says Former Head of Truth and Reconciliation Commission," *Canadian Catholic News*, October 2, 2019, https://grandinmedia.ca/reconciliation-barely-getting-started-says-former-head-of-truth-and-reconciliation-commission/.

8 Potential unmarked graves continue to be located at many former school sites across the country. See Courtney Dickson and Bridgette Watson, "Remains of 215 Children Found Buried at Former B.C. Residential School, First Nation Says," *CBC News*, May 27, 2021, https://www.cbc.ca/news/canada/british-columbia/tk-eml%C3%BAps-te-secw%C3%A9pemc-215-children-former-kamloops-indian-residential-school-1.6043778.

9 Truth and Reconciliation Commission, *Honouring the Truth*, vi.

10 For recent studies of British Columbia's colonial history, see, for example, Daniel Clayton, *Islands of Truth: The Imperial Fashioning of Vancouver Island* (Vancouver: UBC Press, 2000); Adele Perry, *On the Edge of Empire: Gender, Race, and the Making of British Columbia, 1849–1871* (Toronto: University of Toronto Press, 2001); Cole Harris, *Making Native Space: Colonialism, Resistance, and Reserves in British Columbia* (Vancouver: UBC Press, 2002); Ruth Sandwell, *Contesting Rural Space: Land Policy and Practices of Resettlement on Saltspring Island, 1859–1891* (Montreal and Kingston: McGill-Queen's University Press, 2005); John Sutton Lutz, *Makúk: A New History of Aboriginal-White Relations* (Vancouver: UBC Press, 2008); Renisa Mawani, *Colonial Proximities: Crossracial Encounters and Judicial Truths in British Columbia, 1871–1921* (Vancouver: UBC Press, 2009); Keith Thor Carlson, *The Power of Place, the Problem of Time: Aboriginal Identity and Historical Consciousness in the Cauldron of Colonialism* (Toronto: University of Toronto Press, 2010); Adele Perry, *Colonial Relations: The Douglas-Connolly Family and the Nineteenth-Imperial World* (Cambridge: Cambridge University Press, 2015); and Laura Ishiguro, *Nothing to Write Home About: British Family Correspondence and the Settler Colonial Everyday in British Columbia* (Vancouver: UBC Press, 2018).

11 This book focuses on state-supported forms of schooling. Therefore, it does not extensively examine private schools, sometimes called "public" schools in other parts of the former British Empire, as they were not administered directly by the provincial government. In addition, Jean Barman has already covered this topic. She argues that though enrolment in private schooling was small, comprising not more than 3 percent of school-aged children by 1930, this form of education played a key role in reproducing class relations and British elite culture in British Columbia. See Jean Barman, *Growing Up British in British Columbia: Boys in Private Schools* (Vancouver: UBC Press, 1984), 2. The connections between post-secondary schooling and colonialism are similarly outside the scope of my study but need to be acknowledged and further researched, following the lead of Natalie Cross and Thomas Peace, "'My Own Old English Friends': Networking Anglican Settler Colonialism at the Shingwauk Home, Huron College, and Western University," *Historical Studies in Education* 33, 1 (Spring 2021): 22–49.

12 Helen Raptis with members of the Tsimshian Nation, *What We Learned: Two Generations Reflect on Tsimshian Education and the Day Schools* (Vancouver: UBC Press, 2016), 153–54.

13 See Perry, *Colonial Relations*, 15; and Ishiguro, *Nothing to Write*, 19–20.

14 M. Kazim Bacchus, *Education as and for Legitimacy: Developments in West Indian Education between 1846 and 1895* (Waterloo: Wilfrid Laurier University Press, 1994). The literature on schooling in the British Empire is vast. See, for example, J.A. Mangan, ed., *"Benefits Bestowed"? Education and British Imperialism* (Manchester: Manchester University Press, 1988); Linda Tuhiwai Smith, "Kura Kaupapa

Māori and the Implications for Curriculum," in *The School Curriculum in New Zealand: History, Theory, Policy and Practice*, ed. Gary McCulloch (Palmerston North: Dunmore Press, 1992), 26–43; Carmen Whitehead, *Colonial Educators: The British Indian and Colonial Education Service, 1858–1983* (London: I.B. Tauris, 2003); J.M. Barrington, *Separate but Equal? Māori Schools and the Crown, 1867–1969* (Wellington: Victoria University Press, 2008); and Thomas O'Donoghue, "Colonialism, Education, and Social Change in the British Empire: The Cases of Australia, Papua New Guinea and Ireland," *Paedagogica Historica* 45, 6 (2009): 787–800.

15 Memmi, *The Colonizer and the Colonized*, 8, 88–89.
16 Moreton-Robinson, *The White Possessive*, xii.
17 Bruce Curtis, *Ruling by Schooling: Conquest to Liberal Governmentality* (Toronto: University of Toronto Press, 2012).
18 For more on colonial schooling and legitimacy, see Bacchus, *Education as and for Legitimacy*, 305–6. On the concept of a "hidden curriculum," see, for example, Henry Giroux and David Purpel, ed., *The Hidden Curriculum and Moral Education: Deception or Discovery?* (Berkeley: McCutchan, 1983).
19 I use the words "education" and "schooling" interchangeably to avoid repetition, though I acknowledge the difference between them. Education, in a general sense, can be understood as the formal and informal learning embedded in cultures and societies around the globe and across time, whereas mass schooling emerged as a hierarchical kind of learning as a colonizing force during the age of European empires, especially in the nineteenth century. As well, I use "Indian education" to denote the federally funded and church-run scheme for schooling Indigenous Peoples (i.e. Indian Day Schools and Indian Residential Schools) in the nineteenth and twentieth centuries. For more on the difference between education and schooling in relation to Indigenous history, see J.R. Miller, *Shingwauk's Vision: A History of Native Residential Schools* (Toronto: University of Toronto Press, 1996), 16. See also John Willinsky, *Learning to Divide the World: Education at Empire's End* (Minneapolis: University of Minnesota Press, 1998).
20 See, for example, Andrew Porter, ed., *The Imperial Horizons of British Protestant Missions, 1880–1914* (Grand Rapids, MI: Eerdmans, 2003); and Larry Prochner, *History of Early Childhood Education in Canada, Australia, and New Zealand* (Vancouver: UBC Press, 2010).
21 Catherine Hall, "Making Colonial Subjects: Education in the Age of Empire," *History of Education: Journal of the History of Education Society* 37, 6 (2008): 773–87. Hall argues, "Settlers had to become colonisers, had to learn how to define and manage the new world they were encountering. Whether as missionaries, colonial officials, bounty hunters, planters, doctors or military men, they were in the business of creating new societies, wrenching what they had found into something

different ... Europeans made history and made themselves through becoming colonisers." Catherine Hall, *Civilising Subjects: Metropole and Colony in the English Imagination, 1830–1867* (Chicago: University of Chicago Press, 2002), 14.

22 Hall, "Making Colonial Subjects," 774.

23 Eve Tuck and K. Wayne Yang, "Decolonization Is Not a Metaphor," *Decolonization: Indigeneity, Education and Society* 1, 1 (2012): 1.

24 Here I build on Regan's concept of "unsettling," which she describes as the conscious effort of challenging commonsensical or taken-for-granted understandings of Canada's colonial past and present. Regan, *Unsettling the Settler*, 13. See also Arthur Manuel and Ronald M. Derrickson, *Unsettling Canada: A National Wake-Up Call* (Toronto: Between the Lines, 2015), 7–8.

25 R.D. Gidney and W.P.J. Millar, *How Schools Worked: Public Education in English Canada, 1900–1940* (Montreal and Kingston: McGill-Queen's University Press, 2012), 1–11.

26 For more information on the origins of state schooling in British Columbia, see Jean Barman, "Transfer, Imposition, or Consensus? The Emergence of Educational Structures in Nineteenth-Century British Columbia," in *Schools in the West: Essays in Canadian Educational History*, ed. Nancy M. Sheehan, J. Donald Wilson, and David C. Jones (Calgary: Detselig, 1986), 241–64. See also the essays in J. Donald Wilson and David C. Jones, eds., *Schooling and Society in 20th Century British Columbia* (Calgary: Detselig, 1980); and Jean Barman and Mona Gleason, eds., *Children, Teachers and Schools in the History of British Columbia* (Edmonton: Brush Education, 2003). For an important collection of primary sources related to British Columbia's educational past, see Thomas Fleming, ed., *Schooling in British Columbia, 1849–2005: Voices from the Past* (Mill Bay, BC: Bendall Books, 2010).

27 Timothy J. Stanley, *Contesting White Supremacy: School Segregation, Anti-Racism, and the Making of Chinese Canadians* (Vancouver: UBC Press, 2011); Raptis and Tsimshian Nation, *What We Learned*.

28 F. Henry Johnson, *A History of Public Education in British Columbia* (Vancouver: Publications Centre, University of British Columbia, 1964). See also Donald Leslie MacLaurin, "The History of Education in the Crown Colonies of Vancouver Island and British Columbia and in the Province of British Columbia" (PhD diss., University of Washington, 1936).

29 J. Donald Wilson, "Some Observations on Recent Trends in Canadian Educational History," in *An Imperfect Past: Education and Society in Canadian History*, ed. J. Donald Wilson (Vancouver: Centre for the Study of Curriculum and Instruction, University of British Columbia, 1984), 8; and Alison Prentice and Susan Houston, eds., *Family, School, and Society in Nineteenth-Century Canada* (Toronto: Oxford University Press, 1975), 4. See also Alison Prentice, *The School Promoters: Education*

and *Social Class in Mid-Nineteenth Century Upper Canada* (Toronto: McClelland and Stewart, 1977), 13–14.

30 See Paul Axelrod, *The Promise of Schooling: Education in Canada, 1800–1914* (Toronto: University of Toronto Press, 1997); Mona Gleason, *Normalizing the Ideal: Psychology, Schooling, and the Family in Postwar Canada* (Toronto: University of Toronto Press, 1999); Amy von Heyking, *Creating Citizens: History and Identity in Alberta Schools, 1905–1980* (Calgary: University of Calgary Press, 2006); Curtis, *Ruling by Schooling*; Jason Ellis, *A Class by Themselves? The Origins of Special Education in Toronto and Beyond* (Toronto: University of Toronto Press, 2019); and Funké Aladejebi, *Schooling the System: A History of Black Women Teachers* (Montreal and Kingston: McGill-Queen's University Press, 2021).

31 See, for example, Elizabeth Furniss, *Victims of Benevolence: The Dark Legacy of the Williams Lake Residential School* (Vancouver: Arsenal, 1995); Miller, *Shingwauk's Vision*; and Milloy, *A National Crime*. For more recent treatments, see Jan Hare and Jean Barman, *Good Intentions Gone Awry: Emma Crosby and the Methodist Mission on the Northwest Coast* (Vancouver: UBC Press, 2006); Janice Forsyth, "Bodies of Meaning: Sports and Games at Canadian Residential Schools," in *Aboriginal Peoples and Sport in Canada: Historical Foundations and Contemporary Issues*, ed. Janice Forsyth and Audrey R. Giles (Vancouver: UBC Press, 2012), 15–34; Ian Mosby, "Administering Colonial Science: Nutrition Research and Human Biomedical Experimentation in Aboriginal Communities and Residential Schools, 1942–1954," *Histoire sociale/Social History* 46, 91 (May 2013): 145–72; Allan Downey, *The Creator's Game: Lacrosse, Identity, and Indigenous Nationhood* (Vancouver: UBC Press, 2018), 85–117; Jane Griffith, *Words Have a Past: The English Language, Colonialism, and the Newspapers of Indian Boarding Schools* (Toronto: University of Toronto Press, 2019); Crystal Gail Fraser, "T'aih k'ìighe' tth'aih zhit dìidìch'ùh (By Strength, We Are Still Here): Indigenous Northerners Confronting Hierarchies of Power at Day and Residential Schools in Nanhkak Thak (the Inuvik Region, Northwest Territories), 1959 to 1982" (PhD diss., University of Alberta, 2019); Braden Te Hiwi, "'A Lack of Homelike Surroundings': Resident Health, Home, and Recreation Infrastructure at Pelican Lake Indian Residential School, 1952–1962," *Histoire sociale/Social History* 54, 110 (2021): 99–125; and Survivors of the Assiniboia Indian Residential School, *Did You See Us? Reunion, Remembrance, and Reclamation at an Urban Indian Residential School* (Winnipeg: University of Manitoba Press, 2021).

32 Fraser, "T'aih k'ìighe' tth'aih zhit dìidìch'ùh (By Strength, We Are Still Here)." Notable exceptions include Jacqueline Gresko, "Creating Little Dominions within the Dominion: Early Catholic Indian Schools in Saskatchewan and British Columbia," in *Indian Education in Canada*, vol. 1, *The Legacy*, ed. Jean Barman, Yvonne

Hébert, and Don McCaskill 88–111; W.D. Hamilton, *The Federal Indian Day Schools of the Maritimes* (Fredericton: Micmac-Maliseet Institute, 1986); Furniss, *Victims of Benevolence;* and Raptis and Tsimshian Nation, *What We Learned*.

33 For examples of national studies, see Miller, *Shingwauk's Vision;* and Milloy, *A National Crime*. For case studies of residential schools in British Columbia, see Furniss, *Victims of Benevolence;* and Hare and Barman, *Good Intentions Gone Awry*.

34 Exceptions include Jean Barman, "Separate and Unequal: Indian and White Girls at All Hallows School, 1884–1920," in Barman and Gleason, *Children, Teachers and Schools*, 283–302; Joan Sangster, "Domesticating Girls: The Sexual Regulation of Aboriginal and Working-Class Girls in Twentieth-Century Canada," in *Contact Zones: Aboriginal and Settler Women in Canada's Colonial Past*, ed. Katie Pickles and Myra Rutherdale (Vancouver: UBC Press, 2005), 179–201; Helen Raptis, "Exploring the Factors Prompting British Columbia's First Integration Initiative: The Case of Port Essington Indian Day School," *History of Education Quarterly* 51, 4 (Fall 2011): 519–43; Eve Chapple and Helen Raptis, "From Integration to Segregation: Government Education Policy and the School at Telegraph Creek in British Columbia, 1906–1951," *Journal of the Canadian Historical Association* 24, 1 (2013): 131–62; and Helen Raptis, "Blurring the Boundaries of Policy and Legislation in the Schooling of Indigenous Children in British Columbia, 1901–1951," *Historical Studies in Education* 27, 2 (Fall 2015): 65–77.

35 Mary Louise Pratt, "Arts of the Contact Zone," *Profession* 91 (1991): 34. Pratt expands on the concept, describing contact zones as "the space of colonial encounters, the space in which peoples geographically and historically separated come into contact with each other and establish ongoing relations, usually involving conditions of coercion, radical inequality, and intractable conflicts." Mary Louise Pratt, *Imperial Eyes: Travel Writing and Transculturation* (London: Routledge, 1992), 6.

36 E.P. Thompson, *Whigs and Hunters: The Origins of the Black Act* (London: Breviary Stuff, 1975), xi.

37 Moreton-Robinson, *The White Possessive;* and Gina Starblanket and Dallas Hunt, *Storying Violence: Unravelling Colonial Narratives in the Stanley Trial* (Winnipeg: ARP Books, 2020), 24. I use "colonialism" and "settler colonialism" interchangeably to avoid repetition, though I acknowledge the distinction that scholars have made between them. See, for example, Starblanket and Hunt, *Storying Violence;* Patrick Wolfe, *Settler Colonialism and the Transforming of Anthropology: The Politics and Poetics of an Ethnographic Event* (London: Cassell, 1999); and Lorenzo Veracini, *Settler Colonialism: A Theoretical Overview* (London: Palgrave Macmillan, 2010).

38 Patrick Wolfe, "Settler Colonialism and the Elimination of the Native," *Journal of Genocide Research* 8, 4 (December 2006): 388; and Nick Estes, *Our History Is the*

Future: Standing Rock versus the Dakota Access Pipeline, and the Long Tradition of Indigenous Resistance (London: Verso, 2019), 28.
39 Wolfe, "Settler Colonialism," 388.
40 Arthur Manuel, *The Reconciliation Manifesto: Recovering the Land, Rebuilding the Economy* (Toronto: Lorimer, 2017), 67.
41 John Douglas Belshaw, *Becoming British Columbia: A Population History* (Vancouver: UBC Press, 2009), 187; and Allan Greer, "Commons and Enclosure in the Colonization of North America," *The American Historical Review* 117, 2 (April 2012): 365–86.
42 Glen Sean Coulthard, *Red Skin, White Masks: Rejecting the Colonial Politics of Recognition* (Minneapolis: University of Minnesota Press, 2014), 13. See also Leanne Betasamosake Simpson, *Dancing on Our Turtle's Back: Stories of Nishnaabeg Re-Creation, Resurgence and a New Emergence* (Winnipeg: Arbeiter Ring, 2011); and Leanne Betasamosake Simpson, *As We Have Always Done: Indigenous Freedom through Radical Resistance* (Minneapolis: University of Minnesota Press, 2017).
43 Manuel and Derrickson, *Unsettling Canada*, 7–8. See J. Kēhaulani Kauanui, "'A Structure, Not an Event': Settler Colonialism and Enduring Indigeneity," *Lateral: Journal of the Cultural Studies Association* 5, 1 (Spring 2016); and Sarah Nickel, *Assembling Unity: Indigenous Politics, Gender, and the Union of BC Indian Chiefs* (Vancouver: UBC Press, 2019).
44 Wolfe, "Settler Colonialism," 388.
45 Heidi Stark, "Criminal Empire: The Making of the Savage in a Lawless Land," *Theory and Event* 19, 4 (2016), 8 (emphasis added).
46 Moreton-Robinson, *The White Possessive*, xi–xii.
47 Cole Harris, "How Did Colonialism Dispossess? Comments from an Edge of Empire," *Annals of the Association of American Geographers* 94, 1 (2004): 165–82; and Moreton-Robinson, *The White Possessive*. For more on colonization and the origins of capitalism, see Ellen Meiksins Wood, *The Origin of Capitalism: A Longer View* (London: Verso, 2002), 36.
48 Coulthard, *Red Skin*, 125.
49 See, for example, ibid., 6–15; Simpson, "Whither Settler Colonialism?" 440; Simpson, *As We Have Always Done*, 55–82; Estes, *Our History*; and Starblanket and Hunt, *Storying Violence*, 41. For an overview of the connections between colonialism and capitalism in Canada, see Howard Adams, *A Prison of Grass: Canada from the Native Point of View* (Toronto: New Press, 1975); and Terry Wotherspoon and Vic Satzewich, *First Nations: Race, Class, and Gender Relations* (Regina: Canadian Plains Research Centre, 2000), 18–28.
50 See Coulthard, *Red Skin*, 11; and Robert Nichols, "Disaggregating Primitive Accumulation," *Radical Philosophy* 194 (November/December 2015): 18–28.

51 Coulthard, *Red Skin*, 7. For more on these practices, see Harris, *Making Native Space;* Sandwell, *Contesting Rural Space;* and Peter Cook et al., eds., *To Share, Not Surrender: Indigenous and Settler Visions of Treaty Making in the Colonies of Vancouver Island and British Columbia* (Vancouver: UBC Press, 2021).

52 On land pre-emption and the creation of Indian reserves, see Harris, *Making Native Space*. Regarding dispossession and pauperization, I am building on Bryan D. Palmer and Gaétan Héroux, "'Cracking the Stone': The Long History of Capitalist Crisis and Toronto's Dispossessed, 1830–1930," *Labour/Le travail* 69 (Spring 2012): 9–62. Palmer and Héroux make clear that capitalist development is dependent on destructiveness and that dispossession, broadly understood, takes on many different forms and is characterized by successive waves of coercion and expropriation required to fuel ongoing accumulation.

53 In terms of primitive accumulation, dispossession, and the regulation of women's bodies, I draw on Silvia Federici, *Caliban and the Witch: Women, the Body and Primitive Accumulation* (New York: Autonomedia, 2004); and Simpson, *As We Have Always Done*, 54. On gender and colonialism in British Columbia, see Jean Barman, "Taming Aboriginal Sexuality: Gender, Power, and Race in British Columbia, 1850–1900," *BC Studies* 115–16 (Autumn-Winter 1997–98): 237–66. On taxes, money, and the creation of private property, see E.A. Heaman, *Tax, Order, and Good Government: A New Political History of Canada, 1867–1917* (Montreal and Kingston: McGill-Queen's University Press, 2017); Brian Gettler, *Colonialism's Currency: Money, State, and First Nations in Canada, 1820–1950* (Montreal and Kingston: McGill-Queen's University Press, 2020); and Daniel Rück, *The Laws and the Land: The Settler Colonial Invasion of Kahnawà:ke in Nineteenth-Century Canada* (Vancouver: UBC Press, 2021). Regarding schooling and class in British Columbia, see Jean Barman, "'Knowledge Is Essential for Universal Progress but Fatal to Class Privilege': Working People and the Schools in Vancouver during the 1920s," *Labour/Le travail* 22 (Fall 1988): 9–66.

54 David Harvey, *A Brief History of Neoliberalism* (New York: Oxford University Press, 2005), 159. Though "accumulation by dispossession" is Harvey's phrase, positioning so-called primitive accumulation as a permanent force is evident in earlier works. See, for example, Karl Marx, *Capital*, vol. 1, *A Critique of Political Economy* (New York: Vintage, 1977), 873–940; and Rosa Luxemburg, *The Accumulation of Capital* (London: Routledge, 2003). On the origins of capitalism, see Maurice Dobb, *Studies in the Development of Capitalism* (New York: Taylor and Francis, 1963); Bryan D. Palmer, "Social Formation and Class Formation in Nineteenth-Century North America," in *Proletarianization and Family History*, ed. David Levine (New York: Academic Press, 1984), 229–308; Wood, *The Origin of Capitalism;* Michael Perelman, *The Invention of Capitalism: Classical Political Economy and the Secret History of Primitive Accumulation* (Durham, NC: Duke

University Press, 2000); Allan Greer, *Property and Dispossession: Natives, Empires and Land in Early Modern North America* (Cambridge: Cambridge University Press, 2018); David McNally, *Blood and Money: War, Slavery, Finance, and Empire* Winnipeg: Fernwood, 2020); Tyler Shipley, *Canada in the World: Settler Capitalism and the Colonial Imaginary* (Winnipeg: Fernwood, 2020); and Utsa Patnaik and Prabhat Patnaik, *Capital and Imperialism: Theory, History, and the Present* (New York: Monthly Review, 2021).

55 See Wallace Clement and Glen Williams, eds., *The New Canadian Political Economy* (Montreal and Kingston: McGill-Queen's University Press, 1989); Wallace Clement, ed., *Understanding Canada: Building on the New Canadian Political Economy* (Montreal and Kingston: McGill-Queen's University Press, 1997); Wallace Clement and Leah F. Vosko, eds., *Changing Canada: Political Economy as Transformation* (Montreal and Kingston: McGill-Queen's University Press, 2003); Mark P. Thomas et al., eds., *Change and Continuity: Canadian Political Economy in the New Millennium* (Montreal and Kingston: McGill-Queen's University Press, 2019); and Heather Whiteside, ed., *Canadian Political Economy* (Toronto: University of Toronto Press, 2020).

56 Adele Perry, "The State of Empire: Reproducing Colonialism in British Columbia, 1849–1871," *Journal of Colonialism and Colonial History* 2, 2 (Fall 2001).

57 On the complications of Canadian federalism, see Garth Stevenson, *Unfulfilled Union: Canadian Federalism and National Unity* (Montreal and Kingston: McGill-Queen's University Press, 2009).

58 See E.A. Heaman, *A Short History of the State in Canada* (Toronto: University of Toronto Press, 2015). The best collection of writings on the state and British Columbia remains Rennie Warburton and David Coburn, eds., *Workers, Capital, and the State in British Columbia: Selected Papers* (Vancouver: UBC Press, 1988). On the importance of studying state structures, see Thomas et al., *Change and Continuity*, 13–14; Wotherspoon and Satzewich, *First Nations*, 18; and Leo Panitch, ed., *The Canadian State: Political Economy and Political Power* (Toronto: University of Toronto Press, 1977). For a historical overview of federalism and "the state" in Canada, see Michael Howlett, Alex Netherton, and M. Ramesh, *The Political Economy of Canada: An Introduction* (Don Mills, ON: Oxford University Press, 1999), 157–205.

59 Leo Panitch, "The Role and Nature of the Canadian State," in Panitch, *The Canadian State*, 4 and 8.

60 See Ralph Miliband, *The State in Capitalist Society* (London: Weidenfeld and Nicolson, 2009), 36. See also Stanley, *Contesting White Supremacy*, 11.

61 Antonio Gramsci, *Selections from the Prison Notebooks* (New York: International Publishers, 1971), 247 and 350.

62 Terry Wotherspoon, "Introduction: Conflict and Crisis in Canadian Education," in *The Political Economy of Canadian Schooling*, ed. Terry Wotherspoon (Toronto:

Methuen, 1987), 1; M. Patricia Connelly and Pat Armstrong, "Feminist Political Economy: An Introduction," *Studies in Political Economy* 30 (Fall 1989): 5–12; and Thomas et al., *Change and Continuity*, 3–5. I am also building on E.P. Thompson's dual view of "the law" in *Whigs and Hunters*, 202–10.

63 Wotherspoon, "Introduction," 2.

64 On the importance of archives to Indigenous histories, see Mary Jane Logan McCallum's foreword in John S. Milloy, *A National Crime: The Canadian Government and the Residential School System* (Winnipeg: University of Manitoba Press. 2017), xxii–xxvii.

65 Crystal Gail Fraser and Allyson Stevenson, "Reflecting on the Foundations of Our Discipline Inspired by the TRC: A Duty to Respond during This Age of Reconciliation," *Canadian Historical Review* 103, 1 (March 2022): 1–31. The phrase "continuing beneficiaries" is from Harris, *Making Native Space*, xxxi. The editors of the 1997–98 special edition of *BC Studies* elaborate on this point: "we should not forget that British Columbia has been, and largely remains, a highly successful colonial society, one that has been invisible to most people who live here. For most of us, colonialism happened elsewhere, and the recognition of it here, and of ourselves as its agents, suddenly qualifies our fulsome accounts of progress and development of an immigrant society while connecting us with a much less comfortable past." "Editorial," *BC Studies* 115–16 (Autumn-Winter 1997–98): 4.

66 Adam Gaudry, "Insurgent Research," *Wicazo Sa Review* 26, 1 (Spring 2011): 113–14.

67 Mary-Ellen Kelm and Keith D. Smith, eds., *Talking Back to the Indian Act: Critical Readings in Settler Colonial Histories* (Toronto: University of Toronto Press, 2018), 23–25.

68 Linda Tuhiwai Smith, *Decolonizing Methodologies: Research and Indigenous Peoples* (London: Bloomsbury Academic & Professional, 2021), 38 (emphasis in original).

69 Smith, *Decolonizing Methodologies*, 150.

70 See Ann Laura Stoler, *Along the Archival Grain: Epistemic Anxieties and Colonial Common Sense* (Princeton: University of Princeton Press, 2009); Thomas Richards, *Imperial Archive: Knowledge and the Fantasy of Empire* (New York: Verso, 1996); and Antoinette Burton, ed., *Archive Stories: Facts, Fictions, and the Writing of History* (Durham, NC: Duke University Press, 2004).

71 Stoler, *Along the Archival Grain*, 22.

72 See Perry, *Colonial Relations*, 1; Nickel, *Assembling Unity*, 8; and Lutz, *Makúk*, 42.

73 Drawing on the work of Stoler, Kelm and Smith contend that "historians do more than simply read sources; we converse with them. We listen intently to the stories they tell and the silences they allow. We think deeply about the conversations and interchanges that brought our sources into being – the questions and anxieties, the common sense assumptions, the motives of authors and audiences. We ask questions not so much to call our sources out as false or falsifying but rather to lay bare

the remnants of the past embedded within them. We ask our sources to speak to us, from the context of their times, and we talk back to them from the context of our own." See Kelm and Smith, *Talking Back*, 1; and Mary Jane Logan McCallum and Adele Perry, *Structures of Indifference: An Indigenous Life and Death in a Canadian City* (Winnipeg: University of Manitoba Press, 2018), 4–5.

74 Kelm and Smith, *Talking Back*, 23–31. See, for example, Simon Baker, *Khot-La-Cha: The Autobiography of Chief Simon Baker*, edited by Verna J. Kirkness (Vancouver: Douglas and McIntyre, 1994); Bev Sellars, *They Called Me Number One: Secrets and Survival, at an Indian Residential School* (Vancouver: Talonbooks, 2013); and Phyllis Webstad, *Beyond the Orange Shirt Story* (Victoria: Medicine Wheel Education, 2021).

75 Smith, *Decolonizing Methodologies*, 154–55.

76 Gidney and Millar, *How Schools Worked*, xix.

77 Kiera Ladner, "Proceed with Caution: Reflections on Resurgence and Reconciliation," in Asch, Borrows, and Tully, 247.

78 Edward Said uses a contrapuntal perspective to grapple with "intertwined and overlapping histories." Edward Said, *Culture and Imperialism* (New York: Vintage, 1993), 18. I am also inspired by E.P. Thompson's parallel structure in *Whigs and Hunters*. Thompson presents patrician-plebeian relations in eighteenth-century England as a totality but traces the development and perspective of each social grouping separately.

79 Colonization is a continuing process, but the "colonial period" is commonly used to refer to the time between 1849 and 1871, before the Colony of British Columbia joined Canada.

80 Audra Simpson, *Mohawk Interruptus: Political Life across the Borders of Settler States* (Durham, NC: Duke University Press, 2014), 11.

81 Gidney and Millar argue, "We think that the two decades between 1900 and 1920 are best understood as the apogee of a system constructed by the mid-Victorians; despite some modifications after that, the main lineaments remained in place until the 1940s." Gidney and Millar, *How Schools Worked*, xx.

82 Manuel, *The Reconciliation Manifesto*, 56.

83 Murray Sinclair, quoted in Haydn Watters, "Truth and Reconciliation Chair Urges Canada to Adopt UN Declaration on Indigenous Peoples," *CBC News*, June 1, 2015, https://www.cbc.ca/news/politics/truth-and-reconciliation-chair-urges-canada-to-adopt-un-declaration-on-indigenous-peoples-1.3096225.

Part One | COLONIAL ORIGINS, 1849–71

1 On imperial disputes and early Indigenous-newcomer relations in the area, see Clayton, *Islands of Truth;* Jean Barman, *French Canadians, Furs, and Indigenous*

Women (Vancouver: UBC Press, 2014); and Manuel and Derrickson, *Unsettling Canada*, 4–8.
2 On the global connections between colonialism and capitalism, see Wood, *The Origin of Capitalism;* Eric Hobsbawm, *The Age of Capital, 1848–1875* (New York: Vintage Books, 1975); and Patnaik and Patnaik, *Capital and Imperialism.*
3 For more on the development of politics in British Columbia, see Robert A.J. McDonald, *A Long Way to Paradise: A New History of British Columbia Politics* (Vancouver: UBC Press, 2021).
4 Rennie Warburton and Stephen Scott, "The Fur Trade and Early Capitalist Development in British Columbia," *Canadian Journal of Native Studies* 5 (Winter 1985): 28.
5 On the various responses of Indigenous Peoples to settler colonialism in British Columbia, see Lutz, *Makúk;* and Sellars, *They Called Me*, 3–21.
6 See Kiran Van Rijn, "'Lo! the Poor Indian': Colonial Responses to the 1862–63 Smallpox Epidemic in British Columbia and Vancouver Island," *Canadian Bulletin of Medical History* 23, 2 (2006): 541–60.
7 Ned Blackhawk, *Violence over the Land: Indians and Empires in the Early American West* (Cambridge: Harvard University Press, 2006), 148–49.

Chapter One | CREATING COMMON SCHOOLS

1 James Edward FitzGerald to Benjamin Hawes, June 9, 1847, National Archives (NA), Colonial Office (CO) 305/1, 474. For more on FitzGerald, see Jenifer Roberts, *Fitz: The Colonial Adventures of James Edward FitzGerald* (Otago: University of Otago Press, 2016).
2 The strategic value of the Pacific and the role of what Daniel Baugh calls "protective maritime imperialism" in building the British Empire had been debated since the 1770s. See Daniel A. Baugh, "Seapower and Science: The Motives for Pacific Exploration," in *Background to Discovery: Pacific Exploration from Dampier to Cook*, ed. Derek Howse (Berkeley: University of California Press, 1999), 34. Clayton contends that Britain's interest in the Pacific, primarily for commercial reasons, exemplified a "ledger-book imperial mentality." Clayton, *Islands of Truth*, 176.
3 FitzGerald to Hawes, June 9, 1847, NA, CO 305/1, 495.
4 Wolfe, "Settler Colonialism," 388.
5 For more on schooling's role in training colonists, see Hall, "Making Colonial Subjects," 773–87.
6 FitzGerald's objection to company rule was possibly connected to popular critiques of the East India Company's pillaging of India, which, in part, led to resistance movements in the colony. For more, see Priyamvada Gopal, *Insurgent Empire: Anticolonial Resistance and British Dissent* (London: Verso, 2020), 41–82; and

William Dalrymple, *The Anarchy: The East India Company, Corporate Violence, and the Pillage of an Empire* (London: Bloomsbury, 2019).
7 James Edward FitzGerald, *An Examination of the Charter and Proceedings of the Hudson's Bay Company, with References to the Grant of Vancouver Island* (London: Trelawney Saunders, 1849).
8 Perry notes, "Mid-nineteenth-century British Columbia hung precariously at the edge of Britain's literal and symbolic empire." Perry, *On the Edge of Empire*, 3.
9 Wotherspoon, "Introduction," 1, 3. I also draw inspiration from Thompson's critique of the emphasis on consensus over negotiation and struggle. See Thompson, *Whigs and Hunters*, 204–5. Building on Wotherspoon and Thompson, my argument departs from historian Jean Barman's interpretation, influenced by the work of Neil Sutherland, which champions the changes to common schooling as an educational "consensus." Barman is correct to suggest that school structures were not simply imported from central Canada and imposed on local settings but rather emerged from and responded to local needs and interests. Her analysis, however, downplays the key role played by colonial officials in gradually supporting schooling, and eventually agreeing to pay more for it, as a strategic compromise to assume greater power over education to further colonization and support economic development. In this chapter, then, I do not present schooling straightforwardly as either a top-down project or a bottom-up, family-driven initiative, but rather as a negotiated compromise between officials and colonists that ultimately supported colonial social formation. See Jean Barman, "The Emergence of Educational Structures in Nineteenth-Century British Columbia," in Barman and Gleason, *Children, Teachers and Schools*, 13–35; and Neil Sutherland, *Children in English-Canadian Society: Framing the Twentieth-Century Consensus* (Toronto: University of Toronto Press, 1976).
10 See Juliet Pollard, "Growing Up Métis: Fur Traders' Children in the Pacific Northwest," in *An Imperfect Past: Education and Society in Canadian History*, ed. J. Donald Wilson (Vancouver: Centre for the Study of Curriculum and Instruction, University of British Columbia, 1984), 120–40. Pollard points out that four of the first five students to attend the school at Fort Vancouver were recognized as "half-breeds."
11 Alex Colvile to Sir John Pakington, December 1, 1852, NA, CO 305/3, 477.
12 Roderick Finlayson, quoted in Alexander Begg, *History of British Columbia: From Its Earliest Discovery to the Present Time* (Toronto: William Briggs, 1972, originally published 1894). For more on white women, social class, and colonialism in British Columbia, see Perry, *On the Edge of Empire*, 139–93.
13 Perry talks specifically about Emma's negotiation of social status in relation to elite Indigenous women who lived at the fort, including Amelia Connolly Douglas. See Perry, *Colonial Relations*, 133–35.
14 Johnson, *A History of Public Education*, 16.

15 Barman notes, "education was perceived as having two prime functions: preparation to maintain existing place within the social order, and inculcation of denominational religious beliefs." Barman, "The Emergence of Educational Structures," 14.
16 See Perry, *On the Edge of Empire;* and Sarah Carter, *The Importance of Being Monogamous: Marriage and Nation Building in Western Canada to 1915* (Edmonton: Athabaska University Press, 2008).
17 Estes, *Our History*, 81.
18 J.R. Anderson, "Notes and Comments on Early Days and Events in British Columbia, Washington and Oregon Including an Account of Sundry Happenings in San Francisco; Being the Memoirs of James Robert Anderson Written by Himself," British Columbia Archives (BCA), MS 1912, box 9, file 1, 160.
19 J.R. Anderson, quoted in Fleming, *Schooling in British Columbia*, 31.
20 James Douglas to A.C. Anderson, 28 October, 1850, quoted in Donald Leslie MacLaurin, "Education before the Gold Rush," *British Columbia Historical Quarterly* 2, 4 (October 1938): 247.
21 John Sebastian Helmcken, *The Reminiscences of Doctor John Sebastian Helmcken*, edited by Dorothy Blakey Smith (Vancouver: UBC Press, 1975), 114–16, 293. On the "thick mutual histories" shared by elite Métis families in the region, see Perry, *Colonial Relations*, 151–52.
22 Although the policy changed over time, the HBC – adhering to Wakefieldian theory – fixed the price of land in the Vancouver Island colony at £1 per acre and required every purchaser to acquire at least twenty acres. This had the effect of driving many colonists into the local labour pool, but it also drove others to go elsewhere, such as California (which charged only $1 per acre). In showing how Wakefield's theory of colonization, popular with people such as Douglas, helped birth capitalism in British settler colonies, Marx clarified the process: "set an artificial price on the virgin soil, a price independent of the law of supply and demand, a price that compels the immigrant to work a long time for wages before he can earn enough money to buy land and turn himself into an independent farmer." Marx, *Capital*, vol. 1, 938.
23 Douglas would later write, "Mr. Staines unfortunately for himself was a violent party man, and was prudent neither in his conduct nor associations." Douglas to Sir George Grey, December 11, 1854, NA, CO 305/5, 134–35. It is difficult to discern whether the attacks on Staines's teaching were warranted or whether he was purged for his political opposition. Regardless, historian Hollis Slater suggests that, in the end, "pioneer priest, pedagogue, and political agitator" is the label best suited for Staines. See G. Hollis Slater, "Rev. Robert John Staines: Pioneer Priest, Pedagogue, and Political Agitator," *British Columbia Historical Quarterly* 14 (1950): 187–240.
24 Barman, *Growing Up British*, 6. On early religious private schools such as St. Ann's, see Vincent McNally, "Challenging the Status Quo: An Examination of the History

of Catholic Education in British Columbia," *CCHA, Historical Studies* 65 (1999): 74–76.
25 Douglas to Archibald Barclay, October 8, 1851, quoted in J. Forsyth, "Early Colonial Schools on Vancouver Island," *Times,* March 14, 1922, Part 1, BCA, GR 2055, Victoria School District, file 1, newspaper clippings, 113.
26 Douglas to Barclay, May 16, 1850, quoted in MacLaurin, "Education before the Gold Rush," 248.
27 Douglas to Barclay, October 8, 1851, quoted in Forsyth, "Early Colonial Schools," *Times,* March 14, 1922, Part 1, BCA, GR 2055, Victoria School District, file 1, newspaper clippings, 113.
28 Philip Corrigan, Bruce Curtis, and Robert Lanning, "The Political Space of Schooling," in Wotherspoon, *The Political Economy,* 23.
29 Charles E. Phillips, *The Development of Education in Canada* (Toronto: W.J. Gage, 1957), 40–41.
30 Douglas to Barclay, October 8, 1851, quoted in Forsyth, "Early Colonial Schools," *Times,* March 14, 1922, Part 1, BCA, GR-2055, Victoria School District, file 1, newspaper clippings, 113.
31 Douglas to Duke of Newcastle, October 24, 1853, NA, CO 305/4, 92.
32 Iroquois labourers, who travelled west to participate in the fur trade, helped build the mining operations at Nanaimo. They also sent their children to early schools on Vancouver Island and in British Columbia. See Jean Barman, *Iroquois in the West* (Montreal and Kingston: McGill-Queen's University Press, 2019), 132–35.
33 Unlike the mercantilist capitalism of the fur trade, industrial capitalism is a system whereby wage labourers produce commodities for capitalists who own the means of production. The key difference, as Warburton and Scott argue, is the way in which each form acquires surplus value. Using British Columbia as a case study, they write, "Industrial capital creates and retains its own surplus in the production process as wage labourers produce more new value in the form of commodities than they consume in wage goods. Merchant capital acquires surplus in the circulation process by means of exchange of commodities ... The merchant buys commodities not for his own use but in order to sell them again. His goal is to increase his monetary wealth through a process of unequal exchange." Warburton and Scott, "The Fur Trade," 28. See also Starblanket and Hunt, *Storying Violence,* 41.
34 John Douglas Belshaw, *Colonization and Community: The Vancouver Island Coalfield and the Making of a British Columbian Working Class* (Montreal and Kingston: McGill-Queen's University Press, 2002), 194.
35 Belshaw also contends that schooling did not serve the interests of the mining community. He suggests, "boys on Vancouver Island had a role to play in the labour market that was more remunerative than education ... Opportunities for

employment in the mines and in related industries (such as pit-prop making, freighting, work along the docks, and so on) remained a potent lure away from the classroom." Thus, the enrolment of both boys and girls was sparse in common and public schools in the Vancouver Island coalfields. Ibid., 193–97.

36 Thomas Russell, quoted in Fleming, *Schooling in British Columbia*, 37.

37 Thomas Fleming, "In the Imperial Age and After: Patterns of British Columbia School Leadership and the Institution of the Superintendency, 1849–1988," *BC Studies* 81 (Spring 1989): 52.

38 On the emerging political culture during this period, see McDonald, *A Long Way to Paradise*, 15–18. Joan Sangster explains the results of the first election, which excluded Indigenous Peoples: "Forty white men participated (including absentee landlords, who could vote through an agent), producing an assembly with seven representatives. However absurd this exercise seemed, it spelled the future: cheap land and voting rights for white male settlers (though initially excluding the rough-and-tumble transient gold miners) were intended to ensure a white-dominated settlement geared toward the economic development of land and resources." Joan Sangster, *One Hundred Years of Struggle: The History of Women and the Vote in Canada* (Vancouver: UBC Press, 2018), 17.

39 For more on the importance of educational inspectors and state formation, see Thomas Fleming, "'Our Boys in the Field': School Inspectors, Superintendents, and the Changing Character of School Leadership in British Columbia," in Sheehan, Wilson, and Jones, *Schools in the West*, 285–303; and Bruce Curtis, *True Government by Choice Men? Inspection, Education, and State Formation in Canada West* (Toronto: University of Toronto Press, 1992). Curtis contends that "educational inspection played a central role in the formation of new state structures capable of connecting central authorities and local agencies, and educational practice, both as ideology and as administration, was fundamental to the existence of representative government. Educational inspectors ... were placed to promote and, at times, to enforce their cultural conceptions, their moral standards, their sense of justice, and their aesthetic sense as models for the rest of society. Tendencies towards educational standardization embodied their standards." Curtis, *True Government?*, 7.

40 In 1856, and with the assistance of his wife and sister, Cridge also established a private boarding school for elite girls. As Johnson notes, this put him "in the anomalous position of being superintendent of public schools while operating a rival private school." Johnson, *A History of Public Education*, 21.

41 Cridge's report included in Douglas to Newcastle, January 27, 1860, NA, CO 305/14, 46–48.

42 Ibid.

43 Edgar Fawcett, *Some Reminiscences of Old Victoria* (Toronto: William Briggs, 1912), 28, 32.

44 See Philip S. Foner, "The Colored Inhabitants of Vancouver Island," *BC Studies* 8 (Winter 1970–71): 29–33. Not all schools welcomed "coloured" children. John Jessop, who ran a private school in Victoria during the 1860s, yielded to pressure from white parents to exclude Black children. See Jean Barman, "Families vs. Schools: Children of Aboriginal Descent in British Columbia Classrooms in the Late Nineteenth Century," in Barman and Gleason, *Children, Teachers and Schools*, 41–42.
45 Perry, *Colonial Relations*, 10.
46 For more on Douglas and the complications of identity in colonial contexts such as British Columbia, see ibid., 3–4.
47 Victoria School District Register's Account Book, 1861–1865, BCA, GR 2055.
48 I am amending Homi Bhabha's phrase "not quite/not white," as does Renisa Mawani, to address the complexities of racialization at the time. See Homi K. Bhabha, "Of Mimicry and Man: The Ambivalence of Colonial Discourse," *Discipleship: A Special Issue on Psychoanalysis* 28 (Spring 1984): 125–33; and Renisa Mawani, "In Between and Out of Place: Mixed-Race Identity, Liquor, and the Law in British Columbia, 1850–1913," in *Race, Space, and the Law: Unmapping a White Settler Society*, ed. Sherene H. Razack (Toronto: Between the Lines Press, 2002), 47–69.
49 Perry, *On the Edge of Empire*, 197.
50 "Founders of British Columbia," *North Island Gazette* (Port Hardy, British Columbia), April 20, 1966, 10.
51 Sylvia Van Kirk, *Many Tender Ties: Women in Fur-Trade Society, 1670–1870* (Winnipeg: Watson and Dwywer, 1980), 170.
52 See Perry, *Colonial Relations*, 110–12.
53 Van Kirk, *Many Tender Ties*, 237. Amelia Connolly Douglas worried greatly about Martha's distance from the family. See Perry, *Colonial Relations*, 165–66. For more on practices of transimperial schooling, see Erin Millions, "Portraits and Gravestones: Documenting the Transnational Lives of Nineteenth-Century British-Métis Students," *Journal of the Canadian Historical Association* 29, 1 (2008): 1–38.
54 Cridge to Colonial Secretary, May 13, 1862, BCA, GR 1372, B01322, box 45, file 395, 27.
55 Cornelius Bryant to Douglas, June 8, 1863, BCA, GR 1372, B01322, box 45, file 396, 1.
56 Rennie Warburton, "The Class Relations of Public Schoolteachers in British Columbia," in Warburton and Coburn, *Workers, Capital, and the State*, 245.
57 See Barman, *Growing Up British*, 5–6.
58 *British Colonist*, April 4, 1864.
59 Arthur Kennedy to Edward Cardwell, January 24, 1866, NA, CO 305/28, 72.
60 McDonald calls this British Columbia's "great land grab." See McDonald, *A Long Way to Paradise*, 39–45.

61 Douglas to E.B. Lytton, October 26, 1858, *Papers Relative to the Affairs of British Columbia*, Part 2 (London: G.E. Eyre and W. Spottiswoode, 1859–62), 10.
62 On the Fraser Canyon War, see Daniel P. Marshall, *Claiming the Land: British Columbia and the Making of a New El Dorado* (Vancouver: Ronsdale Press, 2018).
63 Carlson, *The Power of Place*, 161.
64 Marx, *Capital*, vol. 1, 915.
65 Virginia Driving Hawk Sneve, *Completing the Circle* (Lincoln: University of Nebraska Press, 1998), 25.
66 On the homosocial nature of mid-nineteenth-century British Columbia, see Perry, *On the Edge of Empire*, 79–96.
67 A few days later, three more bodies were sent downstream and removed from the river between Fort Yale and Fort Hope. Carlson, *The Power of Place*, 166.
68 H.M. Snyder to Douglas, August 28, 1858, BCA, GR 1372, box 126, 1617.
69 On Liquitem's role in abating the conflict, see Carlson, *The Power of Place*, 167–68.
70 Mary Williams, "The Coming of the White Man," in *Our Tellings: Interior Salish Stories of the Nlha7kápmx People*, ed. Darwin Hanna and Mamie Henry (Vancouver: UBC Press, 1996), 130–31.
71 Laura Ishiguro, "'Growing Up and Grown Up [...] in Our Future City': Children and the Aspirational Politics of Settler Futurity in Colonial British Columbia," *BC Studies* 190 (Summer 2016): 15.
72 Douglas to Newcastle, November 14, 1861, NA, CO 60/11, 140.
73 Hellen C. Pullem, *New Westminster: The Real Story of How It All Began* (New Westminster, BC: Hawkscourt Group, 1985), 58.
74 Richard Moody, quoted in Douglas to Newcastle, November 14, 1861, NA, CO 60/11, 141–42.
75 Edward Lugard to Moody, February 24, 1862, NA, CO 60/14, 324. McNally, *Blood and Money*.
76 A.T. Bushby to Colonial Secretary, November 3, 1864, BCA, GR 1372, B01312, box 25, file 242, 14.
77 In 1861, for example, 192 white women (mostly clustered around New Westminster) accounted for only 11.7 percent of the colony's total white population of 1,648. Perry, *On the Edge of Empire*, 13.
78 See MacLaurin, "The History of Education," 59–61.
79 Bushby to Colonial Secretary, January 17, 1868, BCA, GR 1372, B01312, box 25, file 243, 1.
80 On Chinook Jargon and its use in British Columbia, see Lutz, *Makúk*, ix–x. Lutz argues that Chinook was not primarily an Indigenous language; the HBC did business with Indigenous Peoples in Chinook, and several prominent settlers were well versed in it.

81 Barman suggests that British Columbia at this time was "truly multilingual," with many people speaking Indigenous languages, including Michif, as well as Chinook Jargon in addition to Spanish, French, and English. Barman, "Families vs. Schools," 39.
82 See Barman, *Iroquois in the West*, 121–22.
83 Bushby to Colonial Secretary, January 17, 1868, BCA, GR 1372, B01312, box 25, file 243, 1.
84 Chartres Brew to Colonial Secretary, May 8, 1866, BCA, GR 1372, B01310, box 22, file 195, 8.
85 Sarah Brown to Brew, May 19, 1866, BCA, GR 1372, B01310, box 22, file 195, 14.
86 Report included in Colonial Secretary to Brew, June 15, 1866, BCA, GR 1372, B01310, box 22, file 195, 8.
87 Pratt, "Arts of the Contact Zone," 34; Perry, *On the Edge of Empire*, 44.
88 *British Columbia Blue Book Statistics 1868*, NA, CO 64/9, 73.
89 Arthur Birch to Earl of Carnarvon, October 31, 1866, NA, CO 60/25, 237.
90 In the north, the Colony of the Queen Charlotte Islands (1853) and the Stickeen Territory (1862) were created by the Colonial Office in response to gold rushes. They too were overseen by Douglas, merged in 1863, and then joined the Colony of British Columbia in 1866.
91 See Johnson, *A History of Public Education*; and F. Henry Johnson, *John Jessop: Goldseeker and Educator: Founder of the British Columbia School System* (Vancouver: Mitchell Press, 1971). On British Columbia's emerging political culture, and the role of people such as De Cosmos and Robson in shaping it, see McDonald, *A Long Way to Paradise*, 16–18.
92 Johnson, *A History of Public Education*, 25.
93 In addition to De Cosmos and Robson, Leonard McClure and David Higgins were prominent journalists who, according to McDonald, used their newspaper writing in the 1860s to critique the "family-company-compact" and advance populist politics. McDonald, *A Long Way to Paradise*, 16–17.
94 "Editorial," *British Colonist*, August 2, 1865, 2.
95 *British Columbian*, September 21, 1864.
96 Robson, quoted in Barman, "Emergence of Educational Structures," 25.
97 A minority of colonists also opposed non-sectarian education on the grounds that it would lead to the opening of "Godless schools." On these debates, see Johnson, *A History of Public Education*, 34–35. For more on religion generally, see Lynne Marks, *Infidels and the Damn Churches: Irreligion and Religion in Settler British Columbia* (Vancouver: UBC Press, 2017).
98 Seymour brought colonial administrative experience from his posts as lieutenant governor of the Bay Islands and of British Honduras. See Margaret Ormsby, "Frederick Seymour, the Forgotten Governor," *BC Studies* 22 (Summer 1974): 3–25.

99 Seymour, February 27, 1867, *Journals of the Legislative Council of British Columbia* (New Westminster: Government Printing Office, 1867), 29.
100 Barman, "The Emergence of Educational Structures," 23.
101 Seymour, February 27, 1867, *Journals of the Legislative Council*, 30.
102 *An Ordinance to establish Public Schools throughout the Colony of British Columbia*, NA, CO 61/2, 1.
103 Fleming, "In the Imperial Age," 54.
104 Anthony Musgrave to Earl of Kimberly, August 3, 1870, NA, CO 60/39, 248–49.
105 Musgrave to Earl of Granville, May 16, 1870, NA, CO 60/38, 483–86.
106 Attorney General Henry Pering Pellew Crease, April 20, 1870, in Musgrave to Granville, May 16, 1870, NA, CO 60/38, 490–94.
107 *British Columbia Blue Book Statistics* 1870, NA, CO 64/11, 76.

Chapter Two | SETTLER ANXIETY AND MISSIONARY SCHOOLING

1 James Douglas to Earl Grey, October 31, 1851, NA, CO 305/3, 65; Harris, *Making Native Space*, 18.
2 In 1849, a British man-of-war, the *Inconstant*, was sent to protect Fort Victoria against a gathering of reportedly hostile northern Indigenous Peoples. In July 1851, just three months before Douglas penned his letter to the Colonial Office, Indigenous Peoples gathered yet again at Fort Victoria, arousing much anxiety among settlers. See Barry Gough, *Gunboat Frontier: British Maritime Authority and Northwest Coast Indians, 1846–1890* (Vancouver: UBC Press, 1984), 25–28.
3 Douglas to Duke of Newcastle, July 28, 1853, NA, CO 305/4, 73; Douglas to Henry Labouchere, April 10, 1856, NA, CO 305/7, 97.
4 The colony's garrison mentality often found expression in the local press. For more, see Kenton Storey, *Settler Anxiety at the Outposts of Empire: Colonial Relations, Humanitarian Discourses, and the Imperial Press* (Vancouver: UBC Press, 2016).
5 Officials such as Douglas had no accurate statistics on how many Indigenous Peoples actually lived in the colony and the adjacent territories. Gough argues that settlers' fears about Indigenous Peoples were "intensified because they never knew how many Indians they actually faced. They knew there were thousands, but not how many thousands." Gough, *Gunboat Frontier*, 9.
6 Storey, *Settler Anxiety*, 10. The mid-nineteenth century witnessed a number of conflicts across the British Empire: the 1848 Matale Rebellion in Ceylon, the Santhal insurrection of 1855–56 in eastern India, the Second Opium War in China in 1856–57, the Indian Revolt in 1857–58, the New Zealand Wars of 1860–72, and the Morant Bay Rebellion of 1865 in Jamaica, to name only a few. For more on how colonial conflicts shaped imperial policy and Britain's understanding of the empire during this period, see Hall, *Civilising Subjects;* and Gopal, *Insurgent Empire*.

7 Gough argues that Royal Navy gunboats were fitted for service in British Columbia as a "cheap and effective show of power" that could have a "psychological impact" on Indigenous groups and deter their resistance to colonization. Gough, *Gunboat Frontier*, 13. It is important to note that not all Indigenous Peoples responded to colonization in the same way. For more, see Lutz, *Makúk*, 49–162.
8 Douglas to Newcastle, July 28, 1853, NA, CO 305/4, 73; Douglas to Grey, October 31, 1851, NA, CO 305/3, 66.
9 Douglas to Grey, October 31, 1851, NA, CO 305/3, 66–67.
10 Ibid.
11 Susan Neylan, *The Heavens Are Changing: Nineteenth-Century Protestant Missions and Tsimshian Christianity* (Montreal and Kingston: McGill-Queen's University Press, 2003), 9.
12 See Robin Fisher, *Contact and Conflict: Indian-European Relations in British Columbia, 1774–1890* (Vancouver: UBC Press, 1977), 119–45; and E. Palmer Patterson II, *Mission on the Nass: The Evangelization of the Nishga, 1860–1890* (Waterloo, ON: Eulachon Press, 1982). More recent accounts continue to downplay the correlation between security concerns and early government support for missionary education in British Columbia. See Lynn A. Blake, "Oblate Missionaries and the 'Indian Land Question,'" *BC Studies* 119 (Autumn 1998): 28–44; Brett Christophers, *Positioning the Missionary: John Booth Good and the Confluence of Culture in Nineteenth-Century British Columbia* (Vancouver: UBC Press, 1998); and Myra Rutherdale, *Women and the White Man's God: Gender and Race in the Canadian Mission Field* (Vancouver: UBC Press, 2002).
13 Fisher, *Contact and Conflict*, 142. On settler colonialism as a "structure," see Wolfe, "Settler Colonialism," 388. For more on the concept of "settler anxiety" as applied to British Columbia, see Storey, *Settler Anxiety*, 13–15. See also Moreton-Robinson, *The White Possessive*; and Stoler, *Along the Archival Grain*. Stoler argues that colonial records often reflect fears and anxieties not solely over what happened and what can empirically be proven to have happened but also over what *could* happen.
14 Storey, *Settler Anxiety*. For more on the destructive effects of schooling for Indigenous Peoples, often justified by officials as being benevolent, see Woolford, *This Benevolent Experiment*.
15 Vine Deloria Jr., *Custer Died for Your Sins* (Norman: University of Oklahoma Press, 1988), 101–2.
16 On country marriages on the west coast, see Jay Nelson, "'A Revolution in the Manners of the Country': Aboriginal-Settler Intermarriage in Nineteenth Century British Columbia," in *Regulating Lives: Historical Essays on the State, Society, the Individual, and the Law*, ed. John McLaren, Robert Menzies, and Dorothy E. Chunn (Vancouver: UBC Press, 2003), 23–62. For more on marriage and colonialism, see, for example, Van Kirk, *Many Tender Ties*, 155–56; Jennifer Brown, *Strangers in*

Blood: Fur Trade Company Families in Indian Country (Vancouver: UBC Press, 1980); and Carter, *The Importance of Being Monogamous*.
17 Perry, *Colonial Relations*, 219.
18 Rev. Herbert Beaver to the Bishop of Montreal, Colchester, July 31, 1839, Quebec Diocesan Archives, Red River Rupertsland, 1839–1850, 2. Barman shows that a number of Iroquois employees, who had travelled west to work in the fur trade, lived at the fort during the 1830s and 1840s. See Barman, *Iroquois in the West*, 117–44.
19 For more on the Beavers, see G. Hollis Slater, "New Light on Herbert Beaver," *British Columbia Historical Quarterly* 6 (1942): 13–29.
20 Lempfrit was not the first missionary to visit the area. Jesuit missionary Jean-Baptiste Bolduc accompanied Douglas on his 1843 expedition to select a new site for the HBC. Bulduc, with help from local Indigenous Peoples, erected a makeshift chapel but no school was conducted during his short stay. See Begg, *History of British Columbia*, 157–58.
21 Fairfax Moresby to Secretary of the Admiralty, July 7, 1851, NA, CO 305/3, 228.
22 Ibid.
23 See Gough, *Gunboat Frontier*, 51–56, 61–64.
24 Douglas to Grey, May 28, 1852, NA, CO 305/3, 115.
25 McNally, "Challenging the Status Quo," 72.
26 Douglas to Grey, May 28, 1852, NA, CO 305/3, 115.
27 McNally, "Challenging the Status Quo," 72.
28 His reservations also probably reflected his views as an HBC official, since the company only reluctantly supported missionaries in its commercial zones. See Gough, *Gunboat Frontier*, 20–31.
29 Douglas to Grey, May 28, 1852, NA, CO 305/3, 115.
30 Ibid.
31 Ibid.
32 For a recent account of Douglas as a colonizer with "humanitarian motives," see Stuart Banner, "British Columbia: Terra Nullius as Kindness," in Stuart Banner, *Possessing the Pacific: Land, Settlers, and Indigenous People from Australia to Alaska* (Cambridge: Harvard University Press, 2007), 195–230.
33 Gough, *Gunboat Frontier*, 56. Harris argues that Douglas "annoyed many settlers, but had the confidence of the senior management of the Hudson's Bay Company and of the Colonial Office, both in London. With the Hudson's Bay Company inexperienced in such matters and the Colonial Office dithering and increasingly disinclined to become directly involved, Douglas had the creation of Native land policy on Vancouver Island much to himself." Harris, *Making Native Space*, 18. Settler frustrations with Douglas's "forest diplomacy" were no doubt exacerbated by the fact that, like many fur-trade officials, he married a Métis daughter of an

influential fur trader and tried to cultivate a reputation as an Indigenous expert. See Perry, *Colonial Relations;* and Van Kirk, *Many Tender Ties,* 155–56. For the most recent treatment of Douglas and early Indigenous-settler negotiations about land in the region, see Cook et al., *To Share.*

34 Douglas to James Tilton, November 6, 1855, NA, CO 305/6, 158.
35 Ibid.
36 Ibid., 161. On Indigenous workers and the *Beaver,* see Barman, *Iroquois in the West,* 125, 132, 134, 155.
37 Gough, *Gunboat Frontier,* xiv.
38 Douglas to Sir William Molesworth, November 8, 1855, NA, CO 305/6, 153.
39 Ibid.
40 Douglas to Tilton, November 19, 1855, NA, CO 305/6, 194.
41 Isaac Stevens to Douglas, February 17, 1856, NA, CO 305/7, 33.
42 Indigenous Peoples from the north frequently came south for various reasons, most notably to trade in Victoria. Concerned about their increasing numbers, colonists constantly complained about their perceived immorality, poor hygiene, and lawlessness. Storey argues that "every year between 1854 and 1860, Douglas drew the Colonial Office's attention to the discomfort and anxiety of local settlers regarding the presence of northern First Nations in the community." Storey, *Settler Anxiety,* 49–50. For a critical analysis of racialized and gendered discourses about Indigenous Peoples during this period, see Barman, "Taming Aboriginal Sexuality," 237–66.
43 Cridge was the petition's first signatory. Douglas to Grey, March 7, 1856, NA, CO 305/7, 13.
44 Ibid., 17.
45 Douglas to Grey, March 14, 1856, NA, CO 305/7, 5–8.
46 Blackhawk, *Violence over the Land,* 9.
47 Douglas to E.B. Lytton, November 5, 1858, NA, CO 60/1, 366. For more on the Aborigines' Protection Society and "humanitarian imperialism" as justification for empire making, see James Heartfield, *Aborigines' Protection Society: Humanitarian Imperialism in Australia, New Zealand, Fiji, Canada, South Africa, and the Congo, 1836–1909* (Oxford: Oxford University Press, 2011).
48 Douglas to Lytton, November 6, 1858, NA, CO 60/1, 374.
49 Perry, *On the Edge of Empire,* 124–25.
50 McNally, *Blood and Money,* 178; Coulthard, *Red Skin,* 6–15.
51 For more on European philosophical justifications of imperialism during this period, see Harris, *Making Native Space,* xxi–xxii.
52 The HBC fixed the price of land on Vancouver Island at £1 per acre and required every purchaser to acquire at least twenty acres. It retained one-tenth of the revenue from land transactions, with the other nine-tenths to be used for public purposes, such as road construction and the establishment of schools. The colony of

British Columbia, on the other hand, sold land cheaply, fixing the price at only 10 shillings an acre and later allowing settlers to pre-empt 160 acres on the condition that they work and improve the land. Ormsby, *British Columbia*, 178–79. For more on pre-emption policy in British Columbia, see Sandwell, *Contesting Rural Space*, 61–84. Some colonists called for the dissemination of free land, but the Colonial Office continually advised against such a practice. For more, see Perry, *On the Edge of Empire*, 124–38. Indigenous Peoples were initially allowed to pre-empt land, which was unique in the British Empire, but the colonial government changed this policy in the late 1860s, making it almost impossible for them to pre-empt private land off-reserve. See Carlson, *The Power of Place*, 175–77.
53 Moreton-Robinson, *The White Possessive*, xi–xii.
54 Herman Merivale on the back of Douglas to Lytton, February 9, 1859, NA, CO 60/10, 17.
55 Cole Harris, *A Bounded Land: Reflections on Settler Colonialism in Canada* (Vancouver: UBC Press, 2021), 9–10. For more on primitive accumulation as colonial dispossession in British Columbia, see Harris, "How Did Colonialism Dispossess?" 165–82.
56 Earl of Carnarvon to Douglas, April 11, 1859, NA, CO 410/1, 196–97.
57 Rev. A.C. Garrett to Douglas, July 26, 1860, BCA, GR 1372, B01330, box 64, file 634, 1.
58 Garrett to Colonial Secretary, November 24, 1860, BCA, GR 1372, B01330, box 64, file 634, 2.
59 Ibid.
60 Begg, *History of British Columbia*, 305.
61 On early Indian reserves and the "Douglas System," see Harris, *Making Native Space*, 17–44.
62 Garrett to Colonial Secretary, November 27, 1861, BCA, GR 1372, B01330, box 64, file 634, 3.
63 Garrett to A.G. Young, January 24, 1862, BCA, GR 1372, B01330, box 64, file 634, 1. On early land agreements between Indigenous Nations and colonial officials, including the fourteen so-called Douglas treaties, see Paul Tennant, *Aboriginal Peoples and Politics: The Indian Land Question in British Columbia, 1849–1989* (Vancouver: UBC Press, 1990), 17–25.
64 Blake, "Oblate Missionaries," 28. For more on religious debates in British Columbia generally, see Marks, *Infidels and the Damn Churches*.
65 Blake suggests that missionaries used varying methods of outreach, much as fur traders had (i.e., of establishing permanent trade-specific forts versus sending agents into the field to collect furs). Anglicans, such as William Duncan, preferred to erect missions with the goal of attracting permanent settlement. The Oblates

established permanent missions but also travelled extensively, evangelizing in various Indigenous communities. Blake, "Oblate Missionaries," 28–89.
66 Frantz Fanon, *The Wretched of the Earth* (New York: Grove Press, 2004), 17; and Woolford, *This Benevolent Experiment*, 3.
67 Coulthard, *Red Skin*, 4.
68 For a description of Methodist activities in British Columbia, see C.M. Tate, *Our Indian Missions in British Columbia* (Toronto: Methodist Mission Rooms, n.d.).
69 Storey, *Settler Anxiety*, 51–52.
70 For more on Crosby and the importance of his wife, Emma Crosby, to the mission on the Northwest Coast, see Hare and Barman, *Good Intentions Gone Awry*.
71 Douglas to Newcastle, February 17, 1860, NA, CO 60/7, 113–15.
72 Thomas Crosby, *Among the AN-KO-ME-NUMS or Flathead Tribes of Indians of the Pacific Coast* (Toronto: William Briggs, 1907), 43.
73 Ibid., 46.
74 For more on the Chilliwack mission and the creation of the Coqualeetza Home, see Tate, *Our Indian Missions*, 15–16.
75 Crosby, *Among the AN-KO-ME-NUMS*, 192.
76 On how the Sisters of St. Ann shaped female morality in Victoria, see Perry, *On The Edge of Empire*, 185.
77 Downey, *The Creator's Game*, 103–4.
78 For more on the Oblates, Father Fouquet, and missionary colonialism among the Stó:lō, see Carlson, *The Power of Place*, 181–91. On St. Mary's specifically, see Gresko, "Creating Little Dominions," 88–103.
79 Leon Fouquet to Douglas, April 11, 1864, BCA, GR 1372, B01329, box 59, file 584, 2.
80 On the Tsilhqot'in War, see Lutz, *Makúk*, 119–62.
81 In 1865, a sixth Tsilhqot'in warrior, Ahan, was hanged in New Westminster for his part in the attacks. Ibid., 137.
82 Blackhawk, *Violence over the Land*, 55.
83 For more on Begbie, see, for example, David Ricardo Williams, *The Man for a New Country: Sir Matthew Baillie Begbie* (Sidney, BC: Gray's, 1977).
84 Frederick Seymour to Edward Cardwell, August 31, 1864, NA, CO 60/19, 95–97.
85 Carlson also emphasizes that the spectacle helped Indigenous Peoples forge a collective political identity. Carlson, *The Power of Place*, 224, 227.
86 Seymour to Cardwell, August 31, 1864, NA, CO 60/19, 95–97. On the contested meanings of these summits, see Carlson, *The Power of Place*, 211–31.
87 Ibid., 103.
88 Seymour to Cardwell, September 3, 1865, NA, CO 60/12, 548–49.
89 Ibid.
90 Ibid., 549.

91 Ibid.
92 Ibid., 551.
93 Roughly four thousand Indigenous Peoples attended these annual summits between 1864 and 1874.
94 Seymour to Cardwell, June 7, 1865, NA, CO 60/22, 74.
95 Ibid.
96 Ibid., 76.
97 Fouquet to Seymour, August 24, 1865, BCA, GR 1372, B01329, box 59, file 584, 3.
98 Fouquet to Henry Maynard Ball, July 31, 1866, BCA, GR 1372, B01329, box 59, file 584, 6.
99 Fouquet to the Officer Administering the Government, October 25, 1866, NA, CO 60/25, 184.
100 Copy of address presented to His Honour A.N. Birch by the schoolboys of St. Mary's Mission included in Birch to Carnarvon, October 25, 1866, NA, CO 60/25, 182–83.
101 On the Tugwells, see Rutherdale, *Women and the White Man's God*, 50.
102 For more on Clah, see Robert M. Galois, "Colonial Encounters: The Worlds of Arthur Wellington Clah, 1855–1881," *BC Studies* 115–16 (Autumn-Winter 1997–98): 105–48.
103 Neylan, *The Heavens Are Changing*, 5, 9.
104 Edward Cridge to William Duncan, January 4, 1860, NA, CO 60/7, 126.
105 Duncan to Cridge, February 7, 1860, NA, CO 60/7, 133.
106 Edward Cridge, *Sketch of the Rise and Progress of Metlahkatlah, in the Diocese of British Columbia* (London: Church Missionary House, 1868), 8.
107 Douglas to Newcastle, February 18, 1860, NA, CO 60/7, 122.
108 Mr. Elliot on the back of Douglas to Newcastle, February 18, 1860, NA, CO 60/7, 123.
109 Deloria, *Custer Died for Your Sins*, 102.
110 Indeed, the Ts'msyan never formally ceded their lands and, as a result, a struggle for control over Duncan's settlement of Metlakatla broke out in the 1880s between them and the provincial and federal governments. For more on the disputes surrounding the "Indian Land Question," see Tennant, *Aboriginal Peoples and Politics*.
111 Duncan to Cridge, April 24, 1862, BCA, GR 1372, B01322, box 45, file 395, 28.
112 Tennant, *Aboriginal Peoples and Politics*, 29–30. Duncan's request also coincided with the outbreak of smallpox in Victoria, which may have factored into Douglas's support for the relocation strategy. Moreover, Douglas may have thought that Duncan could teach Indigenous Peoples about Western hygiene, which could possibly protect them against the spread of infection to the south. Neylan argues that Duncan gained influence among the Ts'msyan after the move to Metlakatla precisely because he was able to protect the majority of his converts against the spread

of the disease. Neylan, *The Heavens Are Changing*, 211. For more on the devastating effects of smallpox, see Van Rijn, "'Lo! the Poor Indian,'" 541–60.
113 Duncan to Douglas, March 6, 1863, NA, CO 60/15, 368.
114 Ibid., 374–75.
115 Cridge, *Sketch of the Rise*, 11–12. For more on Duncan and Metlakatla, including the possibility of sexual exploitation occurring at the Mission House, see Adele Perry, "The Autocracy of Love and the Legitimacy of Empire: Intimacy, Power and Scandal in Nineteenth-century Metlakahtlah," *Gender and History* 16, 2 (Agust 2004): 261–88.
116 Fisher, *Contact and Conflict*, 162; and Joseph Trutch to Colonial Secretary, November 12, 1866, BCA, GR 1372, B01340, box 82, file 947, 13a.
117 Fisher, *Contact and Conflict*, 136.
118 Patterson, *Mission on the Nass*, 35.
119 Doolan Journal, December 22, 1865, cited in ibid., 41.
120 Tomlinson, cited in Patterson, *Mission on the Nass*, 52.
121 Johnson, *A History of Public Education*, 33.
122 For more on "missionary real estate" in British Columbia, see Pamela E. Klassen, *The Story of Radio Mind: A Missionary's Journey on Indigenous Land* (Chicago: University of Chicago Press, 2018), 112–16.
123 Joseph Trutch, Memorandum on a letter treating on condition of the Indians in Vancouver Island addressed to the Secretary of the Aborigines' Protection Society by Mr. Wm. Green, January 13, 1870, NA, CO 60/32, 80–81.

Part Two | RULING BY SCHOOLING, 1871–1900

1 See Patnaik and Patnaik, *Capital and Imperialism;* and T.J. Tallie, *Queering Colonial Natal: Indigeneity and the Violence of Belonging in Southern Africa* (Minneapolis: University of Minnesota Press, 2019).
2 Speaking to the great transformation that occurred in British Columbia during this period, Harris explains, "The costs and delays of transportation and communication decreased, items other than sea otter pelts became 'resources,' and more corners of land became accessible. In the process, distances shrank; the territory that became British Columbia was repositioned and restructured." Harris, *A Bounded Land*, 173.
3 For more on the history of reserve making, see Harris, *Making Native Space*. On law and colonialism, see Tina Loo, *Making Law, Order, and Authority in British Columbia, 1821–1871* (Toronto: University of Toronto Press, 1994); and Mawani, *Colonial Proximities*.
4 On capitalist development in British Columbia, see, for example, the essays in Warburton and Coburn, *Workers, Capital, and the State*. For more on how the shift

from mercantile to industrial capitalism required a separation of Indigenous Peoples from the land, see Starblanket and Hunt, *Storying Violence*, 41.
5 McDonald argues that early politicians in British Columbia sought to forge an identity around the idea of whiteness and were centrally concerned with issues of immigration and Indigenous lands. See McDonald, *A Long Way to Paradise*, 25–32. See also Patricia Roy, *A White Man's Province: British Columbia Politicians and Chinese and Japanese Immigrants, 1858–1914* (Vancouver: UBC Press, 1989).
6 Axelrod, *The Promise of Schooling*, 25.
7 See Andrew Parnaby, "'The Best Men That Ever Worked the Lumber': Aboriginal Longshoremen on Burrard Inlet, BC, 1863–1939," *Canadian Historical Review* 87, 1 (2006): 53–78; and Baker, *Khot-La-Cha*. Lutz argues that many Indigenous Nations established a mixed or "moditional" economy that selectively combined aspects of subsistence and gift-giving economies with capitalist wage labour. Lutz, *Makúk*, 23.

Chapter Three | PUBLIC SCHOOLS FOR THE PEOPLE

1 Johnson, *A History of Public Education*, 88.
2 Those who favoured a non-denominational system of free public schooling (such as Amor De Cosmos) organized to get themselves elected to the first provincial legislature, where they pushed for their vision. Barman, "The Emergence of Educational Structures," 25.
3 *Daily British Colonist*, April 18, 1872, 3.
4 John Jessop, General Report, British Columbia, *Annual Report of the Public Schools 1874* (ARPS), 1874, 32. McDonald discusses the rhetoric of "the people" and its connections to populist politics in British Columbia during this period. See McDonald, *A Long Way to Paradise*, 15–18.
5 *Daily British Colonist*, April 18, 1872, 3.
6 *Vancouver News*, March 29, 1887.
7 Johnson presents the rise of public schooling as a story of "educational progress." Johnson, *A History of Public Education*, v.
8 Panitch, "The Role and Nature," 11. On politics and ideology in British Columbia during this period, see McDonald, *A Long Way to Paradise*, 14–33.
9 Curtis argues that the "political conflicts about what should be taught, how, to and by whom, on what conditions, and so forth, were at once conflicts about who should rule and be ruled, and of what rule should consist." He notes that schooling was "centrally concerned with political self-making, subjectification and subordination; with anchoring the conditions of political governance in the selves of the governed; with the transformation of rule into a popular psychology." See Bruce Curtis,

Building the Educational State: Canada West, 1836–1871 (London: Althouse, 1988), 14–16.
10 The action was one of the first teachers' strikes in Canada. Warburton, "The Class Relations," 245.
11 Marks explores the lower levels of "religious belief and participation" in British Columbia. See Marks, *Infidels and the Damn Churches*, 11. Though some ministers complained about "godless" public schools, McNally points out that it is perhaps most accurate to see British Columbia's public school system as non-denominationally Protestant, rather than secular. Some school boards allowed Bible readings and other religion teachings. For more on schools and religion in British Columbia, see McNally, "Challenging the Status Quo," 71–91.
12 Barman, *Growing Up British*, 6.
13 Ibid., 2.
14 Alexander Robinson, General Report, ARPS 1899–1900, 192.
15 For more on these processes, see Harris, "How Did Colonialism Dispossess?" 165–82; and Moreton-Robinson, *The White Possessive*. On pre-emption policy specifically, see Sandwell, *Contesting Rural Space*, 61–84.
16 For more on schools and taxes, see Gidney and Millar, *How Schools Worked*, 151–96.
17 Heaman's book on taxation in Canada is an excellent resource outlining the differing layers of taxation. Heaman contends that the federal government preferred indirect taxation on things such as customs, whereas provincial and municipal governments pursued more direct means of taxation on things such as property. On taxation in British Columbia, see Heaman, *Tax, Order, and Good Government*, 88–118. Unlike other provinces, British Columbia, in 1876, pursued direct taxation in the form of a $3 annual poll tax paid by every male resident over age eighteen to support public schools. In its first year, the tax brought in more than $16,000 for local revenues. *Sessional Papers of British Columbia*, Second Session, Second Parliament, 1877, 165. Taxation also intersected with anti-Chinese sentiment. Many white settlers objected to new taxation schemes because they believed, wrongly, that property and income taxes would mean that poor Chinese were not paying their fair share. See McDonald, *A Long Way to Paradise*, 29–30.
18 McNally, *Blood and Money*, 178–79.
19 *Public School Act, 1872*, NA, CO 61/3, 40.
20 For more on the central role of the superintendent in shaping schooling, see Fleming, "In the Imperial Age," 50–76.
21 On Ryerson's educational influence on John Jessop, see F. Henry Johnson, "The Ryersonian Influence on the Public School System of British Columbia," *BC Studies* 10 (Summer 1971): 26–34. Though Ryerson is often lauded for his efforts to bring public schooling to Upper Canada, Milloy also points out that he strongly

favoured separate industrial schooling for Indigenous children. Milloy, *A National Crime*, 15–16.
22 "Without a doubt," Johnson argues, Jessop "was the 'Ryerson of British Columbia.'" Johnson, *John Jessop*, 53.
23 For more on Jessop's work as superintendent, see Johnson, *John Jessop*.
24 James C. Scott, *Seeing Like a State: How Certain Schemes to Improve the Human Condition Have Failed* (New Haven: Yale University Press, 1999), 6.
25 British Columbia, *Supplementary Report of the Public Schools of British Columbia by the Superintendent of Education for the Year 1872*, 36. It is unclear whether Jessop's estimates included Indigenous children living in or near local settlements. The census information for the 1870s is speculative at best; white settlers accounted for approximately 8,576 or only 23.7 percent of the total population, whereas the Indigenous population was approximately 25,661 or 70.8 percent. It seems likely that Jessop's number of 1,768 included some Indigenous children, especially those near remote settlements or those who were racialized as "half-breeds," but his total is probably not accurate.
26 For more on the role and function of trustees in educational operations, see Gidney and Millar, *How Schools Worked*, 4.
27 Heaman, *Tax, Order, and Good Government*, 88.
28 On rural schooling, see Joan Adams and Beck Thomas, *Floating Schools and Frozen Inkwells: The One-Room Schools of British Columbia* (Vancouver: Harbour, 1985).
29 British Columbia, *Supplementary Report of the Public Schools of British Columbia*, 39 (emphasis in original).
30 Barman, "Taming Aboriginal Sexuality," 252–53.
31 Jessop, General Report, ARPS 1874–75, 98.
32 Jessop, General Report, ARPS 1874, 22.
33 Barman, "Taming Aboriginal Sexuality," 252–53.
34 For more about the school, see Wayne Norton, "The Cache Creek Provincial Boarding School, 1874–1890," *British Columbia Historical News* 29, 2 (Spring 1996): 30–33.
35 In 1876, Robert Beaven, who had been the chief commissioner of lands and works under Walkem, alleged that Jessop was taking home a salary of $5,000. Jessop was defended in the legislature by John Mara, who pointed out that the salary was $2,000 plus approximately $500 in travel expenses necessary for school inspections, thus only half of what Beaven had presumed.
36 For more on Walkem and British Columbia politics in the 1870s, see McDonald, *A Long Way to Paradise*, 19, 22–24.
37 Johnson, *John Jessop*, 156.
38 Jessop, General Report, ARPS 1877–78, 183.

39 On the important roles played by superintendents, see Fleming, "'Our Boys,'" 285–303.
40 John A. Gemmill, ed., *The Canadian Parliamentary Companion* (Ottawa: J. Durie and Son, 1891), 373.
41 See MacLaurin, "The History of Education," 155.
42 Johnson, *A History of Public Education*, 90.
43 See Curtis, *True Government?*; and Fleming, "'Our Boys,'" 290–92.
44 Jan Gould, quoted in Fleming, *Schooling in British Columbia*, 83.
45 Scott, *Seeing Like a State*, 6.
46 Robinson, General Report, ARPS 1899–1900, 187.
47 See Barman, *Growing Up British*; and John Porter, *The Vertical Mosaic: An Analysis of Social Class and Power in Canada* (Toronto: University of Toronto Press, 1965), 165–98.
48 Prentice, *The School Promoters*, 66.
49 Belshaw, *Colonization and Community*, 198–212.
50 *Public School Act, 1872*, NA, CO 61/3, 41.
51 *British Colonist*, April 28, 1877, 2.
52 British Columbia, *Supplementary Report of the Public Schools of British Columbia*, 36; Robinson, General Report, ARPS 1899–1900, 193.
53 Roy notes that in many parts of British Columbia informal segregation – the conscious concentration of Chinese and Japanese settlement away from white communities – may have tempered calls for formally segregated schools. See Roy, *A White Man's Province*, xiv, 15.
54 Mawani, *Colonial Proximities*, 4.
55 Constance Backhouse, *Colour-Coded: A Legal History of Racism in Canada, 1900–1950* (Toronto: University of Toronto Press, 1999), 18–55; McCallum and Perry, *Structures of Indifference*, 11–12. Backhouse explains, "The complexity of defining what is meant by 'Indian' is badly obvious. The intricate ways in which people group themselves and live their lives presents a host of enigmatic possibilities. To try to capture such a dizzying array of human combination with a watertight definitional framework is destined for disaster, no matter how earnest or multitextured the effort. The multiplicity of legislative formulae, inconsistent between governments and over time, is reflective of the insoluble difficulties." Backhouse, *Colour-Coded*, 26–27.
56 On the concept of "mixedness" in British Columbia, see Mawani, "In Between and Out of Place," 47–69. On the complications of *métissage*, see Chris Andersen, *Métis: Race, Recognition, and the Struggle for Indigenous Peoplehood* (Vancouver: UBC Press, 2014). Andersen objects to the conflation of "mixedness" and "hybridity" with Métis culture and identity. He argues that scholars and the courts

"misrecognize" Métis as a "hybrid off-shoot of two races – 'Indian' and 'white' – rather than as an *Indigenous people.*" Andersen, *Métis*, 6 (emphasis in original).
57 Anne McClintock, *Imperial Leather: Race, Gender and Sexuality in the Colonial Contest* (New York: Routledge, 1995), 15.
58 For more on this subject, see Barman, "Families vs. Schools," 39–53.
59 Notes Regarding Superintendent of Education's Visits to Schools, BCA, GR 1467, Vancouver Island, Board of Education, file 4.
60 T.H. Mathers to Jessop, April 13, 1876, BCA, Superintendent of Education Correspondence 1872–1892, GR 1445, microfilm reel 1. See Robert A.J. McDonald, *Making Vancouver: Class, Status, and Social Boundaries, 1863–1913* (Vancouver: UBC Press, 1996), 25.
61 Thomas S. to Jessop, May 22, 1876, BCA, GR 1445, B2017.
62 Alex Deans to Jessop, June 26, 1876, BCA, GR 1445, B2017.
63 Jane Trenaman to Jessop, October 25, 1876, BCA, GR 1445, B2017.
64 Barman, "Families vs. Schools," 48.
65 Sherry Farrell Racette, "Returning Fire, Pointing the Canon: Aboriginal Photography as Resistance," in *The Cultural Work of Photography in Canada*, ed. Carol Payne and Andrea Kunard (Montreal and Kingston: McGill-Queen's University Press, 2011), 70–90; Carol Williams, *Framing the West: Race, Gender, and the Photographic Frontier in the Pacific Northwest* (Oxford: Oxford University Press, 2003); Paige Raibmon, *Authentic Indians: Episodes of Encounter from the Late-Nineteenth-Century Northwest Coast* (Durham, NC: Duke University Press, 2005); and Kristine Alexander, "Picturing Girlhood and Empire: The Girl Guide Movement and Photography," in *Colonial Girlhood in Literature, Culture, and History, 1840–1950*, ed. Kristine Moruzi and Michelle Smith (Basingstoke, UK: Palgrave Macmillan, 2014), 197–213.
66 See Krista McCracken, "Archival Photographs in Perspective: Indian Residential School Images of Health," *British Journal of Canadian Studies* 30, 2 (2017): 163–82; and Alexandra Giancarlo, Janice Forsyth, Braden Te Hiwi, and Taylor McKee, "Methodology and Indigenous Memory: Using Photographs to Anchor Critical Reflections on Indian Residential School Experiences," *Visual Studies* 36, 4–5 (2021): 406–20.
67 Philip J. Deloria, *Indians in Unexpected Places* (Lawrence: University Press of Kansas, 2004), 4–5.
68 For more on Indigenous longshore workers, see Parnaby, "'The Best Men,'" 53–78.
69 Stanley, *Contesting White Supremacy*, 6.
70 S.D. Pope to John Robson, Education Office, Victoria, August 11, 1884, BCA, UBC microfilm, GR 450, volume 6, 735.
71 Pope to J.W. Stein, December 20, 1887, BCA, UBC microfilm, GR 450, volume 10, 234.

72 Pope to unknown recipient, 1889, BCA, UBC microfilm, GR 450, volume 178, reel 7377, box 8509.
73 See Barman, *Iroquois in the West*, 149.
74 Pope to Samuel Cutler, October 27, 1893, BCA, UBC microfilm, GR 450, volume 20, reel 7377, box 8513, 680.
75 In Sooke, for example, Indigenous children were let out of class early to avoid conflict with their white classmates. Writing about Black education in Ontario, Funké Aladejebi discusses similar kinds of informal segregation. Aladejebi, *Schooling the System*, 20–21.
76 Robinson, General Report, ARPS 1899–1900, 187.
77 Pope, General Report, ARPS 1890–91, 176.
78 Pope to James McLay (North Gabriola School District, Nanaimo), December 5, 1889, BCA, UBC microfilm, GR 450, volume 10, reel 7377, box 8509, 265.
79 William Burns, Report of Inspector Burns, November 1895, ARPS 1894–95, 214.
80 Jessop, General Report, ARPS 1873, 13 (emphasis in original).
81 Ibid.
82 Gramsci, *Selections*, 247; and Philip Corrigan, Bruce Curtis, and Robert Lanning, "The Political Space of Schooling," in Wotherspoon, *The Political Economy*, 24–25.
83 Jessop, General Report, ARPS 1874, 27.
84 Pope to Miss M.R. Smith, April 11, 1894, BCA, UBC microfilm, GR 450, volume 21, reel 7377, box 8515, 435.
85 Pope, General Report, ARPS 1883–84, 152.
86 For more on women and limited forms of school franchise, see Lara Campbell, *A Great Revolutionary Wave: Women and the Vote in British Columbia* (Vancouver: UBC Press, 2020), 57–59. Campbell points out that the criteria to vote changed over time, though urban white women who owned property were mostly favoured.
87 Sangster, *One Hundred Years*, 238–39. See also Campbell, *A Great Revolutionary Wave*, 57.
88 Pope, General Report, ARPS 1890–91, 261.
89 Appendix B, Public School Teachers and Their Duties, ARPS 1872–73, 19.
90 For discussions of teacher training, see John Calam, "Culture and Credentials: A Note on Late Nineteenth Century Teacher Certification in British Columbia," *British Columbia Historical News* 14 (Fall 1980): 12–15; Terry Wotherspoon, "From Subordinate Partners to Dependent Employees: State Regulation of Public School Teachers in Nineteenth Century British Columbia," *Labour/Le travail* 31 (Spring 1993): 75–110; and Warburton, "The Class Relations," 239–62.
91 Appendix C, Rules for the Examination of Public School Teachers and the Issuance of Certificates of Qualification, ARPS 1872, 21.
92 Robinson, General Report, ARPS 1899–1900, 200.

93 For example, an assistant gaoler made $912, a printer's assistant earned $758, and a convict guard and turnkey, or jailer, made $720. See Warburton, "The Class Relations," 247.
94 See Table C, ARPS 1899–1900, xxxix–li. Johnson confirms that average teacher salaries declined during this period, from $63.10 per month in 1872 to $59.61 per month by 1890. Johnson, *A History of Public Education*, 89.
95 At many provincial schools, whether primary or secondary, men who taught in lower divisions earned approximately $20 to $40 per month more than women, whose salaries typically ranged between $40 and $70 a month. See Table C, ARPS 1899–1900, xxxix–li.
96 For more on gender and teaching in this period, see Jean Barman, "British Columbia's Pioneer Teachers," in Barman and Gleason, *Children, Teachers and Schools*, 171–90.
97 Johnson, *A History of Public Education*, 54.
98 Jean Barman, "Encounters with Sexuality: The Management of Inappropriate Body Behaviour in Late-Nineteenth-Century British Columbia Schools," in Barman and Gleason, *Children, Teachers and Schools*, 196–97.
99 Pope, General Report, ARPS 1894–95, 201 (emphasis in original).
100 The Canadian Series of School Books was a set of revised Irish National Readers with Canadian content that Ryerson introduced to Ontario schools to counteract the American readers in use at the time. The series consisted of "readers" that were based on differing levels of literacy. See Nancy M. Sheehan, "Character Training and Cultural Heritage: An Historical Comparison of Canadian Elementary Readers," in *The Curriculum in Canada in Historical Perspective*, ed. G.S. Tomkins, Sixth Yearbook of the Canadian Society for the Study of Education (Edmonton: Canadian Society for the Study of Education, 1979), 77–84. For more on textbooks and the nineteenth-century curriculum, see Harro Van Brummelen, "Shifting Perspectives: Early British Columbia Textbooks from 1872 to 1925," *BC Studies* 60 (Winter 1983–84): 3–27.
101 Van Brummelen, "Shifting Perspectives," 14.
102 In the 1896–97 school report, the principal of the New Westminster High School explained, "The cleverest girls of New Westminster have from time to time been selected and placed as teachers in the common schools of this city. These young ladies while pupils of the High School, were carefully trained in the art and science of teaching; and so they came to work as well qualified as if they had been for six months or a year in a Normal School. Indeed, I am inclined to believe it is owing not a little to their faithfulness, prudence, and ability that the people here have so much confidence in their teachers, and think the schools of the Royal City are the best in the Province." Hector M. Stramberg, Special Reports on School, ARPS 1896–97, 224.

103 William Francis Collier, *History of the British Empire* (Halifax: A and W Mackinly, 1881), 340–41.
104 Pope, General Report, ARPS 1894–95, 212.
105 On history, curriculum, and textbooks, see Syed Aziz-Al Ahsan, "School Texts and the Political Culture of British Columbia, 1880–1980," *BC Studies* 63 (Fall 1984): 55–72.
106 Starblanket and Hunt, *Storying Violence*, 44–45.
107 Sutherland argues that in the 1880s, a "loose confederation of peoples, interests, and organizations" began to group under the umbrella of "reformers" and gradually "prodded, pushed, and cajoled Canadian schools to change what they were doing." Sutherland, *Children in English-Canadian Society*, 156. The role of reformers will be detailed in Chapter 5.
108 Sutherland argues that Macdonald and Robertson did not invent what became known as "the new education," or progressivism, but they drew inspiration from such ideas in their work, which had the effect of introducing aspects of the new education to many Canadians. He suggests that the Macdonald-Robertson Movement "gave Canadians practical demonstrations of such elements of the 'new' education as manual training, school gardening, nature study, domestic science, consolidated schools, and better methods of training teachers." Ibid., 183.
109 Panitch, "The Role and Nature," 4. For more on the Macdonald-Robertson Movement, see Sutherland, *Children in English-Canadian Society*, 182–201.
110 See Timothy Dunn, "Teaching the Meaning of Work: Vocational Education in British Columbia, 1900–1929," in Sheehan, Jones, and Stamp *Shaping the Schools*, 236–55.

Chapter Four | INVENTING INDIAN EDUCATION

1 John A. Macdonald, January 1, 1884, *Annual Report of the Department of Indian Affairs (DIA Annual Report)* 1883, 105.
2 For more on Duncan's career, see Jean Usher, *William Duncan of Metlakatla: A Victorian Missionary in British Columbia* (Ottawa: National Museums of Canada, 1974).
3 On Duncan's rumoured sexual relationships with young Ts'msyan women and his strict control of Metlakatla, see Perry, "The Autocracy of Love."
4 On Duncan's disputes with church and state, see Peter Murray, *The Devil and Mr. Duncan* (Victoria: Sono Nis Press, 1985), 110–23; and Neylan, *The Heavens Are Changing*, 54–56.
5 "An Account of the Riotous Destruction at Metlakatla: Petition 1882," BCA, F/7/MS 56 a.
6 The DIA did not use the term "residential school" until the 1920s. In this chapter, I discuss "Indian education" and the creation of a system of day, boarding, and

industrial schools, the terminology of the late nineteenth and early twentieth centuries.

7 As John Tobias outlines, section 91, subsection 24 of the British North America Act of 1867 gave the federal government "exclusive jurisdiction over 'Indians and Indian land.'" John L. Tobias, "Protection, Civilization, Assimilation: An Outline History of Canada's Indian Policy," in *As Long as the Sun Shines and the Water Flows: A Reader in Canadian Native Studies*, ed. Ian L. Getty and Antoine S. Lussier (Vancouver: UBC Press, 2014), 39.

8 British Columbia had the highest number of industrial schools (seven), but the North-West Territories – known today as Saskatchewan and Alberta – had the highest number of boarding schools (twenty-six). School Statement, *DIA Annual Report* 1900, 44–45.

9 W. Kaye Lamb, cited in Margaret Ormsby, *British Columbia: A History* (Toronto: Macmillan of Canada, 1958), 257.

10 On the mail's "slow and sometimes ineffective nature" during this period, see Ishiguro, *Nothing to Write*, 39–41.

11 Jean Barman, *The West beyond the West: A History of British Columbia* (Toronto: University of Toronto Press, 2007).

12 The best overview of the development of Canada's Indian Affairs bureaucracy remains Titley, *A Narrow Vision*, 1–22.

13 Marx, *Capital*, vol. 1, 915.

14 For more on the *Indian Act*, see Kelm and Smith, *Talking Back*.

15 In 1900, over fifty thousand acres of "surrendered surveyed Indian lands" were sold, "realizing the sum of $51,115.26." *DIA Annual Report* 1900, 64. Heaman notes that the federal government pursued indirect taxation on lucrative things, such as customs and consumption. Heaman, *Tax, Order, and Good Government*, 6. Robert McDonald outlines how taxes and licensing stemming from British Columbia's "great land grab" helped to expand its capitalist economy. See McDonald, *A Long Way to Paradise*, 39–45.

16 See Gettler, *Colonialism's Currency;* and McNally, *Blood and Money*.

17 For more on the influence of Indian agents in Canada, see Robin Jarvis Brownlie, *A Fatherly Eye: Indian Agents, Government Power, and Aboriginal Resistance in Ontario, 1918–1939* (Don Mills, ON: Oxford University Press, 2003). On the role of Indian agents in Indian education specifically, see Vic Satzewich and Linda Mahood, "Indian Agents and the Residential School System in Canada, 1846–1970," *Historical Studies in Education* 7 (1995): 45–69.

18 On bureaucracy, colonialism, and the work of Indian commissioners, see E. Brian Titley, *The Indian Commissioners: Agents of the State and Indian Policy in Canada's Prairie West, 1873–1932* (Edmonton: University of Alberta Press, 2009).

19 Scott, *Seeing Like a State*, 6. In the context of Indian education, Woolford argues that "knowledge of Indians was viewed as a means for increasing assimilative power over them, and in turn this power allowed schools to know and make legible Indigenous peoples in specific ways that furthered their subsequent management." Woolford, *This Benevolent Experiment*, 177–78.
20 Rück, *The Laws and the Land*, 18–19.
21 On the labour of DIA paperwork, see Bill Russell, "The White Man's Paper Burden: Aspects of Record Keeping in the Department of Indian Affairs, 1860–1914," *Archivaria* 19 (1984–85): 50–72.
22 William Spragge, April 25, 1872, *DIA Annual Report* 1871, 38.
23 F.W. Howay and E.O.S. Scholefield, *British Columbia from the Earliest Times to the Present* (Vancouver: S.J. Clarke, 1914), 2:697.
24 Simpson, *Mohawk Interruptus*, 19.
25 For more on Trutch's policies, see Tennant, *Aboriginal Peoples and Politics*, 40–45. On these jurisdictional disputes, see Harris, *Making Native Space*, 73–103.
26 Panitch, "The Role and Nature," 10.
27 *DIA Annual Report* 1874, 105. The report probably listed these eight schools because they received federal funding. In 1872, a report mentioned a number of other mission schools: of the Church of England at Comox, Nanaimo, Kincolith, Metlakatla, Yale, and Lytton; of the Catholic Church at St. Mary's, Williams Lake, Okanagan, Stuart Lake, Fort Rupert, Cowichan, and Victoria; and of the Methodist Church at Nanaimo, Victoria, New Westminster, and Chilliwack. Thus, the number was probably more than the eight officially listed in 1874, perhaps as high as seventeen.
28 Spragge, March 14, 1873, *DIA Annual Report* 1872, 5.
29 Israel Wood Powell, February 4, 1875, *DIA Annual Report* 1874, 66.
30 Metlakatla and St. Mary's received larger grants, of $500 and $350, respectively.
31 Powell, February 4, 1875, *DIA Annual Report* 1874, 66.
32 Lawrence Vankoughnet, December 31, 1877, *DIA Annual Report* 1877, 7.
33 See Milloy, *A National Crime*, 52. The federal government also called on Duncan for advice on policy. In 1875, he prepared a report for the minister of the interior, advocating the creation of organized settlements based on his Metlakatla mission. He later travelled to Ottawa for further consultation. Appendix C, Copy of part of a letter on Indian Affairs addressed to the Minister of the Interior, Ottawa, by Mr. Duncan, *DIA Annual Report* 1875, ix.
34 For more on American boarding schools, see, for example, K. Tsianina Lomawaima, *They Called It Prairie Light: The Story of Chilocco Indian School* (Lincoln: University of Nebraska Press, 1994); and David Wallace Adams, *Education for Extinction: American Indians and the Boarding-School Experience, 1875–1928* (Lawrence:

University Press of Kansas, 1995). The US historiography on Native American labour, especially regarding boarding schools, is well-established. See Alice Littlefield, "Learning to Labor: Native American Education in the United States, 1893–1930," in *The Political Economy of Native American Indians*, ed. John H. Moore (Norman: University of Oklahoma Press, 1993), 43–59; Alice Littlefield, "Indian Education and the World of Work in Michigan, 1893–1933," in *Native Americans and Wage Labour: Ethnographic Perspectives*, ed. Alice Littlefield and Martha Knack (Norman: University of Oklahoma Press, 1996), 100–21; and Kevin Whalen, *Native Students at Work: American Indian Labor and Sherman Institute's Outing Program, 1900–1945* (Seattle: University of Washington Press, 2016).

35 Nicholas Flood Davin, "Report on Industrial Schools for Indians and Half-Breeds," March 14, 1879, BCA, RG 10, School Files, volume 6001, file 1-1-1, part 1, B-1856, 12.
36 On the National Policy, see, for example, Paul Craven and Tom Traves, "The Class Politics of the National Policy, 1872–1933," *Journal of Canadian Studies* 14, 3 (1979): 14–38.
37 Davin, "Report on Industrial Schools," 11.
38 Ibid.
39 Ibid., 12.
40 Ibid., 2.
41 Ibid., 5.
42 Ibid., 1–2.
43 Coulthard, *Red Skin*, 13.
44 See McCallum's foreword in Milloy, *A National Crime*, xvii.
45 Davin, "Report on Industrial Schools," 2.
46 As Miller notes, money that would normally have been earmarked for other DIA expenditures was diverted into paying for the new schools. In short, this was not new money. Miller, *Shingwauk's Vision*, 103.
47 These schools were intended to satisfy the government's promises of providing education under the terms of the numbered treaties: Qu'Appelle (Treaty 4), Battleford (Treaty 6), and High River (Treaty 7). See Jacqueline Gresko, "White 'Rites' and Indian 'Rites': Indian Education and Native Responses in the West," in Sheehan, Jones, and Stamp *Shaping the Schools*, 91. These were not, however, the first schools in the area. Mission schools had existed there since the 1820s. As well, at the time of the first industrial schools, the Oblates were already running similar boarding institutions in the North-West Territories in St. Boniface, Île-à-la-Crosse, Lac Le Biche, Lake Athabasca, and Fort Providence.
48 Canada, *Debates of the House of Commons*, May 9, 1883, 1107–8.
49 Langevin noted, "The intention is to establish three Indian industrial schools in the North-West ... They have succeeded very well in the United States, and it is quite likely that they will succeed here as well. The fact is if you wish to educate

these children you must separate them from their parents during the time that they are being educated. If you leave them in the family they may know how to read and write, but they still remain savages, whereas by separating them in the way proposed, they acquire the habits and tastes – it is to be hoped only the good tastes – of civilized people." Canada, *Debates of the House of Commons,* May 22, 1883, 1376.
50 Macdonald, January 1, 1884, *DIA Annual Report* 1883, xi.
51 Between 1888 and 1911, 45 percent of the pupils at Coqualeetza had lost one or both parents. At Kuper Island, almost 50 percent of pupils admitted between 1890 and 1906 came from families in which one or both parents were deceased. James Redford, "Attendance at Indian Residential Schools in British Columbia, 1890–1920," *BC Studies* 44 (1979–80): 48.
52 On Canada's connections to this exploitative practice, see Joy Par, *Labouring Children: British Immigrant Apprentices to Canada, 1869–1924* (Montreal and Kingston: McGill-Queen's University Press, 1980).
53 Return on Schools, *DIA Annual Report* 1880, 310–11.
54 See Tennant, *Aboriginal Peoples and Politics,* 55–57.
55 John R. Scott, August 1, 1889, *DIA Annual Report* 1889, 119.
56 W.H. Lomas, August 7, 1885, *DIA Annual Report* 1885, 81.
57 Blackhawk, *Violence over the Land,* 5–7.
58 Scott, August 1, 1899, *DIA Annual Report* 1889, 119.
59 Miller argues that the presence of myriad denominations made British Columbia "one of the most fiercely contested regions." Miller, *Shingwauk's Vision,* 95.
60 *DIA Annual Report* 1884, 121.
61 Gilbert Malcom Sproat and Alexander Caulfield Anderson to Minister of the Interior, July 13, 1877, BCA, GR 0494, Indian Reserve Commission, Correspondence. On the founding of the Kamloops Indian Industrial School, see Celia Haig-Brown, *Resistance and Renewal: Surviving the Indian Residential School* (Vancouver: Tillacum Library, 1988), 36–37.
62 For more on O'Reilly and reserves, see Kenneth G. Brealey, "Travels from Point Ellice: Peter O'Reilly and the Indian Reserve System in British Columbia," *BC Studies* 115–16 (Autumn-Winter 1998): 181–236.
63 Edgar Dewdney, January 1, 1888, *DIA Annual Report* 1888, x. On the transformation of the barracks into a school, see Fred White to Dewdney, October 25, 1888, Library and Archives Canada (LAC), RG 10, School Files, Kootenay Indian Industrial School, C-8773, volume 6452, file 884-1, part 1.
64 Blackhawk, *Violence over the Land.*
65 Nicolas Coccola, July 11, 1891, *DIA Annual Report* 1891, 136.
66 Blackhawk, *Violence over the Land,* 5.
67 Harry Guillod, October 1, 1884, *DIA Annual Report* 1884, 100.
68 Fraser, "T'aih k'iighe' tth'aih zhit diidich'ùh (By Strength, We Are Still Here)," 22.

69 Allyson D. Stevenson, *Intimate Integration: A History of the Sixties Scoop and the Colonization of Indigenous Kinship* (Toronto: University of Toronto Press, 2021), 11.
70 Barman contends, however, that though co-education predominated in the school's early days, racism and the concerns of white parents eventually forced separation between the Indigenous and white boarders. See Barman, "Separate and Unequal," 283–302.
71 On the Williams Lake Indian Industrial School, see Furniss, *Victims of Benevolence*.
72 School Statement, *DIA Annual Report* 1900, 44–45.
73 Harris argues that this philosophy also shaped the government's stingy reserve policy: "It was important to get Indians into the workforce, not to give them land that they would not use, or that, if they became small farmers, would deflect them from wage labour." Harris, *Making Native Space*, 88. For the title of the present section – Learning to Labour – I have borrowed from Paul Willis, *Learning to Labour: How Working Class Kids Get Working Class Jobs* (Farnborough, UK: Saxon House, 1977).
74 Dewdney, *DIA Annual Report* 1890, xii.
75 On teachers and residential schooling, see E. Brian Titley, "Industrious, but Formal and Mechanical: The Sisters of Charity of Providence in Residential School Classrooms," *Historical Studies in Education* 22, 2 (Fall 2010): 58–74.
76 See "Programme of Studies for Indian Schools," *DIA Annual Report* 1896, 396–99.
77 Jean Barman, "Schooled for Inequality: The Education of British Columbia Aboriginal Children," in Barman and Gleason, *Children, Teachers and Schools*, 60.
78 Ibid., 61.
79 Simpson, *As We Have Always Done*, 88–89.
80 Scott, November 2, 1891, *DIA Annual Report* 1891, 170.
81 Coccola, July 11, 1891, *DIA Annual Report* 1891, 136.
82 George Donckele, July 1, 1893, *DIA Annual Report* 1893, 133.
83 Mary Jane Logan McCallum, *Indigenous Women, Work, and History, 1940–1980* (Winnipeg: University of Manitoba Press, 2014), 22.
84 Coccola, July 11, 1891, *DIA Annual Report* 1891, 136.
85 Donckele, July 18, 1892, *DIA Annual Report* 1892, 261.
86 A.M. Carion, August 1, 1893, *DIA Annual Report* 1893, 131.
87 Coccola, July 1, 1894, *DIA Annual Report* 1894, 169.
88 Hayter Reed, December 2, 1895, *DIA Annual Report* 1895, xxii.
89 Coccola, June 30, 1897, *DIA Annual Report* 1897, 290.
90 Reed, December 2, 1895, *DIA Annual Report* 1895, xxiii.
91 See Gresko, "Creating Little Dominions," 101. For more on sport and residential schooling, see Downey, *The Creator's Game*, 85–117.
92 Woolford, *This Benevolent Experiment*, 166–67.
93 Ibid., 295.

94 Mary-Ellen Kelm, "'A Scandalous Procession': Residential Schooling and the Re/formation of Aboriginal Bodies, 1900–1950," in Barman and Gleason, *Children, Teachers and Schools*, 81.
95 Stoler, *Along the Archival Grain*, 22.
96 Woolford, *This Benevolent Experiment*, 215; and Geoffery Paul Carr, "'House of No Spirit': An Architectural History of the Indian Residential School in British Columbia," (PhD dissertation, UBC, 2011).
97 On disease and colonization in Canada, see Kelm, *Colonizing Bodies;* and Maureen K. Lux, *Medicine That Walks: Disease, Medicine, and Canadian Plains Native Peoples, 1880–1940* (Toronto: University of Toronto Press, 2001).
98 *DIA Annual Report* 1891, 170.
99 Woolford, *This Benevolent Experiment*, 238–39.
100 Miller suggests that some schools probably accepted sickly students to secure more lucrative grants, a practice that exacerbated their poor health conditions. Miller, *Shingwauk's Vision*, 132.
101 Sellars, *They Called Me*, 62.
102 Coccola, July 11, 1891, *DIA Annual Report* 1891, 136.
103 J.A. Bedard, July 10, 1899, *DIA Annual Report* 1899, 388.
104 Lavinia Clarke, June 30, 1900, *DIA Annual Report* 1900, 416.
105 Belshaw contends that numerous factors shaped morbidity and mortality rates in British Columbia, including climate, population density, and access to drinking water. He emphasizes that mortality differed from town to town and city to city. Nevertheless, he argues that British Columbia had a high mortality rate in the late nineteenth and early twentieth centuries. Moreover, Indigenous Peoples, who were increasingly hemmed in on reserves and cut off from their subsistence economies by settler encroachment, had a higher-than-average infant mortality rate. Belshaw, *Becoming British Columbia*, 162–85. According to the Truth and Reconciliation Commission, there were 3,201 reported deaths at Indian Residential Schools prior to 1940, with many more going unreported for various reasons. Truth and Reconciliation Commission, *Honouring the Truth*, 94–95.
106 See Peter Henderson Bryce, "Report on Indian Residential Schools," 1909–10, LAC, Black Series, RG 10, volume 3957, file 140754-1.
107 Commentary on Bryce's "Report on Indian Residential Schools," 1907–08, LAC, Black Series, RG 10, volume 4037, file 317021.
108 Michel Hagan, October 1, 1890, *DIA Annual Report* 1890, 125.
109 Albert Memmi, *The Pillar of Salt* (Boston: Beacon, 1992), 259.
110 Sellars, *They Called Me*.
111 Scott, September 10, 1892, *DIA Annual Report* 1892, 259.
112 Scott, July 26, 1895, *DIA Annual Report* 1895, 162.

113 Woolford, *This Benevolent Experiment*, 133.
114 Vizenor defines "survivance" as "more than survival, more than endurance or mere response; stories of survivance are an act of presence ... [Survivance] is an active repudiation of dominance, tragedy, and victimry." Gerald Vizenor, *Fugitive Poses: Native American Indian Scenes of Absence and Presence* (Lincoln: University of Nebraska Press, 2000), 15. For more on Indigenous resistance and resurgence, see Simpson's *Dancing on Our Turtle's Back*.
115 Donckele, July 21, 1891, *DIA Annual Report* 1891, 135.
116 See James C. Scott, *Domination and the Arts of Resistance: Hidden Transcripts* (New Haven: Yale University Press, 1990).
117 Like Scott, Miller argues that children and their parents used the limited means of resistance available to them to register their concerns and critiques. Given the great power imbalance of the schools, everything from breaking the strict rules on the segregation of the sexes and speaking an Indigenous language to absenteeism and arson can be evaluated as contributing, consciously or not, to a school's culture of resistance. Miller, *Shingwauk's Vision*, 343–74.
118 James C. Scott, *Weapons of the Weak: Everyday Forms of Peasant Resistance* (New Haven: Yale University Press, 1985), xvi.
119 Lomawaima, *They Called it Prairie Light*, 167.
120 Hagan, July 27, 1891, *DIA Annual Report* 1891, 134.
121 Hagan, July 8, 1892, *DIA Annual Report* 1892, 259.
122 J.M.J. Lejacq, July 5, 1892, *DIA Annual Report* 1892, 264.
123 Lomas, August 24, 1892, *DIA Annual Report* 1892, 227.
124 Daily Journal, Kuper Island Indian Industrial School, 1895, BCA, MS 1276, volume 10.
125 Conduct Book, Kuper Island Indian Industrial School, 1895, BCA, MS 1276, A01971.
126 *DIA Annual Report* 1899, 405.
127 For more on Crosby and Methodist missionaries at Port Simpson, see Neylan, *The Heavens Are Changing*, 58; and Hare and Barman, *Good Intentions Gone Awry*.
128 As Perry notes, abuse and autocracy also existed at the Metlakatla mission, referenced in the opening to this chapter. For more, see Perry, "The Autocracy of Love," 268–77.
129 Elizabeth Shaw to T.G. Williams, April 19, 1899, BCA, MS 2644, British Columbia Conference, Reports, Clippings and Letters, Indian Affairs, 1881–1899. Extracts from a Letter Regarding the Indian Homes at Port Simpson. The letter may have been written in 1898.
130 Ibid.
131 School Statement, *DIA Annual Report* 1900, 44–45.
132 A.W. Vowell, September 18, 1895, *DIA Annual Report* 1895, 183.
133 Reed, December 31, 1894, *DIA Annual Report* 1894, xxi.

Part Three | REFORM AND RESISTANCE, 1900–30

1 Belshaw, *Colonization and Community*, 3.
2 Cole Harris, *The Resettlement of British Columbia: Essays on Colonialism and Geographical Change* (Vancouver: UBC Press, 1997), 252–53.
3 Tennant, *Aboriginal Peoples and Politics;* and Nickel, *Assembling Unity.* See also Peter McFarlane with Doreen Manuel, *Brotherhood to Nationhood: George Manuel and the Making of the Modern Indian Movement* (Toronto: Between the Lines, 2020).
4 On railways, politics, and capitalist development in British Columbia, see McDonald, *A Long Way to Paradise*, 42–45.
5 The Nine O'clock Gun, which still fires nightly in Vancouver, was cast in 1816 in Woolwich, England. It appears to have been one of sixteen cannons that Britain gave to the British North American colonies in the 1850s. Apparently, three made their way to the west coast to be used as symbols of military strength and imperial connection. Eventually, two were mounted at the entrance to the legislature in Victoria (and were later melted down during the Second World War), whereas the other was sent to Vancouver in 1894, where it was installed in Stanley Park. The cannon blasted for the first time in 1898. For more on time and capitalism, see E.P. Thompson, "Time, Work-Discipline, and Industrial Capitalism," *Past and Present* 38, 1 (December 1967): 56–97.
6 McDonald, *A Long Way to Paradise*, 30. On white supremacy and British Columbia, see Roy, *A White Man's Province;* Kay Anderson, *Vancouver's Chinatown: Racial Discourse in Canada, 1875–1980* (Montreal and Kingston: McGill-Queen's University Press, 1995); Mawani, *Colonial Proximities;* Stanley, *Contesting White Supremacy;* and Manuel, *The Reconciliation Manifesto*, 62–66.
7 These segments of the population were far from homogeneous, and further stratifications existed, especially in urban areas – including the formation of a more or less professional middle class. On the complications of class in British Columbia, see, for example, McDonald, *Making Vancouver*, xvi.
8 Barman, *The West beyond the West*, 444.

Chapter Five | REFORMING PUBLIC SCHOOLS

1 See E.A. Heaman, *The Inglorious Arts of Peace: Exhibitions in Canadian Society during the Nineteenth Century* (Toronto: University of Toronto Press, 1999), 96–97. For more on the politics of exhibition displays, see Anne Clendinning, "Exhibiting a Nation: Canada at the British Empire Exhibition, 1924–1925," *Histoire sociale/Social History* 39, 77 (2006): 79–107; and Paige Raibmon, "Theatres of Contact: The Kwakwaka'wakw Meet Colonialism in British Columbia and at the Chicago World's Fair," *Canadian Historical Review* 81, 2 (June 2000): 157–90.

2 "Today Ends Great Fair," *Daily Colonist*, October 7, 1905, 1.
3 David Wilson, Inspector's Report, ARPS 1905–06, A 19.
4 Ibid., A 18.
5 Ibid., A 19.
6 Here, I build on Harris's understanding of the concept of "modernity" in relation to socioeconomic development in British Columbia: "Modernity may be thought of as a form of social organization characterized by a heightened capacity for surveillance and management of individuals and populations, capitalist enterprises and industrial production, and the centralized control of the means of violence. As such, modernity was accompanied by the changing time-space relations associated with the technologies of transportation and communication that have evolved over the last two centuries. It may also be thought of as the frame of mind associated, some would say, with disenchantment and rational progress. I use the term even more loosely, and with more cultural relativity, to imply the gamut of developments within western European societies and their offshoots that, by the late nineteenth century, had made these societies much the most powerful on earth." Harris, *The Resettlement of British Columbia*, xii.
7 See Gidney and Millar, *How Schools Worked*.
8 Though private schooling would not accommodate more than 3 percent of the school-age population by 1930, it became popular again in the early 1900s. Nevertheless, as Barman writes, the fees charged by private schools in the province, eastern Canada, and Britain were beyond the reach of many families. In 1931, almost 70 percent of employed male British Columbians were labourers, most of whom simply could not afford to send their children to a private school. See Barman, *Growing Up British*, 45–46, 177.
9 Statistical Returns, ARPS 1929–30.
10 In addition to the superintendent of education, there were an assistant superintendent, sixteen elementary school inspectors, two high school inspectors, four municipal inspectors, an organizer of technical education, one home economics director, a director of elementary agricultural instruction, a director in charge of high school correspondence courses, an officer of elementary correspondence courses, a registrar and officer in charge of the Teachers' Bureau, a chief clerk, an officer in charge of free textbooks, two normal school principals, a director of summer school for teachers, one superintendent of Vancouver schools, a principal of the school for the deaf and blind, and a secretary for the Local Committee of the Strathcona Trust. See Timothy Dunn, "The Rise of Mass Public Schooling in British Columbia, 1900–1929," in Wilson and Jones, *Schooling and Society*, 39–40. Sutherland rightly points out that "the growth of the administrative staff in education barely kept pace with the growth in the system as a whole." Sutherland, *Children in English-Canadian Society*, 169.

11 For more on Robinson and Willis, see Valerie Mary Evelyn Giles, "Historical Evolution of the Office of Deputy Minister in British Columbia Educational Policymaking 1919–1945: The Career of Samuel John Willis" (PhD diss., University of British Columbia, 1993).
12 S.D. Pope, General Report, ARPS 1890–91, 169.
13 Alexander Robinson, General Report, ARPS 1900–01, 231.
14 S.B. Netherby, Inspector's Report, ARPS 1900–01, 251.
15 Robinson frequently followed up with inspectors and trustees about parent complaints. In 1904, he asked Inspector A.C. Stewart to mediate a dispute between parents and the Moodyville teacher, Mr. McMillan, which hinged on "an alleged dislike on the part of the children." See Robinson to A.C. Stewart, June 15, 1904, BCA, GR 450, Superintendent of Education Correspondence Outward, volume 56, 1719. The next year, Robinson wrote to E.D. Plaxton, the teacher at Langley Prairie, about complaints that she used "corporal punishment and force to compel" students "to clean and sweep out the Prairie School room." Robinson explained, "I have to inform you that no teacher has authority to force a pupil to do this work." Robinson to Miss E.D. Plaxton, February 6, 1905, BCA, UBC microfilm, GR 450, volume 59, reel 7377, box 8539, 375. For inappropriate body behaviour, including sexual abuse, in public schools, see Barman, "Encounters with Sexuality," 191–214. On punishment, see Neil Sutherland, "The Triumph of 'Formalism': Elementary Schooling in Vancouver from the 1920s to the 1960s," in Barman and Gleason, *Children, Teachers and Schools*, 332–35.
16 J. Donald Wilson and Paul Stortz, "'May the Lord Have Mercy on You': The Rural School Problem in British Columbia in the 1920s," in Barman and Gleason, *Children, Teachers and Schools*, 247. On schooling and class in British Columbia at this time, see Barman, "'Knowledge Is Essential,'" 9–66.
17 Wilson and Stortz, "'May the Lord Have Mercy,'" 234.
18 Stewart, Inspector's Report, ARPS 1903–04, A 30.
19 Robinson to Wilson, October 3, 1902, BCA, UBC microfilm, GR 450, volume 49, reel 7377, box 8532, 2954.
20 Axelrod, *The Promise of Schooling*, 36.
21 MacLaurin, "The History of Education," 151.
22 Ibid.
23 On the complex educational issues in rural areas during the 1920s, see Wilson and Stortz, "'May the Lord Have Mercy,'" 233–57.
24 See Diane L. Matters, "The Boys' Industrial School: Education for Juvenile Offenders," in Wilson and Jones, *Schooling and Society*, 53–70. For a discussion of gender and delinquency, see Joan Sangster, *Girl Trouble: Female Delinquency in English Canada* (Toronto: Between the Lines, 2002).

25 On the role of school inspectors, see Gidney and Millar, *How Schools Worked*, 300–39; and Fleming, "'Our Boys,'" 285–303.
26 Report of the Superintendent of Education, ARPS 1929–30, Q 7. Gidney and Millar point out that although school attendance rates rose across the country in the early twentieth century, the increase was particularly pronounced in the new Prairie provinces and British Columbia. Gidney and Millar, *How Schools Worked*, 12–13.
27 J.C. Shaw, October 20, 1902, ARPS 1901–02, A11.
28 Statistical Returns, ARPS 1900–01, xiv, v.
29 H.H. MacKenzie, Inspector's Report, ARPS 1920–21, F 26.
30 Ibid.
31 Ibid.
32 Robinson clarified to the principal of the Cumberland school that Chinese and Japanese children "cannot be excluded from schools provided they are between the ages of 6 and 16." Robinson to J.B. Bennett, January 17, 1900, BCA, UBC microfilm, GR 450, volume 38, reel 7377, box 8525, 168.
33 See Roy, *A White Man's Province*, 24–27; and Stanley, *Contesting White Supremacy*.
34 Roy, *A White Man's Province*, 27.
35 For more on the strike, public schooling, and racism in British Columbia in the early twentieth century, see Stanley, *Contesting White Supremacy*, 20–44.
36 See Chapple and Raptis, "From Integration to Segregation," 131–62; Raptis, "Implementing Integrated Education Policy for On-Reserve Aboriginal Children in British Columbia, 1951–1981," *Historical Studies in Education* 20 (Spring 2008): 118–46; Raptis, "Exploring the Factors," 519–43; and Raptis, "Blurring the Boundaries," 65–77.
37 Robinson to A.D. Dunbar, 30 September 1904, BCA, UBC Microfilm, GR 450, volume 58, reel 7377, box 8538, 3250–51.
38 See Chapple and Raptis, "From Integration to Segregation."
39 Robert Brown, Indian Agent Report, *DIA Annual Report* 1913, 407.
40 Woolford, *This Benevolent Experiement*, 214–20.
41 T.J. Commisky to J.D. McLean, February 1, 1912, LAC, RG 10, School Files, volume 6042, file 164-6-1.
42 J.R. Brown, Indian Agent Report, *DIA Annual Report* 1915, 207.
43 McLean to Brown, December 7, 1915, LAC, RG 10, School Files, C-8153, volume 6042, file 164-6-1.
44 R.H. Cairns, Inspector's Report, *DIA Annual Report* 1915, 239.
45 Duncan Campbell Scott to George Raley, August 31, 1924, LAC, RG 10, School Files, volume 6422, file 869-1, part 2.
46 *Coqualeetza Residential School: Commencement Exercises, June 1925*, LAC, RG 10, School Files, volume 6422, file 869-1, part 2, 10. Sophia Gladstone married William Reid [not "Read"], and their son, Bill Ried, became a master Haida carver.

47 Deloria, *Indians in Unexpected Places*, 4–5.
48 Williams, *Framing the West*, 7–8.
49 Yearly Report of the Pupils Attending the Moodyville Public School, 1909, Museum and Archives of North Vancouver (MONOVA), Moodyville School, Fonds 82.
50 Deloria, *Indians in Unexpected Places*, 225; Pratt, "Arts of the Contact Zone," 34.
51 Robinson to J.W. Bennett, October 1, 1919, BCA, UBC microfilm, GR 450, volume 189, reel 7377, box 8616, 8476.
52 Sutherland, *Children in English-Canadian Society*, 156.
53 In fact, Van Brummelen shows that religious instruction declined during the early twentieth century in most British Columbia schools. See Van Brummelen, "Shifting Perspectives," 7. For more on growing irreligion, see Marks, *Infidels and the Damn Churches*.
54 Dunn, "Teaching the Meaning of Work," 238. For more on reform politics and social unrest, see McDonald, *A Long Way to Paradise*, 47–51. For health and school medical inspection, see Mona Gleason, "Race, Class, and Health: School Medical Inspection and 'Healthy' Children in British Columbia 1890 to 1930," in Barman and Gleason, *Children, Teachers and Schools*, 133–48. On fears about race and health, see Mawani, *Colonial Proximities*, 51–65; and Anderson, *Vancouver's Chinatown*.
55 Dunn, "The Rise of Mass Public Schooling," 23–24. The transition to an industrial society, as Thompson notes, required "a severe restructuring" of character, a recalibration or great "transformation" of people's habits, values, and desires brought about by discipline, training, and subordination to hierarchical authority. See Thompson, "Time, Work-Discipline, and Industrial Capitalism," 57. For more, see von Heyking, *Creating Citizens*.
56 Axelrod, *The Promise of Schooling*, 105.
57 Stephen Schecter, "Capitalism, Class, and Educational Reform in Canada," in Panitch, *The Canadian State*, 377.
58 For an overview of changing pedagogical methods in Canada, see Phillips, *The Development of Education*, 431–69.
59 On the new education, see Sutherland, *Children in English-Canadian Society*, 155–224; and R.S. Patterson, "The Canadian Experience with Progressive Education," in *Canadian Education: Historical Themes and Contemporary Issues*, ed. E. Brian Titley (Calgary: Detselig, 1990), 95–110.
60 Sutherland, *Children in English-Canadian Society*, 156.
61 Wotherspoon, "Introduction," 2.
62 Jean Mann argues that "no two waves of progressivism were identical: each wave was intimately and intricately related to the economic, political, and social conditions of its time and place." Jean Mann, "G.M. Weir and H.B. King: Progressive Education or Education for the Progressive State?" in Wilson and Jones, *Schooling and Society*, 91–92.

63 Dunn, "Teaching the Meaning of Work," 239.
64 On the national characteristics of the vocational movement, see Gidney and Millar, *How Schools Worked*, 109–11.
65 Canada, *The Royal Commission on Industrial Training and Technical Education* (Ottawa: C.H. Parmelee, 1913), vii.
66 As Schecter notes, Robertson's involvement in the commission is further proof of the early connections between corporate and education elites. Schecter, "Capitalism, Class, and Educational Reform," 391.
67 Canada, *The Royal Commission on Industrial Training*, 8.
68 Ibid., 16.
69 Ibid., 18.
70 I note that manual and vocational training were related though differing kinds of education. As Dunn explains, the former sought only to orient students to the world of work in "superficial" ways. Its goals were general: to introduce pupils to practical and constructive work such as modelling, woodworking, and drawing for boys and sewing and cooking for girls. See Dunn, "Teaching the Meaning of Work," 241.
71 Ibid., 244–45.
72 Karl Marx, *Grundrisse: Foundations of the Critique of Political Economy* (New York: Penguin Books, 1973), 472 (emphasis in original).
73 Not everyone agreed with the new education. Opinion was divided, especially as the true meaning of "practicality" was hard to pin down. In the 1917–18 school report, Inspector A.J. Dove claimed that a "great deal of restless criticism" about educational matters came from the press. He stated, "Insistence has been laid on the suggestion that education should be more 'practical,' and that, to this end, our curricula should be denuded of all studies not directly convertible into dollars and cents. They who urge this do not realize – nor do their dupes – that the most practical education is that which makes the most and the best of the man himself, not that which merely puts a tool into his hand by which to earn a living. 'Practical' studies can be, and should be, so taught to provide a practical training in this higher and truer sense, without less – nay, with actual gain – to their use as means to a 'living.' It will be an imperative necessity in the future for mankind to see that *no* nation shall be allowed to develop a purely 'practical' education." Dove concluded that in the face of great public agitation for change, "The highest moral courage is demanded of those who steer the ship of our education amidst the veering winds and shifting currents of public opinion, in order that she may be held true to her course and that the true flag of humanity may not be displaced by one which, spread to the breeze, shall be found to disclose the skull and crossbones of piratical kultur." A.J. Dove, Inspector's Report, ARPS 1917–18, D 31–32 (emphasis in original).
74 Netherby, Inspector's Report, ARPS 1900–01, 251.

75 Ibid.
76 Netherby, Inspector's Report, ARPS 1903–04, A 24.
77 Wilson, Inspector's Report, ARPS 1900–01, 259.
78 Dunn, "Teaching the Meaning of Work," 244.
79 Schecter, "Capitalism, Class, and Educational Reform," 381.
80 Dunn, "Teaching the Meaning of Work," 250. For more on domesticity, see Cynthia Comacchio, *The Infinite Bonds of Family: Domesticity in Canada, 1850–1940* (Toronto: University of Toronto Press, 1999).
81 Marjory MacMuchy, *The Canadian Girl at Work: A Book of Vocational Guidance* (Toronto: Thomas Nelson and Sons, 1920), iii.
82 John Kyle, Report of the Organizer for Technical Education, ARPS 1925–26, R 58.
83 As Dunn explains, "hierarchically organized schools and a male dominated society complemented one another because the system required subordination, and women were generally subordinate to men." Dunn, "The Rise of Mass Public Schooling," 42.
84 Wotherspoon, "Introduction," 5.
85 On these demands in Canada, see James Naylor, *The New Democracy: Challenging the Social Order in Industrial Ontario, 1914–1925* (Toronto: University of Toronto Press, 1991); and Craig Heron, ed., *The Workers' Revolt in Canada, 1917–1925* (Toronto: University of Toronto Press, 1998). In particular, Allan Seager and David Roth's essay in *The Workers' Revolt* outlines British Columbians' participation in the great labour revolt. Allan Seager and David Roth, "British Columbia and the Mining West: A Ghost of a Chance," in Heron, *The Workers' Revolt*, 231–67.
86 James McCaig, *Studies in Citizenship* (Toronto: Educational Book, 1930), 86 (emphasis in original).
87 Ibid., 122 (emphasis in original).
88 Illich points out that "alienation, in the traditional scheme, was a direct consequence of work's becoming wage-labor which deprived man of the opportunity to create and be recreated. Now young people are prealienated by schools." Ivan Illich, *Deschooling Society* (New York: Harper and Row, 1970), 46–47.
89 Marx, *Capital*, vol. 1, 899.
90 Dunn notes that in the early 1900s, teachers who had trained in Britain and central Canada filled many of the vacant teaching positions. Establishing a normal school was a way of increasing the supply of teachers to meet demand. Dunn, "The Rise of Mass Schooling," 28.
91 See Barman, "British Columbia's Pioneer Teachers," 171–90.
92 For more on the development of normal schooling and its critics, see John Calam, "Teaching and Teachers: Establishment and Early Years of the B.C. Provincial Normal Schools," in Sheehan, Wilson, and Jones, *Schools in the West*, 75–97.
93 In the 1917–18 school report, an inspector observed, "Signs are not wanting that the public is beginning to appreciate that the teacher is worthy of his hire. More

than two thirds of our ... teachers were granted salary increases last year. These increases varied from as high as $50 to $5 a month, but in only five cases was the increase less than $10. While the cost of living has increased fully one-third, the men and women engaged in educational work in many quarters are expected to carry on with their former salary, although the wages of the working men and women and the income of practically all the other classes of our citizens has been increased in proportion to the increase in the cost of living." The inspector also mentioned that Vancouver was one of the few districts to offer teachers a war bonus of eight dollars a month. John B. DeLeon, Inspector's Report, ARPS 1917–18, D 22.

94 MacLaurin, "The History of Education," 255.

95 J. Donald Wilson, "'I Am Ready to Be of Assistance When I Can': Lottie Bowron and Rural Women Teachers in British Columbia," in Barman and Gleason, *Children, Teachers and Schools*, 262.

96 S.J. Willis, General Report, ARPS 1929–30, Q 11–16. The annual salary of $800 was still slightly higher than the average salary in the province, which was $715.07 in 1931. See "Series D512–521: Total Work Force, by Province and Sex, Census Years, 1911 to 1971," Statistics Canada, https://www150.statcan.gc.ca/n1/pub/11-516-x/sectiond/D512_521-eng.csv; and "Series E1–E13: Wages, Salaries, and Supplementary Labour Income by Province, 1926 to 1975," Statistics Canada, https://www150.statcan.gc.ca/n1/pub/11-516-x/sectione/E1_13-eng.csv. Moreover, it must be noted that British Columbia teachers were among the best-paid in Canada. See R.D. Gidney and W.P.J. Millar, "The Salaries of Teachers in English Canada, 1900–1940: A Reappraisal," *Historical Studies in Education* 22, 1 (2010): 4.

97 Dunn, "The Rise of Mass Public Schooling," 41. By 1930, 3,088 female teachers outnumbered just 684 male teachers. See Statistical Returns, ARPS, 1929–30. For more on female educators in Canada, see, for example, Kristina Llewellyn, *Democracy's Angels: The Work of Women Teachers* (Montreal and Kingston: McGill-Queen's University Press, 2012); and Aladejebi, *Schooling the System*.

98 Axelrod, *The Promise of Schooling*, 49.

99 Dunn, "The Rise of Mass Public Schooling," 41. On the feminization of the teaching profession, see Gidney and Millar, *How Schools Worked*, 142–46.

100 Margaret Strong, municipal inspector for New Westminster (1913–15) and the only woman to hold a senior leadership position in the province's school administration prior to the 1970s, was an exception, but her tenure was short. For more on fears about the feminization of society, see Mark Moss, *Manliness and Militarism: Educating Young Boys in Ontario for War* (Don Mills, ON: Oxford University Press, 2001), 44–49.

101 Robinson, General Report, ARPS 1903–04, A 7.

102 Willis, General Report, ARPS 1929–30, Q 7.

103 Robinson, General Report, ARPS 1903–04, A 7.

104 Johnson, *A History of Public Education*, 61.
105 On the emergence of junior high schools, see Mann, "G.M. Weir and H.B. King," 94–96.
106 For more on secondary schooling, see Cynthia Comacchio, *The Dominion of Youth: Adolescence and the Making of Modern Canada, 1920–1950* (Waterloo: Wilfrid Laurier University Press, 2006). The history of post-secondary schooling is beyond the scope of this study, but on the creation of the University of British Columbia in the early 1900s, see, for example, Johnson, *A History of Public Education*, 84–85; William C. Gibson, *Wesbrook and His University* (Vancouver: UBC Press, 1973); and Eric Damer and Herbert Rosengarten, *UBC: The First 100 Years* (Vancouver: University of British Columbia, 2009).
107 Johnson, *A History of Public Education*, 97.
108 On taxes for rural and assisted schools, see Wilson and Stortz, "'May the Lord Have Mercy,'" 234–35. The authors clarify that local tax assessments varied greatly by district.
109 On the continuing challenges of rural schooling in the early twentieth century, see, for example, ibid.; and Johnson, *A History of Public Education*, 93–95.
110 For more on school finances, see MacLaurin, "The History of Education," 271–72.
111 On the myth of schooling as a means for social mobility, see Schecter, "Capitalism, Class, and Educational Reform," 373–416.
112 Here I build on Gidney and Millar, who argue that the war "gave momentum" to educational reform and support for the militarism and imperialism that "were pervasive in English Canada." Gidney and Millar, *How Schools Worked*, 214.
113 Albert Sullivan, Inspector's Report, ARPS 1915–16, A 22.
114 Arthur Anstey, Inspector's Report, ARPS 1913–14, A 55.
115 John Martin, Inspector's Report, ARPS 1914–15, A 37 (emphasis in original).
116 Wilson, Free Text-Book Branch Annual Report, ARPS 1914–15, A 94.
117 Edward Parrott, *The Children's Story of the War* (London: Thomas Nelson and Sons, 1915).
118 On the Free Textbook Branch, see Penney Clark and Yesman Post, "'A Natural Outcome of Free Schools': The Free Text-Book Branch in British Columbia 1908–1949," *Historical Studies in Education* 21, 2 (Fall 2009): 23–45.
119 I. Gammell, *History of Canada* (Toronto: W.J. Gage, 1921), 274. For a discussion about patriotism and curriculum during this period, see Moss, *Manliness and Militarism*, 90–109. On British Columbia textbooks, see Van Brummelen, "Shifting Perspectives," 3–27; and Sean Carleton, "Colonizing Minds: Public Education, the 'Textbook Indian,' and Settler Colonialism in British Columbia, 1920–1970," *BC Studies* 169 (Spring 2011): 101–30.
120 This is not surprising, as many textbook authors were staunch defenders of imperialism. Among the most enthusiastic was George Parkin, whose *Round the Empire*

was a teachers' reference between 1893 and 1906. George R. Parkin, *Round the Empire* (London: Cassell, 1893).
121 Timothy J. Stanley, "White Supremacy and the Rhetoric of Educational Indoctrination: A Canadian Case Study," in Barman and Gleason, *Children, Teachers and Schools*, 113.
122 Ibid.
123 Memmi, *The Colonizer and the Colonized*, 89.
124 I. Gammell, *Elementary History of Canada with British Columbia Supplement* (Toronto: Educational Book, 1907), 9 (emphasis added).
125 Ibid., 28.
126 For more on the Strathcona Trust, see Desmond Morton, "The Cadet Movement in the Moment of Canadian Militarism, 1909–1914," *Journal of Canadian Studies* 13, 2 (Summer 1978): 62–63.
127 Quoted in Moss, *Manliness and Militarism*, 97.
128 Somewhat related is the emergence of the Boy Scouts and Girl Guides movements. On the connections between empire and guiding, see Kristine Alexander, *Guiding Modern Girls: Girlhood, Empire, and Internationalism in the 1920s and 1930s* (Vancouver: UBC Press, 2018).
129 Moss, *Manliness and Militarism*, 98.
130 Sutherland, *Children in English-Canadian Society*, 192–93.
131 J.L. Watson, Report of the Secretary, Local Committee, Strathcona Trust, ARPS 1919–20, C 92. Morton explains that the cadets attracted nearly three times more recruits than the contemporary Boy Scout movement. Morton, "The Cadet Movement," 56.
132 Yearly Report of the Pupils Attending the Moodyville Public School, 1909, MONOVA, Moodyville School, Fonds 82.
133 See Nancy M. Sheehan, "World War I and Provincial Educational Policy in English Canada," in *Historical Perspectives on Educational Policy in Canada*, ed. E.W. Ricker and B.A. Wood (Toronto: Canadian Scholars' Press, 1995), 253–79.
134 It is unclear how many teachers went off to war, but of British Columbia's population of approximately 450,000, 55,570 men enlisted. Ormsby, *British Columbia*, 377.
135 Anstey, Inspector's Report, ARPS 1916–17, 38.
136 Robinson to T.M. Roberts, October 24, 1919, BCA, UBC microfilm, GR 450, volume 186, reel 7377, box 8557, 11666.
137 For more on schooling and British Columbia's agricultural program in the early 1900s, see David C. Jones, "The *Zeitgeist* of Western Settlement: Education and the Myth of the Land," in Wilson and Jones, *Schooling and Society*, 71–89.
138 See Johnson, *A History of Public Education*, 67.
139 Jean Barman and Neil Sutherland, "Royal Commission Retrospective," in Barman, Sutherland, and Wilson, *Children, Teachers and Schools*, 412.

140 B. Anne Wood, "Hegelian Resolutions in the New Education Movement: The 1925 Putman-Weir Report," *Dalhousie Review* 6, 2 (Summer 1982): 256.
141 Putman and Weir were assisted by a number of experts, including J.L. Patron, former headmaster of the Manchester Grammar School; Professor H.F. Angus of the University of British Columbia; Professor S.E. Beckett of the University of British Columbia, who provided a report on finance and schooling; and Professor Peter Sandifold of the University of Toronto, who conducted the testing program in schools. A.W. Crocks was consulted on statistics, and Professor F.C. Ayer of the University of Washington was consulted on questions of educational administration. See Johnson, *A History of Public Education*, 102.
142 Barman and Sutherland, "Royal Commission Retrospective," 413. For more on Weir, see Mann, "G.M. Weir and H.B. King," 92–93.
143 J.H. Putman and G.M. Weir, *Survey of the School System* (Victoria: King's Printer, 1925), 4.
144 Ibid., 6–7.
145 Phillips, *The Development of Education*, 263.
146 Putman and Weir, *Survey of the School System*, 20 (emphasis added).
147 Patterson, "The Canadian Experience," 99.
148 Ibid. Patterson argues that the Putman-Weir Report "stands out as one of the first, if not the first, official document of a department of education to discuss and to recommend ideas and practices of the new education."
149 On the eventual use of IQ testing in Canadian schools, see Gleason, *Normalizing the Ideal*, 119–39. On teacher training, see Calam, "Teaching and Teachers," 75–97.
150 On rural schooling and the Putman-Weir Report, see Wilson and Stortz, "'May the Lord Have Mercy,'" 235–36.
151 Though some pre-school establishments had existed in places such as Vancouver since the 1910s, enrolment in "kindergarten" was not normalized until after the Second World War and was not made compulsory in British Columbia until 1973. For more, see Gillian Weiss, "An Essential Year for the Child: The Kindergarten in British Columbia," in Wilson and Jones, *Schooling and Society*, 139–61.
152 Putman and Weir, *Survey of the School System*, 58, 60.
153 Ibid., 57; see also *Daily Times*, November 28, 1928, 5.
154 Barman and Sutherland note that business elites, who commonly sent their children to private schools, objected to this recommendation, with their "traditional cry of why tax us for other people's children." Barman and Sutherland, "Royal Commission Retrospective," 414.
155 Putman and Weir, *Survey of the School System*, v.
156 Wood, "Hegelian Resolutions," 260.
157 Mann, "G.M. Weir and H.B. King," 93.

158 Eamonn Callan points out that "progressivism" had conservative adherents. See Eamonn Callan, "John Dewey and the Two Faces of Progressive Education," in Titley, *Canadian Education*, 83–93.
159 Ibid.
160 For more about educational debates in British Columbia during the 1930s, see Mann, "G.M. Weir and H.B. King," 96–115.
161 On British Columbia politics during the Depression, see McDonald, *A Long Way to Paradise*, 151–70.

Chapter Six | REVISING AND RESISTING INDIAN EDUCATION

1 A.W. Vowell to Secretary, DIA, March 17, 1902, LAC, RG 10, School Files, volume 6436, file 878-1, part 1.
2 Ibid.
3 For documentation regarding the inquiry, see LAC, RG 10, School Files, volume 6436, file 878-1, part 1. See also Furniss, *Victims of Benevolence*, 62–79.
4 Sworn Information of Witness, Johnny Sticks, February 28, 1902, LAC, RG 10, School Files, volume 6436, file 878-1, part 1.
5 Ibid.
6 Ibid.
7 Ibid.
8 Henry Boening, Report of the Principal, July 8, 1902, *DIA Annual Report* 1902, 424.
9 Furniss, *Victims of Benevolence*, 80–88.
10 Rück, *The Laws and the Land*, 137.
11 For a first-hand account of life at St. Joseph's, see Sellars, *They Called Me*.
12 Miller, *Shingwauk's Vision*, 142.
13 McCallum and Perry, *Structures of Indifference*, 5.
14 Simpson, *Mohawk Interruptus*, ix.
15 Meeting Transcript, 1923, LAC, RG 10, School Files, volume 6459, file 877-1.
16 Coulthard, *Red Skin*, 4.
17 Titley, *A Narrow Vision*, 16. By 1913, the DIA had 651 full-time or part-time employees.
18 Wendy Wickwire, *At the Bridge: James Teit and an Anthropology of Belonging* (Vancouver: UBC Press, 2019), 215. For Scott's views on Indian education, see E. Brian Titley, "Duncan Campbell Scott and Indian Education Policy," in Wilson, *An Imperfect Past*, 141–53.
19 Titley, *A Narrow Vision*, 22.
20 Woolford, *This Benevolent Experiment*, 94–95.
21 Duncan Campbell Scott, LAC, RG 10, School Files, volume 6810, file 470-2-3, volume 7, 55, 63.

22 See Wolfe, "Settler Colonialism," 387–88; and Moreton-Robinson, *The White Possessive*. On Indian education and gencocide in Canada, see Woolford, *This Benevolent Experiment*, 21–45.
23 On Indigenous political organizing, see Tennant, *Aboriginal Peoples and Politics;* Downey, *The Creator's Game*, 118–65; and Nickel, *Assembling Unity*. On Indigenous-settler relations at the municipal level, see Jordan Stranger-Ross, "Municipal Colonialism in Vancouver: City Planning and the Conflict over Indian Reserves, 1928–1950s," *Canadian Historical Review* 89, 4 (December 2008): 541–80.
24 Keith Thor Carlson, "Rethinking Dialogue and History: The King's Promise and the 1906 Aboriginal Delegation to London," *Native Studies Review* 16, 2 (2005): 10. For more on Indigenous Peoples' presence in London, see Coll Thrush, *Indigenous London: Native Travelers at the Heart of Empire* (New Haven: Yale University Press, 2016).
25 See Wickwire, *At the Bridge*, 202–7.
26 Panitch, "The Role and Nature," 10.
27 Gettler, *Colonialism's Currency;* McNally, *Blood and Money*.
28 For more on the McKenna-McBride Commission and land struggles in this period, see Harris, *Making Native Space*, 216–61.
29 On reserve cut-offs and Indigenous organizing, see Tennant, *Aboriginal Peoples and Politics*, 96–113.
30 British Columbia did not transfer full legal title to the dominion until 1938, and even then, Indigenous Nations were dissatisfied with the process and Canada's ongoing refusal to recognize their land and title. As Harris notes, the "province claimed that in agreeing to transfer reserves to Ottawa it had not relinquished rights to surface or sub-surface resources, all of which were under provincial regulations. Moreover, the province maintained that unused reserve land reverted to the province (the reversionary claim), and insisted that the proceeds of sales of reserve land belong to the province. In the face of such claims, it became a central objective of department of Indian affairs policy for years to acquire clear, undisputed title to the Indian reserves in British Columbia, thereby, so it argued, to permit the more effective implementation of the Dominion's fiduciary responsibilities. The other, and even more basic, axis of argument came from Native people, who saw the issue of title not as a jurisdictional dispute between two levels of Canadian government, but as a means of asserting their own prior rights, as original owners, to land they had never ceded." Harris, *Making Native Space*, 217.
31 In 1927, section 141 was added to the *Indian Act*, barring Indigenous Peoples from hiring lawyers, such as Arthur O'Meara, to pursue land claims on their behalf. See Tennant, *Aboriginal Peoples and Politics*, 96–113. For the blacklisting of Indigenous allies, or "white agitators," during this period, see *At the Bridge*, Wickwire's work on James Teit. He worked closely with the Allied Tribes of British Columbia and even travelled to Ottawa to lobby on its behalf.

32 On the myriad demands made during the McKenna-McBride hearings, including the desire for education, see Donald Leland, Deidre Sanders, and Naneen Stuckey, "What the People Said: Kwakwaka'wakw, Nuu-chah-nulth, and Tsimshian Testimonies before the Royal Commission on Indian Affairs for the Province of British Columbia (1913–1916)," *Canadian Journal of Native Studies* 19, 2 (1999): 213–48.

33 On Anglican archbishop Frederick Du Vernet's support for school reform, for example, see Klassen, *The Story of Radio Mind*, 208–15.

34 Titley, *A Narrow Vision*, 75.

35 Scott, Report of the Superintendent of Indian Education, June 1, 1910, *DIA Annual Report* 1910, 273.

36 A.E. Green, Report of British Columbia Indian School Inspector, April 6, 1908, *DIA Annual Report* 1908, 443.

37 Vowell, Report of the Indian Superintendent, July 19, 1906, *DIA Annual Report* 1906, 269.

38 Frank Pedley, Report of the Deputy Superintendent General of Indian Affairs, August 2, 1911, *DIA Annual Report* 1911, xxvi.

39 For more on why the DIA decided to delay compulsory education for Indigenous children, see Miller, *Shingwauk's Vision*, 129.

40 Scott, Report of the Deputy Superintendent General of Indian Affairs, December 1, 1920, *DIA Annual Report* 1920. 13.

41 Summary of School Statement, *DIA Annual Report* 1920, 68.

42 Summary of School Statement, *DIA Annual Report* 1930, 89. Redford suggests, however, that in terms of the overall children of school age in the province, a significant portion – perhaps a third – had been to neither a day nor a residential school. Redford, "Attendance at Indian Residential Schools," 42. Some of these children, as explained in Chapter 5, went to public schools, whereas others were educated, as they had since time immemorial, by parents and community members.

43 See Redford, "Attendance at Indian Residential Schools," 41–56.

44 $60,509.33 was spent on Indian Day Schools; $462,517.45 was spent on Indian Residential Schools. See Indian Education Vote – Expenditure for Year 1929–1930, *DIA Annual Report* 1930, 14.

45 Rück, *The Laws and the Land*, 18.

46 School Statement, *DIA Annual Report* 1901, 38–39.

47 R.H. Cairns, Extract from Report of Inspector on the Hazelton Indian Day School, September 29, 1920, LAC, RG 10, volume 6392, file 814-1, part 1.

48 Statement of Combined Public and Indian Day Schools in the Dominion, *DIA Annual Report* 1930, 86.

49 For more on Indian Day Schools, see Raptis and Tsimshian Nation, *What We Learned*.

50 Cairns to DIA, January 11, 1916, LAC, RG 10, volume 6409, file 839-1, part 1; A.F. MacKenzie to W.E. Collison, November 13, 1920, LAC, RG 10, School Files, volume 6395, file 817-1, part 1.
51 Russell T. Ferrier to Iver Fougner, December 1, 1921, LAC, RG 10, School Files, volume 6384, file 802-1, part 1.
52 Miller contends that Indian Residential Schools had similar problems with staffing: "Unless the young person opted for residential schools out a sense of adventure – and there were many such – a teaching assignment in a residential school was often the resort of someone unable to secure a post in a more attractive, more conveniently located, non-Native school." Miller, *Shingwauk's Vision*, 176.
53 Aladejebi, *Schooling the System*, 6. For more on Indigenous teachers at day schools in a different context, see Alison Norman, "'True to My Own Noble Race': Six Nations Women Teachers at Grand River in the Early Twentieth Century," *Ontario History* 107, 1 (2015): 5–34.
54 Green, Report of British Columbia Indian School Inspector, April 18, 1907, *DIA Annual Report* 1907, 438.
55 See Aladejebi, *Schooling the System*, 53–80.
56 Miller clarifies that calls to de-emphasize boarding and industrial schools in the 1910s came mostly from Anglican and Methodist missionaries; Catholic officials and the Oblates opposed the plan. See Miller, *Shingwauk's Vision*, 138.
57 Scott, Report of the Superintendent of Indian Education, June 1, 1910, *DIA Annual Report* 1910, 274.
58 *DIA Annual Report* 1911, H-75–76.
59 *DIA Annual Report* 1930, Part I-42–43.
60 See Titley, "Duncan Campbell Scott," 147–48.
61 Scott, Report of the Superintendent of Indian Education, June 1, 1911, *DIA Annual Report* 1911, 292.
62 Summary of School Statement, *DIA Annual Report* 1930, 89.
63 *DIA Annual Report* 1930, I-43. Previously, funds provided to Indian bands were used to pay for some day schools on reserves.
64 Scott, Report of the Superintendent of Indian Education, June 1, 1911, *DIA Annual Report* 1911, 292.
65 R.E. Loring, Report of the Indian Agent, Babine Agency, *DIA Annual Report* 1916, 179.
66 Scott, Report of the Deputy Superintendent General of Indian Affairs, November 6, 1924, *DIA Annual Report* 1924, 15.
67 *DIA Annual Report* 1930, 13, Part I-25.
68 Originally, boarding and industrial schools were envisioned as separate though complementary entities. The former were to house younger students who were not

attending a day school, whereas the latter were intended for older and more advanced pupils. In reality, very little differentiated the two aside from the per capita grant they were entitled to receive. In 1923, the DIA created one category of residential schools, known as the Indian Residential School.

69 Pedley, September 10, 1907, Report of the Superintendent General of Indian Affairs, *DIA Annual Report* 1907, xxxii.
70 Cairns, Report of British Columbia Indian School Inspector, *DIA Annual Report* 1915, 240.
71 Coulthard, *Red Skin*.
72 Barman, "Schooled for Inequality," 66.
73 Miller, *Shingwauk's Vision*, 122–23.
74 Barman, "Separate and Unequal," 294–95.
75 On the consequences of these cutbacks for the health of Indigenous students, see Mary-Ellen Kelm, *Colonizing Bodies: Aboriginal Health and Healing in British Columbia, 1900–50* (Vancouver: UBC Press, 1998), 64.
76 Titley, *A Narrow Vision*, 86–87.
77 Scott, Report of the Superintendent of Indian Education, June 1, 1911, *DIA Annual Report* 1911, 294.
78 School Statement, *DIA Annual Report* 1900, 38–39.
79 *DIA Annual Report* 1930, Part I-33.
80 Milloy, *A National Crime*, 51–75.
81 Miller, *Shingwauk's Vision*, 128.
82 Scott, Report of the Deputy Superintendent General of Indian Affairs, November 1, 1925, *DIA Annual Report* 1925, 14.
83 See Mary Jane Logan McCallum, "To Make Good Canadians: Girl Guiding in Indian Residential Schools" (master's thesis, Trent University, 2001); and Downey, *The Creator's Game*, 85–117. See also Evan Habkirk, "From Indian Boys to Canadian Men? The Use of Cadet Drill in the Canadian Indian Residential School System," *British Journal of Canadian Studies* 30, 2 (2017): 227–47; and Alexander, *Guiding Modern Girls*.
84 For more on work and labour at residential schools, see Miller, *Shingwauk's Vision*, 251–88; and Alexandra Giancarlo, "Indigenous Student Labour and Settler Colonialism at Brandon Residential School," *Canadian Geographer* 64, 3 (Fall 2020): 461–74.
85 Harvey Thommasen, ed., *Grizzlies and White Guys: The Stories of Clayton Mack* (Madeira Park, BC: Harbour, 1993), 21–22.
86 Indigenous student labour was also used to run boarding institutions in the United States. See Littlefield, "Learning to Labor," 43–59; and Littlefield, "Indian Education," 100–21. Whalen argues that at Sherman Institute in California, "student laborers performed the vast majority of work as the school expanded the two

decades following its opening. Young men from the school built dormitories for students and employees, a hospital, vocational workshops, farm buildings, and an auditorium. As students constructed the campus, school officials argued that they gained valuable experience as carpenters, masons, engineers, plumbers, electricians, plasterers, painters, blacksmiths, and roofers." Whalen, *Native Students at Work*, 4.

87 For more on gender and residential schools, see Miller, *Shingwauk's Vision*, 217–50.
88 Simpson, *As We Have Always Done*, 109.
89 Barman, "Separate and Unequal," 295; *DIA Annual Report* 1900, 421. For more on residential schooling, gender, and domestic labour, see McCallum, *Indigenous Women, Work, and History*, 21–65.
90 Joseph Hall, Principal's Report, July 1, 1903, *DIA Annual Report* 1903, 427.
91 *DIA Annual Report* 1901, 406.
92 George Raley to Scott, October 21, 1924, LAC, RG 10, School Files, volume 6422, file 869-1, part 2.
93 Summary of Expenses for British Columbia, *DIA Annual Report* 1930.
94 Brittany Luby, *Dammed: The Politics of Loss and Survival in Anishinaabe Territory* (Winnipeg: University of Manitoba Press, 2020), 13.
95 Maracle, *I Am Woman*, ix.
96 Scott, *Weapons of the Weak*, xvi. In a discussion of the Kamloops Indian Residential School, Haig-Brown describes school "counter-cultures" as "groups of children who defined roles, projects, and ways of daily life for and with one another. They did so without sanction, and in some cases, without even the knowledge of those who officially held the power of administration. Although other aspects of the school also influenced the children's development, these opposition movements live clearly in people's memories as times of strength. Fascination and fear are recurring themes for people discussing sub-cultures. There is wonder at the inventiveness of children, and the complexities of the roles which developed, there is fear for the recklessness of those involved and the extents to which students went to define their versions of power and control. At the same time, not one interviewee involved in the thievery, gang warfare, or the other forms of resistance indicated any sense of regret for their actions. In retrospect, these actions can be viewed as the actions of strong people against a system which degraded and dehumanized." Haig-Brown, *Resistance and Renewal*, 114.
97 Blackhawk, *Violence over the Land*, 27.
98 Mary-Ellen Kelm and Robin Jarvis Brownlie, "Desperately Seeking Absolution: Native Agency as Colonialist Alibi," *Canadian Historical Review* 75, 4 (December 1994): 543–56; and Fraser, "T'aih k'iighe' tth'aih zhit diidich'ùh (By Strength, We Are Still Here)," 33–4. Earlier works have been critiqued for glorifying acts of resistance and conveying, intentionally or not, a message of "the schools were not

that bad." For more on these critiques, see Furniss, *Victims of Benevolence*, 32–33. Scott similarly warns against romanticizing "the weapons of the weak," which "are unlikely to do more than marginally affect the various forms of exploitation." Nevertheless, he maintains that everyday acts of resistance are not trivial and that they can teach us much about how oppressed people respond to their circumstances. Scott, *Weapons of the Weak*, 29–30.

99 See Haig-Brown, *Resistance and Renewal*, 52. Surviving testimony of sexual abuse from the early twentieth century is rare; however, the Truth and Reconciliation Commission noted suspected cases, particularly relating to one Oblate priest, in the late 1920s and early 1930s. In 1939, for example, a sexual abuse scandal rocked the Kuper Island school when six boys ran away to escape further abuse by a staff member and were picked up by police. Truth and Reconciliation Commission of Canada, *Canada's Residential Schools*, vol. 1, *The History, Part 1 Origins to 1939* (Montreal and Kingston: McGill-Queen's University Press, 2015), 564–67.

100 Haig-Brown, *Resistance and Renewal*, 82–83.

101 For more, see Kelm, "'A Scandalous Procession,'" 81–111.

102 *DIA Annual Report* 1904, 418.

103 J.D. McLean to Rev. P. Classen, November 16, 1911, LAC, RG 10, School Files, volume 6467, file 889-1.

104 W.R. Robertson to McLean, March 4, 1912, LAC, RG 10, School Files, volume 6455, file 885-1.

105 Giancarlo, "Indigenous Student Labour," 461–74.

106 Jeremy Milloy, "Introduction: Accounting for Violence," in *The Violence of Work: New Essays in Canadian and US Labour History*, ed. Jeremy Milloy and Joan Sangster (Toronto: University of Toronto Press, 2021), 9.

107 See Kelm, *Colonizing Bodies*, 64–65.

108 H. Graham to McLean, August 1, 1919, LAC, RG 10, School Files, volume 6468, file 890-1.

109 Margaret Butcher, Journal, in Kelm, *Colonizing Bodies*, 64.

110 Mary-Ellen Kelm, ed., *The Letters of Margaret Butcher: Missionary-Imperialism on the North Pacific Coast* (Calgary: University of Calgary Press, 2006), 215.

111 McCallum and Perry, *Structures of Indifference*, 142.

112 Peter Henderson Bryce, "Report on Indian Residential Schools," 1909–10, LAC, RG 10, volume 3957, file 140754-1.

113 On denial by government and church officials, see Kelm, "'A Scandalous Procession,'" 89.

114 Peter Henderson Bryce, *The Story of a National Crime: An Appeal for Justice to the Indians of Canada* (Ottawa: James Hope and Sons, 1922). Milloy notes, "Though much of Bryce's 1922 narrative is the self-interested tale of his failed ambitions in the Department and of his unsuccessful attempt to secure the appointment as the first

deputy minister of the Department of Health when it was formed in 1919, the core of his charges was undeniable. Scott was in charge and nothing was accomplished. The evidence and the causes for that were close at hand." Milloy, *A National Crime*, 95.

115 For more on the reception of Bryce's reports, see Titley, *A Narrow Vision*, 83–86; and Kathleen McKenzie and Sean Carleton, "Hiding in Plain Sight: Newspaper Coverage of Dr. Peter Bryce's 1907 Report on Residential Schools," *Active History*, September 29, 2021, http://activehistory.ca/2021/09/hiding-in-plain-sight-newspaper-coverage-of-dr-peter-bryces-1907-report-on-residential-schools/#more-30946. On Bryce's legacy, see Travis Hay, Cindy Blackstock, and Michael Kirlew, "Dr. Peter Bryce (1853–1932): Whistleblower on Residential Schools," *Canadian Medical Association Journal* 192, 9 (March 2020): E223–E224.

116 Jack Usilick, James Usilick, Fred Usilick, and Mrs. Jack Usilick to Frank Devlin, Indian Agent, January 20, 1900, RG 10, School Files, volume 6422, file 869-1, part 1. See also Kelm, *Colonizing Bodies*, 78.

117 Statement of Mrs. Noel Paull, 1923, LAC, RG 10, School Files, volume 6459, file 877-1. For more, see Milloy, *A National Crime*, 59–60.

118 Report of Inspector W.E. Ditchburn for the month of November, 1916, LAC, RG 10, School Files, volume 6426, file 875-1, part 2.

119 NWMP constable Acland to Headquarters, June 8, 1924, LAC, RG 10, volume 6443, file 881-1, part 1.

120 Kay Johnston, *The Amazing Mazie Baker: The Squamish Nation's Warrior Elder* (Halfmoon Bay, BC: Caitlin Press, 2016), 27.

121 See Raibmon, *Authentic Indians;* and Michael Marker, "Borders and the Borderless Coast Salish Peoples: Decolonising Historiographies of Indigenous Schooling," *History of Education* 44, 4 (2015): 480–502.

122 For more on the various reasons for running away, see Redford, "Attendance at Indian Residential Schools," 51.

123 Estes, *Our History*, 248.

124 Eve Tuck, "Suspending Damage: A Letter to Communities," *Harvard Educational Review* 79, 3 (Fall 2009): 416.

125 Simpson, *Mohawk Interruptus*.

126 Joseph Hall to Frank Devlin, January 19, 1900, LAC, RG 10, School Files, volume 6422, file 869-1, part 1.

127 Robyn Maynard, *Policing Black Lives: State Violence in Canada from Slavery to the Present* (Winnipeg: Fernwood, 2017), 4–5. The St. George's school at Lytton, for example, made consistent use of police officers to return students who ran away. Redford, "Attendance at Indian Residential Schools," 52.

128 *Daily Colonist*, August 9, 1906.

129 George Manuel and Michael Posluns, *The Fourth World: An Indian Reality* (New York: Free Press, 1974), 71.

130 Woolford, *This Benevolent Experiment*, 174–75.
131 Baker, *Khot-La-Cha*, 36–37. Striking as a form of protest would be familiar to Baker. As Parnaby explains, Skwx̱wú7mesh lumber workers on the Vancouver docks had been forming unions and using the power of the strike – the withdrawal of their labour power – since the late 1890s. See Parnaby, "'The Best Men,'" 53–78.
132 Baker, *Khot-La-Cha*, 37. After he left school, Baker, like many Skwx̱wú7mesh, became a longshoreman in Vancouver. While working on the docks, he drew on his experience at the school and played an important role in organizing the North Shore Native Longshoremen's Union, which later become Local 500 of the International Longshoreman's and Warehouseman's Union. For more on the labour politics of the Vancouver docks, see Andrew Parnaby, *Citizen Docker: Making a New Deal on the Vancouver Waterfront, 1919–1939* (Toronto: University of Toronto Press, 2008).
133 Simpson, *As We Have Always Done*, 55. For more on Andrew Paull, residential schooling, and Indigenous political networking in British Columbia, see Downey, *The Creator's Game*, 105–8; and Tennant, *Aboriginal Peoples and Politics*, 118–20.
134 For more on fires at residential schools, see Truth and Reconciliation Commission of Canada, *Canada's Residential Schools*, vol. 4, *Missing Children and Unmarked Burials* (Montreal and Kingston: McGill-Queen's University Press, 2015), 152–59.
135 McLean to William May Halliday, January 29, 1918, LAC, RG 10, School Files, volume 6426, file 875-1, part 2.
136 Ditchburn to McLean, January 22, 1918, LAC, RG 10, School Files, volume 6426, file 875-1, part 2.
137 McLean to William May Halliday, October 3, 1924, LAC, RG 10, School Files, volume 6426, file 875-1, part 2.
138 A. O'N. Daunt to McLean, September 25, 1928, RG 10, School Files, volume 6468, file 890-1, part 1. On so-called juvenile delinquency and reform schools for girls, see Sangster, "Domesticating Girls," 180–201.
139 Kelm, *Colonizing Bodies*, 78.
140 Sechelt Band Petition to Charles C. Perry, August 14, 1923, LAC, RG 10, School Files, volume 6459, file 877-1.
141 Simpson, *Mohawk Interruptus*, 11.
142 Meeting Transcript, 1923, LAC, RG 10, School Files, volume 6459, file 877-1.
143 Cairns to Perry, November 6, 1923, LAC, RG 10, School Files, volume 6459, file 877-1.
144 Fanon, *The Wretched of the Earth*, 17; Woolford, *This Benevolent Experiment*, 3–4.
145 Raibmon, *Authentic Indians*, 10.
146 Fanon, *The Wretched of the Earth*, 32.

147 I agree with Woolford that "discussions of the end of genocidal processes is always risky terrain. The reverberations of such processes tend to stretch well beyond supposed end dates, and there is the danger of forcing closure on what is an ongoing and still developing set of harms." Woolford, *This Benevolent Experiment*, 88–95. On the mutations of Canada's assimilative project, see, for example, Stevenson, *Intimate Integration*.

CONCLUSION

1 Mathias Joseph, quoted in Parnaby, "'The Best Men,'" 60.
2 On the history of education and the British Empire, see, for example, Hall, "Making Colonial Subjects," 773–87.
3 For examples, see Perry, *Colonial Relations*; Alexander, *Guiding Modern Girls*; Ishiguro, *Nothing to Write*; Millions, "Portraits and Gravestones," 1–23; and Aladejebi, *Schooling the System*.
4 See Wolfe, "Settler Colonialism," 387–409.
5 Here, I build on and respond to Harris, "How Did Colonialism Dispossess?" 165–82; Coulthard, *Red Skin*; McCallum and Perry, *Structures of Indifference*; and Curtis, *Ruling by Schooling*.
6 Heaman, *Tax, Order, and Good Government*; David Tough, *The Terrific Engine: Income Taxation and the Modernization of the Canadian Political Imaginary* (Vancouver: UBC Press, 2019); Shirley Tillotson, *Give and Take: The Citizen-Taxpayer and the Rise of Canadian Democracy* (Vancouver: UBC Press, 2019); Gettler, *Colonialism's Currency*; McNally, *Blood and Money*; and Patnaik and Patnaik, *Capital and Imperialism*.
7 Wood, *The Origin of Capitalism*, 8. See also Gidney and Millar, *How Schools Worked*; and R.D. Gidney and W.P.J. Millar, "From Volunteerism to State Schooling: The Creation of the Public School System in Ontario," *Canadian Historical Review* 66, 4 (December 1984): 443–73.
8 See, for example, Mary Jane Logan McCallum, "Indigenous Histories of Tuberculosis in Manitoba," 1 (Spring 2014); Fraser, "T'aih k'iighe' tth'aih zhit diidich'ùh (By Strength, We Are Still Here)"; and Stevenson, *Intimate Integration*.
9 Simpson, *Mohawk Interruptus*.
10 See, for example, Barman, "Schooled for Inequality," 57–80; Raptis, "Blurring the Boundaries," 65–77; and Deloria, *Indians in Unexpected Places*.
11 Fraser, "T'aih k'iighe' tth'aih zhit diidich'ùh (By Strength, We Are Still Here)"; and Raptis and Tsimshian Nation, *What We Learned*, 153–54.
12 Truth and Reconciliation Commission of Canada, *A Knock on the Door: The Essential History of Residential Schools* (Winnipeg: University of Manitoba Press, 2016), 144.

13 Ibid., 148.
14 Manuel, *The Reconciliation Manifesto*, 56.
15 Truth and Reconciliation Commission, *Honouring the Truth*, 23.
16 Manuel, *The Reconciliation Manifesto*, 275, 277.
17 Lee Maracle, *My Conversations with Canadians* (Toronto: Book Thug, 2017), 78.

Bibliography

ARCHIVAL SOURCES

British Columbia Archives, Victoria (BCA)
Colonial Correspondence: Correspondence of the Government of the Colony of Vancouver Island, 1849–1866 and of the Government of the Colony of British Columbia, 1858–1871, GR 1372.
Council of Public Instruction, GR 0899.
Education Branch Correspondence, GR 1709.
Kuper Island Indian Industrial School, 1889–1938, MS 1276.
Methodist Church Records, MS 2644.
Metlakatla Indian School, MS 56 a.
Missionaries in British Columbia, PR 1894.
Photograph Collection.
Superintendent of Education Correspondence and Other Material, GR 0450.
Superintendent of Education Correspondence (Inward), GR 1445.

Library and Archives Canada, Ottawa (LAC)
Department of Indian Affairs, RG 10, Red Series, Black Series, and School Files.
Sir John A. Macdonald Papers, MG 26 A.
David Laird Papers, MG 27 I D10.
Edgar Dewdney Papers, MG 27 I C4.
Hayter Reed Papers, MG 29 E106.
Photograph Collection.

National Archives, London (NA)
Colonial Office: British Columbia, Original Correspondence, CO 60.
Colonial Office: British Columbia Acts, CO 61.
Colonial Office and Predecessor: Vancouver Island Entry Books, CO 410.
Colonial Office and Predecessors: Canada, Formerly British North America, Original Correspondence, CO 42.
Photograph Collection.

Vancouver Island Original Correspondence, CO 305.
War and Colonial Department and Colonial Office: Vancouver Island Acts, CO 306.

National Centre for Truth and Reconciliation Archives, Winnipeg (NCTR)
Anglican Church of Canada General Synod Archives.
Anglican Diocese of British Columbia Archives.
Oblates of Mary Immaculate, St. Paul's Province Fonds.
Oblates for Sechelt.
Photograph Collection.
St. Mary's Mission.
United Church Documents Collected by BC Office from United Church of Canada Archives.

Museum and Archives of North Vancouver (MONOVA)
Central School, Fonds 83.
Lonsdale School, Fonds 84.
Moodyville School, Fonds 82.
Photograph Collection.

SPECIAL COLLECTIONS

Historical Textbook Collection. Education Library, University of British Columbia.

PUBLISHED PRIMARY SOURCES

British Columbia. *Annual Reports of the Public Schools.* 1872–1930.
—. *Course of Studies for the Public, High, Technical, and Normal Schools of British Columbia.* Victoria: Department of Education, 1921.
—. *Curriculum Guide: Intermediate Grades.* Victoria: Department of Education, 1920.
—. *Papers Connected with the Indian Land Question, 1850–1870.* Victoria: Government Printing Office, 1875.
—. *Sessional Papers.* 1872–1930.
—. *Statutes of the Province of British Columbia.*
Brown, R.C.L. *British Columbia: The Indians and Settlers at Lillooet: Appeal for Missionaries.* London: R. Clay, Sons, and Taylor, 1870.
—. *Klatsassan, and Other Reminiscences of Missionary Life in British Columbia.* London: Society for Promoting Christian Knowledge, 1873.
Bryce, Peter Henderson. *The Story of a National Crime: An Appeal for Justice to the Indians of Canada.* Ottawa: James Hope and Sons, 1922.

Canada. *Annual Reports of the Indian Branch and Department of Indian Affairs.* 1867–1930.
–. *The Royal Commission on Industrial Training and Technical Education.* Ottawa: C.H. Parmelee, 1913.
–. *Report of the Royal Commission on Indian Affairs for the Province of British Columbia.* Victoria: Acme Press, 1916.
–. *Sessional Papers.* 1867–1930.
Collier, William Francis. *History of the British Empire.* Halifax: A and W Mackinly, 1881.
Cridge, Edward. *Sketch of the Rise and Progress of Metlahkatlah in the Diocese of British Columbia.* London: Church Missionary House, 1868.
Crosby, Thomas. *Among the AN-KO-ME-NUMS or Flathead Tribes of Indians of the Pacific Coast.* Toronto: William Briggs, 1907.
Duane, Patrick. *The School Record: A Guide to Government Archives Relating to Public Education in British Columbia, 1852–1946.* Victoria: British Columbia Archives and Records Service, 1992.
Fawcett, Edgar. *Some Reminiscences of Old Victoria.* Toronto: William Briggs, 1912.
FitzGerald, James Edward. *An Examination of the Charter and Proceedings of the Hudson's Bay Company, with References to the Grant of Vancouver Island.* London: Trelawney Saunders, 1849.
Gammell, I. *Elementary History of Canada with British Columbia Supplement.* Toronto: Educational Book, 1907.
–. *History of Canada.* Toronto: W.J. Gage, 1921.
Gemmill, John A, ed. *The Canadian Parliamentary Companion.* Ottawa: J. Durie and Son, 1891.
Helmcken, John Sebastian. *The Reminiscences of Doctor John Sebastian Helmcken.* Edited by Dorothy Blakey Smith. Vancouver: UBC Press, 1975.
MacMuchy, Marjory. *The Canadian Girl at Work: A Book of Vocational Guidance.* Toronto: Thomas Nelson and Sons, 1920.
Matthews, J.S. *Early Vancouver.* Vol. 2. Vancouver: City of Vancouver, 2011.
McCaig, James. *Studies in Citizenship.* Toronto: Educational Book, 1930.
Parkin, George R. *Round the Empire.* London: Cassell, 1893.
Parrott, Edward. *The Children's Story of the War.* London: Thomas Nelson and Sons, 1915.
Pullem, Hellen C. *New Westminster: The Real Story of How It All Began.* New Westminster, BC: Hawkscourt Group, 1985.
Putman, J.H. and G.M. Weir, *Survey of the School System.* Victoria: King's Printer, 1925.
Tate, C.M. *Our Indian Missions in British Columbia.* Toronto: Methodist Mission Rooms, n.d.

Truth and Reconciliation Commission of Canada. *Honouring the Truth, Reconciling for the Future: Summary of the Final Report of the Truth and Reconciliation Commission of Canada.* Toronto: James Lorimer, 2015.
—. *A Knock on the Door: The Essential History of Residential Schools.* Winnipeg: University of Manitoba Press, 2016.

OTHER SOURCES

Adams, Howard. *A Prison of Grass: Canada from the Native Point of View.* Toronto: New Press, 1975.

Adams, Joan, and Beck Thomas. *Floating Schools and Frozen Inkwells: The One-Room Schools of British Columbia.* Vancouver: Harbour, 1985.

Ahsan, Syed Aziz-Al. "School Texts and the Political Culture of British Columbia, 1880–1980." *BC Studies* 63 (Fall 1984): 55–72.

Aladejebi, Funké. *Schooling the System: A History of Black Women Teachers.* Montreal and Kingston: McGill-Queen's University Press, 2021.

Alexander, Kristine. "Picturing Girlhood and Empire: The Girl Guide Movement and Photography." In *Colonial Girlhood in Literature, Culture, and History, 1840–1950*, ed. Kristine Moruzi and Michelle Smith, 197–213. Basingstoke, UK: Palgrave Macmillan, 2014.

—. *Guiding Modern Girls: Girlhood, Empire, and Internationalism in the 1920s and 1930s.* Vancouver: UBC Press, 2018.

Andersen, Chris. *Métis: Race, Recognition, and the Struggle for Indigenous Peoplehood.* Vancouver: UBC Press, 2014.

Anderson, Kay. *Vancouver's Chinatown: Racial Discourse in Canada, 1875–1980.* Montreal and Kingston: McGill-Queen's University Press, 1991.

Armstrong, Pat, and M. Patricia Connelly, eds. *Feminism, Political Economy, and the State: Contested Terrain.* Toronto: Canadian Scholars' Press, 1999.

Asch, Michael, John Borrows, and James Tully, eds. *Resurgence and Reconciliation: Indigenous-Settler Relations and Earth Teachings.* Toronto: University of Toronto Press, 2018.

Axelrod, Paul. "Higher Education in Canada and the United States: Exploring the Roots of Difference." *Historical Studies in Education* 7 (1995): 141–76.

—. *The Promise of Schooling: Education in Canada, 1800–1914.* Toronto: University of Toronto Press, 1997.

Bacchus, M. Kazim. *Education as and for Legitimacy: Developments in West Indian Education between 1846 and 1895.* Waterloo: Wilfrid Laurier University Press, 1994.

Backhouse, Constance. *Colour-Coded: A Legal History of Racism in Canada, 1900–1950.* Toronto: University of Toronto Press, 1999.

Baker, Simon. *Khot-La-Cha: The Autobiography of Chief Simon Baker*. Edited by Verna J. Kirkness. Vancouver: Douglas and McIntyre, 1994.

Banner, Stuart. *Possessing the Pacific: Land, Settlers, and Indigenous People from Australia to Alaska*. Cambridge: Harvard University Press, 2007.

Barman, Jean. "British Columbia's Pioneer Teachers." In *Children, Teachers and Schools in the History of British Columbia*, ed. Jean Barman and Mona Gleason, 171–90. Edmonton: Brush Education, 2003.

—. "The Emergence of Educational Structures in Nineteenth-Century British Columbia." In *Children, Teachers and Schools in the History of British Columbia*, ed. Jean Barman and Mona Gleason, 13–35. Edmonton: Brush Education, 2003.

—. "Encounters with Sexuality: The Management of Inappropriate Body Behaviour in Late-Nineteenth-Century British Columbia Schools." In *Children, Teachers and Schools in the History of British Columbia*, ed. Jean Barman and Mona Gleason, 191–214. Edmonton: Brush Education, 2003.

—. *French Canadians, Furs, and Indigenous Women*. Vancouver: UBC Press, 2014.

—. *Growing Up British in British Columbia: Boys in Private Schools*. Vancouver: UBC Press, 1984.

—. *Iroquois in the West*. Montreal and Kingston: McGill-Queen's University Press, 2019.

—. "'Knowledge Is Essential for Universal Progress but Fatal to Class Privilege': Working People and the Schools in Vancouver During the 1920s." *Labour/Le travail* 22 (Fall 1988): 9–66.

—. "Schooled for Inequality: The Education of British Columbia Aboriginal Children." In *Children, Teachers and Schools in the History of British Columbia*, ed. Jean Barman and Mona Gleason, 55–79. Edmonton: Brush Education, 2003.

—. "Separate and Unequal: Indian and White Girls at All Hallows School, 1884–1920." In *Children, Teachers and Schools in the History of British Columbia*, ed. Jean Barman and Mona Gleason, 283–302. Edmonton: Brush Education, 2003.

—. *Stanley Park's Secret: The Forgotten Families of Whoi Whoi, Kanaka Ranch, and Brockton Point*. Madeira Park, BC: Harbour, 2005.

—. "Transfer, Imposition or Consensus? The Emergence of Educational Structures in Nineteenth-Century British Columbia." In *Schools in the West: Essays in Canadian Educational History*, ed. Nancy M. Sheehan, J. Donald Wilson, and David C. Jones, 241–64. Calgary: Detselig, 1986.

—. *The West beyond the West: A History of British Columbia*. Toronto: University of Toronto Press, 2007.

Barman, Jean, and Mona Gleason, eds. *Children, Teachers and Schools in the History of British Columbia*. Edmonton: Brush Education, 2003.

Barman, Jean, Yvonne Hébert, and Don McCaskill, eds. *Indian Education in Canada: Volume 1: The Legacy*. Vancouver: UBC Press, 1986.

Barman, Jean, Neil Sutherland, and J. Donald Wilson, eds. *Children, Teachers and Schools in the History of British Columbia*. Calgary: Detselig, 1995.

Barrington, J.M. *Separate but Equal? Māori Schools and the Crown, 1867–1969*. Wellington: Victoria University Press, 2008.

Battell Loman, Emma, and Adam J. Barker. *Settler: Identity and Colonialism in Twenty-First Century Canada*. Winnipeg: Fernwood, 2015.

Battiste, Marie. *Decolonizing Education: Nourishing the Learning Spirit*. Saskatoon: Purich, 2013.

Baugh, Daniel A. "Seapower and Science: The Motives for Pacific Exploration." In *Background to Discovery: Pacific Exploration from Dampier to Cook*, ed. Derek Howse, 1–58. Berkeley: University of California Press, 1999.

Begg, Alexander. *History of British Columbia: From Its Earliest Discovery to the Present Time*. Toronto: William Briggs, 1972, originally published 1894.

Belshaw, John Douglas. *Becoming British Columbia: A Population History*. Vancouver: UBC Press, 2009.

–. *Colonization and Community: The Vancouver Island Coalfield and the Making of a British Columbian Working Class*. Montreal and Kingston: McGill-Queen's University Press, 2002.

Bhabha, Homi K. "Of Mimicry and Man: The Ambivalence of Colonial Discourse." *Discipleship: A Special Issue of Psychoanalysis* 28 (Spring 1984): 125–33.

Blackhawk, Ned. *Violence over the Land: Indians and Empires in the Early American West*. Cambridge: Harvard University Press, 2006.

Blake, Lynn A. "Oblate Missionaries and the 'Indian Land Question.'" *BC Studies* 119 (Autumn 1998): 27–44.

Brealey, Kenneth G. "Travels from Point Ellice: Peter O'Reilly and the Indian Reserve System in British Columbia." *BC Studies* 115–16 (Autumn-Winter 1998): 181–236.

Brown, Helen. "Gender and Space: Constructing the Public School Teaching Staff in Nanaimo, 1891–1914." *BC Studies* 105–6 (1995): 59–79.

Brown, Jennifer. *Strangers in Blood: Fur Trade Company Families in Indian Country*. Vancouver: UBC Press, 1980.

Brownlie, Robin Jarvis. *A Fatherly Eye: Indian Agents, Government Power, and Aboriginal Resistance in Ontario, 1918–1939*. Don Mills, ON: Oxford University Press, 2003.

Burton, Antoinette, ed. *Archive Stories: Facts, Fictions, and the Writing of History*. Durham, NC: Duke University Press, 2004.

Calam, John, ed. *Alex Lord's British Columbia: Recollections of a Rural School Teacher, 1915–1936*. Vancouver: UBC Press, 1991.

–. "Culture and Credentials: A Note on Late Nineteenth Century Teacher Certification in British Columbia." *British Columbia Historical News* 14 (Fall 1980): 12–15.

—. "Teaching and Teachers: Establishment and Early Years of the B.C. Provincial Normal Schools." In *Schools in the West: Essays in Canadian Educational History*, ed. Nancy M. Sheehan, J. Donald Wilson, and David C. Jones, 75–97. Calgary: Detselig, 1986.

Callan, Eamonn. "John Dewey and the Two Faces of Progressive Education." In *Canadian Education: Historical Themes and Contemporary Issues*, ed. E. Brian Titley, 83–93. Calgary: Detselig, 1990.

Campbell, Lara. *A Great Revolutionary Wave: Women and the Vote in British Columbia*. Vancouver: UBC Press, 2020.

Carleton, Sean. "'The Children Show Unmistakable Signs of Indian Blood': Indigenous Students Attending Public Schools in British Columbia, 1871–1930." *History of Education* 50, 3 (2021): 313–37.

—. "Colonizing Minds: Public Education, the 'Textbook Indian,' and Settler Colonialism in British Columbia, 1920–1970." *BC Studies* 169 (Spring 2011): 101–30.

—. "'I Don't Need Any More Education': Senator Lynn Beyak, Residential School Denialism, and Attacks on Truth and Reconciliation in Canada." *Settler Colonial Studies* (June 6, 2021). https://www.tandfonline.com/doi/full/10.1080/2201473X.2021.1935574.

—. "Settler Anxiety and State Support for Missionary Schooling in Colonial British Columbia, 1849–1871." *Historical Studies in Education* 29, 1 (2017): 57–76.

Carleton, Sean and Kathleen McKenzie. "Hiding in Plain Sight: Newspaper Coverage of Dr. Peter Bryce's 1907 Report on Residential Schools." *Active History*. September 29, 2021. http://activehistory.ca/2021/09/hiding-in-plain-sight-newspaper-coverage-of-dr-peter-bryces-1907-report-on-residential-schools/#more-30946.

Carlson, Keith Thor. *The Power of Place, the Problem of Time: Aboriginal Identity and Historical Consciousness in the Cauldron of Colonialism*. Toronto: University of Toronto Press, 2010.

—. "Rethinking Dialogue and History: The King's Promise and the 1906 Aboriginal Delegation to London." *Native Studies Review* 16, 2 (2005): 1–38.

Carr, Geoffery Paul. "'House of No Spirit': An Architectural History of the Indian Residential School in British Columbia," PhD diss., University of British Columbia, 2011.

Carter, Sarah. *The Importance of Being Monogamous: Marriage and Nation Building in Western Canada to 1915*. Edmonton: Athabaska University Press, 2008.

Chapple, Eve, and Helen Raptis. "From Integration to Segregation: Government Education Policy and the School at Telegraph Creek in British Columbia, 1906–1951." *Journal of the Canadian Historical Association* 24, 1 (2013): 131–62.

Christophers, Brett. *Positioning the Missionary: John Booth Good and the Confluence of Culture in Nineteenth-Century British Columbia*. Vancouver: UBC Press, 1998.

Clark, Penney, and Yesman Post. "'A Natural Outcome of Free Schools': The Free Text-Book Branch in British Columbia 1908–1949." *Historical Studies in Education/Revue d'histoire de l'éducation* 21, 2 (Fall 2009): 23–45.

Clayton, Daniel. *Islands of Truth: The Imperial Fashioning of Vancouver Island*. Vancouver: UBC Press, 2000.

Clement, Wallace, and Leah F. Vosko, eds. *Changing Canada: Political Economy as Transformation*. Montreal and Kingston: McGill-Queen's University Press, 2003.

Clement, Wallace, and Glen Williams, eds. *The New Canadian Political Economy*. Montreal and Kingston: McGill-Queen's University Press, 1989.

Clendinning, Anne. "Exhibiting a Nation: Canada at the British Empire Exhibition, 1924–1925." *Histoire sociale/Social History* 39, 77 (2006): 79–107.

Comacchio, Cynthia. *The Dominion of Youth: Adolescence and the Making of Modern Canada, 1920–1950*. Waterloo: Wilfrid Laurier University Press, 2006.

—. *The Infinite Bonds of Family: Domesticity in Canada, 1850–1940*. Toronto: University of Toronto Press, 1999.

Cook, Peter, Neil Vallance, John Lutz, Graham Brazier, and Hamar Foster, eds. *To Share, Not Surrender: Indigenous and Settler Visions of Treaty Making in the Colonies of Vancouver Island and British Columbia*. Vancouver: UBC Press, 2021.

Corrigan, Philip, and Derek Sayer. *The Great Arch*. Oxford: Basil Blackwell, 1985.

Coulthard, Glen Sean. *Red Skin, White Masks: Rejecting the Colonial Politics of Recognition*. Minneapolis: University of Minnesota Press, 2014.

Craven, Paul, and Tom Traves. "The Class Politics of the National Policy, 1872–1933." *Journal of Canadian Studies* 14, 3 (1979): 14–38.

Cross, Natalie, and Thomas Peace. "'My Own Old English Friends': Networking Anglican Settler Colonialism at the Shingwauk Home, Huron College, and Western University." *Historical Studies in Education* 33, 1 (Spring 2021): 22–49.

Curtis, Bruce. *Building the Educational State: Canada West, 1836–1871*. London: Althouse, 1988.

—. *Ruling by Schooling: Conquest to Liberal Governmentality*. Toronto: University of Toronto Press, 2012.

—. *True Government by Choice Men? Inspection, Education, and State Formation in Canada West*. Toronto: University of Toronto Press, 1992.

Damer, Eric, and Herbert Rosengarten. *UBC: The First 100 Years*. Vancouver: University of British Columbia, 2009.

Deloria, Philip J. *Indians in Unexpected Places*. Lawrence: University Press of Kansas, 2004.

Deloria, Vine, Jr. *Custer Died for Your Sins*. Norman: University of Oklahoma Press, 1988.

Dobb, Maurice. *Studies in the Development of Capitalism*. New York: Taylor and Francis, 1963.

Downey, Allan. *The Creator's Game: Lacrosse, Identity, and Indigenous Nationhood.* Vancouver: UBC Press, 2018.

Dubinsky, Karen, Adele Perry, and Henry Yu, eds. *Within and without the Nation: Canadian History as Transnational History.* Toronto: University of Toronto Press, 2015.

Dunn, Timothy. "The Rise of Mass Public Schooling in British Columbia, 1900–1929." In *Schooling and Society in 20th Century British Columbia*, ed. J. Donald Wilson and David C. Jones, 23–51. Calgary: Detselig, 1980.

–. "Teaching the Meaning of Work: Vocational Education in British Columbia, 1900–1929." In *Shaping the Schools of the Canadian West*, ed. Nancy M. Sheehan, David C. Jones, and Robert M. Stamp, 236–55. Calgary: Detselig, 1979.

Ellis, Jason. *A Class by Themselves? The Origins of Special Education in Toronto and Beyond.* Toronto: University of Toronto Press, 2019.

Estes, Nick. *Our History Is the Future: Standing Rock versus the Dakota Access Pipeline, and the Long Tradition of Indigenous Resistance.* London: Verso, 2019.

Fanon, Frantz. *The Wretched of the Earth.* New York: Grove Press, 2004.

Farelle Racette, Sherry. "Returning Fire, Pointing the Canon: Aboriginal Photography as Resistance." In *The Cultural Work of Photography in Canada*, ed. Carol Payne and Andrea Kunard, 70–90. Montreal and Kingston: McGill-Queen's University Press, 2011.

Federici, Silvia. *Caliban and the Witch: Women, the Body and Primitive Accumulation.* New York: Autonomedia, 2004.

Fisher, Robin. *Contact and Conflict: Indian-European Relations in British Columbia, 1774–1890.* Vancouver: UBC Press, 1977.

Fleming, Thomas. "In the Imperial Age and After: Patterns of British Columbia School Leadership and the Institution of the Superintendency, 1849–1988." *BC Studies* 81 (Spring 1989): 50–76.

–. "'Our Boys in the Field': School Inspectors, Superintendents, and the Changing Character of School Leadership in British Columbia." In *Schools in the West: Essays in Canadian Educational History*, ed. Nancy M. Sheehan, J. Donald Wilson, and David C. Jones, 285–303. Calgary: Detselig, 1986.

–. *School Leadership: Essays on the British Columbia Experience, 1872–1995.* Mill Bay: Bendall Books, 2001.

–, ed. *Schooling in British Columbia, 1849–2005: Voices from the Past.* Mill Bay, BC: Bendall Books, 2010.

Fleming, Thomas, Lisa Smith, and Helen Raptis. "An Accidental Teacher: Anthony Walsh and the Aboriginal Day Schools at Six Mile Creek and Inkameep, British Columbia, 1929–1942." *Historical Studies in Education* 19 (2007): 1–24.

Foner, Philip S. "The Colored Inhabitants of Vancouver Island." *BC Studies* 8 (Winter 1970): 29–33.

Forsyth, Janice. "Bodies of Meaning: Sports and Games at Canadian Residential Schools." In *Aboriginal Peoples and Sport in Canada: Historical Foundations and Contemporary Issues*, ed. Janice Forsyth and Audrey R. Giles, 13–34. Vancouver: UBC Press, 2012.

Fraser, Crystal Gail. "T'aih k'ìighe' tth'aih zhit dìidìch'ùh (By Strength, We Are Still Here): Indigenous Northerners Confronting Hierarchies of Power at Day and Residential Schools in Nanhkak Thak (the Inuvik Region, Northwest Territories), 1959 to 1982." PhD diss., University of Alberta, 2019.

Fraser, Crystal Gail, and Allyson Stevenson. "Reflecting on the Foundations of Our Discipline Inspired by the TRC: A Duty to Respond during This Age of Reconciliation." *Canadian Historical Review* 103, 1 (March 2022): 1–31.

Furniss, Elizabeth. *The Burden of History: Colonialism and the Frontier Myth in a Rural Canadian Community*. Vancouver: UBC Press, 1999.

–. *Victims of Benevolence: The Dark Legacy of the Williams Lake Residential School*. Vancouver: Arsenal, 1995

Galois, Robert M. "Colonial Encounters: The Worlds of Arthur Wellington Clah, 1855–1881." *BC Studies* 115–16 (1997–98): 105–48.

Gaudry, Adam. "Insurgent Research." *Wicazo Sa Review* 26, 1 (Spring 2011): 113–36.

George, Ernie, and Sabrina Dungan. *How I Survived Lejac Residential School*. Morrisville, NC: Lulu, 2012.

Gettler, Brian. *Colonialism's Currency: Money, State, and First Nations in Canada, 1820–1950*. Montreal and Kingston: McGill-Queen's University Press, 2020.

Giancarlo, Alexandra. "Indigenous Student Labour and Settler Colonialism at Brandon Residential School." *Canadian Geographer* 64, 3 (Fall 2020): 461–74.

Giancarlo, Alexandra, Janice Forsyth, Braden Te Hiwi, and Taylor McKee. "Methodology and Indigenous Memory: Using Photographs to Anchor Critical Reflections on Indian Residential School Experiences." *Visual Studies* 36, 4–5 (2021): 406–20.

Gibson, William C. *Wesbrook and His University*. Vancouver: UBC Press, 1973.

Gidney, R.D., and W.P.J. Millar. "From Volunteerism to State Schooling: The Creation of the Public School System in Ontario." *Canadian Historical Review* 66, 4 (December 1984): 443–73.

–. *How Schools Worked: Public Education in English Canada, 1900–1940*. Montreal and Kingston: McGill-Queen's University Press, 2012.

–. "The Salaries of Teachers in English Canada, 1900–1940: A Reappraisal." *Historical Studies in Education* 22, 1 (2010): 1–38.

Giles, Valerie Mary Evelyn. "Historical Evolution of the Office of Deputy Minister in British Columbia Educational Policymaking 1919–1945: The Career of Samuel John Willis." PhD diss., University of British Columbia, 1993.

Giroux, Henry, and David Purpel, eds. *The Hidden Curriculum and Moral Education: Deception or Discovery?* Berkeley: McCutchan, 1983.

Gleason, Mona. *Normalizing the Ideal: Psychology, Schooling, and the Family in Postwar Canada.* Toronto: University of Toronto Press, 1999.

–. "Race, Class, and Health: School Medical Inspection and 'Healthy' Children in British Columbia 1890 to 1930." In *Children, Teachers and Schools in the History of British Columbia,* ed. Jean Barman and Mona Gleason, 133–48. Edmonton: Brush Education, 2003.

Gopal, Priyamvada. *Insurgent Empire: Anticolonial Resistance and British Dissent.* London: Verso, 2020.

Gough, Barry. *Gunboat Frontier: British Maritime Authority and Northwest Coast Indians, 1846–1890.* Vancouver: UBC Press, 1984.

Gramsci, Antonio. *Selections from the Prison Notebooks.* New York: International, 1971.

Greer, Allan. "Commons and Enclosure in the Colonization of North America." *The American Historical Review* 117, 2 (April 2012): 365–86.

–. *Property and Dispossession: Natives, Empires and Land in Early Modern North America.* Cambridge: Cambridge University Press, 2018.

Gresko, Jacqueline. "Creating Little Dominions within the Dominion: Early Catholic Indian Schools in Saskatchewan and British Columbia." In *Indian Education in Canada.* Vol. 1, *The Legacy,* ed. Jean Barman, Yvonne Hébert, and Don McCaskill, 88–111. Vancouver: UBC Press, 1986.

–. "White 'Rites' and Indian 'Rites': Indian Education and Native Responses in the West." In *Shaping the Schools of the Canadian West,* ed. Nancy M. Sheehan, David C. Jones, and Robert M. Stamp, 84–106. Calgary: Detselig, 1979.

Griffith, Jane. *Words Have a Past: The English Language, Colonialism, and the Newspapers of Indian Boarding Schools.* Toronto: University of Toronto Press, 2019.

Habkirk, Evan. "From Indian Boys to Canadian Men? The Use of Cadet Drill in the Canadian Indian Residential School System." *British Journal of Canadian Studies* 30, 2 (2017): 227–47.

Haig-Brown, Celia. *Resistance and Renewal: Surviving the Indian Residential School.* Vancouver: Tillacum Library, 1988.

Hall, Catherine. *Civilising Subjects: Metropole and Colony in the English Imagination, 1830–1867.* Chicago: University of Chicago Press, 2002.

–. "Making Colonial Subjects: Education in the Age of Empire." *History of Education: Journal of the History of Education Society* 37, 6 (2008): 773–87.

Hamilton, W.D. *The Federal Indian Day Schools of the Maritimes.* Fredericton: Micmac-Maliseet Institute, 1986.

Hare, Jan, and Jean Barman. *Good Intentions Gone Awry: Emma Crosby and the Methodist Mission on the Northwest Coast.* Vancouver: UBC Press, 2006.

Harris, Cole. *A Bounded Land: Reflections on Settler Colonialism in Canada.* Vancouver: UBC Press, 2021.

—. "How Did Colonialism Dispossess? Comments from an Edge of Empire." *Annals of the Association of American Geographers* 94, 1 (2004): 165–82.

—. *Making Native Space: Colonialism, Resistance, and Reserves in British Columbia.* Vancouver: UBC Press, 2002.

—. *The Resettlement of British Columbia: Essays on Colonialism and Geographical Change.* Vancouver: UBC Press, 1997.

Harvey, David. *A Brief History of Neoliberalism.* New York: Oxford University Press, 2005.

Hay, Travis, Cindy Blackstock, and Michael Kirlew. "Dr. Peter Bryce (1853–1932): Whistleblower on Residential Schools." *Canadian Medical Association Journal* 192, 9 (March 2020): E223–E224.

Heaman, E.A. *The Inglorious Arts of Peace: Exhibitions in Canadian Society during the Nineteenth Century.* Toronto: University of Toronto Press, 1999.

—. *A Short History of the State in Canada.* Toronto: University of Toronto Press, 2015.

—. *Tax, Order, and Good Government: A New Political History of Canada, 1867–1917.* Montreal and Kingston: McGill-Queen's University Press, 2017.

Heartfield, James. *Aborigines' Protection Society: Humanitarian Imperialism in Australia, New Zealand, Fiji, Canada, South Africa, and the Congo, 1836–1909.* Oxford: Oxford University Press, 2011.

Hobsbawm, Eric. *The Age of Capital, 1848–1875.* New York: Vintage Books, 1975.

Houston, Susan, and Alison Prentice. *Family, School, and Society in Nineteenth-Century Canada.* Don Mills: Oxford University Press, 1975.

Howay, F.W., and E.O.S. Sholefield. *British Columbia from the Earliest Times to the Present.* Vol. 2. Vancouver: S.J. Clarke, 1914.

Howlett, Michael, Alex Netherton, and M. Ramesh. *The Political Economy of Canada: An Introduction.* Don Mills, ON: Oxford University Press, 1999.

Illich, Ivan. *Deschooling Society.* New York: Harper and Row, 1970.

Ishiguro, Laura. "'Growing Up and Grown Up [...] in Our Future City': Children and the Aspirational Politics of Settler Futurity in Colonial British Columbia." *BC Studies* 190 (Summer 2016): 15–37.

—. *Nothing to Write Home About: British Family Correspondence and the Settler Colonial Everyday in British Columbia.* Vancouver: UBC Press, 2018.

Johnson, F. Henry. *A History of Public Education in British Columbia.* Vancouver: Publications Centre, University of British Columbia, 1964.

—. *John Jessop: Goldseeker and Educator: Founder of the British Columbia School System.* Vancouver: Mitchell Press, 1971.

—. "The Ryersonian Influence on the Public School System of British Columbia." *BC Studies* 10 (1971): 26–34.
Johnston, Kay. *The Amazing Mazie Baker: The Squamish Nation's Warrior Elder.* Halfmoon Bay, BC: Caitlin Press, 2016.
Jones, David C. "Maleficent Obsession: Social Control and the Schools." *Journal of Educational Thought* 12, 1 (1978): 48–54.
—. "The *Zeitgeist* of Western Settlement: Education and the Myth of the Land." In *Schooling and Society in 20th Century British Columbia*, ed. J. Donald Wilson and David C. Jones, 71–89. Calgary: Detselig, 1980.
Kauanui, J. Kēhaulani. "'A Structure, Not an Event': Settler Colonialism and Enduring Indigeneity." *Lateral: Journal of the Cultural Studies Association* 5, 1 (Spring 2016).
Kelm, Mary-Ellen. *Colonizing Bodies: Aboriginal Health and Healing in British Columbia, 1900–50.* Vancouver: UBC Press, 1998.
—, ed. *The Letters of Margaret Butcher: Missionary-Imperialism on the North Pacific Coast.* Calgary: University of Calgary Press, 2006.
Kelm, Mary-Ellen, and Robin Jarvis Brownlie. "Desperately Seeking Absolution: Native Agency as Colonialist Alibi." *Canadian Historical Review* 75, 4 (December 1994): 543–56.
Kelm, Mary-Ellen, and Keith D. Smith, eds. *Talking Back to the Indian Act: Critical Readings in Settler Colonial Histories.* Toronto: University of Toronto Press, 2018.
Kirkness, V.J. *First Nations and Schools: Triumph and Struggles.* Ottawa: Canadian Education Association, 1992.
Klassen, Pamela E. *The Story of Radio Mind: A Missionary's Journey on Indigenous Land.* Chicago: University of Chicago Press, 2018.
Ladner, Kiera. "Proceed with Caution: Reflections on Resurgance and Reconcilation." In *Resurgence and Reconciliation: Indigenous-Settler Relations and Earth Teachings*, ed. Michael Asch, John Borrows, and James Tully, 245–64. Toronto: University of Toronto, 2018.
Lawrence, Mary. *My People, Myself.* Prince George: Caitlin Press, 1996.
Leland, Donald, Deidre Sanders, and Naneen Stuckey. "What the People Said: Kwakwaka'wakw, Nuu-chah-nulth, and Tsimshian Testimonies before the Royal Commission on Indian Affairs for the Province of British Columbia (1913–1916)." *Canadian Journal of Native Studies* 19, 2 (1999): 213–48.
Littlefield, Alice. "Indian Education and the World of Work in Michigan, 1893–1933." In *Native Americans and Wage Labour: Ethnographic Perspectives*, ed. Alice Littlefield and Martha Knack, 100–21. Norman: University of Oklahoma Press, 1996.

—. "Learning to Labor: Native American Education in the United States, 1893–1930." In *The Political Economy of Native American Indians*, ed. John H. Moore, 43–59. Norman: University of Oklahoma Press, 1993.

Lomawaima, K. Tsianina. *They Called It Prairie Light: The Story of Chilocco Indian School*. Lincoln: University of Nebraska Press, 1994.

Loo, Tina. *Making Law, Order, and Authority in British Columbia, 1821–1871*. Toronto: University of Toronto Press, 1994.

Luby, Brittany. *Dammed: The Politics of Loss and Survival in Anishinaabe Territory*. Winnipeg: University of Manitoba Press, 2020.

Lutz, John Sutton. *Makúk: A New History of Aboriginal-White Relations*. Vancouver: UBC Press, 2008.

Luxemburg, Rosa. *The Accumulation of Capital*. London: Routledge, 2003.

MacDonald, David. B. *The Sleeping Giant Awakens: Genocide, Indian Residential Schools, and the Challenge of Conciliation*. Toronto: University of Toronto Press, 2019.

Mackey, Eva. "The Apologizer's Apology." In *Reconciling Canada: Critical Perspectives on the Culture of Redress*, ed. Jennifer Henderson and Pauline Wakeham, 47–62. Toronto: University of Toronto Press, 2013.

—. *Unsettled Expectations: Uncertainty, Land and Settler Decolonization*. Halifax: Fernwood, 2016.

MacLaurin, Donald Leslie. "Education before the Gold Rush." *British Columbia Historical Quarterly* 2, 4 (October 1938): 247–63.

—. "The History of Education in the Crown Colonies of Vancouver Island and British Columbia and in the Province of British Columbia." PhD diss., University of Washington, 1936.

Mangan, J.A., ed. *"Benefits Bestowed"? Education and British Imperialism*. Manchester: Manchester University Press, 1988.

Mann, Jean. "G.M. Weir and H.B. King: Progressive Education or Education for the Progressive State?" In *Schooling and Society in 20th Century British Columbia*, ed. Donald J. Wilson and David C. Jones, 91–118. Calgary: Detselig, 1980.

Manuel, Arthur. *The Reconciliation Manifesto: Recovering the Land, Rebuilding the Economy*. Toronto: Lorimer, 2017.

Manuel, Arthur, and Ronald M. Derrickson. *Unsettling Canada: A National Wake-Up Call*. Toronto: Between the Lines Press, 2015.

Manuel, George, and Michael Posluns. *The Fourth World: An Indian Reality*. New York: Free Press, 1974.

Maracle, Lee. *I Am Woman: A Native Perspective on Sociology and Feminism*. Vancouver: Press Gang, 1996.

—. *My Conversations with Canadians*. Toronto: Book Thug, 2017.

Marker, Michael. "Borders and the Borderless Coast Salish Peoples: Decolonising Historiographies of Indigenous Schooling." *History of Education* 44, 4 (2015): 480–502.

Marks, Lynne. *Infidels and the Damn Churches: Irreligion and Religion in Settler British Columbia*. Vancouver: UBC Press, 2017.

Marshall, Daniel P. *Claiming the Land: British Columbia and the Making of a New El Dorado*. Vancouver: Ronsdale Press, 2018.

Marx, Karl. *Capital*, vol. 1, *A Critique of Political Economy*. Vol. 1. New York: Vintage, 1977.

—. *Grundrisse: Foundations of the Critique of Political Economy*. New York: Penguin Books, 1973.

Matters, Diane L. "The Boys' Industrial School: Education for Juvenile Offenders." In *Schooling and Society in 20th Century British Columbia*, ed. J. Donald Wilson and David C. Jones, 53–70. Calgary: Detselig, 1980.

Mawani, Renisa. *Colonial Proximities: Crossracial Encounters and Juridical Truths in British Columbia, 1871–1921*. Vancouver: UBC Press, 2009.

—. "In Between and Out of Place: Mixed-Race Identity, Liquor, and the Law in British Columbia, 1850–1913." In *Race, Space, and the Law: Unmapping a White Settler Society*, ed. Sherene H. Razack, 47–69. Toronto: Between the Lines, 2002.

Maynard, Robyn. *Policing Black Lives: State Violence in Canada from Slavery to the Present*. Winnipeg: Fernwood, 2017.

McCallum, Mary Jane Logan. "To Make Good Canadians: Girl Guiding in Indian Residential Schools." Master's thesis, Trent University, 2001.

—. "Indigenous Histories of Tuberculosis in Manitoba." 1 (Spring 2014).

—. *Indigenous Women, Work, and History, 1940–1980*. Winnipeg: University of Manitoba Press, 2014.

McCallum, Mary Jane Logan, and Adele Perry. *Structures of Indifference: An Indigenous Life and Death in a Canadian City*. Winnipeg: University of Manitoba Press, 2018.

McClintock, Anne. *Imperial Leather: Race, Gender and Sexuality in the Colonial Contest*. New York: Routledge, 1995.

McCracken, Krista. "Archival Photographs in Perspective: Indian Residential School Images of Health." *British Journal of Canadian Studies* 30, 2 (2017): 163–82.

McDonald, Robert A.J. *A Long Way to Paradise: A New History of British Columbia Politics*. Vancouver: UBC Press, 2021.

—. *Making Vancouver: Class, Status, and Social Boundaries, 1863–1913*. Vancouver: UBC Press, 1996.

McFarlane, Peter, with Doreen Manuel. *Brotherhood to Nationhood: George Manuel and the Making of the Modern Indian Movement*. Toronto: Between the Lines, 2020.

McNally, David. *Blood and Money: War, Slavery, Finance and Empire*. Winnipeg: Fernwood, 2020.

McNally, Vincent. "Challenging the Status Quo: An Examination of the History of Catholic Education in British Columbia." *CCHA, Historical Studies* 65 (1999): 71–91.

Memmi, Albert. *The Colonizer and the Colonized*. Boston: Beacon, 1965.

–. *The Pillar of Salt*. Boston: Beacon, 1992.

Miliband, Ralph. *The State in Capitalist Society*. London: Weidenfeld and Nicolson, 2009.

Miller, J.R. *Residential Schools and Reconciliation*. Toronto: University of Toronto Press, 2017.

–. *Shingwauk's Vision: A History of Native Residential Schools*. Toronto: University of Toronto Press, 1996.

Millions, Erin. "Portraits and Gravestones: Documenting the Transnational Lives of Nineteenth-Century British-Métis Students." *Journal of the Canadian Historical Association* 29, 1 (2008): 1–38.

Milloy, John S. *A National Crime: The Canadian Government and the Residential School System, 1879 to 1986*. Winnipeg: University of Manitoba Press, 1999.

Moreton-Robinson, Aileen. *The White Possessive: Property, Power, and Indigenous Sovereignty*. Minneapolis: University of Minnesota Press, 2015.

Morton, Desmond. "The Cadet Movement in the Moment of Canadian Militarism, 1909–1914." *Journal of Canadian Studies* 13, 2 (Summer 1978): 56–68.

Mosby, Ian. "Administering Colonial Science: Nutrition Research and Human Biomedical Experimentation in Aboriginal Communities and Residential Schools, 1942–1954." *Histoire sociale/Social History* 46, 91 (May 2013): 145–72.

Moss, Mark. *Manliness and Militarism: Educating Young Boys in Ontario for War*. Don Mills, ON: Oxford University Press, 2001.

Murray, Peter. *The Devil and Mr. Duncan*. Victoria: Sono Nis Press, 1985.

Naylor, James. *The New Democracy: Challenging the Social Order in Industrial Ontario, 1914–1925*. Toronto: University of Toronto Press, 1991.

Nelson, Jay. "'A Revolution in the Manners of the Country': Aboriginal-Settler Intermarriage in Nineteenth Century British Columbia." In *Regulating Lives: Historical Essays on the State, Society, the Individual, and the Law*, ed. John McLaren, Robert Menzies, and Dorothy E. Chunn, 23–62. Vancouver: UBC Press, 2003.

Neylan, Susan. *The Heavens Are Changing: Nineteenth-Century Protestant Missions and Tsimshian Christianity*. Montreal and Kingston: McGill-Queen's University Press, 2003.

Nickel, Sarah. *Assembling Unity: Indigenous Politics, Gender, and the Union of BC Indian Chiefs.* Vancouver: UBC Press, 2019.

Nichols, Robert. "Disaggregating Primitive Accumulation." *Radical Philosophy* 194 (November/December 2015): 18–28.

Norton, Wayne. "The Cache Creek Provincial Boarding School, 1874–1890." *British Columbia Historical News* 29, 2 (1996): 30–33.

O'Donoghue, Thomas. "Colonialism, Education, and Social Change in the British Empire: The Cases of Australia, Papua New Guinea and Ireland." *Paedagogica Historica* 45, 6 (2009): 787–800.

Ormsby, Margaret. *British Columbia: A History.* Toronto: Macmillan of Canada, 1958.

–. "Frederick Seymour, the Forgotten Governor." *BC Studies* 22 (Summer 1974): 3–25.

Palmer, Bryan D. *A Culture in Conflict: Skilled Workers and Industrial Capitalism in Hamilton, Ontario, 1860–1914.* Montreal and Kingston: McGill-Queen's University Press, 1979.

–. "Social Formation and Class Formation in Nineteenth-Century North America." In *Proletarianization and Family History*, ed. David Levine, 224–308. New York: Academic Press, 1984.

Palmer, Bryan D., and Gaétan Héroux. "'Cracking the Stone': The Long History of Capitalist Crisis and Toronto's Dispossessed, 1830–1930." *Labour/Le travail* 69 (Spring 2012): 9–62.

Panitch, Leo, ed. *The Canadian State: Political Economy and Political Power.* Toronto: University of Toronto Press, 1977.

Parnaby, Andrew. "'The Best Men That Ever Worked the Lumber': Aboriginal Longshoremen on Burrard Inlet, BC, 1863–1939." *Canadian Historical Review* 87, 1 (2006): 53–78.

–. *Citizen Docker: Making a New Deal on the Vancouver Waterfront, 1919–1939.* Toronto: University of Toronto Press, 2008.

Patnaik, Utsa, and Prabhat Patnaik. *Capital and Imperialism: Theory, History, and the Present.* New York: Monthly Review, 2021.

Patterson, E. Palmer, II. *Mission on the Nass: The Evangelization of the Nishga, 1860–1890.* Waterloo, ON: Eulachon Press, 1982.

Patterson, R.S. "The Canadian Experience with Progressive Education." In *Canadian Education: Historical Themes and Contemporary Issues*, ed. E. Brian Titley, 95–110. Calgary: Detselig, 1990.

Perelman, Michael. *The Invention of Capitalism: Classical Political Economy and the Secret History of Primitive Accumulation.* Durham, NC: Duke University Press, 2000.

Perry, Adele. "The Autocracy of Love and the Legitimacy of Empire: Intimacy, Power and Scandal in Nineteenth-Century Metlakahtlah." *Gender and History* 16, 2 (2004): 261–88.

–. *Colonial Relations: The Douglas-Connolly Family and the Nineteenth-Century Imperial World.* Cambridge: Cambridge University Press, 2015.

–. *On the Edge of Empire: Gender, Race, and the Making of British Columbia, 1849-1871.* Toronto: University of Toronto Press, 2001.

–. "The State of Empire: Reproducing Colonialism in British Columbia, 1849–1871." *Journal of Colonialism and Colonial History* 2, 2 (Fall 2001).

Phillips, Charles E. *The Development of Education in Canada.* Toronto: W.J. Gage, 1957.

Polanyi, Karl. *The Great Transformation.* Boston: Beacon Press, 1957.

Pollard, Juliet. "Growing Up Métis: Fur Traders' Children in the Pacific Northwest." In *An Imperfect Past: Education and Society in Canadian History,* ed. J. Donald Wilson, 120–40. Vancouver: Centre for the Study of Curriculum and Instruction, University of British Columbia, 1984.

Porter, Andrew, ed. *The Imperial Horizons of British Protestant Missions, 1880–1914.* Grand Rapids, MI: Eerdmans, 2003.

Porter, John. *The Vertical Mosaic: An Analysis of Social Class and Power in Canada.* Toronto: University of Toronto Press, 1965.

Pratt, Mary Louise. "Arts of the Contact Zone." *Profession* 91 (1991): 33–40.

–. *Imperial Eyes: Travel Writing and Transculturation.* London: Routledge, 1992.

Prentice, Alison. *The School Promoters: Education and Social Class in Mid-Nineteenth Century Upper Canada.* Toronto: McClelland and Stewart, 1977.

Prochner, Larry. *History of Early Childhood Education in Canada, Australia, and New Zealand.* Vancouver: UBC Press, 2010.

Raibmon, Paige. *Authentic Indians: Episodes of Encounter from the Late-Nineteenth-Century Northwest Coast.* Durham, NC: Duke University Press, 2005.

–. "'A New Understanding of Things Indian': George Raley's Negotiation of the Residential School Experience." *BC Studies* 110 (1996): 69–96.

–. "Theatres of Contact: The Kwakwaka'wakw Meet Colonialism in British Columbia and at the Chicago World's Fair." *Canadian Historical Review* 81, 2 (June 2000): 157–90.

Raptis, Helen. "Blurring the Boundaries of Policy and Legislation in the Schooling of Indigenous Children in British Columbia, 1901–1951." *Historical Studies in Education* 27, 2 (Fall 2015): 65–77.

–. "Exploring the Factors Prompting British Columbia's First Integration Initiative: The Case of Port Essington Indian Day School." *History of Education Quarterly* 51, 4 (Fall 2011): 519–43.

—. "Implementing Integrated Education Policy for On-Reserve Aboriginal Children in British Columbia, 1951–1981." *Historical Studies in Education* 20 (Spring 2008): 118–46.

Raptis, Helen, with members of the Tsimshian Nation. *What We Learned: Two Generations Reflect on Tsimshian Education and the Day Schools.* Vancouver: UBC Press, 2016.

Redford, James. "Attendance at Indian Residential Schools in British Columbia, 1890–1920." *BC Studies* 44 (1979–80): 41–56.

Regan, Paulette. *Unsettling the Settler Within: Indian Residential Schools, Truth Telling, and Reconciliation in Canada.* Vancouver: UBC Press, 2010.

Richards, Thomas. *Imperial Archive: Knowledge and the Fantasy of Empire.* New York: Verso, 1996.

Roberts, Jenifer. *Fitz: The Colonial Adventures of James Edward FitzGerald.* Otago: University of Otago Press, 2016.

Roy, Patricia. "The Education of Japanese Children in the British Columbia Interior Housing Settlements during World War Two." *Historical Studies in Education/Revue d'histoire de l'éducation* 5 (1992): 211–31.

—. *A White Man's Province: British Columbia Politicians and the Chinese and Japanese, 1858–1914.* Vancouver: UBC Press, 1989.

Rück, Daniel. *The Laws and the Land: The Settler Colonial Invasion of Kahnawà:ke in Nineteenth-Century Canada.* Vancouver: UBC Press, 2021.

Russell, Bill. "The White Man's Paper Burden: Aspects of Record Keeping in the Department of Indian Affairs, 1860–1914." *Archivaria* 19 (1984–85): 50–72.

Rutherdale, Myra. *Women and the White Man's God: Gender and Race in the Canadian Mission Field.* Vancouver: UBC Press, 2002.

Said, Edward. *Culture and Imperialism.* New York: Vintage, 1993.

Sandwell, Ruth. *Contesting Rural Space: Land Policy and Practices of Resettlement on Saltspring Island, 1859–1891.* Montreal and Kingston: McGill-Queen's University Press, 2005.

Sangster, Joan. "Domesticating Girls: The Sexual Regulation of Aboriginal and Working-Class Girls in Twentieth-Century Canada." In *Contact Zones: Aboriginal and Settler Women in Canada's Colonial Past*, ed. Katie Pickles and Myra Rutherdale, 179–201. Vancouver: UBC Press, 2005.

—. *One Hundred Years of Struggle: The History of Women and the Vote in Canada.* Vancouver: UBC Press, 2018.

Satzewich, Vic, and Linda Mahood. "Indian Agents and the Residential School System in Canada, 1846–1970." *Historical Studies in Education/Revue d'histoire de l'éducation* 7 (1995): 45–69.

Schecter, Stephen. "Capitalism, Class, and Educational Reform in Canada." In *The Canadian State: Political Economy and Political Power*, ed. Leo Panitch, 373–416. Toronto: University of Toronto Press, 1977.

Schissel, Barnard, and Terry Wotherspoon. *The Legacy of School for Aboriginal People: Education, Oppression, and Emancipation*. Don Mills, ON: Oxford University Press, 2003.

Scott, James C. *Domination and the Arts of Resistance: Hidden Transcripts*. New Haven: Yale University Press, 1990.

–. *Seeing Like a State: How Certain Schemes to Improve the Human Condition Have Failed*. New Haven: Yale University Press, 1999.

–. *Weapons of the Weak: Everyday Forms of Peasant Resistance*. New Haven: Yale University Press, 1985.

Seager, Allan, and David Roth. "British Columbia and the Mining West: A Ghost of a Chance." In *The Workers' Revolt in Canada, 1917–1925*, ed. Craig Heron, 231–67. Toronto: University of Toronto Press, 1998.

Sellars, Bev. *They Called Me Number One: Secrets and Survival at an Indian Residential School*. Vancouver: Talonbooks, 2013.

Sheehan, Nancy M. "Character Training and Cultural Heritage: An Historical Comparison of Canadian Elementary Readers." In *The Curriculum in Canada in Historical Perspective*, ed. G.S. Tomkins, Sixth Yearbook of the Canadian Society for the Study of Education, 77–84. Edmonton: Canadian Society for the Study of Education, 1979.

–. "World War I and Provincial Educational Policy in English Canada." In *Historical Perspectives on Educational Policy* in Canada, ed. E.W. Ricker and B.A. Wood, 253–79. Toronto: Canadian Scholars' Press, 1995.

Shipley, Tyler. *Canada in the World: Settler Capitalism and the Colonial Imaginary*. Winnipeg: Fernwood, 2020.

Simpson, Audra. *Mohawk Interruptus: Political Life across the Borders of Settler States*. Durham, NC: Duke University Press, 2014.

–. "Whither Settler Colonialism?" *Settler Colonial Studies* 6, 4 (2016): 438–44.

Simpson, Leanne Betasamosake. *As We Have Always Done: Indigenous Freedom through Radical Resistance*. Minneapolis: University of Minnesota Press, 2017.

–. *Dancing on Our Turtle's Back: Stories of Nishnaabeg Re-Creation, Resurgence and a New Emergence*. Winnipeg: Arbeiter Ring, 2011.

–, ed. *Lighting the Eighth Fire: The Liberation, Resurgence, and Protection of Indigenous Nations*. Winnipeg: ARP Books, 2008.

Slater, G. Hollis. "New Light on Herbert Beaver." *British Columbia Historical Quarterly* 6 (1942): 13–29.

–. "Rev. Robert John Staines: Pioneer Priest, Pedagogue, and Political Agitator." *British Columbia Historical Quarterly* 14 (1950): 187–240.

Smith, Linda Tuhiwai. *Decolonizing Methodologies: Research and Indigenous Peoples.* London: Bloomsbury, 2021.

—. "Kura Kaupapa Māori and the Implications for Curriculum." In *The School Curriculum in New Zealand: History, Theory, Policy and Practice,* ed. Gary McCulloch, 26–43. Palmerston North: Dunmore Press, 1992.

Sneve, Virginia Driving Hawk. *Completing the Circle.* Lincoln: University of Nebraska Press, 1998.

Stanley, Timothy J. *Contesting White Supremacy: School Segregation, Anti-Racism, and the Making of Chinese Canadians.* Vancouver: UBC Press, 2011.

—. "White Supremacy and the Rhetoric of Educational Indoctrination: A Canadian Case Study." In *Children, Teachers and Schools in the History of British Columbia,* ed. Jean Barman and Mona Gleason, 113–31. Edmonton: Brush Education, 2003.

Starblanket, Gina, and Dallas Hunt. *Storying Violence: Unravelling Colonial Narratives in the Stanley Trail.* Winnipeg: ARP Books, 2020.

Stevenson, Allyson D. *Intimate Integration: A History of the Sixties Scoop and the Colonization of Indigenous Kinship.* Toronto: University of Toronto Press, 2021.

Stevenson, Garth. *Unfulfilled Union: Canadian Federalism and National Unity.* Montreal and Kingston: McGill-Queen's University Press, 2009.

Stoler, Ann Laura. *Along the Archival Grain: Epistemic Anxieties and Colonial Common Sense.* Princeton: University of Princeton Press, 2009.

Storey, Kenton. *Settler Anxiety at the Outposts of Empire: Colonial Relations, Humanitarian Discourses, and the Imperial Press.* Vancouver: UBC Press, 2016.

Stranger-Ross, Jordan. "Municipal Colonialism in Vancouver: City Planning and the Conflict over Indian Reserves, 1928–1950s." *Canadian Historical Review* 89, 4 (December 2008): 541–80.

Survivors of the Assiniboia Indian Residential School. *Did You See Us? Reunion, Remembrance, and Reclamation at an Urban Indian Residential School.* Winnipeg: University of Manitoba Press, 2021.

Sutherland, Neil. *Children in English-Canadian Society: Framing the Twentieth-Century Consensus.* Toronto: University of Toronto Press, 1976.

—. "The Triumph of 'Formalism': Elementary Schooling in Vancouver from the 1920s to the 1960s." In *Children, Teachers and Schools in the History of British Columbia,* ed. Jean Barman and Mona Gleason, 319–42. Edmonton: Brush Education, 2003.

Tallie, T.J. *Queering Colonial Natal: Indigeneity and the Violence of Belonging in Southern Africa.* Minneapolis: University of Minnesota Press, 2019.

Te Hiwi, Braden. "'A Lack of Homelike Surroundings': Resident Health, Home, and Recreation Infrastructure at Pelican Lake Indian Residential School, 1952–1962." *Histoire sociale/Social History* 54, 110 (2021): 99–125.

Tennant, Paul. *Aboriginal Peoples and Politics: The Indian Land Question in British Columbia, 1849–1989*. Vancouver: UBC Press, 1990.

Thomas, Mark P., Leah F. Vosko, Carlo Fanelli, and Olena Lyubchenko, eds. *Change and Continuity: Canadian Political Economy in the New Millennium*. Montreal and Kingston: McGill-Queen's University Press, 2019.

Thommasen, Harvey, ed. *Grizzlies and White Guys: The Stories of Clayton Mack*. Madeira Park, BC: Harbour, 1993.

Thompson, E.P. "Time, Work-Discipline, and Industrial Capitalism." *Past and Present* 38, 1 (December 1967): 56–97.

—. *Whigs and Hunters: The Origins of the Black Act*. London: Breviary Stuff, 1975.

Thrush, Coll. *Indigenous London: Native Travelers at the Heart of Empire*. New Haven: Yale University Press, 2016.

Tillotson, Shirley. *Give and Take: The Citizen-Taxpayer and the Rise of Canadian Democracy*. Vancouver: UBC Press, 2019.

Titley, E. Brian. "Duncan Campbell Scott and Indian Education Policy." In *An Imperfect Past: Education and Society in Canadian History*, ed. J. Donald Wilson, 141–53. Vancouver: Centre for the Study of Curriculum and Instruction, University of British Columbia, 1984.

—. *The Indian Commissioners: Agents of the State and Indian Policy in Canada's Prairie West, 1873–1932*. Edmonton: University of Alberta Press, 2009.

—. "Indian Industrial Schools in Western Canada." In *Schools in the West: Essays in Canadian Educational History*, ed. Nancy M. Sheehan, J. Donald Wilson, and David C. Jones, 84–106. Calgary: Detselig, 1986.

—. "Industrious, but Formal and Mechanical: The Sisters of Charity of Providence in Residential School Classrooms." *Historical Studies in Education* 22, 2 (Fall 2010): 58–74.

—. *A Narrow Vision: Duncan Campbell Scott and the Administration of Indian Affairs in Canada*. Vancouver: UBC Press, 1986.

Tobias, John L. "Protection, Civilization, Assimilation: An Outline History of Canada's Indian Policy." In *As Long as the Sun Shines and the Water Flows: A Reader in Canadian Native Studies*, ed. Ian L. Getty and Antoine S. Lussier, 39–55. Vancouver: UBC Press, 2014.

Tough, David. *The Terrific Engine: Income Taxation and the Modernization of the Canadian Political Imaginary*. Vancouver: UBC Press, 2019.

Trafzer, Clifford E., Jeam A. Keller, and Lorene Sisquoc, eds. *Boarding School Blues: Revisiting American Indian Educational Experiences*. Lincoln: University of Nebraska Press, 2007.

Tuck, Eve. "Suspending Damage: A Letter to Communities" *Harvard Educational Review* 79, 3 (Fall 2009): 416–47.

Tuck, Eve and K. Wayne Yang. "Decolonization Is Not a Metaphor." *Decolonization: Indigeneity, Education and Society* 1, 1 (2012): 1–40.
Usher, Jean. *William Duncan of Metlakatla: A Victorian Missionary in British Columbia*. Ottawa: National Museums of Canada, 1974.
Van Brummelen, Harro. "Shifting Perspectives: Early British Columbia Textbooks from 1872 to 1925." *BC Studies* 60 (Winter 1983–84): 3–27.
Van Kirk, Sylvia. *Many Tender Ties: Women in Fur-Trade Society, 1670–1870*. Winnipeg: Watson and Dwyer, 1980.
Van Rijn, Kiran. "'Lo! the Poor Indian': Colonial Responses to the 1862–63 Smallpox Epidemic in British Columbia and Vancouver Island." *Canadian Bulletin of Medical History* 23, 2 (2006): 541–60.
Veracini, Lorenzo. *Settler Colonialism: A Theoretical Overview*. London: Palgrave Macmillan, 2010.
Vizenor, Gerald. *Fugitive Poses: Native American Indian Scenes of Absence and Presence*. Lincoln: University of Nebraska Press, 2000.
Von Heyking, Amy. *Creating Citizens: History and Identity in Alberta Schools, 1905–1980*. Calgary: University of Calgary Press, 2006.
Warburton, Rennie. "The Class Relations of Public Schoolteachers in British Columbia." In *Workers, Capital, and the State in British Columbia: Selected Papers*, ed. Rennie Warburton and David Coburn, 239–62. Vancouver: UBC Press, 1988.
Warburton, Rennie, and David Coburn, eds. *Workers, Capital, and the State in British Columbia: Selected Papers*. Vancouver: UBC Press, 1988.
Warburton, Rennie, and Stephen Scott. "The Fur Trade and Early Capitalist Development in British Columbia." *Canadian Journal of Native Studies* 5 (Winter 1985): 27–46.
Webstad, Phyllis. *Beyond the Orange Shirt Story*. Victoria: Medicine Wheel Education, 2021.
Webster, Peter S. *As Far as I Know: Reminiscences of an Ahousat Elder*. Campbell River, BC: Campbell River Museum and Archives, 1983.
Whalen, Kevin. *Native Students at Work: American Indian Labor and Sherman Institute's Outing Program, 1900–1945*. Seattle: University of Washington Press, 2016.
Whitehead, Carmen. *Colonial Educators: The British Indian and Colonial Education Service, 1858–1983*. London: I.B. Tauris, 2003.
Whiteside, Heather, ed. *Canadian Political Economy*. Toronto: University of Toronto Press, 2020.
Wickwire, Wendy. *At the Bridge: James Teit and an Anthropology of Belonging*. Vancouver: UBC Press, 2019.

Williams, Carol. *Framing the West: Race, Gender, and the Photographic Frontier in the Pacific Northwest*. Oxford: Oxford University Press, 2003.

Williams, David Ricardo. *The Man for a New Country: Sir Matthew Baillie Begbie*. Sidney, BC: Gray's, 1977.

Williams, Mary. "The Coming of the White Man." In *Our Tellings: Interior Salish Stories of the Nlha7kápmx People*, ed. Darwin Hanna and Mamie Henry, 130–31. Vancouver: UBC Press, 1996.

Willinsky, John. *Learning to Divide the World: Education at Empire's End*. Minneapolis: University of Minnesota Press, 1998.

Willis, Paul. *Learning to Labour: How Working Class Kids Get Working Class Jobs*. Farnborough: Saxon House, 1977.

Wilson, J. Donald. "Some Observations on Recent Trends in Canadian Educational History." In *An Imperfect Past: Education and Society in Canadian History*, ed. J. Donald Wilson, 7–29. Vancouver: Centre for the Study of Curriculum and Instruction, University of British Columbia, 1984.

–, ed. *An Imperfect Past: Education and Society in Canadian History*. Vancouver: Centre for the Study of Curriculum and Instruction, University of British Columbia, 1984.

Wilson, J. Donald, and David C. Jones. "The 'New' History of Canadian Education." *History of Education Quarterly* 16, 3 (1976): 367–75.

–, eds. *Schooling and Society in 20th Century British Columbia*. Calgary: Detselig, 1980.

Wilson, J. Donald, and Paul Stortz. "'May the Lord Have Mercy on You': The Rural School Problem in British Columbia in the 1920s." In *Children, Teachers and Schools in the History of British Columbia*, ed. Jean Barman and Mona Gleason, 233–57. Edmonton: Brush Education, 2003.

Wolfe, Patrick. "Settler Colonialism and the Elimination of the Native." *Journal of Genocide Research* 8, 4 (December 2006): 387–409.

–. *Settler Colonialism and the Transforming of Anthropology: The Politics and Poetics of an Ethnographic Event*. London: Cassell, 1999.

Wood, B. Anne. "Hegelian Resolutions in the New Education Movement: The 1925 Putman-Weir Report." *Dalhousie Review* 6, 2 (Summer 1982): 254–77.

Wood, Ellen Meiksins. *The Origin of Capitalism: A Longer View*. London: Verso, 2002.

Woolford, Andrew. *This Benevolent Experiment: Indigenous Boarding Schools, Genocide, and Redress in Canada and the United States*. Winnipeg: University of Manitoba Press, 2015.

Wotherspoon, Terry. "From Subordinate Partners to Dependent Employees: State Regulation of Public School Teachers in Nineteenth Century British Columbia." *Labour/Le travail* 31 (Spring 1993): 75–110.

—. "The Incorporation of Public School Teachers into the Industrial Order of British Columbia in the First Half of the Twentieth Century." *Studies in Political Economy* 46 (1995): 119–52.

—, ed. *The Political Economy of Canadian Schooling.* Toronto: Methuen, 1987.

Younging, Gregory. *Elements of Indigenous Style: A Guide for Writing by and about Indigenous Peoples.* Edmonton: Brush Education, 2018.

Index

Note: "(i)" after a page number indicates a photograph or map.

Aboriginal policy of Canada, 3
Aborigines' Protection Society, 56, 76
abuse, culture of, 137–39, 178–79, 195, 199, 203–4
accidents, 195. *See also* conditions in schools
accountability, lack of, 197. *See also* denial
accumulation by dispossession, 9–10, 14, 75, 83–84, 114
Ahousaht, B.C., 202
Aiyansh Day School, 186–87
Aladejebi, Funké, 7, 186, 187, 208
Alaska, 78
Alberni, B.C., 73, 125
Alberni Indian Boarding School, 126(i)
Alert Bay, B.C., 124, 125, 126, 192
Alert Bay Girls' Home, 198, 201–2, 202(i)
Alert Bay Indian Residential School, 202(i)
Alexander, Kristine, 95, 208
Alkali Lake, B.C., 178
All Hallows Boarding School, 125, 190
Allied Tribes of British Columbia, 182, 273*n*31
Alston, Edward Graham, 45
An Act Respecting Public Schools (Public School Act 1972), 81–82

Andersen, Chris, 249*n*56
Anderson, A.C., 25
Anderson, James, 24
Angela College, 26
Anglican Church, 202(i)
Anglican missionaries, 50–51, 60, 69–76, 122, 242*n*65
Anglo-Saxon superiority, 170–71
Anishinaabe Nation, 134–35, 194
Anstey, Arthur, 167–68, 172
apartheid, 151
apology, of Government of Canada, 3
archives, 12
arson, 135, 137, 180, 201–3. *See also* Indigenous resistance
Asian students, 150–51
assimilation, 128, 150, 180, 183, 205
Assiniboine Nation, 121
attendance, school: boarding schools ensuring, 189; coercive measures for, 148; increases in, 176, 264*n*26; of Indian Day Schools, 184, 187; in Indian Residential Schools, 126–27; low in common schools, 30–31, 33–34; low in mission schools, 116–17; low in public schools, 87, 100; reasons for low attendance, 101–2; records of, 40, 75; as target of school officials, 147–48; tied to teacher salaries, 86

attitudes toward Indigenous peoples, 59, 67–68. *See also* civilization attitudes
author identities, 11
authoritarianism, 210
authority, developing student respect for, 103, 161, 163, 171
autonomy, local, 111
Axelrod, Paul, 7, 79, 148, 157, 164

Bacchus, M. Kazim, 5
Backhouse, Constance, 93, 249*n*55
Bailey, Charles, 27–28
Baker, Elder Mazie, 198
Baker, Simon, 200–1, 280*n*131, 280*n*132
Bamfield School, 97(i)
Barman, Jean: on All Hallows Boarding School, 125, 193; on British Columbia's isolation, 113; on desire for school reform after First World War, 172; on government-funded schooling, 44; on independent education review, 173; on Iroquois in wage labour, 240*n*18; on Langley, B.C. origins, 39; on lashing out of male students, 105; on linguistic composition of British Columbia, 237*n*81; on men with Indigenous wives, 94–95; on private school fees, 262*n*8; on residential school curriculum, 128; on schooling in colonization, 210, 231*n*9; on schools and social class, 91, 220*n*11; on segregation in schools, 258*n*70; on teacher training, 164
Barr, Robert, 28
Battleford (trial residential school), 119, 120
Baugh, Daniel, 230*n*2
Beaven, Robert, 248*n*35

Beaver (ship), 53
Beaver, Reverend Herbert, 50, 51
Begbie, Supreme Court Judge Matthew Baillie, 66
Begg, Alexander, 58
Bella Bella, B.C., 124
Bella Bella Indian Day School, 185
Belshaw, John Douglas, 28, 133, 142, 233*n*35, 259*n*105
Bhabha, Homi K., 32, 235*n*48
Blackhawk, Ned, 20, 56, 122, 123, 194
Blake, Lynn A., 60, 242*n*65
Blanchet, Francis N., 51
Blanshard, Richard, 25
Board of Education, 84, 89, 104, 106
Board of Examiners, 104
Board of Indian Commissioners, 115
Boening, Henry, 179
Boer War, 107, 169
Bolduc, Jean-Baptiste, 51, 240*n*20
bookkeeping, 161
Borden, Frederick William, 170
boycotts of residential schools, 203, 204–5
Boy Scouts, 270*n*128
Brew, Chartres, 39–40
Brewster, William, 66
Breyegers Bay School, 93
Britain, 18, 207–8. *See also* British Empire; Colonial Office in London
British Colonist, 41, 42
British Columbia: built by schooling, 4–5; as a capitalist settler society, 10, 13; centralized school system of, 81; coal mining in capitalist economy of, 28; Department of Indian Affairs bureaucracy in, 114–15; early common schools in Colony of, 35–41; on the edge of British Empire, 231*n*8; founding of in 1858, 18; gender in,

143; government resistance to school reform, 44; Indigenous population of, 113, 248*n*25; joining Confederation, 78, 112–13; limited funds of early colony, 56; as a man camp, 36; merging colonies with Vancouver Island, 41; mortality rates in, 259*n*105; multilingual colonial nature of, 237*n*81; official Crown colony status of, 35; percentage of Indigenous land, 9; as priority of Scott's Indian policy, 181; religious belief in, 247*n*11; selling stolen lands, 181–82; social class in, 261*n*7; taxation in, 247*n*17; transformation of, 142, 145, 207; as a white man's province, 79, 246*n*5
British Columbia Clearances, 8
British Columbian, 41, 43
British Columbia Provincial Police, 200
British Columbia Teachers' Federation (BCTF), 164, 172
British Empire, 18, 169, 170, 230*n*2, 270*n*128. *See also* Britain; Colonial Office in London
British North America Act, 7
Brown, Robert, 153
Brown, Sarah, 39–40
Brown, William, 90
Browning, Reverend Arthur, 61
Bryant, Cornelius, 33
Bryce, Peter Henderson, 133–34, 197–98, 278*n*114
budgets, schools, 83, 190. *See also* funding; salaries
Bulwer-Lytton, Sir Edward, 35
Bundy, Edgar, 169
bureaucratic structures, 114, 146–49, 262*n*8

bureaucratic systems for education, 34
Burns, William, 100
Burr, W.H., 33
Burrard Inlet, B.C., 46, 79
Bushby, Arthur Thomas, 37–39
Butcher, Margaret, 196–97
Bute Inlet, 66

Cache Creek, B.C., 87–88
Cache Creek Provincial Boarding School, 87–88, 87(i)
Cadets, 170–71, 171(i)
Cairns, R.H., 153, 184, 189, 203, 204
Calls to Action, of Truth and Reconciliation Commission (TRC) report, 4
Cameron, Agnes Deans, 92
Campbell, Lara, 103, 251*n*86
Canada: 1885 war, 121; historical narratives of, 107
Canadian Civics (British Columbia Edition) (Jenkins), 163
Canadian federalism, 7
Canadian Girl at Work, The (textbook), 162
Canadian history courses, 107
Canadian Pacific Railway, 78, 91, 113, 131
Canadian Series of School Books, 106, 252*n*100
cannons, 261*n*5
Capilano Indian Reserve No. 5, 155
Capilano School, 156(i)
capitalism: development and colonization, 10, 19, 35–36, 143, 207; education reform and, 161; industrial, and schooling, 5, 79, 92, 117, 157–58; labour under, 195–96; mercantile, 19, 233*n*33; normalizing through schooling, 82, 163;

patriarchy and, 161–63. *See also* colonialism; colonization
Cariboo, B.C., 46
Carion, A.M., 130
Carlson, Keith Thor, 35, 67, 181
Carnarvon, Colonial Secretary Lord, 57
carpentry, 128, 193
Carr, Geoffrey Paul, 131
Carter, Perry, 23
Carter, Sarah, 23
Cassidy, Constable, 200
Catholic missionaries, 50–51, 60, 64–69, 122
Cedar Hill, B.C., 46
certification of teachers, 103–4
Cexpe'nthlEm, Chief (David Spintlum), 36
Chapple, Eve, 152
Chessus, 66
chicken pox, 133. *See also* disease and death
Chief Commissioner of Land and Works, 73–74
children, 33–34, 104–5. *See also* Indigenous children
Children's Story of the War (Parrott), 168–69
Chilliwack, B.C., 46, 61, 63–64, 121, 166
Chilliwack High School, 153
Chinese Consolidated Benevolent Association, 151
Chinese Imperial School, 151
Chinese students, 150–51, 264*n*32
Chinook Jargon language, 39, 236*n*80
Chinook language, 39, 68, 236*n*80
Chinook Nation, 39
chores, shirking, 135. *See also* Indigenous resistance
Christianity as contested, 70
churches, role in residential schools, 119
Church Missionary Society (CMS), 50, 75, 118
Church of England, 58, 61, 188
citizens, loyal, 168
civics courses, 163
civilization attitudes: "aggressive civilization," 118; behind Indian Residential Schools, 59, 119–20, 134, 183; in curriculum, 127–28; disease and, 133; of Edward Cridge, 70; of Frederick Seymour, 67–68; of Hayter Reed, 130; on industrial training, 127; of residential school defenders, 199
civil servants, resistance of, 180, 194, 197–98
Clah, Arthur Wellington, 70
Clarke, Charles, 29–30
class hierarchy, 23, 157
Clayoquot, B.C., 124, 202
Clement, W.H.P., 107
Clinton, B.C., 46
clothing and clothes making, 59, 129. *See also* sewing
coal mining, 28
Coast Salish Peoples, 198
Coccola, Nicolas, 123, 128, 129, 130, 133
Collegiate School for Boys, 26
Collier, William Francis, 107
Collison, William, 111
Colonial Administration Buildings, Victoria, 26(i)
colonialism: as a catch-22, 205; invasion as a structure not event, 9; invisibility of in British Columbia, 228*n*65; legitimation of, 169;

maelstrom of, 123; necessity of confronting as history of Canada, 4; requirements of, 113; term notes, 224n37. *See also* capitalism; colonization
colonial legitimacy, 5. *See also under* schooling; schools
Colonial Office in London: Anthony Musgrave's view on early colony, 46; appointment of James Douglas as Governor, 25; approval of missionary work, 71; encouraging land theft, 56–57; on financial self-sufficiency, 35; on Hudson's Bay Company, 21–22; indifference to economy of British Columbia, 78; James Douglas' assurances toward, 48; on Puget Sound War, 53–54; records and correspondence, 12; response to settler anxiety, 55; transfer of jurisdiction, 113
colonial period term, 229n79
colonization: depictions in textbooks, 170; government oversight of, 207, 209; legitimization of, 107; as ongoing process, 208; of Pacific Northwest, 18–19; romanticized history of, 169. *See also* capitalism; colonialism
Columbia Detachment of the Royal Engineers, 36–37
Columbia River, 18
Common School Ordinance, 1869, 44, 45–46
common schools. *See* schools, common
Common Schools Act, 1865, 34
Comox, B.C., 73, 116
compulsory schooling. *See* schooling, compulsory
conditions in schools: as abuse, 178–80, 195, 198; accounts of, 137–40; 203–4; daily schedule, 127; disease and death, 132–34, 197; due to lack of funds, 190; at Indian Day Schools, 187–88; lack of improvement in, 203; at Metlakatla, 122; overcrowding, 149; variety in, 173–74
Confederation, 115
Connolly, Amelia, 32, 231n13
consent *vs.* coercion, 101, 115
contact zones, 7, 40, 91–99, 156–57, 224n35
Coqualeetza, B.C., 125, 126, 257n51
Coqualeetza Indian Residential School, 153, 204
Coqualeetza Industrial Institute, 64, 198, 199
corporal punishment, 104–5, 195, 198, 199, 201, 210, 263n15
Corrigan, Philip, 27, 101
Coulthard, Glen Sean, 8, 9, 10, 56, 119, 180, 189
Council of Public Instruction, 89–90
Council of Vancouver Island, 30
country marriages, 50–51, 239n16
court proceedings, 66
Cowcaelth, 75
Cowichan, B.C., 73, 116, 124
Cowichan Indian Agency, 123
Cowperthwaite, F.M., 90, 91
Craigflower, B.C., 29, 46
Craigflower Farm, 29, 29(i)
Craigflower School, 29, 29(i)
Cranbrook, B.C., 122, 123, 198
Crart, Philip, 37
Crease, Henry Pering Pellew, 46
Cree Nation, 13, 121
Cridge, Mary, 30
Cridge, Reverend Edward, 30–33, 31(i), 55, 70–71, 73, 234n40
crimes, charges of, 179

Critical Indigenous Studies, 8
Crosby, Thomas, 61, 62–63, 137, 139(i)
Crosby Home for Girls, 202
"cult of domesticity," 162
Cumberland, B.C., 166
curriculum: Canadian history, 107; domestic science classes, 162, 172; followed at Indian Day Schools, 187–88; at Fort Simpson school, 70, 72; hidden, 5, 6, 127–28; high school streams, 166; industrial, 127, 159–63; for legitimacy, 106; political conflict over, 246n9
Curtis, Bruce, 7, 27, 82, 90, 101, 246n9

Daily British Colonist, 81
Daily Colonist, 199–200
Dakelh Nation, 64, 174(i), 198
Dakota Sioux Nation, 95
Dalhousie University, 42
Davin, Nicholas Flood, 118, 119, 190
Davin Report, 118
Deans, Alex, 94
death, records of, 133, 178, 196–97
decolonization, 12, 211
Decolonizing Methodologies (Smith), 12
De Cosmos, Amor, 41, 42–43, 75, 81
Deloria, Philip, 95, 154, 210
Deloria, Vine Jr., 49, 71
Demers, Modeste, 51
democratic values, 176
demographics of early common schools, 32
Dene Nation, 8
denial of school problems, 197, 198–99
Denis, J.S., 117
denominational schooling, 27, 44, 83
Department of Agriculture, 108

Department of Education (British Columbia), 146–47, 151, 160, 168–69, 172–73
Department of Indian Affairs (DIA): deaths reported to, 196–97; denial of school problems, 198–99; expansion of Indian Residential Schools (IRS) of, 140; food provision at day schools, 187; funding for, 113–14; funding for residential schools, 190–91; inquiry into St. Joseph's Indian Industrial School, 178–79; investigation of school conditions, 133–34; persisting in mission despite resistance, 180; rationale for industrial training, 127, 130; records from, 12; residential school records of, 131; restructuring of, 180–81; role in establishing residential schools, 122; school reforms of, 182–84; school reports sent to, 110; use of residential school term, 253n6; views on day schools, 188; views on residential schools, 189; views on unqualified teachers, 185–86
Department of the Interior, 113
Derby, B.C., 62
Derrickson, Ronald M., 8–9
de Smet, Pierre, 51
Dewdney, Edgar, 127
Dewey, John, 176
d'Herbomez, Oblate Superior Louis-Joseph, 64
Diocese of British Columbia, 110
Diocese of New Westminster, 125
diphtheria, 133, 196
disease and death, 132–34, 185, 195, 196, 244n112, 259n100, 259n105
dispossession, accumulation by, 9–10, 14, 75, 83–84, 114

Ditchburn, W.E., 198, 201
doctrine of discovery, 56
domestic labour, 129, 193–94
domestic science classes, 162, 172, 188, 193–94
Dominion Exhibition, 145–46, 176
Dominion of Canada, 78. *See also* Canada
Doncklele, George, 128, 129, 135–36, 137
Doolan, Robert, 74–75
Douglas, B.C., 62
Douglas, James: approach to Indigenous relations, 115; autonomy of, 240*n*33; background on, 25–28, 32–33; close involvement in early schools, 30; fearing Indigenous resistance, 48; funding for missionary schools, 71–72; humanitarian motives of, 240*n*32; marriage of, 51; on Mr. Staines, 232*n*23; photo, 54(i); questioning value of missionaries, 52–53; response to Puget Sound War of, 53; response to St. Mary's School, 65; support of missionaries' work, 61
Douglas Nation, 40
Doukhobors, 171
Dove, A.J., 266*n*73
Downey, Allan, 64
Driving Hawk Sneve, Virginia, 36
Duchess of San Lorenzo, 26
Dunbar, A.D., 151
Duncan, William, 58, 69–73, 110–11, 244*n*112, 255*n*33
Dunn, Timothy, 158, 266*n*70, 267*n*83, 267*n*90, 268*n*97
Dunnel, Harry, 159
Durieu, Bishop Pierre-Paul, 64

Earl Grey, 49
economic transition, 79, 246*n*7
economy, colonial, 19, 78, 83, 142
editorials, in newspapers, 42–43
education: attitudes of parents toward, 103; demand for, 38–39; displays of in Dominion Exhibition, 145–46; functions of, 232*n*15; importance of to economic growth, 143–44; increasing parental interest in, 101; inspection of, 234*n*39; philosophy of, 176, 266*n*73; role of in society, 22, 131; service of, 167–72; term note, 221*n*19; views of, 160–61
"educational machinery," 34, 82, 91, 113, 146–49, 176
educational philosophy, 176
1885 war, 121
elections, 234*n*38
Elementary History of Canada (Gammell), 170
elementary school, 175
Elizabeth Long Memorial Home, 196, 203
Ellis, Jason, 7
Empire Day, 169
employability, 161
engineers, 36–37
enrolment, public school, 147, 149. *See also* attendance, school
Esquimalt, B.C., 28, 46, 64, 186(i)
Esquimalt Nation, 186(i)
Estes, Nick, 8, 24, 198–99
Evans, Reverend Ephraim, 61
expropriation of land, 8. *See also* dispossession, accumulation by

Fanon, Frantz, 60, 205
Fawcett, Edgar, 32

fear, culture of, 136, 137, 179
federal government of Canada, 80, 115–16
federalism, Canadian, 7, 159
fees, school, 28, 31, 38, 43, 46, 125, 190. *See also* funding
fighting back, 200. *See also* Indigenous resistance
Finlayson, Roderick, 23
first-hand accounts of Indian Residential Schools, 134, 137–38, 192, 203–4, 278*n*99
First World War, 107, 146, 167–68, 270*n*134
Fisher, Robin, 49, 74
FitzGerald, James Edward, 21, 28, 43
Fleming, Thomas, 30, 90
flu, 132–33. *See also* disease and death
food, 135, 138, 200–1, 203, 204. *See also* conditions in schools; Indigenous resistance
Fort Colville, Washington, 25
Fort Langley, B.C., 51
Fort Simpson, B.C., 69, 70–72, 116, 122
Fort St. James, B.C., 198
Fort Vancouver, B.C., 22–23, 51
Fort Victoria, B.C., 24(i), 25, 27–28, 238*n*2
Fort Ware Indian Residential School, 206
Fouquet, Father Leon, 65, 69, 132(i)
Fraser, Crystal Gail, 7, 124, 194, 209, 211
Fraser Canyon, 73
Fraser Canyon War, 35–36, 56
Fraser River, 37, 51, 63–64, 65, 67, 132(i)
Free Textbook Branch, 169

funding: changing sources of, 166; decreased for Department of Indian Affairs, 180–81; for residential schools, 122–23, 149, 189–91, 256*n*46; for industrial schools, 119; for mission schools, 116–17; for non-denominational schools, 209; Technical Education Act, 172
fur trading, 18

Gammell, I., 169, 170
gardens, school, 172, 188
Garrett, Reverend Alexander Charles, 58–60, 61, 69
garrison mentality, 48, 238*n*4
Gaudry, Adam, 12
gender: binaries, 128, 129, 162, 162(i); gaps in teacher pay, 164; in residential schools, 128, 129, 192–93; political systems and, 143; in public schools, 92–93; schooling, economic development and, 161–62, 172; segregation, 92–93; teachers, 104; teaching and, 268*n*97
Gendre, Father Florimund, 65
General Board of Education, 45
genocide, cultural, 3, 131, 181
Gettler, Brian, 114, 208
Giancarlo, Alexandra, 195
Gidney, R. D., 6, 13, 146, 209, 264*n*26
Girl Guides, 270*n*128
Gitxsan territory, 97(i)
Gladstone, Elinor, 153–54, 154(i)
Gleason, Mona, 7
gold rushes, 35–36, 41, 78
Good, J.B., 73, 73(i), 74
goodwill strategy, 67
Gough, Barry, 53
Gould, Jan, 90

government investments, 79, 117. *See also* funding
Governor-in-Council, 45
Gramsci, Antonio, 11, 101
Grant, Maria, 103
Great Depression, 15, 176
Great Famine in Ireland, 18
Green, A.E., 187
Green, Edgar, 153
Green, William, 76
grounded normativity, 119, 189
Guillet, Félix, 65
Guillod, Harry, 124
Gulf Islands, 93–94
Gwichya Gwich'in Nation, 7, 124

Hagan, Michel, 134, 136
Haida Gwaii, 18, 60
Haida Nation, 55–56, 122, 153
Haig-Brown, Celia, 195, 277n96
Haines, Christine, 178–79
Haisla territory, 196, 203
"half breeds," 93–94, 152, 231n10
Halfway River Indian Residential School, 206
Hall, Catherine, 6
Hall, Joseph, 193
"Hanging Judge," 66
Hargrave, Miss, 139(i)
Harris, Cole, 9, 48, 84, 142, 182, 245n2, 258n73, 262n6, 273n30
Harris, Henry, 153
Harrison River, 65
Harvey, David, 10
Hastings Sawmill School, 95, 96(i)
Hazelton, B.C., 95, 124
Hazelton Day School, 97(i), 188
Heaman, E.A., 86, 208, 247n17, 254n15
hearings, 178–79, 182, 204–5, 274n32

hegemony, 5, 11, 15, 167, 205, 209
Helmcken, John Sebastian, 25
Herring, Emily, 37
heterogeneity in public schools, 93–99
heteropatriarchy, 129, 192–93
"hidden transcript," 136
hierarchy in schools, 267n83
Higgins, David, 237n93
High River (trial residential school), 119
high schools, 106, 165–66, 175
Hills, George, 73
historians, 5–7, 11–12, 228n73
historical materialism, 8, 9
history, transnational, 207
history education, 107, 170
History of Canada (Gammell), 169
History of Public Education in British Columbia, A (Johnson), 6–7
History of the British Empire (Collier), 107
History of the Dominion of Canada (Clement), 107
Holchey, Thomas, 98
"home children," 120
home economics, 159, 161–62. *See also* domestic science classes
Hope, B.C., 46, 61, 62, 73, 94
Hopkins, Miss, 90–91
horseback travel to school, 102(i)
Howe, Joseph, 42
Hudson's Bay Company (HBC), 18, 19, 20; in 1830s, 18; British government ending ten-year lease of, 35; concerns about dominance of, 27; early schools for employees of, 14; as first colonizing activity in Pacific Northwest, 19, 20, 21; investment in settlement through school creation, 20; land price policy of, 232n22,

241n52; in Langley, 39; paternalism and centralization of, 30; role in missionary support, 50–52; support of early schooling of, 22–23; those frustrated with rule of, 25; trade with Indigenous Nations of, 22; use of Chinook language, 236n80
humiliation, 195. *See also* punishment at school
hunger, 200. *See also* conditions in schools; food
Hunt, Dallas, 8, 107
Hupacasath territory, 96(i)
Huu-ay-aht territory, 97(i)
hygiene, 59, 241n42, 244n112. *See also* civilization attitudes

Illich, Ivan, 163, 267n88
imperialism, 18–19, 169–70
independent education review, 172–76
Indian Act, 123, 152, 182, 183–84, 273n31
Indian Affairs, 112–17
Indian Affairs boards, regional, 114
Indian Agents, 153, 199, 200, 254n17
Indian Boarding Schools, 124–25. *See also* Indian Residential Schools (IRS)
Indian Branch, 113, 117, 119
Indian Day Schools: increased practical training at, 183; least funding for, 123–24; Ottawa's commitment to, 14; reform of, 184–88; resistance to, 153, 180; techniques to get children into, 62; as under-studied, 7
Indian Improvement Committee, 58
Indian Industrial Schools, 126
Indian policy, 114, 181–83
"Indian Problem," 115, 130–31, 181, 183, 205

Indian reserves, 9–10, 57, 58, 78, 84, 115, 123, 184
Indian Residential Schools (IRS): attendance in, 126–27, 183–84; boarding vs. industrial schools, 275n68; budgets for, 119; Canadian settler awareness about, 3; closure of, 205–6; as dominant form of education for Indigenous students, 188–94; early justification for, 57; expansion of, 120–27, 140; funding of, 189–90; funding proposals for, 58; graduates becoming Indian Day School teachers, 186; as incarceration, 125–26; increased practical training in, 183; inquiries into, 178–79; international models for, 117–18; justifications for, 119–20; Ottawa's commitment to, 14; punishment at, 136; red flags in plan for, 119; reforms of, 179–80; resistance toward, 180, 194–205; resulting in disconnection from land and community, 119; student experiences at, 131, 134; teacher staffing, 275n52. *See also* conditions in schools
"Indian" term, 249n55
Indian Trust Fund, 114
Indigeneity, 33, 95, 155, 199
Indigenous history, 6–7, 11–12
Indigenous internationalism, 201
Indigenous methodologies, 12
Indigenous Nations: actively negotiating Christianity, 49; conflict with, 35–36, 48, 52–53; differing attitudes toward settler trade of, 19; under federal jurisdiction, 111; lack of consultation with, 18, 35; Ottawa working to avoid conflict with, 115–16; resistance to colonization of, 20. *See also* individual Nations

Indigenous Peoples: bureaucratic management of, 114; as employees of Hudson's Bay Company, 22–23; erasure of and settler colonialism, 8; under federal jurisdiction, 93, 98–99, 112–13, 151–52, 157; grounded normativity of, 189; impact of residential schools on, 124–25, 131; industrial training for, 127; parents understanding implications of residential schools, 124; population in British Columbia, 142, 248n25; portrayals of, 107, 170; reactions to mission schools, 63; research on as extractive, 12; students at public schools, 93–99; trading of, 241n42

Indigenous resistance: attempts to contain, 79–80, 238n2; challenging colonization, 48; of children at residential schools, 134–40, 180, 198–99, 210, 277n96; epicentre at Metlakatla, 121; ever-present nature of, 209–10; fighting back, 200; growing at Metlakatla, 121–22; of Indian Day Schools on reserves, 153; intensifying, 123; of ləkʷəŋən Nation, 52; to mission schools, 62–63, 112; as political catalyst, 65–66; political organizing, 201, 203; potlatches and, 123; Puget Sound War, 55–56; to residential schools, 120, 124, 134–40, 144, 194–205; school boycotts, 203; schooling as a way to prevent, 49, 111–12; settler fear of, 53–54; of Tsilhqot'in Nation, 66; of Ts'mysan Nation at Fort Simpson, 71, 72; to work, 130

Indigenous sovereignty, 20

Indigenous title, 273n30

Indigenous women: Hudson's Bay Company (HBC) officers' intimate relationships with, 23–24; male students having sex with, 88; marriages to non-Indigenous men of, 50–51; relationships with missionaries, 52, 73; violence of miners toward, 36; William Duncan's relationship with, 110–11; as wives of school trustees, 94–95

individualism, 159

industrial capitalism, 79, 106, 108–9, 118, 157–59, 160(i). *See also* capitalism

"industrial efficiency," 158

Industrial Revolution, 18

industrial training, 59, 117, 127–28, 130, 159–61, 160(i), 171–72

inequality, 128

influenza, 132–33, 196. *See also* disease and death

infrastructure development, 20, 23, 79

injuries, 195–96. *See also* conditions in schools

Iroquois Nation, 233n32

Isadore, Chief, 123

Ishiguro, Laura, 5, 37, 113, 208

isolation, geographic, 113

jail time, 198

Japanese students, 150–51, 264n32

Jenkins, R.S., 163

Jessop, John: advocating for school reform, 34; authorizing textbooks, 106; on Indigenous population in British Columbia, 248n25; on parental cooperation in schooling, 101; protest of, 83; as Ryerson of British Columbia, 248n22; salary of, 248n35; school records of, 93–94; as superintendent, 84–89, 85(i)

Jesuit missionaries, 51
Johnson, Charlie, 178
Johnson, F. Henry, 6–7, 81, 82, 248*n*22
Jones, T.T., 88
Joseph, Mathias, 207
Julian, Tom, 203

Kamloops, B.C., 160, 166, 277*n*96
Kamloops Indian Residential School: destroyed by fire, 202; first-hand accounts of, 195; founding of, 122–23; funding at, 191; girls transferred to as punishment, 203; parent resistance of, 134; principal at, 130; student resistance at, 200; Syilx children at, 152; unmarked graves at, 4
Kanaka Maoli, 8
Kaslo, B.C., 166
Kauanui, Kēhaulani, 8
Kelleher, Cornelius, 131
Kelly, Peter, 182
Kelm, Mary-Ellen, 12, 131, 197
Kelowna, B.C., 65
Kennedy, Arthur, 34
Khot-La-Cha, 200–1
Kincolith, 75, 124
Kincolith, B.C., 122
Kincolith Indian Day School, 185
kindergarten, 271*n*151
King, William Lyon Mackenzie, 158
King Edward High School, 162(i)
Kitamaat, B.C., 196, 197
Klatsassin, 66
Klickitat Nation, 53
Kootenay Indian Industrial School, 123, 128, 129, 130, 152, 197–98
Kootenay Indian Residential School, 197(i)
Ktunaxa Nation, 123
Kuper Island, 135(i), 257*n*51

Kuper Island Indian Industrial School, 128, 129, 132, 135(i), 137, 200
Kuper Island Indian Residential School, 122, 123, 195, 196
Kwakwa̱ka̱'wakw Nation, 198
Kyle, John, 162

labour: attitudes toward, 130; manual in schools, 136, 191, 192, 195, 276*n*86; movement, 171; schooling for skilled industrial, 158–59, 160(i); unpaid, 129; wage, 10, 25, 78–79, 128, 183, 194, 246*n*7, 258*n*73
Ladner, Kiera, 13
"la grippe," 132. *See also* disease and death
Lakalsap, B.C., 124
Lake, B.C., 46
Lamb, W. Kaye, 113
land: claims, 273*n*31; dispossession, 8–9, 14, 56–57, 62, 71, 72, 74; grabs, 35, 45; importance of, 8, 56, 115; leasing, 75; rights struggles, 53, 182; sale of, 57, 254*n*15
Landing of the First Canadian Division at St. Nazaire, 1915 (Bundy), 169
Langevin, Hector-Lewis, 120, 256*n*49
Langley, B.C., 39, 46
Langley School, 39, 40
language: learning, 62–63, 68, 127; punishment for, 195; resistance through, 135
Lanning, Robert, 27, 101
lashes, 195. *See also* punishment at school
Latimer, Peter, 75
Laurier, Wilfrid, 181
Legace, Josette, 32
Legislative Council of British Columbia, 44

legitimacy, colonial, 5
legitimacy, learning, 106–9, 163, 169, 175, 207
Lejac Indian Residential School, 198
Lejacq, J.M.J., 137
Lempfrit, Honoré Timothy, 51–52, 58, 64, 240n20
Lenihan, James, 115
Lester, Peter, 32
Lethbridge, A.B., 123
ləkʷəŋən Nation, 19, 24, 51–52, 58, 59, 61, 186(i)
Lheidli T'enneh territory, 155(i)
lice, 198. See also conditions in schools
Lieutenant-Governor-in-Council, 84
Lillooet, B.C., 46
Lillooet, Thomas S., 94
Liquitem, Chief Emmitt, 36
Lolo, Sophia "Martha," 32
Lomas, W.H., 121
Lomawaima, K. Tsianina, 136
loneliness and isolation, 134. See also conditions in schools
Lord Strathcona, 170
Lorne College, 83
love, lack of, 138. See also conditions in schools
Luby, Brittany, 194
Lummi, 198
Lutz, John Sutton, 12, 39, 66, 246n7
Lytton, B.C., 36, 46, 73, 74, 116, 190, 196

Macdonald, Sir John A.: criticism of government, 180; defense of Indian Residential School system plan, 119–20; Macdonald-Robertson Movement, 253n108; as MP for Victoria, 121; plan to "settle the west," 118; as Prime Minister, 117–18; as superintendent general of Indian Affairs, 113–14
Macdonald, William Christopher, 108
Macdonald-Robertson Movement, 108, 158, 253n108
Mack, Clayton, 192
MacKenzie, H.H., 149
man camps, 36
Mann, Jean, 176, 265n62
Manning, William, 66
manual labour in schools, 128, 136, 192, 195, 266n70, 276n86. See also labour
manual training in schools, 107–9, 171–72, 266n70
Manuel, Arthur, 8–9, 15, 211, 212
Manuel, George, 200, 201
Māori People, 12
Maple Point, B.C., 28
Mara, John, 248n35
Maracle, Lee, 194, 212
Marker, Michael, 198
Marks, Lynne, 247n11
marriage as a political tool, 51
Martin, John, 168
Marx, Karl, 35–36, 113, 159, 163, 232n22
Masset, B.C., 124
Matters, Diane L., 148
Maurus, P., 193
Mawani, Renisa, 93
Maynard, Robyn, 199
Mayne Island School Board, 157
McCaig, James, 163
McCallum, Mary Jane Logan, 12, 93, 119, 129, 179–80, 197, 209
McClintock, Anne, 93
McClure, Leonard, 237n93
McDonald, Robert A.J., 143, 246n5
McIlveen, James, 38

INDEX 321

McKenna-McBride Commission and Report, 182, 274*n*32
McKenzie, Colin Campbell, 89, 104
McLoughlin, John, 51
McNally, David, 37, 56, 84, 114, 208
McNally, Vincent, 247*n*11
measles, 133. *See also* disease and death
mechanics of colonial rule, 20
Memmi, Albert, 5, 134
Merivale, Herman, 57
metalworking courses, 161. *See also* industrial training
Metchosin, B.C., 46
Methodist Coqualeetza Indian Residential School, 153
Methodist Coqualeetza Industrial Institute, 193
Methodist Episcopal Church, 61
Methodist missionaries, 60, 61–64, 122
methodology, 11–12
Métis People, 11–12, 78, 121, 124–25, 249*n*56
Metlakatla: circa 1880s, 112(i); as first industrial school in British Columbia, 122; industrial school at, 117, 128; influenza epidemic at, 132; missionary work at, 72–75; mission school at, 116, 121; power struggles at, 110–11, 121, 244*n*110; women working at residential school at, 104
Metlakatla Indian Industrial School, 134, 137
Metlakatla Indian Residential School, 201
Michi Saagiig Nishnaabeg, 8
middle school, 175
military force, 48, 55, 207, 239*n*7, 261*n*5
military training, 170–71
militias, 115

Millar, W.P.J., 6, 13, 146, 209, 264*n*26
Miller, J.R., 7, 190, 191, 259*n*100, 260*n*117, 275*n*52, 275*n*56
Millions, Eric, 208
Milloy, Jeremy, 195, 278*n*114
Milloy, John S., 7, 191, 247*n*21
miners, 35–36, 233*n*32
mining and mineral production, 28–29, 143, 233*n*35
Minnesota, 118
misbehaviour, 136. *See also* punishment at school
Mission, B.C., 116, 121, 125, 196
missionaries: creating villages for conversion, 72; declining interest in Canadian work, 118; denominations of, 60; funding ceased for, 110; ideas about, 139; as key in Indian education, 5–6, 116; outreach methods of, 242*n*65; questioning value of, 52; role in shifting colonial power, 49, 239*n*12; tactics influenced by Puget Sound War, 53, 56; work overview, 20
missionary schools. *See* schools, mission
Missionary Societies of Britain, 49
Mission City, B.C., 65
"mixedness," 249*n*56
modernity, 262*n*6
Mohawk Institute, 117
Moody, Colonel Richard, 37
Moodyville School, 155, 171
morality in school curriculum, 106
Moresby, Anne, 37–38
Moresby, Fairfax, 52
Moreton-Robinson, Aileen, 5, 9, 57
mortality rates, 133–34. *See also* death, records of; disease and death
Morvin, Charles, 187

Moss, Mark, 170–71
Mount Elgin School, 117
Muckleshoot, 53
mumps, 196. *See also* disease and death
municipal property taxes, 166–67. *See also* taxation
Musgrave, Anthony, 46

Nahanee, Edward, 155
Nanaimo, B.C.: Anglican missionaries in, 73; common school at, 28–29, 46; high schools in, 106; Indian Day School in, 124; Methodist missionaries in, 61, 62; mission school in, 116
Nass River, 74, 122
National Indian Brotherhood, 200
National Negro Convention Movement, 32
National Policy platform, 118
Native Brotherhood of British Columbia, 155
Nellie, 138–39
Nelson, B.C., 160, 166
Netherby, S.B., 90, 147, 160, 161
"New Alienation," 163
New Caledonia, B.C., 18, 51
"new education" movement, 158, 183, 266n73
Newman, George, 171
Newman, Nora, 155, 156(i)
newspapers, 41–42, 199–200, 237n93
New Westminster, B.C.: Anglican missionaries in, 73; common school in, 46; domestic science courses in, 162; Dominion Exhibition in, 145; founding of, 37–38; Indigenous people gathering in, 67; Margaret Strong as municipal inspector for, 268n100; Methodist Church missionaries in, 61–62; municipal tax in, 166; Oblate missionary in, 65; Robson as mayor of, 43
New Westminster High School, 106, 252n102
New Westminster School, 38–39, 40
Neylan, Susan, 49, 70
Nickel, Sarah, 8, 12, 142
Nicolaye, Reverend Father, 124
Nine O'clock Gun, 143, 261n5
Nippon Kokumin Gakko, 150
Nisga'a Land Committee, 182
Nisga'a Nation, 74, 75, 121, 122, 181
Nisqually Nation, 53
Nlaka'pamux Nation, 19, 35, 36, 74, 181
Nobili, John, 51
non-denominational schooling, 44, 47, 237n97. *See also* schooling
normal schools, 163–64, 175, 267n90
North Cowichan, B.C., 46
North Shore Native Longshoremen's Union, 280n132
North Vancouver, B.C., 125–26
North-West Mounted Police (NWMP), 123
North-West Territories, 119
Nova Scotia, 42
Nuu-chah-nulth Nation, 18

obedience, 195
Oblates of Mary Immaculate, 60, 64–65, 123, 179, 242n65
Ogden, Peter Skene, 51
Ojibwe Nation, 9
Okanagan Valley, 153
Oliver, John, 173
O'Meara, Arthur, 273n31
150 Mile House, B.C., 178–79
opposition to school, 104–5, 171. *See also* Indigenous resistance

oppression, 128, 136, 199
Order-in-Council of 1892, 126
Oregon Country, 18
Oregon Treaty, 18
O'Reilly, Peter, 123
orphans, 120, 257n51
Ottawa (as federal government): civil servant positions in Department of Indian Affairs, 114, 181; defining Indian status, 93; denial of Indian Residential School conditions, 196; establishing and running Indian Branch, 123; establishing Indian Branch, 113; expansion of Indian Residential Schools, 118–19, 140, 190; Indian Act amendment for compulsory school, 183; on Indigenous children attending public school, 152; McKenna-McBride Commission, 182; passing Technical Education Act, 172; strategy for "Indian problem," 115; wiping debt of British Columbia, 78, 83; working through mission schools, 110, 111–12, 116–17, 122, 189
overcrowding in schools, 132, 149–50, 191. *See also* conditions in schools

Pacific Northwest, 18, 21
Pandosy, Charles, 65
Panitch, Leo, 11, 82, 108, 115–16
parents: attitudes toward school of, 103, 120, 122; boycotts of schools, 203; complaints of, 263n15; fining of, 86; growing to approve of schooling, 167; Indigenous parents preferring day schools, 184; Indigenous responses to residential schools, 124, 134, 180, 198; influence of, 119–20; resistance to school attendance, 101–2, 147, 185, 209–10; school involvement of, 101
Parkin, George, 269n120
Parnaby, Andrew, 280n131
Parrott, Sir Edward, 168–69
participatory democracy, 163
Patnaik, Prabhat, 208
Patnaik, Utsa, 208
patriarchy, 143, 161–63, 192–93, 267n83
patriotism, 168, 169, 170–71
Patterson, E. Palmer III, 74–75
Patterson, R.S., 174–75
Paull, Andrew, 182, 201
pedagogy, 68, 70, 72
Penelakut Island, 135(i)
Perry, Adele: on archival research, 12; British Columbia as a man camp, 36; British Columbia on the "edge of empire," 22; on defining "the state," 10; history of schooling work of, 208; on marriage, 51; mention, 5; on social status, 231n13; state definitions of "Indian," 93; on structures of indifference, 179–80, 197
Phillips, Charles E., 27, 173
photographs, school, 95, 155–56
physical education, 170–71
physical labour, preparation for, 108–9
Piell, 66
Pike Guards, 36
Plaxton, E.D., 263n15
pneumonia, 196. *See also* disease and death
police, 183, 184, 199, 200, 207
political economy, 8, 10–11
political power, 5, 30, 234n38
political reform, 41–42
Pollard, Juliet, 231n10
poor people, regulation of, 10

Pope, Stephen D.: on barring Indigenous children from public schools, 99; on corporal punishment, 105; on importance of parents, 103; on school attendance, 100; on study of history, 107; as superintendent, 89, 98; on women voting for school trustees, 102
population, 142–43
Port Alberni, B.C., 126(i)
Port Alberni School, 96(i)
Porter, John, 91
Port Essington, B.C., 124, 125(i)
Port Essington Indian Day School, 125(i)
Port Simpson, B.C.: boarding school at, 125, 137–38, 139(i), 191, 202; mission school at, 121
Port Simpson Girls' Home, 133
potlatch ceremonies, 123, 182
Powell, Israel Wood, 34, 114–15, 116
power struggles, 110–11
practical training in schools, 107–8
Pratt, Mary Louise, 7
Prentice, Alison, 91–92
Presbyterian Church, 126(i)
Presbyterian Clayoquot Boarding School, 193
Presbyterian missionaries, 122
President (ship), 55
primitive accumulation, 9, 56, 226n54
Prince George, B.C., 174(i)
Prince Rupert, B.C., 160
private education, 23, 83, 220n11, 271n154
private property, creation of, 9–10
programme of studies, 106, 127, 166
progressivism, 158, 265n62, 272n158
propaganda, 168–69

Prophet River Indian Residential School, 206
Provincial Industrial School for Girls, 203
provincial jurisdiction, 6, 7, 115–16, 159
Public School Act, 1872, 81, 83–89, 92
Public Schools Act, 1879, 89
Puget Sound Agricultural Company, 29(i)
Puget Sound War, 53, 55–56, 61, 69, 70
punishment at school, 105, 195, 198–99, 210, 263n15
Puntzi Lake, 66
Putman, Dr. J.H., 173, 174, 175, 271n141
Putman-Weir Report, 175, 176, 271n148
Puyallup, Washington, 53

Qu'Appelle (trial residential school), 119
Queensborough, B.C., 37. *See also* New Westminster, B.C.
Queen's University, 89
Queen Victoria, 37
Quesnel, B.C., 66
Quinwoch, 74–75
Quw'utsun Nation, 52

Racette, Sherry Farrell, 95
racial heritage of early school students, 32, 150–57. *See also* "half breeds"
racism: activated in overcrowded schools, 150–51; changing nature of, 98; creating a white province, 79; gender and, 32–33; illness and, 133; inherent in residential school curriculum, 128, 189; of island colonists, 61; in teacher hiring, 186

Raibmon, Paige, 95, 198
railway development, 78
rank, of teachers, 103–4
Raptis, Helen, 5, 6, 152, 210, 211
reconciliation, 211
Redford, James, 120, 184, 274n42
Red River Resistance, 78
Red Series (textbooks), 106. *See also* textbooks
Reed, Hayter, 114, 130, 140
refusal, school, 101–2, 203
Reid, Bill, 154(i)
relationships, reciprocal with land, 8
religion, 22, 247n11, 265n53. *See also* missionaries; specific churches
Renax, Mr., 128
"Report on Industrial Schools for Indians and Half-Breeds" (Davin), 118
research questions, 13
reserve systems, 79, 132, 182, 258n73, 259n105, 273n30
resistance to school, 101–2, 104, 136. *See also* Indigenous resistance
resource exploitation, 8, 36, 56, 143. *See also* gold rushes
Revelstoke, B.C., 160
Richard, Pierre, 65
Richards, Mr., 139
Ridley, William, 110–11, 122
road building, 66
Robertson, James Wilson, 108, 158, 253n108, 266n66
Robinson, Alexander, 147, 148, 151, 157, 172, 263n15
Robson, John, 41, 43, 75, 98
Robson, Reverend Ebenezer, 61, 62, 63
Rossland, B.C., 166
Round the Empire (Parkin), 269n120
Roy, Patricia, 150, 249n53

Royal Commission on Indian Affairs for the Province of British Columbia, 182
Royal Commission on Industrial Training and Technical Education, 158
Royal Navy, 239n7
Rück, Daniel, 114, 179, 184
"ruling by schooling," 82. *See also* schooling
running away from schools, 136, 137, 178, 199–200. *See also* Indigenous resistance
Rupert's Land, 78
Russell, Thomas, 29–30
Ryerson, Egerton, 43, 84, 247n21, 252n100

Saanich, B.C., 46, 73
safety, 195. *See also* conditions in schools
salaries: of superintendent, 34, 85, 88, 248n35; of teachers: at common schools, 33, 38, 39–40, 45; at Indian Day Schools, 187; at public schools, 84, 104, 164, 252n94, 267n93, 268n96; tied to attendance records, 86; of various professions, 252n93
Saltspring Island, B.C., 46
Sangster, Joan, 103
Sapperton, B.C., 37
Sapperton School, 37–39, 40
Saulteaux Nation, 121
Schecter, Stephen, 157, 161, 266n66
schedule for school year, 103, 127. *See also* conditions in schools
school fires. *See* arson
schooling: blurred boundaries of, 210–11; as a civilizing project, 59, 111–12, 146, 211; common, on Vancouver

Island, 27–34; as contested from beginning, 11, 28–29; debating free, 43; early, on Vancouver Island, 22–26; emergence of, 14; funds for, 59–60, 69; history of, 5–7; as ideological, 163; to legitimize colonization, 11, 49, 67, 79, 158, 161, 167, 177; non-denominational, 44–45; non-sectarian, 81; potential for both oppression and transformation through, 11; purpose of denominational, 27; relationship to colonization, 4, 22; to reproduce class hierarchy, 23–24, 30, 44; rise of state, 14; "ruling by schooling," 82; snapshot of public, 173–74; state (*see* schools, common); structural functions of, 13; term note, 221n19; as used by British colonies, 5–6

schooling, compulsory: acceptance of, 144; clause in School Act, 87, 146–48; in for Indigenous children, 183–84; as norm by 1930s, 177; resistance to, 101–2; secondary, 175

school inspectors: A.C. Stewart, 147–48; A.E. Green, 172; arrival accounts of, 90–91; Arthur Anstey, 167–68, 172; David Wilson, 145; H.H. MacKenzie, 149; Netherby, 160–61; R.H. Cairns, 203; W.E. Ditchburn, 198, 201

school refusal, 101–2, 203

schools: as agencies of legitimacy, 11, 49, 67, 79, 158, 161, 167, 177; boarding, 87; boards, 45, 102–3, 166; fees, 28, 43; high schools, 106, 165–66, 175; preferences for, 33; private, 262n8; rural, 102(i); segregation in, 249n53; specific colonizing role of, 21, 42–43; trustees, 94–95, 102

schools, common: appropriation of public land for, 42, 43; background on, 21–22; in colony of British Columbia, 35–41; on colony of Vancouver Island, 27–34; conflicting visions for, 41–45; demand for tuition-free, non-denominational, 34, 43; early problems with, 30–32; funding for, 45, 57; Indigenous students in, 210; as key to attracting settlers, 81; as key to social mobility, 82; low attendance in early, 30–31, 33–34; ordinances for, 45–46; power and, 82; reform of, 14, 34, 41–42, 44; as settler infrastructure, 20; state of by 1870, 82–83; transition to public schools, 86; on Vancouver Island, 22–26

schools, mission: in British Columbia in 1880s, 121; concerns about, 239n12; deemed inadequate by Ottawa, 117; early work and intentions for, 60–61; funding for, 69, 71–72, 75–76, 112, 116–17, 122, 255n27; low attendance at, 116–17; in Nlaka'pamux territory, 73(i); in Quw'utsun territory on Vancouver Island, 50(i); rise of, 112–17; as sites of hegemonic struggles, 70, 110; techniques to get children into, 62; as a tool of legitimation, 67

schools, public: amalgamation of, 175; attitudes toward, 91–92; budgets of, 83; changes to, 143–44; classroom composition of, 149–57; compulsory nature of, 144; costs of, 166–67; daily schedule of, 103; enrolment of, 147, 149; expansion of, 146–47; gender in, 92–93; increases in, 88–89, 91; Indigenous students in, 151–57, 210; low attendance in, 87, 100;

public acceptance of, 109; race in, 93–99; reform for industrialization, 146, 157–67; in Sidney, B.C., 150(i); social hierarchies and, 91–92; stolen lands paying for, 83–84; streams of, 166; systems under strain, 146–49; values promoted at, 103
Scott, Duncan Campbell, 181, 183, 188, 190–91, 192, 198
Scott, James C., 86, 91, 136, 194
Scott, John R., 122, 128, 132, 134
Scott, Stephen, 233*n*33
Sechelt, B.C., 203
Sechelt Indian Residential School, 180, 198, 203, 204(i), 205
secondary education. *See* high schools
Secwépemc Nation, 8, 123, 178, 181, 200
segregation, 249*n*53
Sellars, Bev, 133, 134
settler anxiety: about Indigenous peoples traveling to southern B.C., 241*n*42; fear of insurrection, 66–67; of Governor James Douglas, 54–55; Indigenous grievances and, 79–80; informing colonial policy, 122; military force and, 238*n*2; missionaries and, 14; in missionary work, 51–52, 61, 71–72, 111; nature of, 239*n*13; over Indigenous resistance, 121–22, 123
settler capitalism, 9, 79, 129, 194, 209, 210. *See also* capitalism
settler colonialism, 8, 9, 179–80, 197, 208, 224*n*37. *See also* colonialism
settler conflicts. *See* settler anxiety
settlers, early of British Columbia, 19, 43, 78
"settle the west," 118
sewing, 129, 162(i), 188, 193–94

sex at school, 88
sexual abuse, 179, 278*n*99
sexual misconduct, 104–5
Seymour, Frederick, 44, 66–68, 237*n*98
səl̓ílwətaɬ Nation, 155
Shaw, Elizabeth, 137–38, 139–40, 179
Shaw, J.C., 149
Sheehan, Nancy, 171
Shingwauk School, 117
shíshálh Nation, 180, 198, 203, 204(i), 205
Shoshone Nation, 56
Sidney, B.C, 150(i)
silencing, 198
Similkameen, B.C., 153
Simpson, Audra, 15, 115, 180, 199, 201, 203, 210
Simpson, Leanne Betasamosake, 8, 128, 192–93
Sinclair, Murray, 4, 15
singing, 68
Sioux Nation, 8
Sisters of St. Ann, 64
"Siwash" term, 40
Sḵwx̱wú7mesh Nation, 79, 155, 171, 181, 198, 200, 207
Slater, Hollis, 232*n*23
Sm'algyax language, 70
smallpox, 19, 66, 196, 244*n*112. *See also* disease and death
Smart, James A., 114
Smith, Keith D., 12
Smith, Linda Tuhiwai, 12, 13
Smith, Miss M.R., 102
Smith, William Alexander, 42
Snuneymuxw Nation, 28, 62–63
Snyder, Captain H.M., 36
social hierarchies, 24, 27, 30, 44, 82, 91–92, 163, 261*n*7
socialization, 91–99

social studies, 163
Society for the Propagation of the Gospel (SPG), 56, 60, 69, 73, 74
socioeconomic development, 78
Songhees Indian Day School, 186(i)
Songhees Indians. *See* ləkʷəŋən Nation
Sooke, B.C., 98(i), 99, 99(i)
South Africa, 151
South Cowichan, B.C., 46
South Fort George School, 154–55, 155(i)
sovereignty declarations, 66, 121
spanking, 105. *See also* punishment at school
Spences Bridge, 90–91
Spragge, William, 116
Squamish Indian Residential School, 198
"squawtocracy," 53
Staines, Emma, 23, 24, 26, 231*n*13
Staines, Robert John, 23, 24–26, 51, 232*n*23
Stanley, Timothy J., 6, 98, 150, 169
St. Ann's Academy, 26
Starblanket, Gina, 8, 107
Stark, Heidi Kiiwetinepinesiik, 9
Starrett, Clara Smith, 104
state: as an educator, 11, 101; control over education, 10, 22, 82; defining the, 10–11; state-church model of residential schools, 119
St'át'imc Nation, 40, 196
status *vs.* non-status "Indians," 93, 152
St. Augustine's School, 204(i)
Steele, Sam, 123
stenography, 161
Stevens, Isaac, 55
Stevenson, Allyson D., 125, 206, 209
Stewart, A.C., 147–48, 263*n*15

St. George's Indian Residential School, 190, 196, 200
Sticks, Duncan, 178, 193(i), 205
Sticks, Johnny, 178
Sticks, Mary, 179
St. Joseph's Indian Industrial School, 130, 178–79, 193(i)
St. Mary's Indian Residential School, 131, 132(i), 196, 203, 205
St. Mary's Mission, 132(i)
St. Mary's School, 65, 67–68
St. Michael's Indian Residential School, 192, 202(i)
stolen lands, 62, 71–72, 79, 84, 143, 181–82, 254*n*15. *See also* accumulation by dispossession; land
Stoler, Ann Laura, 12, 131
Stó:lō Nation, 36, 63–64, 196, 198
Storey, Kenton, 61
"storying," 107
Story of a National Crime, The: An Appeal for Justice to the Indians of Canada (Bryce), 198
St. Peter's College, 89
strap, 195. *See also* punishment at school
Strathcona Trust, 170
strikes, 200–1, 280*n*131
Strong, Margaret, 268*n*100
student body of early common schools, 32
student opposition to school, 104–5
student-teacher ratios, 149
Studies in Citizenship (McCaig), 163
Sumas, B.C., 46
superintendent of education, 34, 85–86, 85(i), 147
Survey of the School System, 173, 175–76
survivance, 134–35, 260*n*114

INDEX 329

Sutherland, Neil, 157, 158, 172, 173, 253*n*107, 253*n*108
Sylix Nation, 65, 152, 153, 181

Tahpit, 66
Takla Lake Indian Residential School, 206
Tate, Henry, 139(i)
taxation, 46, 84, 166–67, 247*n*17, 271*n*154
teachers and teaching: attitudes towards, 33; authoritarian nature of, 210; certification of, 103–4; experiences with school inspectors, 90–91; at Indian Day Schools, 185–86, 198; job duties of, 103; male enlisting in military, 171–72; ratios to students, 149; relationships with parents, 102; training for, 163–64, 175, 267*n*90; wages of, 33, 38, 39, 104 (*see also under* salaries); working at Indian Day Schools, 185–86
technical class, 160(i)
Technical Education Act, 172
Teit, James, 273*n*31
Telegraph Creek, 152
Tellot, 66
Tennant, Paul, 142
Terrace, B.C., 186–87
terra nullius, 56
textbooks, 45, 106, 107, 163, 169–70, 252*n*100, 262*n*10, 269*n*120
Thompson, E.P., 8, 231*n*9
Thompson River, 73
Tillotson, Shirley, 208
Tilton, James, 53
title rights, 182
Tk'emlups te Secwepemc Nation, 4
Tod, Isaac, 32
Tod, William, 32

Tomlinson, Robert, 75
Toronto Normal School, 84
Tough, David, 208
transnational histories, 207–8
transportation to school, 101–2, 102(i), 187
Transvaal, South Africa, 151
Traveller (ship), 53
treaties, 181, 256*n*47
Trenaman, Jane, 94
truancy, 100–1, 102, 109, 198–99, 205
Trutch, Joseph, 74, 75, 76, 84, 115
truth, grappling with, 3, 211
Truth and Reconciliation Commission (TRC), 3, 4, 15, 211, 212, 278*n*99
Truth and Reconciliation Commission (TRC) report, 3–4
truth telling, 207
Tsartlip Indian Day School, 185
Tseshaht territory, 96(i)
Tsilhqot'in Nation, 66, 79
Tsilhqot'in War, 67
Ts'msyan Nation, 5, 69, 71, 110, 111, 121, 122, 211, 244*n*110
tuberculosis, 133, 185, 196. *See also* disease and death
Tuck, Eve, 6, 199
Tugwell, Reverend Lewin S., 69
tuition fees, 31, 166

Ucluelet Indian Day School, 185(i)
Unangax̂ Nation, 199
Union of British Columbia Municipalities, 172
unions, 280*n*132
United Church, 126(i)
United States, colonizing activity of, 18
University of British Columbia, 173
unmarked graves, 4, 133, 219*n*8
"unsettling" concept, 222*n*24

Upper Canada, 43
urban-rural divide, 147, 164

vaccination, 196
values promoted at school, 103, 106
Van Brummelen, Harro, 106, 265n53
Vancouver, B.C.: becoming a world-class port, 142–43; high schools in, 106; industrial training in, 159–60; municipal tax in, 166; Nine O'clock Gun in, 261n5; normal school in, 164
Vancouver Island, B.C.: British colonization of, 18, 19, 21; early schooling on, 22–26, 46; heterogeneity of students at schools on, 93–94; limited funds of, 56; merging colonies with British Columbia, 41; mission school on Quw'utsun territory, 50(i)
Van Kirk, Sylvia, 33
Vankoughnet, Lawrence, 114, 120
Vernon, B.C., 166
Victoria, B.C.: Anglican missionaries in, 73; British colonization of, 19, 23; Colonial Administration Buildings of, 26(i); domestic science courses in, 162; early schooling in, 46; industrial training in, 159–60; Methodist missionaries in, 61; mission school, 59–60, 116; municipal tax in, 166; normal school in, 164; regional Indian affairs board in, 114; Sisters of St. Ann's private school in, 64; as site for first Indian Residential School, 58; William Duncan's students in, 70
Victoria Board of Education, 103
Victoria Boys' Public School, 89
Victoria High School, 105, 106, 165(i)
violence, cultures of, 137, 195
violence, fears of, 55–56, 111

violence, state, 199
Vizenor, Gerald, 134–35, 260n114
vocational training, 266n70
von Heyking, Amy, 7
Vowell, A.W., 115, 140, 179

wage labour, 10, 25, 78–79, 118–19, 128, 183, 194, 246n7, 258n73. See also labour
wages of teachers. See salaries
Wakefield, Edward Gibbon, 25, 232n22
Walkem, George Anthony, 88, 89
war, 167–68, 169
Warburton, Rennie, 233n33
Washington Territory, 53, 55
Weir, G.M., 173, 174, 271n141
West Coast Agency, 124
White, Mr., 99
White, Reverend Edward, 61, 63
white supremacy, 79, 143, 150–51
whitewashing, 107
whooping cough, 133, 196. See also disease and death
Wikwemikong School, 117
Williams, Carol, 95, 155
Williams, Elder Mary, 36
Williams Lake, B.C., 126, 130, 134, 136, 178
Williams Lake Indian Residential School, 193(i)
Willis, S.J., 147, 268n96
Wilson, David, 90, 145–46, 161, 168
Winnipeg, M.B., 114, 118
winter weather, 31. See also conditions in schools
Wolfe, Patrick, 8, 9, 21
women: importance of high school education for, 165; as low-paid teachers, 164; recruitment of for school involvement, 102–3; regulation of,

10; as teachers, 104; voting rights of, 251*n*86
Wood, Ellen Meiksins, 19
Woodpecker School, 174(i)
Woods Lake School, 153
woodworking courses, 161
Woolford, Andrew, 60, 131, 133, 134, 153, 181, 206, 255*n*19, 281*n*147
Work, David, 32
Work, James, 26
Work, John, 32
work, resistance to, 130
working class families, 91–92
Wotherspoon, Terry, 11, 22, 163, 231*n*9

X̱wemelch'stn Nation, 155
xʷməθkʷəy̓əm Nation, 155
Xz'xtsa Nation, 40

Yale, B.C.: All Hallows Boarding School in, 190; Anglican missionaries in, 73; boarding school at, 125; common school at, 40, 46; land provided to churches in, 62; missionary land grants at, 74; mission school at, 121
Yale School, 40
Yang, K. Wayne, 6